100

W9-CSC-483

A Paradise of Birds

Also by Helen Gere Cruickshank

Bird Islands Down East
Flight into Sunshine
Water Birds
Wonders of the Bird World
Wonders of the Reptile World
1001 Questions Answered About Birds
(*with Allan D. Cruickshank*)

EDITED BY HELEN GERE CRUICKSHANK
Fun with Birds in Florida
John and William Bartram's America
Thoreau on Birds

Photographs illustrating *A Pocket Guide to Birds,
Eastern and Central North American* by
Allan D. Cruickshank

A PARADISE OF BIRDS

When Spring Comes to Texas

By Helen Gere Cruickshank
Photographs by Allan D. Cruickshank

DODD, MEAD & COMPANY · NEW YORK

The jacket and book illustrations are reproduced
by courtesy of the National Audubon Society and
by special permission of Allan D. Cruickshank.

Library of Congress Catalog Card Number: 68-16876

Printed in the United States of America
by Vail-Ballou Press, Inc., Binghamton, N. Y.

Acknowledgments

TO ALL THE PEOPLE who made our spring visits to Texas more interesting and rewarding I am most grateful. I am particularly grateful to two presidents of the National Audubon Society: John H. Baker and Carl W. Buchheister, and to their research biologist, the late Robert Porter Allen. Their wardens were always helpful. Among these the John Larsons (Senior and Junior), Douglas Plummer, Louis Rawalt and Will Russell gave us special assistance.

We visited many refuges administered by the United States Bureau of Sports Fisheries and Wildlife and at each were met with courtesy and help. James Stevenson and Luther Goldman, both now in the Washington office, were particularly helpful. The entire staff of the Aransas Refuge was unfailingly kind and Earl Benham several times rescued us from unfortunate predicaments.

Robert Gibbs of the National Park Service helped us greatly in the Big Bend. We remember with appreciation the kindness of the McConnells in charge of Bentsen State Park.

Dr. Richard Albert of Alice gave me some of his peyote plants and dug up valuable information about them for me.

Mr. and Mrs. Irby Davis of Harlingen gave us some days

of spectacular birding in the Rio Grande Valley and also taught us much about the plants in that region.

Conger Hager, whose knowledge of birds around Rockport changed the entire picture of migration in that area and made her home a mecca for bird-watchers, was always a highlight on our trips to Texas, and we were sad that our projects were so demanding that we could stop only for a short call.

Glen Evans of Midland told me about the Rucker bat cave and the Ruckers, who were our hosts when we visited it.

Armstrong Price was generous with information about the geology of southeast Texas. The Whiteheads of Smith Point contributed much to our frequent visits to that interesting area. Mr. and Mrs. Robert Hopper of Hopper's Landing were often our hosts when we worked at Aransas Refuge. All of these enriched and made more exciting our Texas springs.

Contents

Illustrations

xi

A curve-billed thrasher flew toward us.
The whole chisos range was in a cloud shadow.
We saw the beautiful and unique pronghorn.
A resident of the prairie dog colony posed for us.
The small brown burrowing owl lives with the prairie dogs.
A grizzled badger entered a prairie dog tunnel.
A lark sparrow flushed from beside the road.
Avocets displayed long blue legs and upcurved bills.
Willets showed lovely black and white wing patterns.
The verdin is a member of the chickadee family.
A fairly common bird was the greenish olive sparrow.
The vermilion flycatcher is the brightest of the family.
The red eyes of the male bronzed cowbird shone like rubies.

Following page 302

Of all the herons the snowy egrets are the most graceful.
The roseate spoonbill's plumage was glorious.
Like a Ubangi belle's lips their bills were fashioned.
Twice the heat drove the Louisiana heron from its nest.
The blue eyes of the white ibis glistened.
Wild nutria average twenty pounds or less.
On the cattle egrets' heads fell delicate plumes.
We heard the frantic wild cry of black-necked stilts.
Great blue herons used a cactus plant for a nest.
A colony of royal terns leaped into the air.
The terns shrieked in shattering decibels without ceasing.
Brown pelicans are rare in Texas although once common.
In the air white pelicans are beautiful beyond compare.
Really good photographs of oystercatchers are rare.
We caught the graceful pose of a reddish egret.
A handsome male pyrrhuloxia was discovered at the nest.

MAP OF TEXAS
showing location of National Audubon Sanctuaries
and major places of interest mentioned in this book

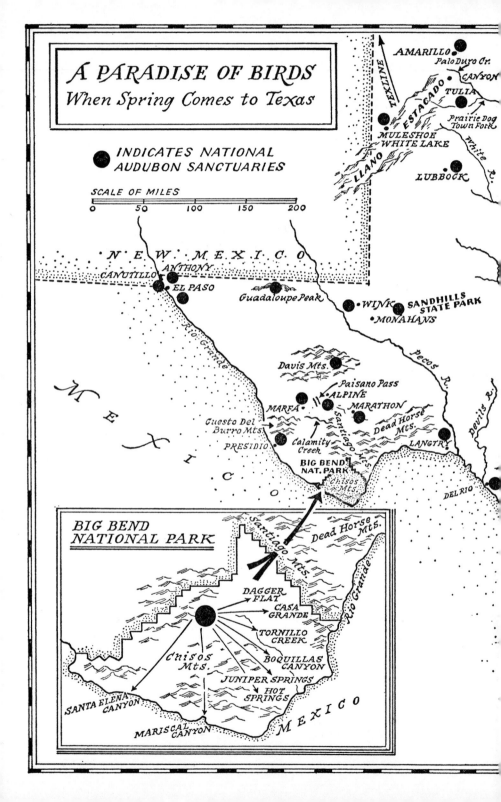

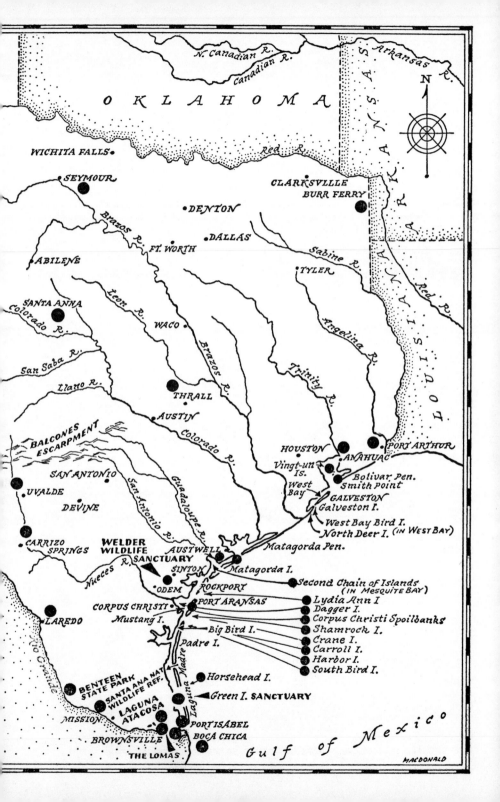

A Paradise of Birds

1

The Time of Singing Birds

> To see a world in a grain of sand
> And heaven in a wild flower,
> Hold infinity in the palm of your hand
> And eternity in an hour.
> —William Blake

A SHOWER HAD wakened us more than an hour ago and lightning guided us to our car on the twenty-first day of March. We set out through slackening rain. The car lights glinted briefly on dimpled puddles before they were sprayed away in great fans by our wheels. Then the rain no longer slanted out of the dark and Allan switched off the windshield wipers. In a few more minutes the tune of the wheels changed to a hollow clang. Below we saw the faint steel shine of water. We had come to the Burr Ferry crossing of the Sabine River well ahead of dawn on the first day of spring.

Allan pulled off the road on the Texas bank and switched off lights and motor. The Sabine whispered faintly as it slid toward the gulf, but the world was hushed, waiting for the end of night. We breathed deeply of pine-scented air and the perfume of wet earth and awakening seeds and burgeoning leaves. A few stars sparkled overhead.

Now we waited expectantly for the rising of the spring sun at the farthest east bulge of Texas touched by a highway. Somewhere a mockingbird wakened and broke the stillness with a rehearsal. *"Do do do"* he sang over and over again until, satisfied with that note, he climbed to *re* and finally to *me*. He dropped back to *do* and continued to practice those three notes until abashed into silence as three balanced minor chords floated deliberately on the still air. A wood thrush had wakened and the singular beauty of his crystalline yet solemn music was as stirring as the opening of Beethoven's *Fifth Symphony*. The leisurely chords fell gently in a serenade to spring.

The music died away, and as if they had waited breathless for it to end birds everywhere burst into song. Perhaps the early shower had delayed the usual dawn chorus, for suddenly now the air shook with their robust salute to spring. The mockingbird cast rehearsal to the winds and exploded into an emphatic rollicking cadenza. Chickadees called, and a tufted titmouse shouted *"Peter, Peter, Peter!"* A jaunty Carolina wren sang its loud, cheery song, and as if to outdo its larger cousin a house wren burst into a long laughing rippling carol. Cardinals chipped dryly and began to sing. Redwings, blue jays, crows and a host of other birds joined in the rousing joyful cacophony.

A flash of light shot across the river, and there was a startled *quak* from a yellow-crowned night heron fishing near the bank. I got out of the car into the wet grass to look down the steep bank. Moored below was the tiniest houseboat I had ever seen. A fat woman in something shapeless came out onto the narrow deck, set a kerosene lantern on a bench and dipped a bucket of water from the river. A man padded after her, yawning. He pulled on rubber boots, then poured some water into a pan, splashed it on his face and wiped it off without removing the towel hanging from a nail. He dropped into a dinghy nearly filled with some kind of gear, tossed off the painter and rowed upstream and out of sight with the heron, squawking loudly, leading the way.

The stars faded and the sky grew lighter. The moment we waited for approached, and our eyes were glued to the east. Soft yellow tinted the horizon and then sudden glory flared across it. At exactly 6:17 a fiery thread glittered, and quickly the sun rose above the horizon, too bright for eyes to endure. Rosy light flooded the pine forest and slid down dark trunks and over the steep bank onto the water, turning its sullen steel to merry blue and casting a path of melted gold across it. We looked again at the forest and now shadows, long and crisp, were flung behind each tree. Spring had come to Texas.

There was a sharp slam. A gate rattled behind a red Buick that rumbled over the bridge and stopped beside us. A smiling man leaned out the window.

"Car trouble," Can I help?"

"No trouble," Allan replied. "We have been listening to the dawn chorus and watching the sun rise. We thought this was an appropriate way and place to begin our spring wildlife photography in Texas."

"Sure enough, this is the first day of spring! You chose an historic place to watch its arrival. Steamers once traveled up the Sabine as far as Logansport. The river was deeper and narrower then. 'Kitchens' of logs floated down to Orange. Cotton was piled on top of the logs. When the cotton was sold, the farmers bought their entire year's supplies at once. My family bought out the Burrs in 1898 and ran the ferry until the bridge was built in 1936. The Burrs were descendants of Aaron Burr."

"But I thought Burr's wife died before he attempted to start a colony that some said was planned as an empire, and that his only child was a brilliant daughter, Theodosia."

"It happens in the best of families, even among royalty," the gentleman stated. "Burr's descendents here were highly respected members of the community. Three other illegitimate children were mentioned in his will. I have read that Burr lived for a period of several months with a son in New York."

Allan caught sight of a red-tailed hawk beautifully lighted by the low sun. He seized his camera and made a flight shot of the large bird.

"So you are going to spend the spring photographing in Texas. You will find plenty of variety there. I once had a visitor who wanted most of all to see Texas. So we set out at sunup and we drove all day long as fast as we could and never went on the same road twice, and it was sundown when we came back to this bridge. My visitor said Texas is surely a big place. I said it sure is because we have been driving in it from sunup to sundown but you have seen just one little bitty corner of it."

We agreed with this as we took leave and continued southwestward. We drove for a long time through country quite like that of other gulf states, but our mind's eyes were fixed on far horizons as unlike the pines, moss-hung oaks and sweet gums of this forested and rural area as day is different from night. Texas is so big and so varied that if anybody claims not to like the state he either knows too little about it to have found the kind of country he likes or he is blind to the wonders of this earth spaceship on which we travel through the solar system. Our days sparkled with excitement from the moment we knew our spring would be spent in Texas. No other place in the entire United States offers as much to a bird photographer as Texas in spring.

Since the beginning of time, the titanic forces of creation have been molding Texas into a paradise for birds. It lies where the continental land mass narrows sharply, and birds from the vast expanse of North America funnel into it. Texas is the last part of the United States seen by many birds as they stream south on their autumnal migration and the first they see on their return in spring.

Though ornithologists do not agree about the exact number of species found on this continent north of the Rio Grande, it is somewhere between 700 and 800. I cannot give a precise figure because some scientists separate birds into full species that others, equally distinguished, lump together as subspecies. Whatever the exact number actually is, Roger Tory Peterson's *Field Guide to the Birds of Texas* includes 542 species or about three-fourths of all the birds ever recorded in our country.

Some birds found nowhere else in the United States come into the Rio Grande Delta and the high Chisos Mountains. Moreover, Texas claims one species as its very own. The lovely little golden-cheeked warbler is known to nest nowhere in the world except in the cedar-and-oak-clad hills of Texas. Ornithologists employ the 100th meridian as a dividing line between eastern and western species. This meridian nearly bisects Texas, which has a generous share of birds both of the East and the West.

Texas is far more than a highway for countless hosts of birds bound for distant places. It posseses an infinite variety of habitats where many species are at home either during the winter or in the nesting season. In fact, Texas is so varied that a birder simply cannot know all the good birding places in it. It is bigger than life. Too varied. Too complicated. It is necessary to pick and choose from the enormous wealth of places where birding is excellent or unique or secret.

Its broad expanse is sometimes overwhelming. My road map informs me that I must drive 862 miles from Port Arthur to reach El Paso. If I plan a trip from Brownsville near the mouth of the Rio Grande to Texline at the top of the Panhandle, 910 miles lie ahead of me.

East and west, north and south, astonishing changes of landscape and climate occur. Miles and miles of varied country—hundreds and thousands of them—lie across the

face of Texas. Within its far-flung borders Texas contains
nearly 267,000 square miles. No wonder the breeding birds of
Texas are as varied as those from the tip of Florida all the
way to northern Maine.

The sun was launched above the Sabine at 6:17, but the
swift turning of the earth would require nearly an hour to
swing El Paso into sunlight. As spring advances toward
summer, the sun slants more and more to the north until on
June 21, Amarillo near the center of the Panhandle enjoys
fifty-one minutes more of sunlight than Brownsville far to
the south.

Rainfall in Texas is as varied as its surface, which lifts
irregularly from sea level to nearly nine thousand feet. Port
Arthur in the east receives an average of about 55 inches of
rainfall annually while El Paso receives less than 9 inches.
Extremes are always entertaining, and Texas provides these
to an astonishing degree. Clarksville in northeast Texas recorded a staggering 109.38 inches in 1873, while Wink in
west Texas was parched in 1956 when only 1.76 inches fell.
The greatest single rain in a twenty-four-hour period spilled
38.2 inches on Thrall on September 10, 1921. On June 17,
1961, Allan and I were forced to seek refuge on a high bluff
above the main highway through Del Rio when a 6-inch
rain turned the street into a wild torrent. The same storm
killed ten people and collapsed the International Bridge
across the Rio Grande between Del Rio and Ciudad Acuna.

Normal rainfall in Texas varies all the way from copious
through moderate to light. Some parts of the state are positively arid. Paradoxically, though a good part of the state has
a light rainfall it is garnished by water. The coastline alone
stretches about 380 miles. For over a thousand miles the Rio
Grande separates Texas from Mexico with an erratic flow of
sweet water, sometimes so shallow a child can wade across it,
and again so swollen it overflows high, wide banks spreading
death and devastation in its wake.

Scattered over the state are many rivers, streams and arroyos, and some of these dry to beds of dust and boulders in periods of drought, then burst into roaring lethal monsters when the rains come. Then flash floods run wild and sweep trees, people and livestock to their death. Natural and man-made lakes, springs gushing from the earth, ephemeral playas, salt marshes and fresh-water swamps all offer homes for many kinds of wintering birds and breeding species that demand a watery habitat.

Off the coast lies a chain of barrier islands shielding the mainland from Port Arthur to Port Isabel. Between these barrier islands and the mainland are shallow waters where numerous shell bars rise above the surface. The vast shallows teem with aquatic life and offer food for many species of birds and for man. Practically all harbors, ship basins and boat channels are man-made. Coastal plains, grassy prairies, deserts, mountains, forests, fruit groves, grainfields and cattle ranges all attract particular species of birds. The same is true of truck gardens and cotton fields, city parks and gardens and even garbage dumps. Each has its particular bird inhabitants, and only by searching many habitats can we appreciate the enormous variety of birds present in the state.

The vital climate of Texas throbs with change and variety. A high temperature of 120 degrees was recorded at Seymour on August 12, 1936, and Presidio near the Big Bend frequently reports the highest temperature, usually in the nineties, in Texas during the summer. The winter climate of this vast state varies from almost subtropical warmth in the Rio Grande Delta to frigid on the high plateau of the Panhandle. Tulia reported a low of 23 degrees below zero on February 12, 1899, and the freeze-free growing period of the Panhandle is only 180 days in contrast to 320 such days in the lower Rio Grande Valley.

From east, west and north to the brink of the Arctic and beyond, armies of birds swarm into Texas in winter, each seeking its preferred haunt that often has a subtle resemblance to its far-off breeding place. In the marshes, on the estuaries, along the beaches and sand dunes, in mesquite thickets and chaparral tangles, on rocky slopes and parched deserts, on prairies that reach away to a dim horizon of distant hills, on mountains and in deep-gouged canyons, each species seeks the kind of place where it can find the food and shelter that mean home to it.

We have seen hundreds of white-necked ravens at the El Paso city dump, and thousands have been reported from other cities. Companies of sandhill cranes gather in noisy conventions at Muleshoe, where occasionally more than sixty thousand have been counted in a single day. By tens of thousands, ducks and geese flock to coastal marshes and waters, particularly at Aransas, Rockport and Laguna Atascosa. In search of weed seeds, tribes of lark buntings so big they darken acres at a time drift about the chilly plateaus. Bands of doves settle uneasily and then flash up and away in zigzag flight. Before the whistling stoop of a pigeon hawk, a cloud of shorebirds rises, swerves and circles, governed by some mysterious sense of unity so it moves like parts of a single well-coordinated body. Daily flocks made up of dozens of redwings, cowbirds, Brewer's blackbirds and grackles chatter and whistle in the marshes and suburbs; then, as evening draws near, the scattered groups converge and unite. Gathered together in a compact mass they roost in unnumbered multitudes.

Large flocks of herons are seldom encountered in winter. More often a lonely individual here and another there feeds in the marshes and shallow waters where throngs gather in spring. Who knows what it is that causes many solitary-nesting birds to seek their kind in winter and many colonial birds to desire solitude at that season? Perhaps in a fashion birds share a characteristic with man, who needs association with his fellow men, yet, to remain at his best and develop to his highest capacity, must have time alone, time that is shared by no one, no matter how beloved and congenial, time when his thoughts may turn inward and he can survey the person he is and think his deepest thoughts.

The spirit of spring in Texas arises, slow-paced and unobtrusive, long before the calendar calls the turn of the season. Early in the year the husky bass of great horned owls booms a love song under the winter moon. Soon the bell-like honking of geese clangs down from the cold sky as their chevrons and wavering lines aimed northward cleave the air. Then ducks with many voices pick up the chant of spring. Sandhill cranes bugle in harshly resonant choruses and perform their traditional dances. At Aransas Refuge a pitifully small remnant of a once mighty host of whooping cranes sound their deep sonorous trumpets and turn their faces toward the wilds of Wood Buffalo Park where in a place almost inaccessible to man they rear their young.

In northeast Texas instrumental music is made in the dusk of late winter evenings when woodcocks mount for their sky dance. Giving short nasal calls they rise in great spirals, accelerating as they gain height, then fan their wings so rapidly that the wind whistles through curiously long, slim primaries. The snipe, too, sweeps up and up with wild abandon and draws a huge circle perhaps a mile in circumference, and as it circles, it dives, rises and dives again and again, its wings half-closed and quivering and its tail feathers spread so the air rushes through and vibrates them with a drumming sound. Often the snipe is so high in the twilight sky that it is difficult to discover the bird, and the mysterious sound seems to emanate from some ghostly spirit.

Where the ancient prairie remains uncultivated, male prairie chickens still gather to spar in the earliest dawn. They inflate strange orange-yellow sacs on their necks and produce an explosive sound like a cork pulled from a huge champagne bottle followed by a breath blown across the neck. The hollow sound of their wooing carries for a mile and more over the open country as the prairie chickens stamp like Apaches performing their war dance.

Though wild turkeys have disappeared from more than two-thirds of their former range, they still strut in Texas. The turkey cocks spread their great tails, fluff their feathers, and droop their wings that quiver as they touch the ground.

Before Aries, the first sign of the zodiac, speeds the sun to the vernal equinox, the symphony of the birds is well under way. Some of the voices like those of the green jay and chachalaca are harsh and dissonant. The clicking of tiny green Texas kingfishers, the incisive snapping of roadrunners, the sharp cries of flycatchers and the drumming of woodpeckers cannot be called musical, yet they are part of the symphonic chorus of spring. Though they lack melody, they add beat and rhythm. As the bass and tenor notes fade away and the wind and percussion instruments lose their urgency, alto and soprano voices swell the spring chorus. These voices gain strength with the coming of March.

Spring in Texas is a season of winds. As the wind rises, the chorus of bird song grows. Lyrical, challenging, gay and poignant, songs surge up and break like a wave over the country. Some of the finest melodies are sung by birds that mount into the air as if in rapture. Cassin's sparrows make abrupt little flights to repeat plaintively, *"I sing to thee."* Horned larks and lark buntings tower high in the sky and sing as they drop back toward earth. Of all the small aerial singers that visit Texas perhaps Sprague's pipit climbs highest into the sky where for a long time it sings its tinkling thin melody without ceasing. We once timed one of these pipit songs that lasted for 42 minutes.

Some birds trickle slowly back to Texas in spring while others arrive in massive waves. Once near Denton we were wakened by a host of scissor-tailed flycatchers singing *chuck, chuck, chuckle* in the moonlight, and next morning they were everywhere in trees, on fences and power lines. Some lively individuals towered toward the sky, plunged down only to rise again and finally fling themselves backward in two or three somersaults, all the while spreading and scissoring their tails so long that they make these small-bodied flycatchers the longest in the entire family. While displaying they held their silken wings high so the salmon patches underneath glowed.

The mockingbird is a fitting state bird for Texas. They are found in all kinds of habitats from the sultry woodlands hung with Spanish moss to the cities and towns, mountain slopes and even the desert. Their singing ability varies greatly; some individuals are true virtuosos. One lived for a time beside our cottage at Smith Point. Its own song was incomparably rich and varied, and in addition it was a most accomplished mimic. It imitated the mewing of a cat and the calls of guinea fowl and crowed like a rooster. We listed fourteen wild bird songs that it rendered beautifully. We were particularly impressed by its crow, blue jay and bobwhite calls. Apparently it heard these only from a distance, and as the mocker reproduced them, they sounded a half mile off. Then one day I heard some children shouting and went to investigate. By the time I arrived they were lying on the ground peering under a cottage. A cat cowered in the darkness as it chewed on a mockingbird. It was evidently our gifted bird, for we heard no more mimicked songs or rich carols.

Suddenly all the birds are on territory, the males lustily announcing their claims. Colonial birds with shrill or guttural notes gather on low islands in the shallow waters. Woodpeckers chisel nest cavities in dead trees and utility poles. Swallows turn into masons and plaster their nests on the sides of cliffs or under bridges. Orioles weave their intricate baskets and parasitic cowbirds skulk about searching with Machiavellian cunning for the nests of birds smaller than themselves in which to deposit their eggs. The desert birds nest hurriedly as if they remember the blazing heat that follows so quickly on the heels of cold days of early spring.

One day we went to Santa Ana Refuge with Luther Goldman who was then the manager of both it and Laguna Atascosa National Wildlife Refuge. We came to a high bank above the Rio Grande. In the muddy stream below us two logs rudely bound together with wire bumped against the shore.

"Its a raft made by a wetback—a *bracero* without a permit to work in the fields here in Texas. They cross illegally to earn as little as twenty-five cents an hour under the broiling sun in the fields. Look—here you can see a path worn through the chaparral. They wear sandals made of old automobile tires. Bandits know these secret trails and often rob and sometimes kill the *braceros* when they return to Mexico with their pitifully small earnings."

Not far away was a small pond and in a low tree standing in the water was a bulky nest.

"Groove-billed anis," Luther said. "They build communal nests and I believe three pairs are using this one. There is a comic deliberation in their movements. They built this nest in perfect harmony, each pair working as a team but without any conflict with the other pairs."

Something moved. A head poked out of a hole and then a fat, coal-black young ani with a short tail but with its high, thick bill like an enormous hooked nose fully grown moved languidly and rather unsteadily onto a branch. It was followed by another and another. Finally seven young anis were scattered through the branches where they clung uncertainly.

Santa Ana has been called the gem of the Federal Refuge System and in its towering primeval river forest it represents a habitat that has largely vanished from Texas. The bird chorus early in the morning is almost deafening, and to this chorus, gray chachalacas add their harsh cackles. Usually the species is very secretive but they frequently run ahead of cars on the roads of Santa Ana.

A short distance up the Rio Grande from Santa Ana lies Bentsen State Park and here Mrs. Luhe McConnell guided us to a dell shaded by towering trees. About sixty feet above our heads hung a three-foot-long nest built by nine-inch Lichtenstein's orioles. The bright orange builders looked alike and busily hurried in and out of the pendulous nest, for the young were well grown.

A hundred feet from the long oriole nest was a globular nest as big as a football. Six-inch rose-throated becards slipped back and forth putting the finishing touches on it. The birds were rather plain but the throat of the male was brushed with lovely pale rose.

A rather low but extremely dense thicket of *huisache* and other thorny chaparral trees surrounded the dell and in this a big-headed kiskadee flycatcher had placed its nest. It reminded us of an enormous cactus wren nest, as the giant flycatchers went in through a side entrance.

These flycatchers come only as far north as the Rio Grande Valley. Once we watched one perched quietly on a dead branch above the river. It sighted a water insect and plunged after it as adeptly as other flycatchers dart from similar perches to seize flying insects. Kiskadees also snatch minnows from the water.

We think of flycatchers as eating only insects, yet the diet of most is varied with berries and fruits. The kiskadee appears to be alone in catching fish and water insects, and for some time a few scientists claimed it was the only flycatcher that did not eat fruits of any kind. Several years ago kiskadees were introduced to Bermuda, and there people quickly discovered those scientists were mistaken. The kiskadees eat so much fruit there that desperate efforts were being made, Allan found the last time he was in Bermuda, to eliminate the unfortunate introduction.

While we watched the kiskadees, green jays watched us inquisitively from behind a latticework of thorny twigs. These are the only green jays in the world, and their extraordinary color is enhanced by a black throat patch, bright blue on top of the head and a streak of yellow on either side of the tail. The green jays refused to leave the deep shade, so the pictures I made of them, using available light, showed far softer, almost misty colors rather than the vibrant hues they actually wore.

We walked through a dense thicket to the river, and all the way we were surrounded by a low thunder, the thunder of thousands of doves. It beat upon us until we were a part of the universal sound. The chorus rose and fell with soft, insistent urgency. White-winged doves led all the rest. At close range their cooing resembled soft, flatted, muffled crows of roosters. Joining in the solid body of sound that varied only slightly in pitch was the moan of ground doves and mourning doves. Inca doves sobbed *"no hope, no hope,"* and occasionally we picked out the low-pitched ghostly *"co-whooooo"* of a white-fronted dove. Several times the uniform lament was punctuated by a more emphatic note from a red-billed pigeon. Never, anywhere, have we heard so strange and pervasive a sound as the thunder of those doves. It was arresting and mystifying, and it wrapped itself about us and penetrated our bodies and minds until we were a part of the throbbing intonation.

It is a strange thing, but many of the happiest, sunniest and most comfortable days we had in Texas are soon told, or perhaps even forgotten, while the cheerless days when our bodies were miserable and our thoughts were dark, are longest remembered and most cherished. The days most joyfully recalled are those when we were taxed physically and mentally to the very limit we could give. Those days remain most alive and best of all.

A day we will always remember came when Dr. Carl
Buchheister, then president of the National Audubon Society, sent us to Texas to make a sanctuary film. That season
Will Russell was acting as warden for the Second Chain of
Islands lying between Matagorda Island and the Aransas
Refuge. Will and his university had temporarily parted
company because he cut too many classes to look at birds.
That he was doing a splendid job of guarding them I found
one morning when we left Allan on Island Number Two to
photograph a colony of gull-billed and Forster's terns. Will
and I continued toward Number Eight away across the bay
so I could film some reddish egrets nesting there. On the
way Will say a dory too close to Carroll Island, on which
one of the largest and finest colonies of herons and spoonbills in the entire chain is located. We detoured toward a
tall, heavy man waist-deep in the water setting a net. As we
sailed close we saw he was leaning on a crutch. The fisherman apologized for having come too close to the island sanctuary, pulled up his net and threw it into the dory. Then he
pulled himself aboard, and we saw he had only one leg. We
have sometimes encountered gulls, a heron and occasionally
a tern or a black skimmer with only one leg—cripples that
succeeded in fishing well enough to stay alive—but this was
the only human commercial fisherman with one leg that we
have met.

We had a rough, wet trip to Number Eight Island. I
didn't like the look of the pewter-colored sky, and the air
was ominously still.

The island was flat. Most of it was grassy, and the few
bushes were scattered and low. I chose a nest with three
fuzzy young reddish egrets in it. A sooty tern flew over as we
put up my blind. Roseate spoonbills gathered on a bar,
where they watched us uneasily. Laughing gulls cackled
overhead. As soon as I was concealed in the blind, Will went
back to his boat and returned to the mainland to write a re-

port and notes. The birds watched him leave and streamed back to their nests, some of them landing on my blind before dropping down to their young.

Soon all the birds were back, busy with nest duties. I shot a hundred feet of reddish egrets, pleased with the varied action they presented. It was great being surrounded by egrets, white ibis and spoonbills in the midst of a noisy, active community of birds. Great, that is, until 11:20.

I heard the rumble of thunder and raised my eyes from the birds. A grim steel curtain was approaching. It blotted out the distant mainland and then the islands vanished. Hurriedly I packed away the cameras and placed them under my small canvas stool for what slight protection it offered. There were no other preparations I could make for the advancing storm.

The wind came first, and my arms strained to hold the blind. Then the rain struck savagely. More wind came. Though I held on with all my strength, the blind toppled. By the time I had extricated myself from the clinging wet cover, the wind had abated slightly. I righted the blind, rescued the stool that, propelled by the powerful gusts, had blown toward the shore. Hoping the cameras and the birds had not suffered irreparable harm, I had little time for further concern.

A new onslaught hit. I could scarcely breathe, for the air was almost solid with water. The heavy rain pounding down and the thunder almost deafened me. Lightning stabbed continuously, and I shook with fright, for my blind was by far the highest object on the island and the most likely target for one of the flaming bolts.

Another terrible gust smashed across the island. My resisting muscles were as nothing. Over went the blind, and I was past caring. Bruised, shivering and half drowned, I pulled the blind and cameras close to the shore, again put the stool over the cameras, lay face down across it and let the wind tear at me and the cataract of rain sluice over me, flailing my lightly clad body.

At last the storm began to abate. Not long after, I glimpsed through rents in the sheet of rain Will's aluminum outboard boat bobbing wildly in the angry waters. Finally I could see him huddled under a survival-red air mattress we had used to cover the cameras on the way to the island. Soon the wind fell off enough so it was safe to bring the boat to the shore. It was almost full of water. We had to turn it over to empty it before loading the soaked blind and the equipment. I did not dare inspect the nests but I hoped the birds had been so dazed by the fury of the storm that they had covered the eggs and young even when my blind was dashed to the ground.

Will accused me of reckless disregard for the safety of the birds.

"You should not have come out of your blind until I came back, so the birds would leave without being scared."

I knew this, so what was the use of explaining that the storm was powerful beyond my ability to cope with it. A few days later Will forgave me, for I found a hummingbird nest near the tip of an oak branch in a grove where he frequently birded. It was the first breeding record for a hummingbird on the Aransas Refuge.

Allan fared better than I. Either his greater strength had enabled him to keep his blind upright throughout the storm or the most tempestuous gusts had bypassed Island Number Two. The Corpus Christi weather station reported that 5.69 inches of rain fell in about two hours that day and wind gusts reached forty-seven miles an hour.

Spring in Texas is always a time of adventure for birdwatchers and bird photographers. National Audubon sanctuaries are necessarily off bounds for all visitors. They are set aside and guarded by wardens for one purpose only—that the colonial birds may nest in peace and security so people can enjoy them at other places. The Welder Wildlife Sanctuary near Sinton is host to a fascinating variety of wildlife. Scientists work there on wildlife projects as varied as the animal and plant life. Scientific work is carried on at many federal refuges, and while they are set aside primarily for game species, other wildlife is both welcomed and protected in them. At headquarters of the refuges permits may be obtained to visit at least a section of the reserve.

Both national and state parks protect all wildlife at all times and are excellent places to enjoy birds and other animals. The state parks of Texas vary from bare, rippled Sandhills State Park near Monahans where a bird on the dunes is an accident, to Bentsen near Mission, which is literally crowded with rare and interesting birds. The national forests of Texas are rich in wildlife, and so, with an entirely different population, is the National Grasslands in the northern Panhandle.

No birder should go to Texas without Peterson's *A Field Guide to the Birds of Texas* and Pettingill's *A Guide to Bird Watching* (West). Armed with these, a good pair of binoculars and maps from the highway department and literature from the park department, both located in Austin, even a stranger to Texas will find keen pleasure in watching birds there.

That spring morning as we sped away from the Sabine, going deeper and deeper into Texas, we met tree swallows already moving swiftly northward in a broad sheet that stretched from horizon to horizon. Touched by the early sun, their white breasts were streaks of silver.

We moved against the tide of migration that would soon sweep northward as the shifting of an enormous cloud that is pushed along by contrary currents. Sometimes it would stream as swiftly as a mountain brook plunges down a steep slope, sometimes as slowly as a butterfly drifts from flower to flower on a lazy day. But swiftly or slowly, the flocks are drawn steadily northward by the pull of spring, the increasing light and the longer days.

Then we saw our first mesquite tree, an indisputable indicator that we had left the east and were in Texas. Ahead were three months when we would be out-of-doors every day, always watching wildlife. We knew ourselves to be the luckiest people in the world.

I thought of a stage character I find particularly poignant; Thornton Wilder's Emily of *Our Town*. Returned from the grave to live again her twelfth birthday, she cannot look at anything enough. So much goes on, so much is beautiful. But nobody will *look*. Nobody notices the wonderful things around them; people rarely see each other.

"Oh, earth," mourns Emily, "you're too wonderful for anybody to realize you."

How true it is that we go blindly through life and seldom see the extraordinary world we live in. But during the spring months when we are in the field with wild life all day every day, we enter for a time that unseen world. We move out of our limited spheres into a world far older and better adjusted than the human world. It is a world without sentimentality where each animal lives within primitive laws or is quickly transmuted into some other form of life by way of a meal for the still strong and vital. Perhaps we would be no wiser at spring's end. But we would see bright birds and strange flowers. We would see lustrous eyes looking at us and wonder what they saw. We would marvel at the incredible variety of living things, each different from any other. Perhaps we would understand a little better the truth that no single species is desirable above all others, while each is important in its own way.

2

Twilight for Whoopers

THE FIRST TIME we saw whooping cranes, America's tallest, most regal bird, they were too far away for our cameras to record the thrilling sight. Already the species was one of the rarest in America and faced imminent extinction.

Imprinted in our memory of the eventful day was a picture of those cranes that stirred our pulse and aroused dreams of the time when we could know the great birds better and photograph them. Almost a decade would pass before that dream was realized. During the intervening years the fate of the whoopers would hang in delicate balance, even as it does today.

Chances are we should never have seen a wild whooping crane, had the Aransas National Wildlife Refuge not been established in 1937. This refuge spreads over more than 47,000 acres, mostly on Blackjack Peninsula, and has a shoreline of almost 45 miles of shallow water. It was set aside to provide a wintering place for hundreds of thousands of waterfowl. Once the salt marshes from the Sabine to the Rio Grande teemed with ducks and geese in winter, but those seemingly limitless coastal marshes were vanishing before varied developments that threatened to engulf the entire shore. Yet wintering places are quite as vital to the survival of ducks, geese and other birds as are their breeding grounds. Like people, they demand food and a suitable home the year around.

In this refuge for game birds, other species found a haven, too, and among them was a tiny band of whooping cranes. Since the turn of the century there had been steadily mounting alarm as the already small number of whooping cranes continued to decline. Until the Aransas Refuge was established, however, no concrete step had been taken to preserve the magnificent birds. That first winter fourteen whooping cranes set up territories in the new refuge.

James O. Stevenson left a comfortable office in Washington to become the first manager of the refuge and immediately succumbed to the spell of the cranes. He began publicizing their grim circumstances. People who had never given a thought to the rights of wildlife began to realize they were shirking their responsibilities as monarchs of all lesser creatures if they did nothing to protect endangered species.

The National Audubon Society had long urged that action be taken to preserve the dwindling cranes. In this they were supported by many groups including the Wilson Club and the American Ornithologists Union. Though the United States Bureau of Sports Fisheries and Wildlife is primarily charged with the care of game species, in 1945 the bureau joined the National Audubon Society in a project to study the whooping crane, with its preservation as the goal. Later the Canadian Wildlife Service joined this effort.

That autumn Dr. Olin Sewall Pettingill, Jr., one of the most distinguished ornithologists this country has produced, was given leave from Carleton College to begin the study. He inventoried all the wild and captive cranes, studied the whoopers on the refuge, and the following summer amid clouds of mosquitoes and swarms of tormenting gnats aptly called *no-see-'ums* by the Indians, searched the muskeg for nesting sites in the region of Lake Athabacka in Canada. He chose that area on the best available evidence as the most likely nesting place of the rare birds. He was too far east but almost a decade of continued search by both Americans and Canadians passed before a nest was finally found in Wood Buffalo Park in 1954.

By the time Dr. Pettingill's leave of absence ended, the late Robert Porter Allen, then research director for the National Audubon Society, had been discharged from army duties during World War II. He took over the study of the cranes. The wild flock then numbered twenty-five birds. The results of Bob Allen's studies have been told in many magazine articles, in his book, *On the Trail of Vanishing Birds*, and in his masterly reports: *"The Whooping Crane,"* and its sequel, "The Whooping Crane's Northern Breeding Grounds." All of these are not only fascinating to read but they contain the most important facts known about the rare and majestic birds. If the whooping cranes are saved for the years to come, this can be credited in a large measure to the remarkable effort made on their behalf by Robert Porter Allen for the National Audubon Society and the Bureau of Sports Fisheries and Wildlife.

About two years after the establishment of the Aransas Refuge in 1937 we made our first spring trip to Texas. A Stevenson, the manager. He said two cranes still lingered in the refuge, though usually they all left sometime in April. He urged Allan to hurry. There was a chance that he could photograph the rare birds if he arrived while the birds loitered on the marsh.

So it happened that early on May 6 we piled into a refuge truck at Headquarters and set off for Blackjack Peninsula, scattering herds of white-tailed deer having a final morning browse, sending flocks of wild turkeys scurrying into the brush and chasing jackrabbits that bounded with incredible leaps ahead of us. We paused by a pond where Wilson's phalaropes spun in circles like so many whirligig beetles as they stirred up their breakfast. From a watery thicket we flushed a pair of tawny fulvous tree ducks, long-legged and long-necked as geese.

Jim stopped by an oak motte where great horned owls had nested. It was still occupied by one fully fledged youngster that glared at us with huge wild yellow eyes. A white-tailed hawk carrying a stick glided over us. Jim showed us its half-built nest on top of a yucca, the daggerlike leaves circling it like bristling bayonets. Everywhere we saw new birds and old friends and no wonder, for almost three hundred species of birds have been recorded on the refuge.

As we advanced the road faded to a track. Live oaks and sweet bay became more widely scattered. Brush was lower. Far in the distance rose a few bare sand ridges. A great salt marsh nearly two miles wide and reaching to the horizon both north and south opened before us. The marsh was broken by shallow ponds and mud flats. Here and there slim fingers of water probed the green plain.

The air was filled with sweet plaintive whistles of shorebirds on their way north. For the first time I saw noisy long-billed curlews, largest of American shorebirds, with down-curved bills as long as seven inches, almost a third of their entire length. Stilt sandpipers and chunky dowitchers bound for arctic breeding grounds rested in compact flocks, and others, their legs twinkling, sped about probing the mud with their bills.

Pink spoonbills and white herons started up from small pools. We watched reddish egrets in a wide shallow pond spread their wings and dart and swoop erratically, swaying as they cavorted. Far from dancing for art's sake, the odd but graceful motions were their way of catching minnows. Above us a great flock of white pelicans alternately beat their great wings and soared in unison as they circled with measured dignity toward the clouds.

"We are close to the whooper territory now," Jim told us.

"Get your camera ready, Allan, so you can shoot the instant we are near enough for a picture. The cranes are wary and will not allow us to approach near them."

Just then Jim glanced at a grassy tongue of land thrust far into open water.

"Look," he yelled. "Five javelinas! Biggest bunch I've ever seen. I'll try to cut them off so you can get a shot of them."

We surged forward and already the javelinas, aware of their distance from the nearest cover, raced to escape from the trap Jim hoped to close. Javelina (have-a-lena) is the Mexican name for the only American pig, the collared peccary. It has coarse blackish bristles, a broad dirty-white collar, long tusks, and a very short tail.

I was scared. I had read stories about hunters who had barely escaped with their lives when attacked by a band of peccaries, of others held prisoner for days while the beasts took turns patrolling around and around the tree where they had taken refuge, and of less fortunate people torn to bits by them. So my heart beat fast as I thought of Allan getting out of the safety of the truck to take their picture even if the speed they were displaying showed caution if not downright timidity.

Later I learned such tales were tall ones. Often to save travel time when he was studying the cranes on territory, Bob Allen slept in a tent far down Blackjack Peninsula. One night he was wakened by footsteps and a strong musky smell. In the moonlight he saw a javelina in the small tent, exploring it thoroughly. It sniffed all around Bob's sleeping bag while he lay motionless. Finally it wandered out and Bob went back to sleep.

Javelinas do appear to resent and sometimes attack dogs.

One day one of the staff wives at the refuge heard her cocker whining and at the same time a strange whoofing and grunting outside her kitchen. Looking out the window she saw a heaving, shoving band of javelinas apparently trying to dig their way under the house where the dog had taken refuge. She snatched up a broom and began laying about with it. The javelinas appeared to think their companions were responsible for the furious thrashing and they redoubled their pushing and began to bite each other. Suddenly there was a pause, and they all swung about and tumbled over one another in a mad rush to escape.

Now as we sped headlong to cut off the javelinas, Allan clutched his camera and unlatched the door, ready for a quick leap to the ground.

"The instant I step on the brakes, jump and shoot your picture," Jim shouted over the roaring motor. "Those fellows are really traveling. NOW!"

I toppled forward like a rag doll and Allan was halfway out of the truck when, quicker than anybody could think, he reacted to a furious buzz directly beneath his foot, and he was inside again, slamming the door. A thick four-foot rattler shot out of the very spot Allan's foot had reached for. If Allan was fast, no TV triggerman ever acted faster than Jim. With one smooth motion he caught up a rifle, was out and around the truck and with a single shot straight through the head killed the reptile.

"This place is alive with rattlers," Jim wiped his face. "They give me nightmares. In my charge is a CCC camp of city boys put here to help build roads and dikes. Those boys can't tell the difference between the buzz of a cicada and a rattler. They are so ignorant about the country there is no telling what fool thing they may do. I wouldn't put it past them to pick up a rattler by the tail."

Silence gripped us as we stared at the dead rattler. Allan had had a narrow escape, but we were even more impressed by the accuracy of Jim's single shot through the head of the speeding, raging snake. Then Jim groaned.

"The whoopers. There they go. Listen!"

We had forgotten the object of our early morning journey to the marsh. Now two great white birds ran lightly on tip-toe over the plain and rose into the air. A loud, rather harsh trumpeting, a sound that stirred the spirits and lifted the heart, shook the east wind. With tranquil, unhurried strokes the wings, reaching more than seven feet from tip to jet-black tip, carried them away, and they vanished in the hazy distance. Long after they passed beyond our vision we heard their wild free bugles ringing from afar.

Gradually our memory of that morning when the two majestic birds winged away and the music of their bugles slowly died, lost its clarity and merged into all the accounts we read of whooping cranes from modern times back to 1722 when Mark Catesby, who never saw a living whooping crane obtained a dried skin of one from an Indian and from this painted and described the species. We saw and heard the cranes through the eyes and ears of Bartram, Hearne, Audubon, Coues and many others. Included was a description by the botanist Thomas Nuttall of a vast assembly of whooping cranes in the Mississippi Valley on a December night in 1811. He listened to "vast migrations of the whooping cranes assembled by many thousands. . . . The clangor of these numerous legions passing along high in the air seemed almost deafening; the confused cry of the vast army continued with the lengthening procession and as the vocal call continued nearly throughout the night without intermission, some idea may be formed of the immensity of the numbers now assembled. . . ."

One evening we talked with Bob Allen about bird songs at night and recalled the music of Leach's petrels coming through dense fog to their Maine island nests, and the single notes of northbound songbirds above the Dry Tortugas here

and there from all parts of the sky until the emigrants wing-
ing by seemed as numerous as the stars. We spoke of loons
calling across a mountain lake in New Hampshire and the
honking of geese on cold winter nights at Mattamuskeet,
North Carolina, just west of Cape Hatteras.

"We have heard a lot of wonderful bird sounds," I commented, "but I feel cheated because I can never hear a
whooping crane chorus like the one Nuttall described."

Bob objected. "If Nuttall heard that many cranes, he
heard sandhills, not whoopers. Look here," Bob rummaged
through some magazines and held out a book review, pointing to a sentence that read ". . . when James Fenimore
Cooper was writing the first notable American adventure
stories, whooping cranes were as numerous as buffalo." There
have always been gullible people ready to accept stories of
former abundance of birds and mammals, but as far as
whooping cranes are concerned, facts don't support them.
Catesby never saw a live one and Hearne, writing about the
Hudson's Bay country late in the eighteenth century, mentioned them as regular but usually seen only in pairs and
then not very often. Bartram usually called all the cranes in
Florida whooping cranes, but then people there today still
call sandhills whooping cranes. Early in the nineteenth century McCall traveled along the Texas coast, and occasionally
saw pairs and even three or four together but no real flocks.
When Elliot Coues published *Birds of the Northwest* in
1874 he gave the range of the whooping crane as the interior
of America up through the Mississippi Valley and spreading
into the fur countries, but he noted that no specimens were
obtained by collecting expeditions into that area.

"I don't believe," Bob continued, "that whooping cranes
have been really numerous since Columbian days. Probably
they looked as they do today before man made his appearance on earth, reached their peak of abundance late in the
Pleistocene and have been slowly declining ever since. But

don't think for a minute that the coming of Europeans to America didn't have a decisive impact on their population!"

"Our growing numbers and the fantastic habitat changes we have engineered may have given the cranes a fatal shove toward quick extinction. They are darned near it right now. I estimate the whooping crane population at about fourteen hundred birds by the time Coues wrote *Birds of the Northwest*. Now their numbers are so reduced and their nesting and wintering places so limited we may not be able to save them."

There was never any doubt, however, that black as the future for the cranes might be, Bob Allen would do everything within his power to save the tiny wild group of twenty-two adults and three young birds that made it back to the Aransas Refuge in 1946.

That conversation led us to search accurate accounts of the nineteenth century for reports of whooping cranes. The Lewis and Clark Expedition cut across the migration route of the species when they should have been conspicuous had they been numerous. On April 11, 1805, the expedition was moving up the Missouri near the mouth of the Little Missouri at a point now beneath the Garrison Reservoir, and Lewis noted: "Saw some large white cranes pass up the river. These are the largest bird of that genus common to the country through which the Missouri and Mississippi pass. They are perfectly white except the large feather of the first two points of the wing which is black."

On October 26, 1805, when the southbound migration of the cranes would be under way, the expedition had reached a place near the present Dallas Dam on the Columbia River. Clark wrote: "a great number of white crains flying in Different directions very high."

We suspect these "crains" were not whoopers. More likely they were snow geese or white pelicans, which are often misidentified as whooping cranes as are wood storks in the southeast. Both the geese and pelicans still occur there in good numbers. No whooping cranes were collected by the expedition.

Alexander Wilson never saw a whooping crane until Audubon showed him some near Louisville in 1810. Audubon proved his acquaintance with the species, for his painting of it is detailed and accurate. He wrote of flocks numbering twenty to thirty individuals moving southward in November. Audubon so loved the dramatic that had he observed larger flocks, surely he would have noted them with enthusiastic rhetoric. Audubon saw few whooping cranes in Florida but quantities of their beautiful feathers, which were sought by Spaniards and Indians for use in fans and fly brushes. Coues, mentioned earlier, never saw the species alive except in northern Dakota. Though he failed to find a nest he suspected they bred in that area.

There are reliable records of nests with eggs during the nineteenth century from Iowa, Minnesota, North Dakota and Illinois. No nest has been found in the United States this century except for some belonging to a peculiar, non-migrating group in southwest Louisiana that has now been extirpated.

The wild, wary whooping cranes, so closely identified with extensive spaces and primitive solitudes, continued to nest in widely separated parts of central Canada as late as 1922. That summer the "last wild whooping crane nest" was found near Muddy Lake southeast of Unity in Saskatchewan's great prairie country. Then decades passed when not a single nest was found anywhere in spite of intensive search.

Hidden somewhere in the vast, seldom visited wilderness of north-central Canada a few whooping cranes persisted in building their high, wide nests. Somewhere among tangled streams bordered by dense willow thickets or in watery marshes or in the muskeg, eggs were laid and young were hatched. Over a twenty-two-year period, eighty-four young cranes accompanied the adults to Aransas. This was an average of fewer than four young whoopers a year successful in making the long flight south to the cranes' remaining wintering ground, a pitifully small number to sustain the fading species.

In 1954 the nesting country was finally located in Wood Buffalo Park, an enormous national park sprawled over northern Alberta and southern Northwest Territories. From a plane above that primeval wilderness in a section where neither Indian nor white man had ever set foot, tiny rust-colored young were observed. They were in a pothole muskeg where open waters reflected the sky, and thickets of dwarfed spruce, willows, birch and larch bordered the ponds. There on tiny islands or long fingers of bulrushes the cranes built up their nests until they stood high and dry above the water.

Each time Bob Allen made a flying visit to New York for a National Audubon Society conference, the keen interest of the staff in the cranes and their precarious future was lifted even higher. Sometimes one of his visits aroused attention in far wider fields as when he went to see *Where's Charley?* and without doubt was the most fascinated member of the audience that night. In Ray Bolger's energetic, leaping dances Bob saw several steps identical to some whooping crane steps. There in the darkened theater he delightedly sketched a composite Bolger-whooping crane dance, which was published in LIFE.

The time came when Allan had to make a new film for the National Audubon Society's Wildlife Films program. Profoundly impressed by Bob's concern for the whooping crane and remembering the many spectacular Audubon sanctuaries we had visited so long ago on our first short trip to Texas, Allan considered making his film there. The ex-

tremes in climate and altitude, its varied habitats and the vital role of conservation being played in Texas provided
plentiful material that he could film.

The very wealth of Texas bird life was impressive. Depending on the authority consulted, the total number of
bird species in North America varies. Dr. Roger Tory Peterson puts the total at about 650. In his *A Field Guide to the
Birds of Texas* he treats fully 487 species and lists an additional 55 species that have been identified in the state less
than five times, making a grand total of 542 Texas species.
One of these is the only surviving band of wild whooping
cranes.

When Allan consulted him about film opportunities in
Texas Bob was fired with enthusiasm.

"Come straight to Aransas," he urged. "You must have
whoopers in your film and you can surely get some from my
blind. Aransas in spring is a great place. The majority of
wintering ducks and geese will be gone but you will find
plenty still here. The wild turkeys will still be strutting,
too."

The blind Bob offered Allan was not the first he had
constructed. For some time before it was built, he made his
observations of crane behavior from a distance using a telescope. Bob possessed, among other talents, the ability to
sketch quickly and accurately. He wanted to reduce the distance to permit more accurate sketches. Noting the cranes
were not alarmed by cattle that sometimes grazed on the
marsh, he molded a beautiful bull of wire and canvas and
painted it realistically. Once inside his Trojan bull he could
see fairly well, though his movements were uncertain. The
fake bull was given to canting right or left unexpectedly.
Still, he was quite pleased with his blind, and one morning
before dawn he transported it to the salt marsh, climbed inside and with his legs acting as the forelegs of the mimic
bull, moved away while the jeep was driven back to refuge

headquarters. Far in the distance as dawn broke he saw the cranes. Joyfully he waited for them to come close, but just then he heard a peculiar sound on one side. It was a huge Santa Gertrudis bull pawing the ground and snorting with lowered head. Bob wished then that he could travel as fast as a crane, and through the air at that. Finally the bull lost interest and went away. So did the cranes. They were too wary and alert to be fooled by the patiently built contraption and Bob abandoned it on the marsh. Finally, remembering Allan's repeated successful use of blinds for photography, he built a tiny low one and baited the ground in front of it with grain. The whooping crane family in that territory accepted the grain and ignored the blind, which gave Bob the intimacy of observation he desired and later was used by Allan for his photography of the birds.

So when spring and photography time came we made straight for Aransas, having reserved one of the Hopper cabins between Austwell and the refuge, only to find a hitch in our plans. Every cabin had been commandeered for workmen constructing a new wharf. Since there was no place to stay within forty miles of the refuge, Mrs. Hopper won our undying gratitude by persuading the reluctant owner of a weekend cottage just up the road to rent it to us. He held out against her pleas for some time because he had to come down weekends to care for his hygrangeas of which he was justly proud. Finally he gave in but with a condition. We must use the double bed in the living room, leaving the bedroom for him. So shelter was found for us while we worked at the refuge. Life in that cottage was to be more exciting than we dreamed when we unlocked the door. Biologically it offered many surprises, some downright unnerving.

The bathroom was an architectural afterthought, a dark cubbyhole reached by going through the kitchen, out the back door and across a small cement porch. Wasps, industriously building nests entirely around the four walls where they joined the ceiling, buzzed with animosity whenever we intruded.

Black widow spiders lurked in considerable numbers. Unlike the wasps, they moved stealthily in ominous silence. Fortunately they are not aggressive, for their colorless venom is said to be more virulent drop for drop than that of a diamondback rattler. Edwin Way Teale tells in *Grassroot Jungles* of acquiring the silk pouch of a black widow spider. When he cut it open out rolled about three hundred eggs, each as small as the head of a pin, and translucent with a purplish sheen. We searched for egg sacs but failed to find one.

It was not until we turned on the shower that we discovered that scorpions, those omens of evil, lived under the baseboard. Apparently the falling water aroused them, and they came out militantly with stingers swung above their backs and ready for action. There was no room in the cubbyhole for the lavatory, so it was fastened to the outside wall where we washed, brushed our teeth and Allan shaved under the interested gaze of fishermen going to and fro on the road.

A perverted rat managed to squeeze into the bathroom every night through some small opening and then was too stupid to find its way out again. In a panic it racketed madly about until finally, unable to sleep, we got up and let it out. Had we left the door open a rattler might have decisively ended our troubles with the rat, but the bathroom, dark and comparatively temperate, might be so attractive to the well-stuffed rattler that it would remain. Thoughts of meeting even a lethargic rattler when, sleepy-eyed, we stumbled into the bathroom next morning, deterred us from taking advantage of the snake's skill as a rat disposal.

The first evening when Allan took the garbage to the pit there was a big rattler in possession, probably waiting to catch one of the rats that visited it. After that he always took the garbage out by daylight and looked around until in some shady nook he located the reptile. In Texas rattlers are called lords of the night. Though we prefer to walk at night with only the stars or moon to give us light, it was wise in the Aransas area to carry a flashlight after dark, for then the heat-sensitive reptiles came out to hunt and we met them suddenly in unexpected places.

All snakes are vulnerable to the intense heat experienced for part of the year by our southern states, so they hide during hot days. Staff members of the Arizona–Sonora Desert Museum near Tucson have told us that snakes are so sensitive to heat that just keeping them alive is a serious problem when they are needed for programs in the city only twenty or thirty minutes away. Often to keep these sensitive reptiles alive and active, the snake cages are wrapped in wet towels to provide cooling by evaporation, and sometimes chunks of ice are added. As long as the days were cool at Aransas we had to remember that snakes were active and might come into our blinds. Once the heat set in, a cautious inspection before we entered our blinds in the morning was enough. Barring some disturbance that chased the snakes from their chosen hiding place they were inactive all day.

Before our first night at the cottage advanced much further, we were awakened again, this time by mysterious taps on the floor. When these went on and on unabated, Allan seized his flashlight and we went out into the night and lay flat on the ground while he played the light back and forth in the narrow space beneath the cottage. Several pairs of tiny eyes gleamed in the pencil of light. A family of big-eared, pink-nosed armadillos digging in the earth under the cottage were bumping the floor with their shell-covered backs. Once we had identified the mysterious tapping, the sound of the busy armadillos no longer kept us awake.

As the days went by, we found these peculiar mammals were actually abundant on the refuge. As long as the cold days continued, they stayed out to feed late in the morning and came out early again in the afternoon. The first time we saw one in a field with its armored head and tail hidden in the grass, Allan remarked that its rounded body looked rather like a football. Perhaps the association with sport awakened his old track-team spirit because he decided to catch it for a closer look. Somebody at the refuge had told him if he caught one to seize it by the lower edge of the shell between the front and back legs, otherwise he could be badly scratched by toenails meant for digging. So off dashed Allan and away went the armadillo. He gained on it and bent to pick it up, whereupon the armadillo shot off at right angles. Again Allan gained on it and again the armadillo changed course while Allan took longer to change his direction. Each time he thought he had it the armadillo swung abruptly and made its escape. Finally it swung in its tracks and raced back toward me as I cheered Allan on. This time the armadillo went to ground. After a few more defeats by other armadillos, Allan won a race. I looked curiously at the strange animal he held, one that had stirred Kipling's imagination so much he wrote one of his most charming *Just So Stories* about the beginning of the armadillos. They are more odd than Kipling's delightful flight of fancy suggests. If they want to cross a narrow stream they simply plunge in and walk along the bottom. Should the body of water be a broad one they can inflate themselves enough to bob over the surface rather like toy balloons or dried gourds. The females give birth to identical quadruplets, all of the same sex. The quads are born with their eyes open; their soft shells soon harden. While juveniles, they are much paler in color than the adults. As Allan held the squirming armadillo I looked at its toenails, which are efficient digging tools. They were a beautiful oval and shiny pink. Its big ears looked rather like leaves and probably are most effective in trapping sounds, but its pinkish-rimmed eyes looked weak and almost blind. Coarse black hairs grew at random. A sort of gusset of tough skin joined the shell to the soft and vulnerable underparts. Nine bands of shell across the middle of the back also are joined by tough skin, and these give the armored back considerable flexibility. For a long time armadillo baskets, made by bending the shell somewhat and bringing the armored tail forward into the mouth to make a handle, were popular.

Armadillo flesh is good, it is said, and is often called poor man's pork. They have not learned to beware of speeding cars and great numbers of them are killed every night on our highways, where they become food for vultures and other carrion-eaters.

If Allan enjoyed his races with armadillos, I enjoyed a game with them also. One day I stood motionless to watch a pair of scissor-tailed flycatchers build their pale soft nest. An armadillo came slowly along the trail, and noting an obstruction in its way, stood on its hind legs to sniff. Apparently I carried no scent of danger, and it dropped down and went its way. This led to a more passive game than Allan's armadillo races. I tried to sneak up on those I saw busily digging for insects and grubs. Sometimes I managed to pat one on the rump. Then it would keep right on digging and only notice the pats by heaving up its rump and giving a small kick. This was great fun, but about 75 per cent of the games were won by the armadillo, which raced away with erratic shifts of direction before I could pat it.

Though we went peacefully back to sleep after seeing the armadillos under the cottage, we did not rest undisturbed for long. In the first fading of night before dawn something large pressed against the window screen until it twanged. We heard heavy breathing, then stamping, and a soft whinny. Two horses were trying to push the screen out of the window. The wall of our sleeping room formed part of a corral for horses. The horses, sensing the presence of people, were demanding attention. We surrendered all thoughts of further sleep. Already birds were waking and soft notes from here and there gathered quickly into a resounding chorus.

Before the sun cleared the horizon, Bob, driving a green jeep, came by and we were off at a merry pace. This quickly slackened to a sluggish uncertain speed of no more than twelve miles an hour, for the refuge roads were badly rutted and had become one long quagmire from heavy rains that continued to fall at intervals. Unprotected in the small jeep, the brisk wind wrapped us in a wintery blast and set us shivering like so many aspen leaves. Though I was blue with cold, birds sang their independent vernal songs enthusiastically, and these all blended by some magic into a symphony.

Soon the marsh ahead of us blazed with golden light, and everywhere blue water in lively motion tossed sparkles from wave to wave. A spring of teal leaped from sheltering bulrushes. Then ducks by the hundred became uneasy, held their heads high and quacked in alarm. They skipped with spirited paddles across the surface and then, airborne, wove tangled skeins above us. Laughing gulls had donned their springtime black hoods and now wheeled and cackled.

Lurching unsteadily and throwing long streamers of mud from the wheels, we neared the intercoastal canal, which had been driven straight across the finest crane wintering marsh.

"It would have been easy to locate the waterway beyond the marshes which are so crucial to the future of the cranes," Bob told us, "but the National Audubon and other conservation groups couldn't budge the Corps of Engineers from their chosen route. They couldn't think beyond the machinery they use and the earth they displace to the all-over welfare of the land. It is discouraging to struggle for what you know is right today and will be even more right in the future, only to be defeated by bureaucrats. The canal is one more great hazard against the survival of the whooping cranes; the result of narrow, restricted thought."

We had drawn close to Mustang Lake and Bob's head swiveled from side to side. Suddenly he slammed on the brakes and grabbed his binoculars.

"I see them, too." Allan's binoculars were aimed beyond the open water.

"Three of them here, and all accounted for." Bob said. "You can pick out the male because he is definitely taller than his mate. Even at this distance you can see the rusty wash on the head of the young bird. Chalk up three whoopers!

We slogged on through the squelching road. I turned to keep the shining white birds in view as they receded in the distance. All three walked with great dignity in Indian file and then, just before I lost sight of them, they stopped, gathered in a close group; apparently they had found some choice morsel that all shared.

When the inspection ended that morning, we had seen a total of eighteen cranes, more than half of all the wild whoopers in the entire world. All were in widely separated family groups of two or three, except for one crane all by itself.

"The ones with young always claim the best territories," Bob told us. "Even though a single crane or a pair arrive first and claim a particularly good area, they are displaced by parents with one or two young birds. The territory boundaries are not particularly rigid but there is strife if an established territory is invaded very deeply."

Always our view of the whoopers was a distant one, and we found that we must use the 30X of the telescope for really careful study of them. That morning not a single crane flew. All were either striding across a marsh or shallow water or intent upon feeding.

"It is difficult to tell what they are eating," Bob said, "because I can't get close enough to be sure what they pick up so I have to rely to quite an extent on droppings for exact information. I've found, though, that the tracks tell something. When they are catching blue crabs they move around in a circle, and when they probe for mud shrimps and worms, they stalk along the pond edges in single file."

One pair of whoopers, far out in a shallow pond, slowly swung a crude circle as we watched.

"Blue crabs. They are having blue crabs for breakfast." We felt we had learned some crane lore.

That morning set a pattern often followed in days to come. We joined Bob on his inspection trips whenever we planned to work in blinds on Blackjack Peninsula, for, the tour ended, he could drop us off well ahead of good photography light. Each day we were more eager to work in Bob's blind, but he advised us to wait for a really good morning that promised acceptable light throughout the day. Otherwise when or if the cranes came, we might be frustrated by dense clouds. Impatiently we waited for that desirable morning and in the meantime worked with ducks and wild turkeys and red-tailed hawks. We also had many small adventures.

One morning as we turned back from the inspection trip we stopped to watch a party of vultures gathered on a dead cow. Down came a caracara, and the vultures bounced away into a respectful circle well removed from the cow. The caracara ate its fill and stood quietly for a few moments, then walked close to the ring of vultures and stretched its neck forward and stood still. With their bouncing gait, several vultures gathered around the caracara and began to run their bills through the head feathers of the caracara. All the time the vultures maintained a fawning, servile attitude. Finally the caracara appeared satisfied with the attention given its head and neck by the vultures and flew away. Then the vultures returned to their interrupted feast.

We have had pet blue jays and crows probe our hair and around our ears with their bills, but it was with an affec-

tionate air of an equal caressing a friend, and never obsequious in manner. Accounts of explorations of other animals
by birds are fairly numerous. It is believed that many times
when cattle egrets run up and down the backs of elephants,
water buffalo or domestic cattle, they are eating flies or other
insects. The crocodile bird or crocodile plover was named
for its habit of inspecting those big saurians, even on occasion picking around the formidable teeth. William Henry
Hudson in *Birds and Man* noted a jackdaw scramble about
the back of a cow, where it busied itself with its beak to the
evident enjoyment of the mammal. Another time in Saver-
nake Forest he watched a jackdaw explore the face of a deer.
Unlike the caresses of a pet crow or jay, which apparently
stem from an affectionate attitude, these other birds mentioned obviously seek food from the bodies of the animals
they search. The vultures like bird pets with humans, appeared to caress the caracara and gave no indication of
plucking anything from it. Only in their cringing, subser-
vient attitude did the vultures' behavior differ from that of
bird pets, while the caracara behaved like a monarch demanding service from his inferiors.

Sometimes when the sun burned through the clouds, turtles, stirred by the sudden heat, climbed onto high dry places
where the road, lying across a shallow pond area, was built
well above flood level. Using their hind feet alternately in
rhythmic but slow shoveling, the turtles scooped cavities for
their eggs, which were covered, again by using the hind feet,
and left alone to be hatched by the heat of the sun. One day
we sat on the road near a snapping turtle fully a foot across
its shell that had already begun to lay its eggs in the grassy
shoulder on the south slope. The eggs were perfectly round
and white. We decided, when she completed laying, that she
had deposited about twenty eggs in the cavity. The snapper
was large enough to be potentially dangerous. She could
strike with the speed of a rattler and her jaws were strong

enough to snap a broomstick in half. But now, intent on depositing her eggs in the cavity she had excavated, she aroused, not thoughts of danger, but of Alice in Wonderland, for tears coursed from her eyes as she labored. Unlike Alice's Mock Turtle, with large eyes full of tears, the snapper's face was wet by tears from small very dark brown eyes.

One day as we turned toward headquarters, Bob suddenly veered off the road, pushing the gas pedal to the floor at the same time.

"A red wolf." His eyes sparkled with gusto. "Let's chase it. The more we can put fear of people in it the longer it will live," and we rocketed across the plain while I, in the back seat, hung on for dear life and gruesome visions of hitting some stump or rock and all of us hurled from the jeep flickered across my mind.

"They are another of our vanishing animals," Bob told us, "and another tragic loss immediately before us. Once there were red wolves in Florida and Louisiana, but they are all gone. The Texas red wolf, the only exclusively North American wolf, is disappearing fast. They eat a few things people want, and there are plenty of men who can't stand that; so they are varmints to be shot, trapped and poisoned. I'm afraid they will soon be extinct. They seldom weigh as much as seventy pounds, a hundred pounds less than some of the arctic timber wolves."

How that wolf did travel! It seemed to flatten into a long streak, and its flying legs were a blur as it raced over the open prairie toward shelter where it vanished into a mesquite thicket.

The few red wolves still living are slightly larger than their successful relatives, the coyote, which have extended their ancient range in the face of man's persecution. For one brief period we had a fairly intimate acquaintance with one of the small wolves. John Davenport, who lived on a farm near Austwell, found a weak, almost starved pup. Probably its mother had been a victim of the local enmity against wolves. John fed and cared for his pup. Shortly it regained its normal vigor and became as lively and affectionate as a wire-haired puppy. Its bright mischievous eyes and pointed ears were in constant motion as it caught every sight and sound. It was as charming a pet as any boy ever had, and John adored it. When he was not playing with his pet, John snapped on its collar a chain leash that ended in a ring that slid freely along an overhead wire so the wolf could frisk up and down. One day when the Davenports were away from home the red wolf disappeared and was never seen again. Some callous individual with no pity for a child's grief over the loss of a beloved pet, a man to whom hungry animals are evil pests, had trespassed on another's property and disposed of the red wolf, cynically leaving the leash where it was with the clasp undamaged.

One morning the sun glittered on the horizon with no sign of its usual aureole. All the sky was cloudless and the wind drifted gently as a whisper.

"This is your day, Allan," Bob announced. "Now, if ever, you should have ten to twelve hours of good light. No matter when they come, if the whoopers show up, you should have adequate light for your shots."

That evening when Allan crawled out of the tiny blind he was beaming with joy.

"What a day! The cranes came twice. I know I have some excellent footage of them and some good stills, too."

I was so eager to get into the blind that I couldn't sleep that night. Next morning, with clouds once more hiding the sky, Bob and Allan put me in the blind, a tiny boxlike affair of wood and canvas, about seven o'clock. I was able to sit upright, something that neither of the tall men could do, for the top was very low. As soon as my camera was fixed on the tripod and swung into sharp focus on the grain Bob had scattered, they left, making as much confusion as possible so the sharpeyed cranes would observe their departure.

All that day I waited in vain. Not a crane did I see. Once I heard their stirring bugle ringing across the marsh. I listened intently but heard no more of the distant sound. Audubon claimed he could hear the calls of whoopers three miles away, and I believe the sounds I heard came from nearly that distance. The whoopers produce their resonant calls with an exceptional instrument, for their trachea is almost five feet long. It is coiled and packed in loops into the bony cavity of the sternum. This unique organ provides volume and resonance to a high degree. Texans long called the species bugle cranes. Whether their calls are regarded as buglelike or trumpetlike, comparison to either brass wind instrument indicates the power and clarity of their voices. When two or more cranes trumpet together there is a dissonant clangor as stirring as the final movement of Tchaikovsky's *1812 Overture* played by a great orchestra. Compounded of far horizons and lofty skies, of chill salty winds and tall birds trumpeting, the music of the cranes will never be truly captured on tape or wax for posterity. Only a recording of notes can be preserved, notes to be studied and analyzed; but the music of the cranes will be gone forever if whoopers pass into oblivion.

There were many birds to watch and many songs to hear that day, but the cranes did not show themselves. My vigil was lightened by a white-footed mouse that had moved into Bob's blind. At times it crept to the grain and, having collected some, frisked back to its dark home. After stowing the grain it paused near me to wash its long quivery whiskers and look at me with interest but no fear. At lunch time it accepted a piece of cheese from my sandwich with caution and then delight. By five o'clock I was cold, stiff and weary. Allan and Bob swung my almost rigid body into the jeep, but I begged for another day in the blind.

Again the next morning I was left there and Allan,

who knows well that there is one thing I can do even better than he, and that is keep very still for a very long time, went away shouting, "No singing and yelling in the blind today! If you do you'll keep the cranes away again."

I made an indignant face at him and settled down. My fingers were stiff with cold, and each time I checked to make sure the camera was still focused on the grain the view finder fogged. The sun swung higher and the blind slowly became more comfortable. No man-made sounds could be heard except for the chug of an occasional boat moving along the distant inland waterway. With loud whistles yellowlegs dropped down to feed, hurriedly jabbing their slender bills into the mud. In the shallow water baldpate and blue-winged teal consorted in amiable conventions. Three heavy-bodied white pelicans slipped onto a mud bar while I was looking another way, and my heart lurched for an instant as my eyes swung over them. I thought the cranes had come. Though the distance was great, their huge bills and short legs corrected my swift impression.

A horned lark sprang from the grass and mounted steeply into the sky until its distant volatile tinkling song, a spirit voice, floated down as lightly as gossamer. A meadowlark established an uncertain perch on a yellow-edged red gaillardia blossom, threw back its head, and with clear poignant whistles sang of its love of spring, of sunny days, and of its mate as truly as if the scientific world had not relegated bird song to a triggered defense of territory.

Once more I heard the distant sputter of a motorboat. This one brought me luck. The crane family must have been feeding close to the channel for I heard a sudden burst of trumpets. Three cranes lifted above the horizon and flew straight toward the blind, bugling as they advanced. Their necks extended before them as stiffly as lances, and their long legs trailed straight behind. Great wings beat in strong shallow thrusts, and like sandhill cranes in flight, they gave a quick flick of the tips with each powerful stroke. These birds, which stride with grace and freedom across wide marshes, are equally at home in the air. Then the cranes dipped down to land, and I recalled Audubon's remarks as he heard

> . . . from on high the notes of the swiftly traveling but unseen Whooping Crane. . . . Gradually they descend, dress their extended lines, and prepare to alight on the earth. With necks outstretched, and long bony legs extended behind, they proceed, supported by wings white as the snow but tipped with jet, until arriving over the great savannah they wheel their circling flight, and slowly approach the ground, on which with half-closed wings, and outstretched feet they alight, running along for a few steps to break the force of their descent.

Now the cranes landed while still some distance from the blind, and gave a final resonant shout. Shaking their feathers into place, they walked like kings with stately dignity across a shallow pool, still advancing directly toward the blind. The smallest of the three was their young of last summer, whose face was an odd reddish buff, all that was left of its infant rust color The young bird led the procession. Upon reaching the grain it daintily picked up and ate some corn. Its poised deliberate choice of a kernel here and another there was in sharp contrast to the gluttonous behavior of gulls and many other birds when they find a concentration of food.

In the meantime the adults with measured tread moved to and fro, placing each foot with deliberate precision. Then the male halted, bowed, flapped his wings and leaped stiffly into the air. He dropped down again with his legs held at an awkward angle and his bill pointed upward. The female, definitely smaller, forgot her dignity and ran toward him, pumping her head up and down very much as a young heron does when begging for food, and flapping her wings.

Then both birds bounded into the air, their snowy wings gleaming and the black tips flashing in the sun, but they rose only two or three feet and then dropped back. I believe they bowed, then, but surprised by my good fortune to see even an abbreviated whooping crane dance at close quarters as if we had been in a ballroom, I let my notebook fall unnoticed to the ground.

The rusty-faced crane stopped eating and stared at its parents, then forgot about food and walked toward them. But their latent desire to dance, which never completely forsakes them even in midwinter, was satisfied for the time being by the few steps executed, and the adults swung about and faced the east. Now as they had advanced, they retreated in a precisely spaced straight line, and the cranes marched off toward the horizon with a stately gait reminiscent of royalty making a public appearance.

That afternoon visit by the crane to the blind climaxed a day that will forever be a thrilling memory. The mud-stained page where my open notebook fell to the wet ground and was forgotten in the presence of America's most regal and perhaps rarest birds is enough to bring the day alive. The burst of trumpets beyond the horizon challenging the intrusion in their territory of a hostile presence, their shining wings spreading far wider than a tall man can reach and their imposing march across the plain tenderly colored with spring green presented a unique sequence of events. The small family had made last autumn a 2,500-mile journey from the muskeg country of Canada to the Aransas Refuge when their route bristled from beginning to end with the guns of sportsmen at the height of the waterfowl season. In another couple of weeks or so they would set out to reverse that hazardous journey to the far-off muskeg. There the young would be expelled from the family group before the new nest was built. The three would leave Aransas while that remote nesting area was still gripped by winter cold. In

The mockingbird is a fitting state bird for Texas. They are found in woodlands, cities, towns, mountain slopes and even in the desert. (Chapter 1)

Once near Denton we were awakened by a host of scissor-tailed flycatchers singing in the moonlight. (Chapter 1)

The chorus rose and fell with soft, insistent urgency. White-winged doves led all the rest. (Chapter 1)

In search of weed seeds, tribes of lark buntings so big they darken acres at a time drift about the chilly plateaus. Migrant through the western half of Texas, and wintering south of the Panhandle, a few return to the Panhandle region to breed. (Chapter 1)

Whooping cranes, America's tallest, most regal birds. (Chapter 2)

The whooping cranes walked like kings with stately dignity.
(Chapter 2)

I looked curiously at the strange animal that had stirred Kipling's imagination so much that he wrote one of his *Just So Stories* about the beginning of the armadillos. (Chapter 2)

I found the blue-winged teal more beautiful than I had thought. (Chapter 3)

Turkey gobblers with their feathers puffed and their huge tails erect. (Chapter 4)

When the time came to decide on a national bird, Benjamin Franklin urged with eloquence that the wild turkey be chosen. (Chapter 4)

The ladder lurched and swayed as I climbed down into the cavern. Now I could hear the incessant, very high-pitched chatter of bats, innumerable bats. (Chapter 5)

One spring I ran across a reference to peyote. It stated that it has the effect of changing sound into light—the ticks of a watch are received as a rapid succession of beautiful colors. (Chapter 6)

Scaled quail, round soft-gray birds, their breast feathers edged with dark, giving them a genuinely scaled look. These were true Western birds, usually associated with cactus, yucca and other thorny plants. (Chapter 7)

Painted buntings spend the winter with us in Florida. Beyond the
Pecos in Texas we saw a male bird. Song burst enthusiastically from
its quivering throat. Between songs it gave a sharp cluck we had
not heard our wintering buntings give. (Chapter 7)

The roadrunner jerked and switched its tail erratically. It bristled all over and raised a shaggy crest on its head. (Chapter 8)

During our explorations of the Big Bend country we looked in vain for either a panther or a coyote. Now at last one of the small predators was right before us. (Chapter 8)

stages of about two hundred miles a day they would make their way northward in time to meet the advancing spring warmth. I took particular delight in the thought that Allan had already recorded similar activities on film from the blind and that people all across the continent would become more deeply concerned with the future of the whooping cranes because of this.

We were present when tragedy struck at the refuge. We had worked at a red-shouldered hawk's nest near the road until late afternoon when we stopped at headquarters. Bob was there, his face white and his eyes hot with fury. Staff members gathered around him might have been turned to stone by a Medusa and every face reflected Bob's anger. He held a mortally wounded crane. He had found it crumpled beside the inland waterway that for ten miles cuts across the refuge marshes. Somebody on the deck of a passing boat had disregarded the flying goose sign that identifies national wildlife refuges from coast to coast as well as the posters stating that guns must be cased during the passage through the refuge. Seeing a large living target, the gunner had fired at it. Another bird was lost from the little band of whooping cranes. Not only was the killing an illegal act, but it was stupid; the arrogant, useless destruction of a valued bird.

Even as death approached the great white bird was beautiful. Long soft feathers drooped almost like plumes over the tail. Its black legs were slender but the upper parts were muscular as one would expect in so vigorous a walker. Strong fliers though they are, whooping cranes prefer to walk over both their winter and summer habitats. There was bare pebbled bright red skin reaching up and over the forehead and also extending almost to the ears between the eyes and the bill. This red skin had a sparse scattering of black hairs, coarse as horse hair, sprinkled over it. The red skin bordering about half the eyes gave the clear yellow iris an orange cast.

The crane gave a slight shiver and died in Bob's hands. As the lids gently closed, the eyes kept their clear yellow. Quickly Bob hurried to a local freezing plant and had the crane frozen before deterioration began. Later, having made arrangements for the plane to be met in Washington, he packed the crane in dry ice and shipped it to the Smithsonian Institution where it was rushed to the laboratory. Whooping cranes are so few in number that they may not be able to survive. The loss of a single bird is a calamity. But Bob's quick action made it possible for that particular bird to contribute to the scientific knowledge of the species. Its crop would reveal especially valuable facts about the food it had eaten.

The rains lessened, the sun grew hotter and strong winds blew from the east. The roads dried up except for the deepest mud holes. The cranes were leaving Aransas, and Bob made a careful count of them from the air. Less than half the winter group remained. Two days later Bob left, too, and for several weeks to come he would range widely across the sub-Arctic air-ways in search of the nesting place of whooping cranes. There had been so many interesting birds and mammals to photograph at Aransas we had stayed longer than we had planned. It was time for us to leave and catch up on our tight schedule.

Allan wakened me while it was still dark and stars glittered above a quiet sky.

"Come on," he shook me awake. "Let's get started. We can take a last drive down Blackjack and then head for Del Rio."

The stars faded and a yellow glow lighted the east. We passed the place where we had photographed wild turkeys and Salada Pond. The windmill towering above it was quiet but ducks quacked and leaped up and away. We came to the turnaround overlooking Bob's blind and the territory of the three cranes we had photographed. No sooner had Allan switched off the motor than we heard the cranes. We leaned against the mud-spattered hood of the car and braced our elbows on it to steady our binoculars.

Though they were far off on the marsh we quickly located the cranes, but something was new. Five cranes, not three, moved restlessly in a close group. All were bugling and the wind carried to us their wild yet solemn *Ker-looo ker-lee-ooo ker-lee-ooo*. Their music was stirring as the warlike blast of trumpets in the opening scene of *Aïda*. Then, as if a signal had been given, all five cranes leaped into the air and spiraled upward. As they rose the sun on the horizon haloed the snowy birds with fire and flames darted from their ebon wingtips. Higher and higher they ascended until they were surely a thousand feet or more above the marsh, and as they rose they appeared to drift. Then swiftly they moved into a line reaching toward the north. Clouds, quickly formed, hid them, but as they moved away their bugles rang more and more faintly until they died away. Had they begun their migration? We are not sure. But next morning when he checked the crane territories, Earl Benham reported to Bob that the family occupying the blind territory was missing.

The following spring we were busy in the Big Bend and then moved down to the valley. For weeks we might as well have been out of this world, for we neither read a newspaper nor listened to a radio. Having completed our work, we left the valley on May 25 to go straight to the Audubon Camp of Maine. We decided to detour the few necessary miles to Aransas. At headquarters we were told that Bob Allen was down at the tower and the eggs were infertile. Eggs? Yes, two captive cranes, one from Nebraska and the other from New Orleans had been put in an enclosure of about a hundred and fifty acres. The birds had built a nest and laid two eggs. After twenty-three days of attentive care the cranes had broken the eggs. They had been infertile, and when the cranes smashed them only dry contents remained.

So we drove along a smooth and dusty road, for spring rains had ended weeks ago, and came to the fence and the fifty-foot tower overlooking the crane pasture. Bob was not alone. Dr. Lawrence Walkinshaw, who has studied cranes for many years and in 1964 would photograph a whooping crane's nest with two eggs, the first such photograph for forty-two years, had come from Battle Creek, Michigan, to attend the hatching of the eggs at Aransas. Distinguished Texas naturalist, the late Roy Bedichek, was there, too, with his binoculars pointed toward a pair of cranes feeding in a distant part of the enclosure. All three men had the slightly glazed eyes one sees so often in hospital waiting rooms. They had gathered to be present when an event of great importance to the world of conservationists took place, an event comparable to a royal birth in a monarchy. They hoped the young would be the forerunner of many whooping cranes hatched in captivity by birds that could no longer journey through the skies with the wild flock to the far north, once known vaguely as the fur countries.

Bob led us down the ladder, through a gate and across marshy ground. Near some cattails he pointed to a place where a rattler had recently been killed, and close by was the abandoned crane nest, rather crushed and beaten after twenty-three days of incubation, but it still stood well above its surroundings. Though both birds had long been captives their building instinct had lived on. The flat platform was contructed of marsh plants such as ox-eye, cattails and spike grass. It was about six feet across. Fragments of spotted buffy eggs lay on the deserted nest.

The following year a wild crane newly crippled so it could never fly again was placed in the enclosure. After about thirty-three days of incubation one of the eggs hatched and the downy crane was named Rusty because of its color. It lived four days and vanished, nobody knows how for sure, though a maze of raccoon tracks near the spot where the crane was last seen suggests its fate.

Cranes in the wild may live for many decades, but this is only a guess. Dr. Oliver Austin believes their span of life is less than a century. If properly cared for, they may live longer in captivity than under the many hazards of natural conditions. In 1966 an Asiatic White Crane that had been in the Washington zoo since it was eighteen months old reached the age of sixty.

In Japan cranes are a favorite symbol of longevity, and in popular belief they are said to live for a thousand years. This surpasses the western symbol, Methuselah, by several decades, for according to the book of Genesis he died in his nine hundred sixty-ninth year.

Many distinguished ornithologists believe the way to save whooping cranes for the future is to round them up, trap them, clip their wings and put them in large enclosures with plenty of elbow room between pairs. One of the telling points of these ornithologists is the fact that cranes belong to the group of birds that, while their normal clutch of eggs is two, if an egg is removed soon after it is laid, will lay far more than their normal quota. Flickers normally produce a clutch of no more than 8, but one flicker on record laid 71 eggs in 73 days when eggs were experimentally removed. A closely related wryneck of Europe once laid 62 eggs under similar conditions, and domestic hens lay up to 350 eggs annually. The eggs taken from the cranes would be hatched in incubators and, hopefully, the annual production of young whooping cranes would rise sharply.

But more people are vehement in urging, "Let's do all we can to protect the wild whooping cranes. They were here before we were and are entitled to living room. Provide them with as much suitable wintering area as we possibly can. Let us protect their breeding grounds from any kind of destructive intrusion. Let us be willing to sacrifice material gain for the spiritual values these regal birds contribute to our lives."

If, despite our best efforts, the whooping cranes join the ever-swelling ranks of extinct species, let them go as wild, free birds, and not as captives pinnioned so they can never fly again. Let them on their dangerous migrations rise under their own power and wing their way across the unmarked sky. But never chain them to earth by mutilating them so they are earth-bound cripples.

Bob Allen's life was cut short by a heart attack before planned studies, books and especially children's stories he hoped to write and illustrate could be realized. The whooping cranes he studied and worked to save remain in twilight, their future uncertain. Storms, thoughtless gunners, outbreaks of disease, disturbance of their habitat—one of these or any combination of unforeseen factors could send this incomparable bird into total extinction. Perhaps if we care enough, the twilight of whoopers will swing, like the twilight of an arctic summer, straight into a blazing dawn, and their numbers will multiply until the species is safe.

3

Always in the Present

THOUGH THE PHOTOGRAPHY of whooping cranes was our foremost goal that spring when we spent many weeks at the Aransas Refuge, we found so many other interesting subjects for our cameras that we were forever pressed for time. Many more or less permanent ponds are scattered over some 47,000 acres of the great Aransas National Wildlife Refuge. Beside one of these, Salada Pond, we placed a blind in early April. Within the narrow confines of my yard-square blind on the seventeenth of that month I lived a day to remember always. I watched birds carry on their activities as they have through thousands of years gone by and as they will continue to through the years to come. The birds, whose demands do not vary from year to year or increase as old needs are satisfied, found in Salada Pond not only water but food and a place to rest undisturbed by man. On this way station of their journey toward distant goals they had found what was for them a small garden of Eden, and for a while I shared that Eden with them.

Salada Pond lies on Blackjack Peninsula about twelve miles from headquarters. Its name properly means a hollowed plain from which water has evaporated, leaving behind a deposit of salt. But now, swollen by heavy spring rains, the round depression was filled to its outermost edge. Its banks were sharply defined except on the south side where the water thinned to a film and bulrushes formed a rank border that spread inward more and more sparsely as the depth increased.

This pond is not solely dependent on rain and surface drainage, for additional water is fed into it by a creaking, rattling windmill that hoists to the surface some of the fossil water trapped aeons ago deep in underground recesses. From the beginning of spring until its end, the windmill never ceases its noisy complaint. Then constant winds from the gulf howl across the barrier islands and bays, and over coastal marshes to slam against the oblique vanes of the lofty wheel. The water lifted by the windmill fills a large round cement tank where cattle can drink. Excess water slops over the edge of the tank spreading out in a thin sheet, so the tank is stained bright orange by deposited minerals and a growth of algae, and then trickles into the pond.

The spring rains that raised the level of the pond and spread a delicate film of green over the prairie also made one long mudhole of the dirt road. Then only a truck or a four-wheel-drive jeep could travel the normally good track. Daily we were thoroughly shaken as we slued and churned and splashed through the series of deep chuckholes and washouts to one of the blinds on Blackjack Peninsula, now to the whooping crane blind, now to one baited for turkeys, now to one beside a large yuccca called Spanish bayonet where a white-tailed hawk had its nest.

The first time we approached Salada a plump of ducks streamed from it and dropped into a smaller pond not far off. Their behavior, Allan said, was further proof of his conviction that people who planned to attract wild ducks to their land would be wise to provide not one but two ponds so when the waterfowl were frightened from one pond they

did not have to go far to other water. The ducks we saw that
first day were winter species that had spent the bitter months
on or near Aransas Refuge when northern waters were ice-
bound. Soon they would feel the irresistible pull of the
north, and at some unpredictable moment the warming
April sun and the chemistry of their bodies would trigger
their departure.

The ducks were in their finest plumage, and it took but
two or three trips past Salada to impress us with the benefits
that would follow if a blind were placed beside it. So one
cold windy morning we stopped the jeep, dragged out a
framework and a cover that had cushioned the cameras
during the jolting trip from headquarters, and chose a place
for it close to the muddy shore where a maze of tracks indicated a favorite resting place for ducks. The ground was
soggy, and we cut armsful of rushes, spread them on the
ground in the blind and covered them with burlap bags.

While we worked a kingfisher rattled steadily. Once the
blind was set up, Allan drove a stake into the water in front
of it.

"There isn't a perch anywhere near the blind. Maybe the
kingfisher will use this," he said.

The kingfisher never did perch on it while I was in the
blind, but other birds often settled there.

Directly in front of the blind Allan built a long narrow
mud island. If the ducks wanted to sun themselves, he provided a fine place at good camera range. Finally we scattered
grain generously in the water, on the artificial island and on
the shore close to the blind.

That night the wind tossed the blind into the pond. This
was not unexpected, for the wind was a constant handicap at
our other blinds. Once we complained about the incessant
wind at headquarters. The staff just laughed.

"This isn't the worst Texas weather," they told us. "It

won't be long until this searing wind is heated by a scorching sun. Then you'll wish for the cold winds we are having now."

Next morning we pulled the blind, muddy and dripping, from its tumble into the pond. This time we fastened ropes to all four corners, pulled them taut and secured them with tent pegs. The ropes held it upright and the pond birds came to accept it as a part of the natural landscape and perched on it and beside it as confidently as if it were a bush.

Days full of activity hurried by, but each morning we paused at Salada to scatter more grain for the ducks. On April seventeenth Allan said I had better make use of the blind. At any moment the ducks might respond as the geese and most of the whooping cranes already had to the pull of the north.

To step into a blind accepted by birds gives me a feeling much like the one Alice had when she stepped through the looking glass. There is the same prairie touched with delicate green and dotted by coreopsis bending before the wind, and the same gnarled live oaks sheared by the constant wind from the gulf. But everything, though the same, has suddenly shifted in emphasis. I enter a new world, no longer the world of man, but a world of wild animals, and the natives of that world speak an unknown language. They have strange habits. They live by a different code of laws. Their civilization is far older than man's and is more perfectly tuned to the laws of their universe. They eat, sleep, provide for future generations and protect themselves from enemies, which inevitably reap a certain number of them for food. In an eat-or-be-eaten world their needs are elemental, and they survive only as long as they are sufficiently alert and their physical condition is equal to the demands made upon it. If there is sudden wailing by bereaved parents when their young are eaten, some other creature has just had a fine meal. Chances are the grieving parents will quickly forget their loss and produce another family. For birds the present is everything and most of it seems filled with joy.

So with keen expectancy I unzipped the back of the blind and then jumped away. A deermouse, white-footed, long-tailed and with tawny upperparts topping pale underparts darted out. The mouse was in a panic and dashed blindly around until it crashed against a crayfish tower. Apparently thinking any hole offered escape it pushed its head into the small opening. But struggle as it would with waving hind feet and lashing tail, the mouse could not push its way into the small opening. Our laughter must have been as terrifying to the cowering mouse as the "fee fi fo fum" of the giant was to Jack. In despair, the mouse backed out, ran to a clump of grass and then as a small checkered milk snake slithered away it scampered down the recently vacated snake hole.

In spite of the rushes we had piled on the floor of the blind it was very wet, so I pulled on rubber boots. In a few minutes the blind was zipped tight, my camera was in place and the strident labor of the jeep plowing through the mud died away. I shivered in my dark little room that broke the force of the wind but let in the numbing cold of early morning.

Through the narrow slit of my window I saw glittering white puffs skid across a sky of intense blue. Never is the sky so blue as when it is seen between bright clouds. The shining pond repeated the blue of the sky and it danced in the wind, scattering sparkles with lavish extravagance.

The whistle of duck wings rose on the wind as the shy flock, adding wildness to the sky, swung around their favorite pond, inspecting it for danger. Then came a companionable chatter as they circled closer and closer. There was a rush and a swish, and they descended with a sliding splash, skated briefly on the surface and settled with contented quacks.

Through the narrow window I could see more ducks circling the pond. Round and round they went, some dropping down with each swing. Widgeon whistled loudly as new groups joined the flock on the water. Many of the widgeon separated into pairs, and each pair was quarrelsome when approached by another pair. The drakes whistled, raised their wings stiffly over their backs, and the ducks growled with bass voices. Francis Kortwright, the distinguished authority on duck, says that widgeon probably do not mate until they reach their breeding ground, but these birds had already selected their future mates, and were ready for the nuptial ceremonies that would take place after their flight to some northern lake or marsh.

Long ago, on April 17, 1852, Henry David Thoreau was struck by the fact that a fence in the landscape confined his attention to a small undulation of land and helped him to consider it by itself. The fence, which defined and framed the field, presented it to him as a picture. So, too, the narrow window of my blind confined my vision and heightened attention to details of the scene before me where the ducks were as unconscious of my presence as if I did not exist. The ground glass of my camera narrowed still further the field of my observation so at times, as through a telescope, I watched only the yellow-brown eye of a widgeon or examined the usually concealed flashy speculum of a gadwall or noted that female redheads had dark eyes while their mates had orange-red eyes in exquisite harmony with their red heads. I counted the number of bobs a minute made by an ardent drake blue-winged teal before the duck of his choice while she remained preoccupied with feeding.

Except for a single pair, the blue-winged teal were still unattached. Nevertheless the drakes were ardently courting and whistled wheezy, monotonous notes and bobbed their heads vigorously, all the time swimming in a circle around a heedless duck. The drakes were unselective and moved from one duck to another hoping to find one, any one at all, that would respond. But if the blue-winged teal ducks were insensible of the wooing by the drakes, one day soon they would become receptive, and as a drake bowed rapidly a duck would return the bows, as many as thirty in a minute.

Never before had I been so close to blue-winged teal, and to my delight I found them far more beautiful than I had thought. They were quietly colored but glowed gently with a delicate sheen. The white beside the bill of the drake can be seen for a long distance, but his faintly pink bloom, far paler than that of a widgeon, can be seen only for a few feet. I discovered that the pale blue on the middle wing coverts that gives the teal its name is, close at hand, a lively cobalt, and the iridescent green of the speculum is dazzling. During much of the day blue-wings stood on the bank close to the blind, and when individuals left on various errands, others took their place. Whenever action lagged on the pond, I had only to swing my folding canvas chair to the right and look out through the side window at ducks and drakes so close that I could have reached out and touched them. Not only are the blue-wings that monopolized that particular spot the latest migrants to leave for the north, but they are one of the swiftest fliers of all ducks.

Shovelers sneezing like cats added to the noise of the steadily growing congregation on Salada. Males of this species outnumbered the females three to one. Though they have a reputation for feeding at night, these shovelers were evidently very hungry. They skated onto the pond, immediately formed a line and with heads half submerged they drove through the water, occasionally swinging as a unit in a broad ellipse; and all the time their heads swung from side to side. They were picking up bits of floating vegetation and straining it through their clattering bills. Nobody had ever told those ducks that it is polite to eat quietly. The big bill of this species is all out of proportion to its over-all small size and has more prominently developed "teeth" or lamellae than any other duck. It is not surprising that scientists have located exceptionally sensitive nerves in the roof of the mouth of shovelers; this nerve center provides them with an unusually delicate sense of touch and taste.

Part of the courtship of shovelers—and this is true of many ducks, including the widgeon, gadwall and redheads that outnumbered the shovelers on Salada—is conducted in the air. Both sexes engage in aerial pursuits when they circle, twist and turn erratically. But these shovelers were still unmoved by sex, and as soon as their feeding was satisfactorily concluded, they drifted aimlessly on the water. Their green heads glowed, and the chestnut bands on their sides appeared to expand and contract as the wind-ruffled water lifted and lowered them.

Unlike the other migrants on Salada, which are largely confined to the Americas, shovelers occur on every continent, including Australia. They also are found on such romantic far-off islands as Borneo and Ceylon, and they travel behind the Iron Curtain and into Red China. The shoveler added a genuine cosmopolitan touch to Salada Pond.

From the moment when the first duck, a widgeon, returned to the pond there was constant action and sound. If the ducks were quarrelsome at times, no injury was inflicted during their fleeting squabbles. They fed. They sunned themselves on the bank or on Allan's small island. They drifted and slept on the choppy waters. Some courted. They watched the sky for danger, springing almost simultaneously into the air when an alarm was signaled. Fears were transient, and they resumed their contented activities quickly when they settled after a threat of peril from the skies had sent them whirling into the air. Nobody wants to be a duck, yet we cannot help but envy the satisfactory way their lives are ordered. They are self-sufficient. They make their way across the vast reaches of the sky and arrive unerringly at their destination without maps, charts, roads, machines, compasses and all the paraphernalia required by man when he makes a journey. They find their food skillfully at a time in history when the vast majority of Americans are dependent on the supermarket and when three-fourths of humanity goes to bed hungry each night.

The nest required for their eggs is built without attention to the kind being favored by the Joneses and without shortages and government restrictions. Battles with their kind are bloodless. Each lives his own life in complete obedience to natural laws. Each is bursting with health. Each will live as long as he remains sufficiently alert, agile, and healthy to cope with the dangers of his existence.

It is good life in spite of natural dangers and the eternal rigors of intense heat and profound cold that they must endure and the ever-multiplying man-made hazards that confront them. It is probable that man would be happier and less given to mental and emotional aberrations if he would steer his course toward the highest possible development of himself as an individual instead of into narrow restraining channels bound by steadily increasing ties of governmental controls from the cradle to the grave. In seeking security, man is casting away self-reliance. Lurking outside the false security are the fundamental laws of the universe, which he cannot ignore with impunity. His machines give him the power of geologic time. His chemicals can eliminate forms of life he does not appreciate. He can litter his habitat until the earth's surface becomes a garbage heap. He can pollute and destroy the life-giving elements, water and air. He can encourage his kind to multiply beyond the carrying capacity of this earth.

But man is subject to the same laws that govern wildlife.

He must breathe air. He must drink water. He must reproduce his kind. As *homo sapiens* removes himself farther and farther from the natural world and shrugs off his responsibility to it, the specter of disaster to his race looms ever greater.

Now as widgeon, blue-wings, shovelers, gadwall and redheads appeared in turn in my camera's field, I was impressed by the perfect grooming of each, and the exuberant health they displayed, and by the serene confidence with which they met each small crisis that presented itself. We know dogs, cats, zoo animals and occasionally wild animals may become neurotic, but among the untamed and unconfined a neurotic animal seldom survives very long.

A new subject appeared before my camera as a lesser yellowlegs settled in front of the blind and shook its wings with satisfaction. This, he indicated, was a good place, and he immediately claimed it for his own. When a second yellowlegs dropped down with the same idea, the two birds faced each other, and breast to breast began leaping into the air. Finally the second comer withdrew but the title of the first yellowlegs was not yet firmly established. First several killdeer, then a black-necked stilt and finally a small flock of dowitchers alighted in the shallow water to stake out a feeeding claim. But the yellowlegs met each intruder with loud cries and darted at it again and again until it withdrew. At last it was left alone and spent the rest of the day peacefully sleeping, sunning and searching for food. The conqueror, having established an undisputed claim to a territory, was free to enjoy it—until such time as other birds arrived and successfully challenged his authority over it.

Several hours passed and much film was exposed. I looked beyond the water to a small live oak motte. The interlaced branches of the trees formed a smooth arc and on its summit several common egrets were sunning themselves. I realized that I no longer shook with cold, and even my feet were comfortable though an inch or two of muddy water rose around them. The scent of earth warmed by the April sun, the fragrance of expanding plants and opening flowers filtered into the blind. Beneath the live oaks turkey cocks strutted and boomed before hens preoccupied with their search for breakfast. In the shelter of the gnarled, lichencoated branches mourning doves moaned langorously. A pair of cardinals, busy with nest building, called softly to each other. A scissor-tailed flycatcher darted forth, caught a dragonfly and returned to its perch with the glittering transparent wings of the big aeshnid bristling like a moustache on either side of its bill.

Suddenly I was transported to our home in Florida as the sweet, deliberately spaced warble of a painted bunting reached me. Eagerly I searched the tops of all the plants that stood above the fairly uniform prairie vegetation. Finally I detected the singer perched on a yellow spike Baptisia flowers. The sapphire head of the bunting was thrown back and his small body throbbed with the verve of his song. How can anybody call this beautiful bird gaudy? This exquisite jewel so aptly called nonpareil by South Carolinians? Of course, this may be a matter of semantics, and it is granted that *gaudy* is a word of several meanings. To Shakespeare a gaudy night was a jolly night and probably a noisy one. But to most of us *gaudy* means garish, raw, cheap finery, a lack of breeding and has other unpleasant connotations. To call a painted bunting gaudy is simply to repeat thoughtlessly an adjective used by early ornithologists who probably never watched a living painted bunting and knew the species only from lifeless skins or inadequate paintings.

The ominous tread of many feet squelching through the soggy earth erased all thought of the bunting. A long string of Santa Gertrudis, each marked with the running W of the King Ranch, which developed the breed, strode purposefully toward the pond and my frail cloth blind. We had been warned to use caution when near the cattle, for the big bulls have notoriously short tempers. Even when we were in the comparative safety of the little jeep we always drove quietly, making a polite detour, whenever we encountered one of the big bulls standing like a statue with lowered head and flaming red eyes. Santa Gertrudis is the only genuine breed of cattle ever developed in the United States. While the King Ranch records of its development are a closely guarded secret, the breed is a combination of Brahman and shorthorn. They can withstand intense heat and grow fat on grass without additional feed. Now the herd surrounded the blind and drank noisily from the pond. They moved about restlessly, snorting heavily as they gulped the muddied water. Not until the herd filed away did I breathe freely.

Half an hour later another herd of Santa Gertrudis came to drink. Again the tank was ignored, and the cattle surged around the blind, sending the ducks away in confusion and further muddying the water as successive waves of the big animals went deeper and deeper to drink. They did not stay long, but soon a third herd surrounded the blind. I was really terrified then, for almost all were massive bulls with heavy pointed horns. They snuffled the blind and circled around it. They pressed so close that the fragile blind shook with their movements. A veritable sea of horns shifted and tossed. Momentarily I expected the blind to topple. One bull licked the stick Allan had driven as a kingfisher perch and then another stuck out a long tongue and licked my camera lens, my precious 400 mm. telephoto lens. This was too much. My legs trembled and my heart raced. I could not endure another second of such terror. In desperation I shouted weakly, "Go away!"

The response was sudden and startling. With a rush the herd stampeded over the gently rolling prairie with their tails swinging wildly over their backs. Old time cattlemen would have said they were high-tailing it for the next county. Rigid with surprise, I realized the blind still stood. I was alive and untrampled. The wind still blew and the sun lighted the plain and the clouds. The ducks swung around the pond and returned with satisfied quacks and the yellowlegs resumed its patrol in front of the blind.

My heart had scarcely steadied to normal when I saw a cottonmouth moccasin fishing in front of the blind. Only its head and three or four inches of its muscular neck rose above the surface as it pursued minnows and struck at them from above with such lightning speed the eye could scarcely follow. Suddenly I realized there was a snake at my feet. Unnoticed it must have entered while the cattle milled around the blind. Once more my heart raced, but it was only a harmless olive and yellow ribbon snake. My sudden movement sent the snake slithering out in a rush but I was still not alone in the blind. The cloth cover waved, and a triangular little face topped by big ears looked at me through a hole in the double fabric of the blind cover. Long whiskers quivered, and a small nose trembled. The deermouse was back, staring at me with beady black eyes. From then on it spent the day between the layers of the blind cloth only leaving when hungry to gather corn spread for the ducks. Each time it came back to the blind its cheek pouches bulged with corn, which it stored in a fold of the fabric. Though I was an enemy when I opened the zipper that morning, once inside apparently I was accepted by the mouse as a fixture in its adopted home. It often pushed its long-whiskered face through an opening to look at me without showing any fear. Sometimes as it moved about between the cloth layers I tickled it and then it became still as if it enjoyed the caress.

Meantime the ducks, egrets and yellowlegs that frequented Salada Pond showed that they were better adjusted to the blind than I. Though I had gone through a period of tension and fright, they continued their feeding, courting and bathing quite unconcerned by the blind or the camera that clicked over and over again. A mixed flock of blue-winged teal and widgeon discovered that the blind made a fine windbreak and they settled down to enjoy the brilliant sun so close that I could touch them with my toes.

Not far to the right of the blind was another favorite sunning bank. Large numbers of ducks congregated there to preen and sleep. A snowy egret entered that group but did not become a part of it. Energetically it darted from the bank into the water after minnows. Quick stabs with its pointed black bill seldom missed the target. The common egrets left the treetops to join in the fishing. Sliders, dull blackish turtles with hind feet as broad as flippers, lumbered onto the bank. Overhead Sennett's white-tailed hawk with its short whitish tail widely fanned glided low above the pond, sending the sliders splashing into the water and the ducks up with a burst of noisy wings.

A boat-tailed grackle perched on top of the blind and gave a loud squawk. The several races of this large blackbird look alike, though the eastern race has a dark eye while the western races have a whitish eye. The Texas race, often called mesquite grackle, has a voice that exceeds all others in raucousness. If a sheet of tin and one of canvas could be glued together firmly and then ripped, it would make a noise like the opening notes of a mesquite grackle's "song." These notes are followed by a buzz like the sound of winding the spring in a shoddy toy; it ends with a loud grating squawk.

Having surveyed the pond and expressed approval of it while standing almost on my head, the grackle hopped down, ate some corn and then skipped onto the kingfisher stick, where it continued its discordant solo accompanied by grotesque fluffing of its iridescent feathers and contortions of its body. Apparently a frightful effort was required to expel the strident sound from its bill.

Louisiana herons and snowy egrets indicated the presence in the sky of other birds by tilting their heads and staring upward. Sometimes their alert turns of the head signaled the approach of a plump of ducks, sometimes it was a flock of white ibis scaling by or a turkey vulture hanging as if from an invisible wire as it fronted the wind. Once it was a ragged flock of black vultures hurtling along on a tail wind. As they split around the windmill, one dropped from the company to perch just below the creaking vanes and there it stayed, motionless, hour after hour.

The bright puffs of early morning swelled and consolidated their ranks into huge wet-looking clouds. Each now dragged a bulging dark belly and its movements were ponderous. Shadows deepened across the pond and the prairie, only to be shattered by bursts of blinding light as the sun stabbed through an opening. In spite of the wind it grew hot in the blind. The ducks became silent except for occasional tranquil quacks and whistles. The splash of bathing birds rose and fell in a soothing murmur.

A common egret with apple-green lores strode past the blind. It was followed by a snowy egret with lores as red as yew berries, and I recalled the day at East River in the Everglades when I first saw a lovesick snowy egret with bright red lores. Now as this egret paused to scratch an ear and then to groom its recurved plumes that look as delicate as snowflakes, I saw that its normally golden feet were red; not the clear red of the lores, for they made me think of a piece of glazed yellow paper that has been crumpled, then dipped in red watercolor and held up by one corner until the surplus paint has drained away. The red was most intense at the edges of the scales, while the smooth part of each scale remained largely yellow.

"Never," I thought for the thousandth time, "is it possible to spend a day in a blind without seeing something new and surprising."

More ducks skimmed onto the pond. My eyes blinked with astonishment. Three drake cinnamon teal had come. They swam quickly around the pond as if to inspect it and then began to bathe vigorously, splashing water over their backs and dipping their heads. How far had they come to reach this small pond? Perhaps from Nicaragua or Costa Rica, or even the Cauca Valley of Colombia. These were not wintering ducks, but travelers from far away, now in passage to their nesting place, perhaps in some Dakota or Manitoba marsh. One came close to the blind, where it seemed to stare straight at me with its golden-orange eye. Then it continued to splash and turned on its side to toss water on its breast. How beautiful its wings were! Bright chalky blue lay on the forepart and its speculum was a wide band of brilliant emerald. As the slanting Texas sun touched it I thought it the most brilliant duck I had ever seen. Though its pattern was chaste in comparison to that of a wood duck or a mandarin, its feathers were radiant as if newly minted copper had united with rich burnished mahogany. Its bill was deep midnight blue tinged with green when the sun touched it. Perhaps if those teal had arrived at midday they would have been less sensational, but the lowering sun intensified their colors, which normally are subtle in hue, so they gleamed like theatrically lighted gems.

More egrets on wide slowly undulating wings came to the pond and many of them began to bathe. With heads held high and with stately pace they marched deeper and deeper into the pond until the water came halfway up their bodies. They bent their heads until submerged; then, opening their wings and laying them flat on the surface for a moment, they began to beat them vigorously, splashing water wildly. Now they relaxed and stood quietly for some moments before having another go at hurling water about.

There is much to learn about the habits of birds, and I saw that day a long-held notion demolished. I was both surprised and delighted to see the herons bathe, for I had recently read in a book by a distinguished British ornithologist that the heron tribe has not been known to bathe. Probably all birds bathe to some extent. Screech owls, held by many to avoid water, bathe regularly in our Florida birdbath.

Recently Herbert H. Mills, the energetic conservationist, received a permanently injured red-tailed hawk that, kept in captivity, had not had an opportunity to bathe for some weeks because "hawks do not bathe." Disbelieving this ancient idea, Mr. Mills supplied water, and the hawk spent much of the first day in its new flying cage sitting in the water and bathing with evident enjoyment. It clearly delighted in an opportunity to bathe, a need that had long been denied it.

Out of the sky dropped a olivaceous cormorant and immediately it dipped beneath the surface of the pond. It popped out first on one side and then another, swimming beneath the surface for nearly the entire diameter of the pond. The ducks were thrown into confusion by the newcomer and appeared greatly alarmed and highly agitated by the big fish-eater. They moved rapidly about, chattering their displeasure. Some of them left the pond as if refusing to associate with the primitive-looking diver. Finally the cormorant stopped behaving like an unpredictable submarine, hopped onto a stump near the far shore, spread its wings and became still as a stone. The ducks irritably settled down and stopped their grumbling. Once more all was serene and the pleasant chatter of the ducks rose and fell. Listening to these garrulous creatures I fancied that I not only recognized the voices of the different species, but understood some of their meaning.

The day was almost spent and the clouds had grown until they were a solid cover from horizon to horizon when suddenly a large flock of white ibis drifted down on fluttering wings and alighted in the shallow water on the left side of the blind. Their black-tipped white wings were held stiffly over their backs and they moved slowly in unison as if in some intricate quadrille. A brilliant shaft of sunlight pierced the clouds, and like a spotlight it singled out the white ibis, lighting their snowy plumage and brightening the pink skin showing through the feathers at the wrist. Their faces and bills, already flushed with breeding intensity, became as red as wild hibiscus blooms.

I heard a voice chanting over and over again, "What wonders my eyes have seen. What wonders my eyes have seen," and, embarrassed, I realized I was talking to myself.

Then as if a switch had been pulled the clouds cut off the searchlight and the bevy of ibis lost their celestial beauty. The whole flock suddenly rose from the pond with a sibilant whisper as air rushed through their wings, and then they were gone.

Now the heavy clouds melted and flowed together and a few drops splashed on the pond and the birds. The herons spread their wings, mounted into the air and were carried from sight in broad, slowly undulating flight. The ducks began to gabble and shift restlessly. Suddenly they sprang straight into the air, spun into a single string and circled away. With a wild and poignant whistle that told of far-off places, of unbearable beauty and unattainable longing the yellowlegs followed. I heard the churning of the jeep creeping painfully over the rough and muddy road and I packed away my camera, unzipped the blind, and after ten hours and more in a strange wild world, stepped back through time into the world of men.

4

The Dance of the Wild Turkey

THE FIRST MORNING when we left Refuge headquarters at Aransas with Bob Allen to explore some of its remote wilderness the symbol of our American Thanksgiving was far from my thoughts. Sluing and splashing along the rutted trail the jeep sidled like a crab as often as it moved straight forward. About half way down Blackjack Peninsula I caught sight of three large creatures moving about with ponderous dignity. I caught Bob's arm.

"Look! Under those oaks!"

"Turkeys," Bob and Allan told me in a single breath. Bob braked the olive-green jeep and I swung binoculars to my eyes. Sure enough, now I could see the big animals were turkey gobblers with their feathers puffed, their huge tails erect and widely spread and their wings drooping to the ground. Near the strutting toms a few hens, much grayer and slimmer, were feeding.

"They look almost as big as burros," I said, surprised by the apparent bulk of those birds under the oaks.

Allan, of course, wanted to photograph the turkeys, and Bob knew just the place for him to do it.

"I always see them near Salada Well when I pass it on my way to check the cranes on the lower peninsula. The turkeys

71

have been strutting since the middle of February, but they will keep on for a couple weeks more."

Having completed the whooping crane count for the day, we returned to Salada Well. Allan chose a sunny spot for the blind close to some small gnarled and sparse-looking live oaks. Near the blind was an outcrop of sand so beaten and trampled by the turkeys that we knew it must be a favorite place for dust bathing. With Salada Pond and the well close by, with a dust bath, and the chick feed that we scattered for them the turkeys would surely not lose interest in the place in spite of the blind.

Before my turn came to spend a day in the turkey blind, I had a chance to watch the big birds at close range. Young toms with dull heads and short, blunt spurs frequently splashed into Salada Pond where I was photographing ducks. They drank and ate grain sprinkled for the ducks. They hopped onto the edge of the cement cistern behind the blind and drank there, too. These young toms were always solitary as were the females that came to drink. Occasionally I was treated to a turkey race, usually run around the pond with a handsome adult gobbler in pursuit of an upstart male. Then I recalled an account written by William Wood in Massachusetts in 1629:

"He [the turkey] hath the use of his long legs so ready that he can run as fast as a Dogge, and flye as well as a Goose."

The races were exciting. Both birds, with flattened plumage, stretched out long and thin and their heads reached forward like those of racehorses approaching the finish line. Most races ended after one lap around the Pond, but occasionally two laps were run with the contestants finally shooting off across the rolling prairie where they vanished from sight. Inevitably bits of turkey lore drifted into my thoughts.

No one seems to know for sure how the turkey got its name, but in the fifthteenth and sixteenth centuries, all lands outside Europe including Africa were often referred to as Turkey, though that Moslem nation in fact occupied a very small part of the world. Europeans habitually prefaced their names for anything from the non-Christian world with *turkey* or *turk*. For instance, maize was first called turkey wheat, and guinea fowl from Africa were called turkeys. Many people believe Europeans confused the two species of fowl, but it seems more likely that, upon seeing strange birds from an un-Christian land, people simply called them turkeys, too.

To which European goes the credit for seeing the first turkeys? We are not sure, but Francisco Hernandez de Cordova while on a slave-hunting expedition in 1517 discovered Yucatan and sailed as far northwest as Campeche, so he could have seen turkeys domesticated by the people he sought to enslave. Slight records, however, are left of that trip, and Cordova shortly died of wounds received there. Juan Grijalva is credited with the discovery of Mexico in 1518 when he was searching for wealth in the form of slaves and gold. Again, we are not sure whether he and his crew actually saw turkeys. Then in 1519 Cortez invaded Mexico, and now the past becomes clearer. We know he saw domesticated turkeys in the care of the Aztecs. It was not, however, until 1527, when Oviedo published an account of the West Indies and Mexico, where he spent several years, that a description of the domesticated American bird appeared in print.

By 1530 the Spaniards had introduced turkeys to Europe, where they caught the popular fancy and rapidly spread across the continent. By 1540 they had reached England, where their popularity grew to such an extent that early English colonists brought the turkey back to America. Now, as domestic birds they are scattered around the world. The Mexican race from which our domestic strain came has white tips on the tail feathers while the wild turkey of most of the United States has chestnut-tipped tail feathers.

The turkey is a genuinely American bird. It is native only to the Western Hemisphere. Oliver Austin in his *Birds of the World* states that all seven known fossil species of turkeys were confined to the Americas. Today only two species remain: our wild turkey and the ocellated turkey of British Honduras, Guatemala and Yucatan. The latter turkey is smaller than ours and receives its name from the eyelike design on its handsome tail feathers. Its warty head is blue, and red encircles its eyes. There are red protuberances on its forehead, and some of these stand almost crestlike in a shaggy row along the top of the head.

Originally the wild turkey was a very abundant and widespread species, occurring in suitable habitat from southern Canada to the gulf and into Mexico. According to notes made by Clark during the Lewis and Clark Expedition of 1804–1806, it was found as far west as Kansas, Nebraska and South Dakota. Long before that expedition, on April 12, 1680, Father Hennipen claimed that after cooking seven or eight recently caught turkeys on the shore of Lake Pepin, he blessed the food and at that moment he and his companions were taken prisoner by Indians.

Thomas S. Roberts wrote in *The Birds of Minnesota* that he doubted turkeys occurred as a native species in that state. It is indeed ironic, if Dr. Roberts was right in believing that wild turkeys never were native to Minnesota, for today that state, and California, where the turkey did not occur, are the largest turkey-producing areas anywhere.

The turkey is the only species of American bird, with the exception of the muscovy duck, that has been truly domesticated. Many strains of domestic turkeys have been developed from the original southern race tamed by the Indians, who used them chiefly as a source of decorative feathers rather than of meat. Their value in a single year is greater than all the treasure acquired by the conquistadores in the first century after the discovery of the New World. With increased perfection of strains that conform to modern tastes, the domestic turkey population in America has skyrocketed. Over 8,500,000 were grown here in 1940.

In 1953 young Tom Draper, appropriately the son of the supervisor of the National Turkey Improvement Plan, won, in Dallas, the awards for the Grand Champion and the Reserve Champion dressed turkey in the junior division. This Grand Champion junior dressed bird weighed fifteen pounds and was purchased at $95 a pound, which still stands as the highest price per pound ever paid for a turkey.

By 1954 the United States Department of Agriculture was sending out releases urging those in the turkey business to guard against excessive production, which would lower the price of the birds. That year the output was some 61,000,000 turkeys. Now it frequently exceeds 100,000,000 young birds annually.

Back in 1952 the champion turkey of the year was raised in Texas and weighed 68½ pounds. Modern turkey breeders are seeking not larger, heavier birds, but small, more tender and broader-breasted turkeys to satisfy the ever-increasing demands of shoppers in supermarkets.

It may be said with confidence that no wild turkey ever equaled the weight of the Texas champion. There are authentic records and fairly substantial reports of exceptionally large wild tom turkeys. William Bartram while traveling in Georgia in 1773 saw at the M'Intosh plantation on a branch of the Sapello River not far north of Darien a huge gobbler:

I saw here a remarkably large turkey of the native wild breed. His head was above three feet from the ground when he stood erect. He was a stately, beautiful bird, of a very dark dusky-brown color, the tips of the feathers of his neck, breast, back, and shoulders edged with a copper color which in a certain exposure looked like burnished gold, and he seemed not insensible of the splendid appearance he made. He was reared from an egg found in the forest and hatched by a hen of the common domestic fowl.

Of one wild turkey raised under similar conditions, Henry E. Davis in *The American Wild Turkey* records a gobbler that weighed 47 pounds. However, he believed that no genuinely wild turkey ever exceeded 40 pounds, and Richard H. Pough in his *Audubon Bird Guide* gives 15 to 20 pounds as the average weight of wild turkeys. Alexander Sprunt, Jr. in *South Carolina Bird Life* gives 22½ pounds as the heaviest authentic record for wild turkeys in that state.

The story of the wild turkey with its chestnut-tipped tail is almost as dark as that of the domestic turkey is bright. Several subspecies of this largest American game bird once roamed through Central America, Mexico and north to the Dakotas and eastward to Maine. Early explorers seldom failed to note with astonishment the enormous numbers of this noble bird. In fact, accounts written about wild turkeys through the days of the colonies and the early years of the Republic convince the reader that they were present in numbers almost incomprehensible to us today. In 1637 Thomas Morton in Massachusetts wrote:

Turkies there are which divers times in great flocks have sallied by our doores. . . . They daunce by the doore so well. . . .

They are many degrees sweeter than the tame Turkies of England feede them how you can.

I had a Salvage who hath taken out his boy in the morning, and they have brought home their loades about noone.

I have asked them what number they found in the woods, who have answered Neent Metawna, which is a thousand that day; the plenty of them is such in those parts. They are easily killed at rooste, because the one bing killed, the other sit fast. . . .

In the same colony John Josselyn said "I have seen three-score broods of young Turkies on the side of a marsh, sunning themselves in a morning betimes."

Because of their abundance in the early days of the English settlements, the wild turkey's delectable flesh played an important role in the colonists' food supply. It was natural that the turkey which had already had a part in their feasts before they left England should hold a central role in their harvest festivals.

Fruits of their summer's labor in the earth, so history tells us, were arranged on that Thanksgiving table around fat and succulent roasted turkeys. So the wild turkey that abounded in the forests of the first Puritan New England settlement and often came to feed with the domestic animals became in just one long agonized and fear-filled year inseparably interwoven into our history.

Year after year the plough, ax, dog and gun forced wild turkeys from their ancient haunts. Writers following Morton began to complain of the lack of turkeys, but they still told of shooting five, a dozen or twenty of the birds with a single shot. Let it not be said that wild creatures never change their habits. As their number decreased, the turkeys changed from birds that "daunce by the doore" to extremely shy wily creatures that could outwit men and their dogs.

Legends grew and multiplied about individuals displaying such acumen that repeated forays into known habitats by the most skilled hunters and the best stalkers were unavailing. At last, their time running out, the turkeys simply died of old age, leaving behind them a multitude of yarns about the ingenious and imaginative tricks they employed to baffle and elude all their pursuers.

As the tide of population rolled south and west, the turkeys retreated in ever-dwindling numbers to whatever remote and inaccessible wilderness they could find. In 1774 William Bartram camped beside the St. John's River between Picolata and Palatka in Florida. Great stands of cypress then bordered the river on both sides, and he wrote:

I was awakened in the morning early, by the cheering converse of the wild turkey-cocks [*Meleagris occidentalis*] saluting each other from the sun-brightened tops of the lofty Cupressus disticha and Magnolia grandiflora. They begin at early dawn, and continue till sunrise, from March to the last of April. The high forests ring with the noise, like the crowing of the domestic cock, of these social sentinels; the watch-word being caught and repeated, from one to another, for hundreds of miles around; insomuch that the whole country is for an hour or more in a universal shout. A little after sunrise, their crowing gradually ceases, they quit their high lodging-places, and alight on the earth, where expanding their silver-bordered train, they strut and dance round the coy female, while the deep forests seem to tremble with their shrill noise.

A few years later when the time came to decide on a national bird, Benjamin Franklin urged with eloquence that the wild turkey be chosen, and like so many politicians since his time, he pulled no punches in his attempt to discredit the more popular bald eagle while lauding his choice. This was one political skirmish that the wily diplomat lost. Usually his judgment was impeccable, but a pompous and portly turkey gobbler emblazoned on state documents and perched aloft on flagpoles would be a humorous rather than a dignified figure. Though the turkey is a genuinely American bird while the bald eagle is not, we must confess the bald eagle was the better choice, for it looks majestic and inspiring.

The native turkey gobbler would lend a ludicrous note while performing his national-bird duties.

Though the retreat of wild turkeys continued before the rising tide of white invaders, naturalists, carried on the crest of the westward-flowing wave, had much to say about them. On October 17, 1820, John James Audubon observed them flying across the Ohio River.

"The turkeys extremely plenty and Crossing the River hourly from the North Side, a great Number destroyed falling in the Stream for want of strength."

Two days later one of Audubon's companions bagged three turkeys with a single shot on his very first turkey hunt.

On December 10, 1820, Audubon walked from the Mississippi River to the Old Post of Arkansas, and no blanket being furnished by the inn, he was saved from a miserable night when he discovered about ten pounds of wild turkey feathers into which he burrowed and so saved his rounder parts from the sharp edges of the rude bed and also warded off the bitter cold.

One of Audubon's finest life histories is that of the wild turkey, and we are as charmed with it today as his readers were a century ago. As we read it, we feel a sense of nostalgia for those far-off lavish days when flocks of a hundred and more wild turkeys were encountered frequently in the autumn of the year. If all the Audubon prints, the turkey usually has the highest price tag when an elephant-folio is broken up and the prints sold individually.

Audubon was the last of the great naturalists to record an abundance of wild turkeys in many places on his extensive journeys. In 1851 the last wild turkey shot in Massachusetts was killed in the Holyoke Range, but the last one seen in Connecticut had been long ago in 1813. In Bent's *Life Histories of North American Gallinaceous Birds* it is said that some remained in northern Vermont along the Ontario bor-

der as late as 1856. Wild turkeys were last seen in Michigan
in the 1890's, though the latest preserved specimen was shot
in 1886 near Reese in Saginaw County. They have vanished
from roughly 70 per cent of their once great range, says
Richard H. Pough in his *Audubon Water Guide*.

In recent years federal and state game departments and
many hunting clubs have joined in an effort to save and re-
store this magnificent game bird to a population great
enough so it will enjoy a margin of security. Undoubtedly
this effort will be successful, but in the face of our shrinking
wilderness and increasing population there is left comparatively little wild country suitable for this variety-loving bird.
It demands for normal life a combination of swamps, for the
sly bird likes to roost in trees growing in water, and forests
where oaks, dogwood, grape and sumac grow interspersed by
open fields so it can range widely and find a great variety of
foods, both vegetable and insect. Today many active birders
have never seen a wild turkey in its native habitat. Those
whose good fortune leads them to many of the wilderness
areas still left in our country can count on the fingers of
their hands all the places where they have seen wild turkeys.
Most such fortunate people would place their estimate of the
number of individuals they have seen at well under a thousand.

Ironically enough, it was misuse by overgrazing that destroyed the original grassy prairie and permitted the influx
of brush and scrub trees on what is now the Aransas Refuge.
This abuse of the land created an almost ideal situation for
turkeys. Texas has been particularly successful in rebuilding
its wild turkey population, but nowhere in the state has this
gone forward more effectively than on the Aransas Refuge.

All this is far afield in both time and space from our three-
foot-square, five-foot-tall blind close to stiff scrawny, lichen-
crusted live oaks and fronted by about a square yard of bare
sand. My first day in the turkey blind began when I opened

my notebook about eight o'clock that sunny warm April morning. My camera was already on the tripod and trained on the patch of sand where we had scattered chick feed with a lavish hand.

Two turkey cocks strutting near the blind when the jeep slued to a stop augured well for my day. Now a pair of scissor-tailed flycatchers were making a noisy to-do as they built a nest in the nearest live oak. In the distance a white-tailed hawk drew lazy circles above the yucca where its nest with two white eggs lay protected by a circlet of daggers. As a caracara walked through yellow coreopsis, its head, red-faced, black-crested above brown shoulders, bobbed in and out of sight. Finding a small stick to its liking, the caracara sprang into the air and flew off toward a distant mesquite thicket.

"Probably nest-building, too," I thought as I watched the scissor-tails dart after it, scolding harshly. A pair of mourning doves cooed fatuously on and on and on.

Few minutes are more filled with anticipation than those first tense, eager ones in a blind. Hopefully the curtain is about to rise on a play full of action. It will be a play that can never be previewed and one that will never be repeated in exactly the same way. Now I looked across the prairie and listened to the sounds floating across it. It was time for the leading actors to appear.

In the distance I heard a turkey gobble. It was answered by another. A chorus of gobbles broke out. I could distinguish at least four voices. Then silence fell.

Swift footfalls approached the blind. A turkey hen giving a high-pitched *cut cut cut cut* ran to the grain. While she ate she continued her monotonous calls. Her naked head was wrinkled and warty. A loose wattle swung from her upper throat and a very short "horn" stood upright between her eyes. The brown of her feathers was sprinkled with ash, giving her a grayish look. This was the alluring creature that played the feminine lead in the turkey-blind play.

Shortly two magnificent cocks approached. They moved in unison—one, half a step in advance of his companion. The heads of both were pulled tightly against their shoulders and their feathers were puffed and loose. Their wings were spread and drooped to the ground and their sweeping tails were fanned until they almost made a circle. They looked longer than their four feet, and though it is doubtful that they weighed twenty pounds, they looked bulky as a Shetland pony. Their dark brown body feathers were lightly burnished with copper and iridescent in the morning light. The upper wings were deeply brown but the primaries and secondaries were barred with cream. Their spectacular tails were dark brown with bars and tips of chestnut that looked translucent in the sun.

With pompous dignity the gobblers advanced on stiff legs by a series of short running steps. Then came a pause accompanied by stamping feet as they stood in place. This was followed by a click and a boom. It appeared that the click was caused by the sudden downward snap of the wings and the boom was made by rapid vibrating of the wings as they drooped to the ground. Over and over again the tom turkeys repeated their short quick steps. It was step, step, step, pause and stamp, click and boom. As they danced, the long black tassels hanging from the center of the breast like pieces of frayed tarred rope swayed in time with their energetic movements.

The hen stopped eating but appeared unconscious of the dancing gobblers. She preened delicately and looked off into the distance.

A tom turkey at rest has a blue face and grayish-white, liberally sprinkled with red tubercles, spreads over the remainder of his warty wrinkled head and neck A fleshy protuberance, larger than that of the female's, stands between his eyes. Two bulbous swellings cluster at the base of the throat, and a loose flangelike wattle shaped like a limp sail lies under the bill.

The turkeys near my blind were definitely not at rest. As the dance progressed, color ebbed and flowed across the performers' faces and necks. The red intensified and spread over all the naked skin. The globular swellings at the base of the throat grew bigger and bigger until they were the size of ping pong balls, and became more and more vividly red as the dance continued. The "horn" lengthened and flushed deeply red. Like the tassel in the middle of the breast, it swayed and shook as the turkey cocks strutted, clicked and boomed before the inattentive hen.

Slowly the colors of the gobbler half a step in advance began to change. Creamy flecks appeared on his ping pong ball swellings, and the red flush slowly ebbed until they had turned all creamy white. The gobbler had danced himself almost to exhaustion. Then his partner, as if he had deliberately conserved his strength, swung energetically forward and led the dance by half a step.

On and on went the dance for twenty-three minutes without a pause or break in the rhythm, though there was a very slight acceleration when the gobblers changed their relative positions. The sun blazing down on the stage made an adequate spotlight and repeatedly as the turkeys moved in their dance their feathers suddenly turned to fiery bronze. The unimpressed hen finally wandered off toward another dust bath and the gobblers followed after, stepping, stamping, clicking and booming.

One of the gobblers had about two inches broken from a feather near the middle of his tail, so we knew he was the same individual who danced by the blind each day. Tweedledum and Tweedledee quite naturally became the names of our dancers, and while they were sometimes beyond our limited vision for an hour or more at a time, we kept them in view at least six of the nine hours one of us daily spent in the blind from April ninth through the eighteenth. During the time we had them under observation, Tweedledum and Tweedledee spent more than five hours of each day either strutting energetically in their dance, or standing quietly in strutting posture with tail spread and wings drooping. We never saw more than five females at a time near our blind.

While the dance I watched that first hour in the turkey blind was typical, there were variations that involved the turning of the dancers in opposite directions, then their slow swinging around until they faced each other. Without missing a step they swung on until they were again side by side and facing the same direction for the typical routine. The turning apparently was employed to check on males attempting to intrude on the territory. Usually the intruders were young birds with short spurs. Occasionally the turning step was used to search for females that had scattered but were lingering within sight of the gobblers and me.

Most often the dance was broken off when an aggressive young male entered the dancing preserve and arrogantly began to dance. If they persisted for any length of time, the solitary males were chased away by one of the dominant gobblers in the territory. Usually these solitary gobblers, after assuming the strutting posture, lost interest almost immediately and withdrew without any challenge by the dancers. Certainly the hens appeared not even to see them.

Occasionally one or even two adult males came to the food by the blind while Tweedledum and Tweedledee were in the midst of a dance. Those gobblers always slipped in with a meek and ingratiating air and their plumage was snugged tight against their bodies so they looked small and submissive. Quietly they ate their fill and slipped away as unobtrusively as they had come while the dancers ignored them as if they were invisible.

April was drawing to a close when we left Aransas Refuge. It is doubtful that any place in the entire country can boast of a healthier population of wild turkeys; turkeys that are completely wild and uncontaminated by domestic breeds.

We returned for a single day in early June. Not a turkey gobbler did we see. They had all secreted themselves in some hidden fastness, perhaps driven there by the intense heat of late spring. Perhaps they were quietly awaiting the renewal of their strength so severely tried by the courting season now ended some weeks past. Again and again we glimpsed a large brown shape in the grasses and then many smaller brownish-gray forms scattered as we came too close to a turkey hen and her brood of poults. The dancing of the turkey gobblers had achieved its purpose. A new generation of turkeys was already replacing natal down with a covering of feathers.

5

The Cave of a Million Bats

WE BRAKED THE CAR and studied our map. It was drawn with meticulous detail on a sheet of paper bearing an E. T. Rucker Ranch, Edwards County, Texas, letterhead. We had come forty-two miles north from Del Rio, driving through country that was new to us. Low, smoothly rounded hills undulated off into the distance while the whole country tilted gently upward. Bare, gravelly earth was sparsely dotted with clumps of creosote bush, yucca, cactus and other plants characteristic of a semidesert.

Now we had reached a slight uphill curve where a dirt road led from the highway through an offset in the right-of-way fence. Our map indicated that here we should leave the pavement. On our left stood a water trough. Beyond, exactly as the map promised, towered a windmill with slowly revolving blades. A round rock storage tank squatted beside it. The precise directions on Mr. Rucker's map encouraged us. We needed encouragement. Only a few days ago our ignorance of a wild area coupled with misleading directions had led us into a terrifying situation where we could not retrace our way up steep, boulder-paved slopes, and only by plunging forward and finally fording a river a couple of times had we extricated ourselves. But this time our directions were clear and accurate.

No sooner had we left the highway than the country that had rolled away so smoothly closed around us. The barren hills and great ledges took on a forbidding look. Somewhere in the desolate ranch land ahead of us was a great bat cave unknown to speleologists or spelunkers.

At home we had sometimes found bats hanging upside down behind the shutters and heard them squeaking in attic crevices. Their swift, darting flight as they pursued their insect prey over New England fields had been one of the marvels of migration we enjoyed each year. Sometimes in the twilight of a hot summer night we had teased a bat by tossing tiny pebbles into the air near it. Mistaking the pebble for an insect, the bat sometimes shifted its course to follow it almost to the ground.

Our casual interest in bats intensified when Dr. Charles Mohr, who is not only an outstanding all-round naturalist but also a speleologist and an authority on bats, learned we were going to Texas. He suggested we visit Ney Cave and check on the hawks that preyed on bats during their evening flights. His suggestion reminded us of a letter just received from geologist Glen Evans, who wrote that while searching the Rucker ranch for Indian shelters and caves he had witnessed a great bat flight, the most impressive he had ever seen. Charles read the letter but could not recall ever having heard of a bat cave on a ranch by that name. He referred to *Caves of Texas,* which he had edited. This book was compiled from information gathered by the leading speleologists and bat experts in Texas. Nowhere was the Rucker ranch mentioned.

We would rather check hawk predation on a bat flight at an unknown cave than at one so famous as Ney Cave. We enthusiastically agreed to trace Glen Evans' bat flight to its source. We knew he was even then on an expedition in the wilds of Mexico, and since people in the field have no time to answer mail, we decided to send a letter blindly to the Rucker ranch, asking if we might visit the bat cave. The response was immediate.

"We will be happy," Mr. Rucker wrote, "to have you as our guests and to take you to see our bat cave. We will drive you there in our ranch-trained truck; no other conveyance except a horse could carry you to it."

The warm hospitality offered by the letter was delightful. We looked forward to meeting this gracious rancher quite as much as seeing his cave. Now with the highway behind us, we followed the dirt road deeper and deeper into a dry and stony country. Repeatedly we consulted our map and directions.

"You will pass seven gates, all 'bumpers.' Approach these on the right side, come to a complete halt, then with the bumper touching the gate, shift into low gear and push gently. When the gate is about to leave the bumper, accelerate. They are self-closing."

With considerable trepidation we stopped at the first gate. Tensely we set the car in motion, then raced through the opening like a jackrabbit with a greyhound on its tail. We had negotiated the first of our seven barriers without having our rear bumper spanked.

Now as the narrow dirt road led us farther into wilderness country we began to feel the charm of the harsh rocky arid land. Lacy mesquites grew close to the road and we heard the staccato notes of vermilion flycatchers fluttering slowly among them in courtship flights. Behind the mesquites, the hills rose steeply but kept their rounded contours except where great ledges thrust forward. On the faces of some of the larger cliffs, black shadows hinted of caves and suggested Indian shelters and dens for panthers. Precipitous draws revealed scars made when past floods roared down, ripping out rocks and tumbling them violently from their beds. Trees torn up by their roots had been pitched headlong down the slopes.

Everywhere there were birds. Ash-throated flycatchers explored old woodpecker holes. Families of scaled quail ran by, their skinny little legs as stiff as those of wooden soldiers, while cottonlike pompons on their heads bobbed in time with their twinkling feet. Beside one bumper gate the remains of a golden eagle hung on barbed wire. Allan looked at it with a stricken face. Texas once had a large population of those magnificent birds but that tattered carcass on the fence was the first one, living or dead, we had yet seen in the whole state.

It took far longer to drive the twelve miles of dirt road than the forty-two miles of pavement from Del Rio. We examined the limestone cliffs. We photographed gay fields of yellow bitterweed. We tasted the sour red berries on gray and prickly algarita with its hollylike leaves. We breathed the fragrance of tiny white flowers on black persimmons.

Finally we came to the seventh gate with a large "No Hunting" sign nailed to the top board. Beyond, in a grove of live oaks, stood the Rucker ranch house. A tall, handsome woman crossed the deep porch, and the warmth and charm of her greeting made us welcome. In another moment Mr. Rucker had joined us, and such was their Texas hospitality that right away we forgot we were strangers.

We talked about the ranch of fifteen thousand acres on which sheep and angora goats were raised. Then our conversation turned to caves. There are at least a hundred of them on the ranch. Many were once used as shelters by Indians. Perhaps ten are really big caves. Swallow Cave is the handsomest. During the black days of the 1930's, when stockmen were compelled to reduce their herds, as Mr. Rucker had sadly watched his sheep hands throw dead sheep into one of the caves his thoughts had gone to far places of the world where people always went to bed hungry. The bones of those sheep thrown into the cave so long ago still lie in heaps, a ghostly reminder of the wanton destruction of good food.

We mentioned bats and our thoughts became brighter. The bats were confined to one cave about five miles from the ranch house.

In 1910 three thousand tons of guano were taken from the cave. No doubt this represented an accumulation of decades. For the next twenty years from forty-five to fifty tons were removed annually. Then the guano yield fell off sharply to about twenty tons, and that figure was maintained through the fifties. Mr. Rucker believed the drop was the result, to some degree, of the bats' use of inaccessible chambers.

He leased the guano rights to a man who "mined" bat guano from ten caves, including Ney Cave, scattered over four or five counties. The guano brought about forty-five dollars a ton, and from each ton mined in his cave, Mr. Rucker received a royalty of fifteen dollars. The mining was done in winter, usually in December, when the bats were hibernating and therefore undisturbed by the activity.

We were surprised that a cave where such extensive mining had been carried on for so many years had remained unknown to speleologists.

Mr. Rucker smiled. "The guano men are a close-mouthed bunch. They don't tell where their best caves are because they don't want them disturbed. So unless somebody interested in caves and bats stumbles on information about them, they remain unknown except to a few people."

We showed him our copy of *Caves of Texas*. He looked through it with keen interest. He knew many of the caves described in the book but he was loyal to his cave and believed the bat flight from it compared favorably with the best that Texas could offer. He estimated that millions of bats swarmed out in the spectacular evening flights. His conviction carried authority, and when we finally went to bed we were filled with anticipation of the excitement to come.

Early the next morning we padded the truck as much as possible and tucked the camera equipment securely in the padding. It was only five miles to the cave, but the road leading to it was a really tough one. To be sure it was pleasantly smooth at first but grew progressively rougher. Finally we paused by a windmill and tank on a hill about half a mile from the cave. The trail leading into the shallow valley was paved with huge jagged boulders. It looked impassable by any wheeled vehicle. I had been shaken quite enough and decided to walk. Allan stayed in the truck to cushion the cameras as much as possible against jolts. The truck growled down the slope in low, lurching from side to side. Several times Mr. Rucker brought it to a stop in order to climb more gently over a particularly large boulder.

It was easy to outdistance the truck, though broken rocks eroded by weather and hot from the sun hurt my feet. My nostrils stung from the heat and pungent odor compounded of dust, drying cedar and a multitude of aromatic desert plants.

Then a wide black mouth sloping lightly toward the south yawned downward in the blazing white limestone. It looked as if a great bubble had solidified and then a fragment of the bulging surface had broken away. I peered over the edge into the depths below and a shiver curled along my spine. I was on a thin shelf hanging far out over the abyss. Carefully I retreated to more solid rock and looked around. Cerise petaya cactus flamed in a crevice on the north rim and in its slender shadow a plump rock squirrel with a black face watched me. A few stunted mesquites found sufficient soil and water to maintain a hold on life. It was a desolate and forbidding place; a place of extremes. Only this morning a sheet of ice had covered the water in that tank on the hilltop, yet now the rocks were painfully hot to the touch.

A crude tripod stood on the south rim of the orifice. It had been built by the guano miners many years ago. Near the tripod rested a ladder made of 2 by 6 timbers anchored firmly to the rim and extending down into the cavern. So huge was the yawning adyss that the ladder looked flimsy and unsafe.

But now the truck shuddered to a stop, and Allan, the Ruckers, and their cocker Honey joined us. Immediately excitement mounted as it always does when Allan appears. He swung down the ladder and a great horned owl, perched unseen on a ledge, suddenly flew out of the cave. The rock squirrel flirted its dusky tail and ran for the shelter of a rock. A canyon wren began to sing its loud poignant song, and its series of liquid descending notes echoed faintly by the cavern walls had a depth and beauty equal to those of a veery.

Allan paused halfway down the ladder and examined the rock walls. Quickly he pointed to the wren's nest high in a jagged cavity some sixty feet above the floor of the cave. We came to associate the canyon wren and its song with caves, for we heard them in all the Texas caves we visited. Each time they approached their nests, their songs rang out, and again when they left, the air trembled with the cascading melody like hollow crystal balls bounding down a glass slide or little silver bells shaken in a goblet. Only in a large cave where the song of the canyon wren is held within rounded rock walls that amplify and echo it can the song be heard at its best. In the open, resonance is lost and the notes become separate and thin. The flowing stream of melody and the magic spell woven by the song within a cave vanishes.

Canyon wrens are reddish-brown with delicate bars of slightly deeper brown. The white throat and upper breast contrast sharply with the dark belly. Chirping softly as they hunt for insects, they scuttle like mice over the floor of a cave, going around and under and over tumbled rocks.

Their little tails are held upright like tiny masts and are constantly bobbed as they scurry about. Many times as I sat quietly within a cave, my eyes have been drawn to a moving spot of white, and there would be a canyon wren, its throat almost luminescent in the dim light that nearly hid its dark body.

Mr. Rucker told us the mouth of the cave is about 90 feet long and 60 feet wide. Through this the sunlight falls in a moving patch to the cave floor 80 feet below the rim. He cautioned us to use care as we climbed down the long ladder.

"Be watchful," he urged. "Just a few days ago one of the ranch hands killed a rattler at the foot of the ladder."

Before descending into the cave I found a shady place and took a temperature reading. The rocks were uncomfortably hot yet the air was only seventy-five degrees. Even that was an abrupt change from the twenty-eight-degree reading at the ranch house at dawn.

The ladder lurched and swayed as I climbed down into the cavern, but I was smaller than those who had gone before me, so I hoped it would not collapse. Soon I stepped from the last rung, and there lay the remains of a large rattler. As I clambered down the steep mound on which the foot of the ladder rested I looked sharply from side to side but saw nothing more fearful than one small dusky lizard. Then I was on the cavern floor and felt as if I were in a great rough bowl whose rim curved inward. Now I could hear the incessant wiry high-pitched chatter of bats, innumerable bats. Shifting air currents carried the stench from their chamber. Again I took a temperature reading. In the cave it was fifty-eight degrees F.

"The temperature is so constant down here," Mr. Rucker told us, "that during winter mining operations the guano men always make their camp down here. It eliminates the need for a tent and heavy bedding. Moreover the sun reaches into the cave for a few hours every day to make it dry and cheery.

"Once a family of eight—that was back in the winter of 1910–1911—spent the entire winter here and was very comfortable. They lowered their supplies on a cable. Since they needed wood only for cooking there was plenty close to the cave, and after cutting it, they simply threw it over the rim. In those days the drip from the stalactites there on the west side of the cave gave them sufficient water for cooking and drinking. And I doubt," Mr. Rucker added dryly, "if they were too much concerned about water for bathing."

The high chamber where we stood was pocked with holes and chimneys. From one cavity a steady procession of honeybees moved in and out. Under the canyon wren's nest we found a tiny white eggshell with a dusting of fine reddish specks that had fallen after one of the young birds hatched. Small mottled gray lizards scuttled about far too fast for us to catch them.

Then we turned toward the back of the cave, where we could see the black opening of the bat chamber. I tied a rain hood over my head and drew on rain boots. We climbed a seventeen-foot ladder to the main bat chamber, and with every rung we mounted, the stench grew worse and worse and the thin high cries of the bats more piercing. I gasped for breath as I clung to the top of the ladder and the full force of the fumes and the heat blasted against me.

I paused there long enough to pull out my thermometer and turn on the flashlight, for now we were in darkness. From fifty-eight degrees in the great outer chamber, the temperature had risen to seventy-five, exactly the same as it had been above ground. I found a place where I could hang the thermometer. Soon it registered ninety-six degrees.

Masses of bats in incredible, overwhelming numbers covered the upper walls and ceiling of the chamber so thickly that no rock was visible. They clung to every inch and in places appeared piled on top of one another. The whole mass quivered and trembled like a bowl of gelatin held upside down or some loathsome slime about to be released upon us.

Hummingbirds are said to become torpid at night with slow heartbeats and respiration. Bats are exactly the opposite. They become torpid by day. Now our entrance into the cave had aroused them. Some of them began to fly. Those that hit us with a gentle thud clung like soft leeches. Their very softness added to our revulsion. They felt as though they would squash if sufficient force to dislodge them were exerted. Those flying between us and the dim opening of the chamber looked almost like night-flying moths, for their swiftly moving wings created an illusion of pale transparency.

Our eyes and nostrils were tortured by the pungent fumes of ammonia. There was a steady rain of excrement upon us. Our feet plunged deep into soft spongy brown ordure on the floor of the chamber.

No matter how many bats left their places on the congested ceiling, so many remained that the stone to which they clung was hidden from the shafts of our flashlights. Yet this year's young, which would increase the population by a third or more, had not yet been born.

Often we were forced to go to the mouth of the bat chamber to gasp for air, even though it was better there only by degrees for it, too, was fetid. But having shaken off incipient faintness and suffocation, again we moved deeper into the cavern where the walls sloped down, bringing the bats clinging to it close to our cameras. So far as we could tell, all were Mexican free-tailed bats (*Tadaria mexicana*) aptly termed the "guano bat." It was guano from this species that was used by the Confederate Army during the Civil War to produce niter for gunpowder after the northern blockade had cut off other sources of it. As a fertilizer the bat guano today is a valuable agricultural commodity.

It was this species of bat that was used in the fantastic Project X-Ray of World War II. Incendiary bombs weighing three times as much as these third-of-an-ounce bats were attached to the loose skin beneath the wings. Then the bats were refrigerated until they became dormant. In that state of artificially induced hibernation they were placed in cases resembling egg crates. Still refrigerated, it was planned to fly the bats to targets in Japan. Above the target, the crates would be opened and attached to slow-falling parachutes. During the slow fall earthward, the bats would regain normal body temperature and awaken. Naturally they would immediately seek shelter in dark places by crawling into the crevices of buildings, thus triggering the incendiaries, which would set entire cities on fire.

Thousands upon thousands of bats were expended in this strange project before the technique was perfected. Not only did the bats successfully burn down a demonstration town built in the desert, but when two bats equipped with live incendiaries escaped from their handlers they burned down an auxiliary air station at Carlsbad. Fortunately for the bats and for all people who enjoy wildlife, this project was abandoned upon perfection of the atom bomb.

Because of the vast quantities of food required by so enormous a number of bats, they are generally protected for their effectiveness in controlling insects. Mr. Rucker was well aware of the value of bats. Mosquitoes were almost unknown within a radius of several miles of the cave. As long ago as 1910 a Dr. Campbell of San Antonio had recognized their service in controlling malaria mosquitoes. He persuaded the city to build a tower for a bat roost near Mitchell Lake, then on the outskirts of the city. Malaria had been rampant in that section of San Antonio for years, but after the successful establishment of the man-made bat roost, mosquito-borne diseases were sharply reduced.

Recently the numbers of Mexican free-tailed bats have dropped alarmingly. Many people attribute their decrease to the growing use of insecticides. Most insects quickly become immune to pesticides, so increasingly deadly ones must be used to fight them. In bats nature created a most effective mosquito control; yet they are dying out, and man is using instead poisons that harm man and may kill him.

Allan made a sweep with his insect net as some bats flew by him and caught three. He released two and with the third bat still in the net, we left the chamber and climbed down the ladder into the huge grotto.

The shock of brilliant light after the blackness of the bat chamber was painful to our eyes, but there was active pleasure in each draught of fresh cool air.

Then Allan opened the net and lifted out the bat, carefully spreading its wings. It was yellowish-brown and the fur was soft and velvety. I was surprised by the naked, mouselike tail with skinlike appendages near the body. The long narrow wings looked quite powerful, yet they were so transparent that the arm bones showed red against the light. I touched the wings, and they were softer and more delicate than the finest suede used for costly gloves. From tip to tip of the wings, the bat measured 8⅜ inches.

"It is really a flying mouse," I thought. But I quickly changed my mind as I studied the dark wizened face with huge forward-cupped ears and deep vertical wrinkles in the upper lip. It reminded me of the shrunken heads I had seen at the Explorer's Club, human heads that had sent a chill through me as I looked at them. Now I remembered that certain primitive people are said to have regarded bats with veneration because of a fancied resemblance to humans.

Bats are among the few species of mammals that, like humans, suckle their young at two breasts. When the young is born, the mother catches it in her wings, which she folds into a basket for it. For two or three weeks she carries her young with her on flights through the night in search of food. When the young bat—for Mexican free-tailed bats seldom have multiple births—becomes too heavy for such excursions, it remains hanging in the cave while the mother feeds. One wonders how the mother ever again finds her child in the darkness among the multitudes crowding the cave.

Thinking of the strange lives of these cave animals, we fell silent, gazing at the bat, a member of an enormous community which appeared to have solved all important problems and lived at peace with the world. We watched as Allan stood up, held the bat high over his head and opened his hand. Swift as a bullet, the bat swooped into the bat chamber and vanished.

Then I noticed that orange-yellow lice were crawling on Allan's hands. Suddenly I realized that I too was covered with unwelcome wildlife. I had thought it quite bad enough to have the stench of the cave clinging to my clothes and skin, but this was much worse. Allan and Mr. Rucker, after looking at themselves with consternation, disappeared toward the slender concealment of some cedars.

I could tolerate none of their half-measures. Remembering the water tank half a mile away at the top of the hill, I started toward it, unmindful of the reassuring calls to the effect that bat lice would not stay on me, that they would crawl off before I could reach the tank. I continued on my way, toiling up the rough hot hill, swerving only to avoid cactus.

Quickly I stripped and plunged into the tank that early in the morning had been covered with ice. Though the ice had all melted, the tank was slippery. Its sides and bottom were coated with a thick growth of green algae. The cool water soothed my itching skin, and when finally I climbed out, I tossed my clothes into the tank and swished them about furiously, then wrung them out and flattened them on the hot rocks. Back into the tank I went while my clothes dried. The nylon things dried almost instantly but blue jeans are made of sterner stuff. Finally I decided damp jeans would have to do and after examining them and my body to make sure I was free of bat lice, I dressed.

In spite of the bath, the offensive smell of the bat cave clung to my clothes and body. Slowly I made my way back down the hill to the others now clustered beside the cave. Around us all, except Mrs. Rucker and Honey, the stench of bats hovered like an invisible cloak.

In the meantime Mr. Rucker had built a fire that blazed merrily, then slowly crumbled into a bed of red coals. A pot of coffee soon bubbled fragrantly.

The valley grew hotter as the afternoon hours passed. The brilliant light was intensified by the white rocks that paved the valley, and everything from rocks to pale gray-green cactus shimmered, and their outlines were vague. Heat waves like ghostly flames trembled above them. Our eyes grew heavy, and we became as torpid as the collard lizard, big-headed and long-tailed, that lay in a horizontal crevice of limestone rock close to us.

Suddenly there were flying shapes near the opening of the cave, and lethargy vanished. Were the bats about to fly? No, it was a flock of cave swallows, very much like cliff swallows but with pale cheeks and dark chestnut foreheads. We had noted some of their last year's nests in the cave. Unlike the jug-shaped nests of cliff swallows, these were open mud cups. As the swallow circled above the cave opening, their numbers swelled. Round and round they wheeled, gathering newcomers into their ranks. Now they swooped into the upper part of the cavern and spiraled out again. Soon several hundred swallows whirled around the mouth of the cave. Then, as if spilled from the air, they flowed into the cave and clung to the upper walls, fluttering and chattering.

The sun dropped lower, and shadows stretched long and thin across the valley. Silently we waited and watched. Then came a rush of many wings, and we gasped. By the time our stunned eyes carried the message to our disbelieving brains, the flight of bats had reached the horizon at the valley rim and was breaking into black clouds that whirled off into the distance.

The stream of bats, perhaps twenty feet in diameter, brought the fetid stench of the cavern with them. The column rose from the southwest side of the cave and twisted off across the valley like a gigantic fire hose out of control, like the twisting funnel of a tornado. The flight was silent except for the soft whisper of a multitude of wings on the air. The wiry, incessant chatter of the roosting bats was stilled, though it may be they were giving the supersonic calls, inaudible to the ears of man, that they employ to guide themselves around obstacles and in the darkness of caves and at night. The incredible swiftness of the flight held us spellbound. According to Charles Mohr, the wings of the free-tailed bats closely resemble in shape those of the swifts, the speed kings of the bird world. Indeed, the Indian swift is said to attain speeds of more than two hundred miles an hour in ordinary flight. So it is fitting that the free-tailed bats should hold the record as the fastest flying species of bat.

Spellbound, we watched the stream of bats lash from the cave and splinter into fragments that rolled away like puffs of dark smoke and vanished from sight. There was a beautiful synchronization in the mass movement from the cave, as there is when a great flock of tree swallows alternately spins itself into long streamers and contracts into wide ribbons as the fever of migration builds within them, and in swarms of bees weaving such exact figures that no single individual breaks the fluid outline of the undulating mass, and as shorebirds swing and dart like a single body above a mud flat. The beauty, speed and size of the flight left us breathless and marveling. I doubt that any sight I will ever experience can excel in fantastic strangeness that great bat flight.

Not once during the day had we seen a hawk but suddenly

they appeared as if by magic. A peregrine stooped at the living river and darted away with a bat in its talons. A second and a third falcon flashed into and through the column of bats with the same success. A sharp-shinned hawk was equally adept and went off with a bat dangling from its claws. Two red-tailed hawks were not so agile. Nevertheless after two or three attacks, they made a catch. All of us thought one redtail caught two bats in a single strike, one in each talon, but such an observation would need further verification. The attacks of the hawks failed to turn the bat flight, which deviated only with a slight expansion of the column at the point of assault.

Eight minutes passed, and the flight ended as suddenly as it had begun. Allan figured if 300 bats a second had emerged from the cave, in eight minutes about 144,000 bats had swarmed by us. Allan and I were jubilant. We had watched a sight we would never forget as long as we lived. But the Ruckers were depressed. They had promised us millions of bats and they thought Allan's figures were fairly accurate. Therefore they had let us down. But their regret in no way affected our delight with the experience we had just had.

Now we had to leave the vicinity of the cave. The full moon, which would soon be hidden by a total eclipse, was rising in the east as the rim of the sun slid behind the western hills. We decided that, heavy as the cameras were, it would be wiser to walk the half mile to the water tank carrying them rather than subject them to the shaking and bouncing of the truck as it growled and heaved itself over the boulders. With night creeping up the valley it was essential that the truck pass the worst of the trail while some light remained. So we labored up the hill, still gripped by a stunned feeling of disbelief in the witness of our eyes, so amazing was the spectacle we had watched.

We reached the water tank, and in a short time the truck, lurching from rock to rock, roared to a stop beside us. Allan swung a camera toward the bed of the truck, then whirled with a wild shout that rose high above the whining motor.

"Here they come again!"

A second flight of bats, in a column even larger than the first, was pouring from the cave, up the side of the valley, and over our heads. So great was this flight of bats that the multitude of wings created a soft roar like the sound of distant surf. On and on they streamed against the sky, red with the last fading banners of sunset. Directly over our heads the stream of bats broke, whirled into compact balls, and disappeared in the deepening twilight.

On and on they came. How many were there? Where were they going? How far must they fly to find food enough to satisfy such a multitude? Where in this semidesert could they find the insects their hunger demanded? Dazed and almost awed by the sight of the lengthening stream, we forgot that ahead lay some rugged road that the truck would cover more slowly than we could walk. We forgot the bat odor that clung to us and the need to soak in hot baths with fragrant soap.

The Ruckers were serene. Their cave had measured up to their claims for it. As for Allan and me, this was the most memorable experience we had ever had. For twenty-three minutes we watched the second flight of bats. How long it continued we do not know. We heard the silken rustle of many wings and saw dim shapes against the night sky when Mr. Rucker reluctantly started the motor and our slow, bumpy journey back to the ranch house began. The earth's shadow had crept far across the face of the moon, dimming its brilliant light. The passage of the bats was but a whisper of wings above us and a hint of vile smell that soon faded away altogether in the darkness of the early spring night.

6

A Look of Innocence

SPANNING TEXAS, the migrating birds stream north like a vast shifting cloud that is pushed by contrary winds, sometimes swiftly as snow water tumbles down a mountain slope, sometime lazily as a butterfly drifts from daisy to primrose on a still day, and again all forward motion is halted by opposing winds or deep cold. But swiftly or slowly, the flocks are drawn steadily northward by the pull of spring and the increasing light and lengthening days.

At the same time other clouds are gathering force, clouds tied to the earth by roots, yet they are gay as the sunrise and the sunset. Somehow, someway, a new generation must be born, and with stupendous prodigality, the plants prepare for the event. Bright colors and perfume attract the eyes and delight the nose by day, and white flowers shine dimly in the night and release great quantities of scent into the air. In their various methods of flowery propagation, the plants provide man with one of his most cherished delights, but the enormous effort involved in the arrangements for continuing their kind is directed not toward the enjoyment of man but toward those creatures that can be enticed to transport pollen from the stamens of one flower to the pistil of another of the same species. A bat, a few species of birds and many kinds of

insects have become intermediaries in this essential gamble of
the flowers. In payment, the flowers dispense a modicum of
nectar to those unaware sexual assistants attracted by the
colors and perfumes.

Swinburne wrote, "Blossom by blossom the spring begins,"
but not in Texas. Flowers burst forth in all the lavish exuberance of numbers and variety traditionally attributed to
the prodigious, larger-than-life activities of Texas men.
Wherever areas of relatively undisturbed prairie remain,
bluebonnets, the state flower, billow mile after mile in misty
azure carpets. Masses of white, pink and yellow primroses
dance in the wind. Orchid sand verbenas sprawl over inhospitable shoulders of highways. Nodding on slender stems,
millions and millions of sunny coreopsis shine in the sun,
and gaillardias' broad ray-flowers sometimes measuring a full
two inches across splash the land with color. Associated with
them are other flowers of infinite variety and hue.

Travelers across Texas in spring ride between gay ribbons
of many-colored wild flowers and can find elsewhere no equal
for the brilliance and variety of native flowers in that state.
At the same time the air is filled with heady perfume, sometimes subtle but often an insistant fragrance, and on every
breeze intriguing scents drift by. Along wooded streams gum
elastic and saffron plum put forth little flowers with a strong
scent. In more arid places the hooked barbs of catclaw are
hidden beneath abundant catkins hanging from slender stems
and under spiny stiff leaves tiny yellow flowers like miniature
narcissus blossoms open on algarita. Huajillo's sweet scented
clusters of white flower balls yield heavy white Uvalde honey
considered the best produced in all Texas.

With the first warm rains of spring one of the most beautiful small trees in all the world bursts into bloom in low moist
places. If an artist were given the task of imagining and then
drawing the most dainty and elegant tree possible, he would
likely reproduce a retama, also called *lluvua de oro* (shower

of gold) by our Mexican neighbors. As *Parkinsonia aculeata* it is planted in gardens and along highways throughout the south. Its foliage is a mist of feathery drooping leaves of tiny leaflets on long mid-ribs. Its five-petaled golden flowers nestle in profusion among the filmy leaves. A day or two after it opens one petal of each blossom becomes lightly spotted with red near the throat, and by the time another day has passed, that petal blushes red all over and lifts above the plane of its yellow companions. Then the flower is ready to yield its pollen to any insect that visits it.

All animal life on this earth depends, in the final analysis, on plants. The food chain of even those animals that eat only flesh in the end goes back to plants. These alone of living things are able to take the raw materials of the earth and the air and sunlight and turn them into substances animal life can assimilate into its own body. The panther eats the deer that ate the yaupon leaves. In searching the earth for plants that can give us food or pleasure or cures for our ills, many dark and mysterious secrets have been discovered through the ages.

Delicate paintings remain of an expedition sent out by Queen Hatshepsut of Egypt more than 3,500 years ago to collect plants, and men are still at it. Alexander the Great, Marco Polo, Columbus and David Fairchild all searched for plants that man could use in one way or another. We did not think of their potential dangers when we enjoyed the oleanders of Galveston, oleanders that are poisonous in every part: roots, stems, leaves and flowers. Nor did we think of the harm they do when we photographed sweeping carpets of golden bitterweed lying beneath mesquite trees. We enjoyed locoweed flowers without thinking of the torment of livestock that may browse those members of the great legume family. Our first reaction to the wild flowers of Texas was sheer delight in their color, variety and perfume. Among those we came across, we found three that typified for us the sinister, a complexity of good and evil and a touch of mysticism.

We were slow to grasp the sinister qualities of the first. The truck rocked to a halt, for the motor was boiling over. We were on our way to the Rucker bat cave; and nighttime frost still lingered in the air, though the sun already glared feverishly on the white rocks thatching the hills. Springing from the white rocks already trapping the sun's heat was an eight-foot, dark green shrub. With an exclamation of delight, Ethel Rucker darted from the cab and in an instant was beside the shrub and had swept several of its large wisterialike flower clusters together and buried her face in them.

"Mummmm! Wonderful!" she breathed happily, her voice muffled by the pea-shaped flowers ranging from pale lilac to amethyst.

I promptly plunged my face among the cool flowers. They did have an exquisite scent, and following hard on the flowery bouquet came a tantalizing afterscent. A picture of the Hudson River highway above Nyack in autumn sprang to my mind, and I saw roadside stands of farm produce: mounds of gay pumpkins, heaps of russet potatoes, piles of shiny red apples, and, yes! Baskets of dark Concord grapes bursting with juice. These wisterialike flowers reminded me particularly of Concord grapes.

"It is mountain laurel," Ethel told me. "No, it is not a Kalmia. It belongs to the pea family. I consider it the most beautiful native shrub of the Edwards Plateau. The dark compound leaves are evergreen, so it is attractive all year. It should be planted more often in gardens, for no exotic shrub is more decorative."

"I suspect," Ethel added, "That some homesick New Englander who came to here in colonial days—which weren't so very long ago in this section of Texas—was reminded of home when the loveliest shrub of all came into bloom; and wrapped in nostalgia, he transferred a dear familiar name to it from the East as the colonists so often transferred English names for birds and plants they knew at home to similar species in their new land."

That evening we had a delicious tapioca pudding for dessert, and I mentioned my long-standing wonder that primitive Indians along the Amazon had learned to take the deadly poison tapioca plant and by a fairly complicated treatment make it not only safe but actually the mainstay of their diet.

Ed Rucker broke in. "That mountain laurel you admired this morning contains a deadly poison. It has been called many names: mescalbean, frijolita, coralbean and big-drunk bean are some of them. Its scientific name is *Sophoro secundiflora*. The flowers are pretty, but the Indians committed suicide by eating the seeds. Sometimes they disposed of unwanted prisoners by forcing them to drink a concoction spiked with powdered mountain laurel beans.

"You have seen agave growing all through south Texas. Well, the Indians for countless centuries brewed a colorless liquor from any one of several species, but maguey [*Agave atrovirens*] is the one they preferred. The Spaniards learned from the Indians how to make their intoxicating mescal.

"The early settlers in Texas soon learned to drink mescal. Apparently it wasn't potent enough to satisfy those hardy pioneers. They often ground up mountain laurel seeds and added it to their mescal for an extra kick. This made the mescal wildly exhilarating at first, and this stage was followed by profound sleep. It is claimed that during the Civil War some of the prisoners held in camps along the Rio Grande not only managed to make mescal but they, too, added ground-up mountain laurel seeds to it so enthusiastically that many never wakened from their drinking spree."

Ed seized a flashlight. "Come on. There is a mountain laurel by the shed that finished blooming some time ago, and it must have good-sized beans right now."

Sure enough, heavy green pods hung all over the shrub. They were densely covered with silvery hairs having a sheen that reminded me of the coat of young harbor seals. Ed broke one open. It contained three pea-sized green seeds.

"I'll send you some when they are ripe," he promised me.

In September the mailman delivered a small box from the Ruckers. In it were several seed pods coated with a tawny bloom. Where the bloom had rubbed away they were pale yellowish-tan. The shells were swollen over each seed and then contracted sharply, making a partially enclosed compartment for each. The pods ranged from about two inches to slightly more than six inches in length. Some pods had only two seeds, while one had six in it. When shaken, the seeds rattling in the pods sounded like a child's toy. I tried to break one with my fingers as Ed Rucker had the green pods in April but it was too tough. A knife made no impression on the pod. Finally I resorted to a hammer and struck the pod sharply. It shattered. Five round orange-red seeds rolled out. They were hard as pebbles.

Nothing could have looked more innocent; yet had I eaten half of one it would have put me to sleep for days, and a whole one would have been fatal. I still have those seeds and some unopened pods. Kept in my workroom I expect they will remain unchanged indefinitely. Though Florida, where we live now, is a place of many insects, not one has ever attacked the mountain laurel seeds. If the powerful alkaloid they contain has any medical value it has eluded my search. Those foolish enough to add it to a drink hazard life itself.

Mountain laurel is not the only "Bean" that produces sinister reactions in humans. Away back in the time of Homer some 850 years or more B.C., pilgrims desiring to speak to departed relatives or friends undertook a journey to Necromanteion, and there priests gave them dried beans that produced hallucinations and stimulated their senses so they believed they were at the bleak entrance to Hades and in the presence of the spirits of those who had entered the world of the dead.

The weird quality of the *Sophoro secundiflora* seeds awakens wonder that the large pulse family, at home in deserts, in tropical swamps and in temperate forests and fields can produce so great a variety of forms with so many qualities. Beans, peas and clover are so tied to human economy that a disaster to them would be a disaster to us. It may be that the world's first candy came from the roots of a tall pulse herb, licorice; today the long black whips flavored with it are beloved by children. Indigo is only one pulse that gives us a fine dye. Acacias and mimosas are sources of excellent honey, perfumes and timber, while other pulses such as the Japanese pagoda tree are appreciated chiefly for their beauty. *Sophoro secundiflora* may be put in this group. It clearly deserves Emerson's "Beauty is its own excuse for being."

For a while we worked out of Alpine. South of that town and not far from Calamity Creek lay a barren area covered with coarse gravel. We noted it because growing here and there around its edges were a few clumps of prickly poppies, sure signs of impoverished soil, but most pleasing camera subjects. The conspicuous flat white flowers have yellow centers and are often called cowboy's fried eggs. Their stems drip orange-colored juice when cut, and the seeds are said to contain a narcotic more potent than opium. We passed that way at intervals and were astonished one day to find a tight bouquet of rank gray-green leaves had erupted in a compact mound in the center of that seemingly lifeless earth. It was as if a place of great honor had been cleared and reserved for royalty.

Perhaps a week later we approached Calamity Creek shortly after dawn. Our plant that had appeared so magically was covered with a dozen or more seven-inch white flowers faintly tinted near the base with violet. Even before we sniffed the fragrant white flowers, we recognized them as datura, often called sacred datura by the Indians. Perhaps because of the poor soil, this particular plant did not sprawl as they often do over as much as fifty square feet of ground, but kept instead its fountainlike bouquet shape.

Every part of the plant is extremely poisonous, yet it belongs to the same nightshade family as potatoes, tomatoes, and lovely deep purple eggplants. The huge family has some three thousand members around the world. We had enjoyed several species of wild nightshade that added to the roadside beauty of Texas. Petunias, those invaluable garden flowers, and tobacco are also in the nightshade family, and so is henbane which was brought to this country from Europe. Planted in gardens, it escaped and has made itself at home across the continent. Henbane was well known by witches, who used it in their brews, and it is believed to have contributed, along with datura, to their delirium, making them dream vividly of wild flights through the air and even wilder dancing. Doctors say this brew caused uneven heartbeats and breathing, which induced the frantic dreams.

Like *Sophoro secundiflora*, sacred datura has many popular names including devil's trumpet, thornapple and jimson weed. An eastern variety grew in Virginia, and the early colonists, hungry for plants to enhance their monotonous diet, gathered the large leaves and cooked them like spinach. It brought suffering and death. So it came about that datura was called Jamestown weed and this was corrupted to jimson weed.

Unlike the beans of *Sophoro secundiflora*, which have been employed for murder, by suicides and to increase the exhilaration and oblivion of drunkenness, datura has been used for countless centuries by witch doctors, medicine men—especially those of Central and South America—by laymen administering self-medication and has long been particularly favored by gypsies as an ingredient in their folk medicine. Today such alkaloides as atropine and hyoscyamine are obtained from it for medical purposes and psychiatric studies. In nonlethal quantities datura produces hallucinations and was frequently used by the Indians for this purpose.

Around the world, datura has been put to strange uses. Among some tribes of Colombia, Indian wives and slaves were buried with their dead masters. A datura brew was given the living to put them to sleep before the burial. In India wives were once burned on the funeral pyre of their husbands, and they too were put to sleep with datura before being placed on the fire. It was in India, also, where there was often great disparity in the ages of married couples, that quite a different use was made of datura. Young wives gave their old husbands sufficient datura to stupefy them. Then they were free to enjoy themselves as they wished as long as the old husband continued to breathe.

The Indians of Darien combined superstition and datura. Making a brew of the plant, they gave it to children, who then raced about in a wild state of exhilaration until at last they collapsed in a stupor. It was believed children who had imbibed the brew would fall on deposits of gold. Since gold was plentiful in Darien, perhaps the datura-witching for gold was quite as effective as water-witching with a forked hazel stick is in New England.

Unlike *Sophoro secondiflora,* which can intoxicate and kill but to our present knowledge has nothing but its beauty to offer humans, daturas have contributed to medical treatments since history began. During the Middle Ages, one of its products, belladonna, was used to make the eyes of fashionable beauties darker and more luminous, and today it is used to dilate our pupils during eye examinations. It was used half a century ago when twilight sleep was popular during childbirth and is administered today before anesthetics for surgery are given. Many a parent gives children prone to car sickness pills made partly from datura. While many factors of datura are known to have medical value, some scientists believe many more secrets and mysteries of the plant are still unknown.

Later in the season I gathered some seed pods of that datura that had erupted so suddenly from the bare ground near Calamity Creek. They were round and bristled with a hundred stiff prickles. Between the stem and the pod a small scalloped cap flared. Should I cut one open, I could remove from the four compartments of the pod seeds less than a sixth of an inch long, flattened and wrinkled and almost black. They are said to have a bitter nauseous taste. This does not encourage me to experiment so I rely on hearsay while I look at them with continued fascination. How many people through how many ages have been affected by datura in so many strange ways.

One spring, before going to Texas, when LSD and other "mind expanding" drugs had not yet occupied the limelight, I ran across a reference to peyote, *Lophophoro williamsii*. It said the little cactus grew sparsely in Texas. It stated that if peyote is eaten it has the effect of changing sound into light: for instance, the ticks of a watch are received as a rapid succession of beautiful colors. It added that doctors and psychologists at the National University of Mexico had embarked on a project concerned with possible medical use of peyote.

In response to my inquiry, the university wrote that they were not engaged in such research, but sent me a copy of an official publication in Spanish about the cactus: The Magic of Peyote. This was illustrated with wildly confused and nightmarish drawings of writhing serpents and dragons. At its conclusion was a long list of references, some dating back to the early days of the Spanish exploration of Mexico, while most of the modern ones were by Americans.

Investigating the card catalog in the Forty-second Street Library in New York, I found more than half a drawer devoted to references about peyote. Reading these, I discovered

considerable conflict in the information. As early as 1560 peyote was mentioned by Spanish explorers as a narcotic cactus
used by the Indians in religious rituals. The first botanical
description of the cactus was written in 1638 by Hernandez,
the naturalist in Mexico for Philip II. He called it "glittering
medicine." A few years later Malino spoke of peyote as "shining water of the fields." Back in the seventeenth century laws
were passed to prohibit the use of peyote, and today though
peyote has neither thorns nor horns I could be arrested in
some states because I cherish three of these small plants in
flowerpots. One of these bloomed not long ago, and the single
lavender-pink flower stood upright like a small parasol. After
it shriveled a club-shaped rosy fruit with a reddish tinge began to swell. The gray-green top of this cactus that grows
above the ground and is eaten either fresh or dry is called the
peyote button.

In spite of scientific studies of peyote that prove it does not
fit within the definition of a narcotic, it is viewed by many
with alarm, though it is not addicting nor does it cause un-
seemly or orgiastic behavior. It is generally agreed that the
color hallucinations are very beautiful and that a feeling of
well-being lasts for some time after a peyote ceremony. It appears that people having an abnormal psychology often have
frightening visions, and should even the well-balanced take
too many peyote buttons they, too, would suffer very disagreeable effects. Since the cactus is rather rare and has a
most disagreeable taste, overuse of it is never likely to become
a social problem. It takes about eight to cause hallucinations.

Peyote has collected many names for itself, and these tend
to be misleading. Some of these are diabolical root, devil's
root, dry whiskey, white mule, Indian dope and mescal button. The "mescal button" has nothing to do with mescal
bean (*Sophoro secundiflora*) or with the drink mescal made
from maguey nor brandy distilled from agave beer. Never-

theless, the alkaloid in peyote that causes color visions is called mescaline. Mescaline is now made synthetically in laboratories; and this is preferred by doctors for studies and experiments, since its potency is controlled whereas its concentration varies greatly in peyote.

The more one explores reports concerning peyote, the more evident it becomes that fear and even hatred of it result chiefly from its association with a culture different from ours. The Indians had their ancient religion taken from them and Christianity forced upon them. As time passed and more and more they lost their identity, something of their very own took on increasing importance. Many feel they have found this in a truly Indian religion. During this century the Native American Church has spread northward across our country. The Indians have adapted the peyote rites that Mexican tribes followed a thousand years ago and added them to Christianity to make them their own. Far from its being bizarre and heathenish, unbiased observers report that the Native American Church fits the fundamental traits found in the best types of all religions but is based on the Ten Commandments and the Christian God. The ceremony conforms to traditional Indian practices and beliefs, and the peyote is eaten sacramentally in a solemn and reverent ceremony as is bread and wine in holy communion. The Indians say the peyote "takes us where God is."

It is conceivable that peyote can be abused, but so can wine. It would appear that the conflict between Americans and Indians where peyote is concerned is largely a matter of mores, not reason, and the illogical desire to compel them to keep to our ways and forget their own. While the very rarity of peyote is sufficient to preclude real danger from it by those who might eat the unpleasant-tasting vegetable for reasons other than sacrament, the same is not true of synthetic mescaline. This potent chemical can be very dangerous and should only be used under the direction and supervision of competent doctors.

The Doors of Perception was written by Aldous Huxley after he had swallowed 4/10 of a gram of synthetic mescaline. He believed it made him see truly as only the greatest poets and artists are able to see. It is clear that he was deeply interested in the folklore, mysticism and romance that envelop the small cactus, peyote. While it made him see beauty where he had not seen it before, it also diminished his desire to act. He was content merely to sit and do nothing except look.

Having immersed myself in literature concerned with peyote, I wanted to see it growing in its native surroundings, but everything indicated its rarity, its secretiveness, and the difficulty of finding it. Even the pre-Columbian Indians had traveled far and under hazardous conditions to collect it for their periodic religious ceremonies. Botanists noted that it was a rarity on some of the mesas of Pecos County and some hills southeastward to the Rio Grande and was most abundant in Starr and Zapata counties; large counties with very few roads.

Whenever we were in arid country, I touched small round cactus heads just poking from the surface, hoping to find one without spines. Always prickles clung to my exploring fingers. Then Ed Rucker told us he knew where some grew down in Zapata County. We looked at our official Texas road map. It showed only two roads: one paralleling the Rio Grande, the other, Route 16, bisecting it. Ed made a telephone call to a Zapata rancher, and we were off toward Uvalde, Carrizo Springs and Laredo. Here and there dainty sprays of yellow retama streamed in the hot wind. Ceniza bushes were covered with delicate lilac flowers, which meant it had rained fairly decently though flying dust belied this. In the old days, tea made from the leaves of ceniza was the standard remedy for bad cases of fright.

We turned north on an unsurfaced road. Hills rolled

gently and thickets of brush enclosed us. Heat and dust
wrapped around us. Deeper and deeper into the brush country we went. We passed through a gate and another and still
another. Ed pulled the car off the rough ranch road. Following his lead we slid through a narrow gate onto parched barren range from which most of the brush had withdrawn and
even opuntia was low and shriveled with thirst.

"It is a small pale gray-green dumpling of a cactus," Ed
said. "And there is more of it underground than above.
When you find one you will be astonished at its uninteresting
look. You just can't believe that so much has been said and
written about so small a plant."

We separated and wandered about. Soon my fingers bristled with almost invisible spines from small cactus plants. I
came to a stony ridge, and on a small level plateau above it I
suddenly saw five small cacti whose rounded tops scarcely
broke the baked surface. They were veiled by a tangle of
grayish threads. Gingerly I touched one. No spines. They
were peyote plants, Ed assured me. The gray silklike threads
were centered on the top and spread down the sides. They
were fine as those of an artist's camel's hair brush. I rubbed
them away from one peyote and lay flat on the ground and
sunk my teeth into it. Even before my tongue touched my
teeth I had had quite enough of the cactus. It tasted awful.
No wonder there has never been a case of peyote addiction in
any hospital. Nobody could possibly want to eat much of that
untasty cactus.

"I wish I could take one home with us."

"You can," Ed was already pulling up a plant. "I arranged
for that when I telephoned. You don't have to worry about
their dying. They can live a long time just this way. When
you get home, plant them in light sandy soil in a pot and
water them occasionally."

The roots were much longer and almost as thick at the top
as the gray-green dumpling above the ground. Only the top,

either fresh or dried, is eaten during peyote ceremonies.

It was one of these plants from Zapata that bloomed recently. So far as I can see they have not grown any larger since they were pulled from that hot Texas hillside. If I neglect to water them for a long time, they grow quite wrinkled, and then when they are watered they swell out and become firm and plump.

Once there were many plants that Indians held in veneration, for they believe them incarnations of spirits. Some were good and others decidedly evil. Of them all, peyote held a leading place and was considered good, tough and powerful. Modern medicine has followed up few leads concerning the properties of peyote other than in the treatment of mental illness, where it seems to have definite value.

Today our world has become a shore from which man will take off into a universe far more hostile than the one faced by ancient Polynesians on their great voyages or by Columbus sailing westward on the Atlantic. But surely the proportion of people who will venture into distant space will remain small for centuries to come. Yet there will be no lack of the unknown for the earth-bound to explore right here. In the plant world alone our knowledge barely scratches the surface. Oh yes, we know many plants that give us food, many that add beauty to our lives and yield perfumes, many that contribute cures for disease, many that are deadly.

But why do plants build strange chemicals in their tissues? How many of these may be useful to humanity? Why do some call forth beautiful visions from unknown depths of our being?

Primitive people stumbled upon some of the secrets of the plants and made use of them in strange ways. Through the ages there has been a steady increase in the knowledge of plants and their qualities. Tomorrow scientists in laboratories will discover secrets beyond our comprehension today. So many mysteries are hidden in the plant world that it requires an imagination like William Blake's made vivid with a "stronger and better light than his perishing mortal eye can see" to conceive what lies hidden among the flowers of the field, innocently smiling in the sunshine and dancing in the springtime breeze.

7

Where the West Begins

THE PINY WOODS of Texas, an extension of eastern forests, were far behind us that spring day. So were the gray clouds scudding before a bitter wind that tossed feathery mesquites and sprayed bursts of fine drizzle as we sped across the black-land prairies. There mile after mile of bluebonnets, blue as any sky, blue as the Gulf Stream on a bright day, covered the plain like a vast misty carpet. Golden coreopsis, pink prim-roses and orchid sand verbenas bordered the road with rib-bons of gay colors.

The prairie sank away and the road went on and on and flung itself up the Balcones Escarpment. We were on our way to find and photograph birds of the west in the land of cowboys, Indians, badmen and sudden spectacular riches. If that land is largely mythical, the romance of times long gone lingers and adds a special luster to wildlife living there.

Admittedly the West is distorted by our imaginations, but there is a dramatic change from east to west and this is espe-cially true in south Texas. The 100th meridian has become a generalized boundary between east and west for botanists, ornithologists and entomologists. No wonder they have all settled on the same meridian, for plants, birds, insects and mammals are inseparably associated. Not that the boundaries

119

of eastern and western plants and their associates follow any such rigid line as the 100th meridian. In reality a boundary between the two bulges far to the east in some places and far to the west in others, while detached islands of either would have to be drawn in far beyond that meridian. Men drew the straight lines on the map for their convenience. For the same reason, writers of guidebooks to plants, birds, mammals, insects, reptiles and so on have used the 100th meridian as the dividing line between east and west. That there is overlapping matters very little, for there is a good balance between the number of species listed on either side of the line. The same meridian satisfies the imagination, too, for Abilene, Dodge City and Broken Bow, all identified with the Wild West, lie very close to it.

Many species of life overlap this meridian, but it must also be remembered that some species of plants and animals span the continent. One of the dogbanes is found from Maine to British Columbia. Dandelions, which arrived in America as stowaways with the Europeans, have spread from coast to coast as have introduced house sparrows and starlings. Cattle egrets seem bent on doing this also.

Killdeers, mourning doves and raccoons are among native species found from the Atlantic to the Pacific. We have photographed eastern kingbirds in western Montana incubating eggs in nests made largely of bison fur. Once we rescued for a museum a male western tanager illegally shot with a beebee gun within sight of the space-age gantrys of Cape Canaveral. That wildlife refuses to be confined within set boundaries and may be discovered where it has never been seen before provides some of the most exciting moments of field work.

We crossed the Nueces River and shortly afterward Allan said we were west of the 100th meridian. I was not satisfied. We were not yet in the West I imagined.

Beyond Del Rio the country was drier. The road began to undulate. Signs beside it warned of dangerous air currents.

Great ribs of pale rock were thrust through bare hills rising higher and higher ahead of us. An occasional windmill marked a lonely ranch but more often stood over a water tank in the midst of a stark and empty land. Dry washes torn as if by giant fingers from rearing slopes incongruously spoke of raging floods on parched and desiccated hills. Wind whistled and sang in the telephone wires. We heard the bleating of sheep and goats.

We came to Devil's River. It was dry except for a few red-brown pools half hidden by huge boulders tumbled every which way in the river bed. Higher and higher grew the circling hills, and they pressed closer to us.

Suddenly we poised on the verge of a great canyon. Below us yawned a frightening abyss, and our road plunged into its depths. Far below shone a pale silver thread bordered with narrow bands of green. It was the Pecos River.

Allan threw the car into low, proceeded cautiously over the brink, and we dipped sharply down the dizzy yellow and gray wall that fell vertically below the road. I held my breath and my right foot pushed hard against the floor. It seemed forever until we rumbled onto the long narrow bridge swung about fifty feet above the river.

At the western end Allan pulled into a turnout and slowly my breathing became normal. Downstream we saw the end of the Pecos Canyon, cut off as if some giant knife had sliced it away. Here the Rio Grande, which also flowed between mighty walls, swallowed the Pecos. At right angles to the Pecos, its south rampart blocked our view. All we could see of Mexico was a dark frowning perpendicular cliff built of layer upon layer of dull rock.

The Pecos Canyon was starkly impressive and vaguely threatening. Also it presented a strange and puzzling familiarity. In sudden recognition of the place we began to laugh. It was the land of Indians, cowboys and charging cavalry come to life. It was the land of Pecos Bill reared by coyotes who taught him all they knew. It was Pecos Bill who in turn taught Texans to be cowboys and to round up longhorns and brand them with irons heated in mesquite fires. This was the land where Commanches and Apaches were brave and noble one day and bloodthirsty savages the next, changing characters to fit the tale of a storyteller. We could almost hear the bugles signaling the charge of a detachment of cavalry. We could see scouts peering from the high mesa and renegades lurking behind boulders to ambush an unwary traveler carrying a treasure of gold or silver. We could smell the dust stirred by thundering herds of longhorns. This was truly the wild West, a land of extremes and romance. Its extremes extend to man's efforts, for it is in Pecos County that the world's deepest oil well, a dry one at that, was driven 25,340 feet into the earth.

Between the soaring canyon walls we were literally enclosed in history; a haunted place where spirits of long-gone people linger. We followed a rough trail toward the mouth of the Pecos. It had first been traced by the feet of prehistoric cave dwellers. Above us were cavelike slits eroded from the rock walls where West Texas cave dwellers lived and died long ago. There is no record of their departure, but they left paintings on the walls and some of their artifacts behind.

When Fray Augustin Rodriguez struggled through the inhospitable canyon-riven arid Pecos country in 1518, Commanches and Apaches were already there. These Indians continued to use the canyon long after Texas was settled and became in 1845, a state. It remained a fabled place well into the twentieth century.

There was plenty of scope in the early days for the growth of tall tales about it, for the Pecos Canyon was avoided. It was a dangerous and almost impassable barrier to westward travel across southern Texas. In 1849 Colonel Jack Hays of the Texas Rangers was ordered to find a southern route across the Pecos. Commanding a force of seventy civilians and rangers, he managed to lead them into the canyon but then was unable to find a way out of it. Food gave out and the mules were eaten one by one. Before anybody starved to death they were found by a band of Mescalero Indians who guided them out of the Pecos trap. Defeated by formidable cliffs, Hays was so disgusted he resigned from the Rangers after frankly announcing his expedition was a failure.

For many decades after Hays's failure, the Pecos remained a barrier across south Texas. Finally a crossing was located, but getting down to the ford and up the other side was time-consuming and dangerous. In 1892 the Southern Pacific achieved the difficult feat of throwing a bridge across the gorge, an event of such importance that a highway pullout is presently maintained so travelers may stop, read the historical marker telling about one of the highest railroad bridges in the world, and then gaze at the structure far in the distance where it looks as fragile as a spider web.

In the meantime restless Americans moving east and west demanded that something be done about the Pecos Canyon, and in 1923 the ford became obsolete when an iron bridge above any recorded flood level spanned the river. This was the bridge Allan and I crossed when I first found my West. Here and there pale sage-green ceniza, often incorrectly called purple sage, clung to a crevice and was covered with delicate purple flowers. Close to the water stood a half dozen tall cottonwood trees and in their shade two male blue grosbeaks bathed in the shallows, throwing sparkling drops about as though enjoying their bath even on so chilly a day. Suddenly Allan grasped my arm.

"Look! Under that huajillo," he spoke softly. "A covey of scaled quail."

Seven round soft-gray birds with white tufts on their heads stared at us with round black eyes. All faced us, their breast feathers edged with dark giving them a genuinely scaled look. These were true western birds, usually associated with cactus, yucca and other thorny plants. They, like the plants, are able to survive long periods of drought. The scaled quail crouched low under one of the many species of acacia that are at home on the desert. This one was covered with newly opened white balls of fragrant flowers. It was fitting, we thought, that so sweet a sight as the quail presented was enhanced by huajillo, from which the famous Uvalde honey of Texas is made.

Back in the car I found the climb out of the canyon quite as breathtaking as the plunge into it. I wished I could help the wheels up the steep incline that hugged the palisade rising like a curtain on the left while it fell away so abruptly on the right that all I could see was the river growing thinner and more threadlike as we climbed.

Since our first sight of the Pecos Canyon, great changes have occurred. Late in June, 1954, a tremendous storm caused by a tropical disturbance spilled thirty-four inches of rain onto the lower Pecos River. This built up an incredible wall of water eighty-six feet high. Roaring down the canyon, it swept away a border patrol cabin and corral and the cottonwoods by the pool where we watched the grosbeaks bathe and ripped the bridge from its abutments and tore out the lower part of the road on both sides of the canyon. Traffic along U.S. 90 detoured north of the canyon until late April, 1957 when a new bridge stretching from one rim of the canyon to the other was opened.

Remembering the old days when crossing the Pecos was an adventure, we always stop at the east end of the new bridge and look for vultures roosting in one of the caves. At the same time we search the river for a great blue heron that looks like a small stake as it stands in shallow water almost three hundred feet below us. If the scaled quail have returned to the canyon they are too far below for us to see them. We listen to the silvery cadence of canyon wrens echoing from side to side across the narrow gorge and the brooding wail of mourning doves rising softly.

Soon the Pecos Canyon will change again. According to schedule, the Armistad Dam across the Rio Grande about twelve miles above Del Rio will be completed in 1969. Then waters behind it will rise and push into the Diablo and the Pecos, affecting the rivers for seventeen miles and more. The caves where prehistoric cave dwellers lived and painted pictures will be drowned, and the herons will be forced upstream to shallows where they can fish.

Beyond the Pecos the hills are covered with creosote bushes that almost alone of the native plants survived overgrazing by sheep and goats. We came to a fine stand of ocotillo, and all the thorny branches were thickly furred with yellowish leaves. Following a good rain a few weeks ago they had covered themselves with small green leaves. Now they were preparing to drop them again as trees of the north do in winter. In a brief time they had stored sufficient food in their tissues to last them through a prolonged drought while they remained dormant, asleep.

Turkey vultures glided by. We watched two Swainson's hawks soar leisurely past, each appearing to nibble its toes. Allan said they were probably eating insects they held in their talons.

In one place the road was cut through rock stacked up in exact layers like those of a slate quarry. But these rocks were colored like Talisman roses; delicate yellow and bright rosy pink. Soon the railway swung close to the road and we noticed that colorful slabs of the handsome yellow and rose sandstone were used to bolster the railway bed. We would have overlooked this, but Allan saw a male painted bunting on a telephone wire and we pulled over. Its head was thrown back and song burst enthusiastically from its quivering throat. Between songs it gave a sharp *chick* we had not heard our wintering buntings give.

Painted buntings spend the winter with us in Florida. We coax them to stay instead of going on southward perhaps as

far as Mexico or Panama by putting one of their favorite
grains, white proso millet, in cages with sides made of 1 inch
by 2 inch crab-trap wire. The buntings, as well as chipping
sparrows, go in and out of the cages as if the wire did not
exist. There the small birds eat their millet undisturbed by
the big birds. Blackbirds, jays and cardinals, try in vain to
force their way into the cages after the grain that they, too,
prefer to the cheaper chick feed that we offer them in abundance.

The sapphire head of the male is brightened by a thin ring
of red around the eye. The wings are dusky pleated silk of
changeable black, brown and green. His throat and breast
are bright red. The back has a luminous quality that in shadow may appear dark emerald and becomes chartreuse when
well lighted. Its full splendor is seen only when the sun
strikes it and turns it to fiery gold. While that fiery gold is a
rare color in birds and so far as I know is not shared by any
other North American species, I have seen the identical hue
soon after the sun rises in the brilliant sky of a clear and
windy dawn. Then when the first strong rays strike the tossing fronds of a sabal palm outside my bedroom window, liquid gold darts and flashes with the same rare splendor that so
startles us when we see the back of a painted bunting illu-
minated by slanting rays flame into volatile gold.

To say the breast of the male bunting is ruby or rose-cerise
or carnelian fails to indicate its changeable radiance, which
in some conditions is like a coal shining in the dark. Yet
when a squirrel leaps onto the roof of the cage or a blue jay
gives an angry scream so the bunting is frightened away from
its food and leaves the cage to perch in a nearby eucalyptus,
we are always astonished that the bunting, brilliant as a fire
opal, becomes almost invisible among the leaves. Its pattern
then is effective camouflage.

To attempt a word description of a painted bunting is useless. Colors mean different hues to different people. Yet the

names of colors are beautiful and stir the imagination. Once I determined to be accurate and precise in my use of them. Robert Ridgeway's *Color Standards and Nomenclature* has long been an authority on color for scientists, but it is out of print and available only in the reference section of libraries. Therefore it cannot serve as a guide in the field.

My search continued for some time, and finally I anticipated success when I read an advertisement that promised duplication of colors anywhere in the world from New York to Hong Kong and from Rio de Janeiro to Paris, Delhi and Johannesburg. In hot pursuit of this wonderful system I soared high in the Empire State Building, and the receptionist smilingly confirmed the advertisement. She added that more than twelve hundred colors could be precisely matched on any surface, whether velvet, satin, pebbled, ridged or glazed. But even as my heart leaped with satisfaction it fell, for the young woman went to a shelf and began lifting down case after case, which she opened on a table of truly impressive dimensions. This color system was far too massive for my purposes. Disappointed, I noted the colors were not named: instead each had a number. With no emotion I heard the receptionist say their color service cost more than a thousand dollars. She had nothing I wanted at any price. I was looking for flying-duck green, peacock blue, pansy violet and jonquil yellow; color names that soared or sang, were velvety soft or sweetly scented, colors of the sea and the woodland, the harsh dry desert and the plants and animals that lived in each.

Finally, for about fifty cents I obtained a set of cards with the names of shades used by philatelists in identifying stamp colors. While limited in range, this set is useful in naming colors of flowers and other objects that can be held in the hand. It is less helpful with birds. Moreover it lacks many of the enchanting names for an almost endless range of hues, of brilliance and saturation and is woefully lacking in such luminous tones as pearl, pungent hues like marigold yellow, and willow green that carries in its name the tender freshness and exuberance of burgeoning spring.

Desert sparrows, black-throated and trim, collected grass seeds blown under a large opuntia and sang their musical varied trills. Cassin's sparrows must have been migrating, for a large flock was gathered there. It was difficult to see those inconspicuous sparrows perched on top of small bushes, many of them huajillo in full bloom and casting a delicate fragrance on the spring air. Seized with a wish to sing, a Cassin's leaped straight up from its perch, spread its wings widely and began to sing before it reached the summit of its flight. It would hold the highest note as it hovered perhaps ten feet above its perch, and slowly conclude the melody as it fluttered back. To me they sang "I *Sing* to thee!"—*Sing* being the highest note and held longer than the others. No sooner did one Cassin's sparrow resume its perch than another, until then unnoticed, sprang up into the air to repeat, "I *Sing* to thee!" They were like so many jumping beans, with only one springing up at a time.

Mockingbirds, probably the most regularly seen species all across Texas, perched in a mequite to watch us and occasionally sang a few bemused notes. Allan investigated and found they had made a bulky nest in a mesquite and already one spotted greenish-blue egg lay in it.

We watched a pair of scissor-tailed flycatchers build their nest, also in a mesquite but a dead one. The pale nest was conspicuous in a fork of the dark branches. There was no secrecy about their building activities, for they expended great energy with their loud stuttering calls and looped about scissoring their long tails and flashing the soft bright salmon patches under their wings. The half-built nest was scarcely more than three feet above the ground, and Allan could scarcely pull himself away from it for it was in a perfect situation for photography.

Flocks of lark buntings streamed by, and occasionally one

of the males, though still rusty black and far from wearing spring jet-satin garb, bounded higher than the others and sang a few aerial tinkling notes, a faint preview of the gusto with which he would pipe his clear trills above his nest in June over some open prairie, perhaps in Montana.

Having stopped because chance directed our eyes to a painted bunting and then to the colorful stones by the railway, we decided the great diversity of vegetation must surely have attracted the throng of birds to it. No overgrazing was evident. By accident we had stopped beside a block of habitat that remained little changed from what it had been before cattle, sheep and goats replaced the herd of bison that once wintered in Texas. We learned a sound lesson that day. Watch for places where many species of plants grow in a complex association and when you find one, look for birds. In such bird-rich places we saw for the first time many species new to us.

Twenty miles from the canyon we came to Langtry. As distances go in west Texas, Langtry might as well have been on the brink of the canyon. This hamlet has a colorful history and most of it is related to notorious Judge Roy Bean. Late in the nineteenth century he became the self-proclaimed law west of Pecos. His combination saloon and courtroom is now a state park, and some of the desert plants growing beside it have been labeled to help interested strangers become acquainted with the semidesert vegetation of the locality.

I once asked the ranger about the hanging tree, an essential part of legendary western justice. Sheepishly he pointed to a dead mesquite. It was a small tree, and its branches were delicate. Even as a living tree, any outlaw hanged from the biggest, most sinewy branch of that small tree would have been gently lowered to the ground by the flexible limb before the rope could snap his neck. According to tales often recounted about Langtry, a horse thief named Carlos Morales was among those hanged to that particular tree, but its slender branches sorely tax my credulity. Probably drunken prisoners, as legend insists, were chained to it while they sobered up.

In its earliest days Langtry was called Vinegaroon because of the abundance of those big but almost harmless whip scorpions that give off a vinegary smell when alarmed. In the boom days of railroad building, the name was changed to honor a construction official named Langtry. Later Judge Roy Bean fell in love with a picture of The Jersey Lily, Lily Langtry, and named his saloon for her and plastered its wall with her pictures. Apparently he wrote her fan letters that went unanswered until he stated that he had named the town in her honor, a legend that persists today. He never did meet Miss Langtry, but it is said that after his death the English actress, on her way west, left her private car and had the train held up while she paid a brief visit to the hamlet. What she thought of it is not recorded.

Judge Bean scandalized the orthodox by his peculiar brand of justice based solely on his one law book *The Revised Statutes of Texas* and enforced with his sixshooter. There was no jail, so culprits hailed into his court were either hanged or fined. When he fined the guilty a round of drinks for all present in the court, his saloon did a booming business. The building of the Southern Pacific Railroad and the prolonged work on its Pecos High Bridge, not completed until 1892, brought a period of great prosperity not only to Judge Bean's Jersey Lily Saloon but to his court. Some of the work crews were quite abstemious Chinese, but most were dedicated Irish drinkers, and though very clannish, were given to intramural battles that were often quite spectacular.

One tale often repeated concerns a Chinese who was murdered. All evidence pointed to a particular Irishman as the murderer. Judge Bean was in a quandary. The Chinese were not good clients of his saloon and the Irish were. He did not want to lose his standing with the latter. The problem was indeed a knotty one. Finally he announced his verdict. He had studied his law book with care. There was not a single mention anywhere of Chinese, let alone any prohibition about killing one. Therefore no crime had been committed and the Irishman went free. Another time Judge Bean was presented with a newly made corpse. In an inner pocket he found a gun and forty dollars. He fined the corpse forty dollars for carrying a concealed weapon.

We soon lost interest in The Jersey Lily, for noise, profaning the name of music, blared from a nearby tourist attraction and drove us toward the Rio Grande. The river was low, and wide sand beaches bordered each shore as they had in 1896 when Judge Bean staged there a world's championship heavyweight boxing match between Australia's Bob Fitzsimmons and Ireland's Peter Maher. Ireland's pride was knocked out in exactly one minute and thirty-five seconds, and naturally this sorrowful debacle was solaced in the judge's saloon.

Boxing was then illegal in Texas, and the crafty judge, the administrant of law west of the Pecos, counted on the river remaining low enough to enable the boxers and their enthusiastic supporters to wade across to the Mexican shore where they could thumb their noses derisively in complete security, should his bailiwick be invaded by more law-abiding officers.

The Rio Grande at Langtry runs between impressive walls, and the vertical cliffs are quite sensational. Circling in dizzy erratic flight above the cliffs was a swirling cloud of white-throated swifts, birds I had never seen before. Their loud high voices filled the air with excited twittering. Suddenly I saw two of the black-and-white swifts come together and, like a pinwheel, whirl and spin until I held my breath, fearing they would strike the cliff. They separated but a few yards above the rim, and the wild circling went on. Their velocity was so great they could surely outstrip the racing flight of chimney swifts. Again we saw a pinwheel as two swifts deliberately collided and joined, and their black-and-white pattern was blurred by the whirling of their bodies. This aerial spin was part of their courtship.

The swifts rose to exalted heights and swooped downward with an audible swish of air against their narrow bowed wings. As the wild giddy flight continued, vertigo seized me, and I moved away from the edge of the precipice. So closely do these swifts associate with rocks—nesting in crevices of high mountain cliffs and rock stack, resting in them when on migration as these swifts were and hunting insects about them—that once they were called white-throated rock swifts.

In the meantime Allan was swinging his binoculars along the Mexican wall of the canyon. Suddenly he stiffened and became intent.

"A golden eagle nest," he said, "in that slitlike cave about fifty feet below the top of the canyon wall."

Allan had located a page straight out of history, an ancient landmark noted by early explorers and trappers but sadly enough a nest that had not been used for at least three quarters of a century. As Indian artifacts in dry caves remain undamaged so this eagle nest will probably stand for a century or more to come, for what would dislodge those firmly intertwined sticks? Surely no man would make his way down to it on a rope, and like a vandal destroy a famous landmark. I had read of that nest, but until Allan located it, it had never occurred to me that it still lay in its sheltering cave where searching eyes could see it.

Robert Hill, who led the first expedition through the canyons of the Rio Grande in 1899, terminated the strenuous journey at Langtry. By that time the expedition members were so weary they no longer appreciated their noble surroundings and only looked upon them as a prison. Hard rowing and frequent hauling of heavy boats over dangerous rapids, constant wetting, baking by the merciless sun and a scant diet made worse by Serafino's (the cook) unhygienic cooking had everybody highly nervous and quarrelsome. Desperately weary, they finally sighted that large eagle's nest, the longed-for landmark that signaled the end of their remarkable passage down the uncharted Rio Grande. Hill wrote:

Opposite the village of Langtry, near the top of a vertical cliff some three hundred feet high, is a small bluff cavern. Poised on the edge of this inaccessible cavern is a huge pile of sticks skillfully entwined into what is perhaps the largest bird's nest in America. Since the trans-Pecos country was first known this nest has been a landmark, and until lately was inhabited by a pair of eagles which here annually brought forth their young. A few years since, however, a company of colored soldiers were stationed near this place, and with the instinct which prompts men to shoot at every living thing, they killed the birds, which even the hardened frontiersmen had long protected.

". . . A messenger proceeded a mile and a half to the village of Langtry and secured a packhorse, which conveyed our belongings to the railway station. It was gratifying to see once more even the crudest habitation of man. We were received by a famous old frontiersman, whose hospitable house is decorated with a peculiar sign reading:

LAW WEST OF THE PECOS
ROY BEAN
JUSTICE OF THE PEACE AND NOTARY PUBLIC
SAN ANTONIO LAGER BEER

Today *The Jersey Lily, Ice* and *Billiard Hall* also appear outside this landmark of the West. Judge Roy Bean ran a busy varied establishment. It looks now much as it did when Robert Hill saw, with a sense of profound relief, the ancient eagle nest that marked the end of his ordeal and the first

habitation, that of the man who is today a part of the legendary West.

Judge Roy Bean's combination saloon and courtroom will
continue the legend of its owner while the golden eagle nest,
unused even in 1899, will remain on its protected shelf for
another century or more before the sticks that form it and are
protected from weather disintegrate into dust. It may still be
there after the last golden eagle vanishes from the Trans-
Pecos. They have been relentlessly persecuted by ranchers
and hunted down by planes. Though they were placed on the
list of nationally protected birds in October, 1963, there has
been constant agitation to have them removed.

Golden eagles range widely across the world, and history
indicates that of all birds this species is the most admired. Its
image appears on state seals, on banners, on coins and in
paintings and sculpture from the most ancient times.

In North America they have decreased sharply in recent
years until fewer than three thousand breeding pairs are believed to inhabit this entire continent. Each pair needs a territory ranging from twenty-five to a hundred square miles.
Their food is small mammals. In winter they must move
south, for many small mammals in the north hibernate then.
During the cold months they scour the semiarid country of
the Southwest in search of jackrabbits, ground squirrels and
other rodents. This same open arid country is grazed by
sheep and goats by the tens of thousands and they drop their
young on bleak, exposed hills where eagles, coyotes and
other predatory creatures seek to alleviate their hunger.

In the past twenty-five years since hunting with planes has
become popular, it is believed that at least twenty thousand
golden eagles have been killed in the semidesert country of
our Southwest. Dr. Walter R. Spofford made the first scientific investigation of the golden eagle-domestic mammal relationship in the trans-Pecos of Texas in 1963. He found that
when adult eagles are shot, immature eagles fill the vac-

cuum, and they too are killed. Dr. Spofford flew with some of the eagle-killing pilots and saw them follow eagles into the wildest, most remote canyons. Pilots usually repeated each flight the following day in order to kill any eagle that escaped the first day's flight. One pilot claimed to have killed forty eagles in a day. Another killed over nine hundred during the 1960–1961 winter.

Some ranchers claim the eagles actually threaten their livelihood. They claim the eagles take anywhere from scores to hundreds of lambs and kids annually. They base their figures on the difference between the number they mark in early spring, and the number remaining at harvest time. Since eagles eat an average of ten ounces of meat daily and the maximum number of eagles wintering for four months of the lambing season is not more than a thousand, they could not possibly consume even 1 per cent of the lambs and kids charged against them were their diet exclusively domestic animals with never a rodent included. Yet among golden eagle crops studied, jackrabbits were found to be their preferred food. Often the eagles did not kill the jackrabbits but merely utilized road kills, which are frequent. Runoff from dew and the extremely light rains of that semidesert country provide enough extra moisture so the roadside plants are often green, when away from it the country is parched and brown. So the jackrabbits congregate there to eat the juicy green plants and are often hit by cars at night.

As far as eagles and lambs are considered the rough highlands of Scotland bear a certain resemblance to the arid Southwest; for they have been overgrazed, and cover is slight. Yet researchers working over a five-year period could find only seven lambs killed by eagles during that entire period though at least five thousand ewes (one thousand annually) over that period were under study. Eagles do kill lambs, most often those that are lost from their mothers and would die anyway, but the number they kill is small indeed.

Those employed to kill eagles have been far more blind to reason than the ranchers. Dr. Spofford found the ranchers quite receptive to facts about eagles and their stock in spite of long-lasting and deep-seated dislike of them. On more than one occasion Dr. Spofford on an early morning inspection tour was accompanied by a rancher when an eagle was frightened from a meal of lamb. Ranchers, knowing that eagles do not begin hunting until dawn, accepted the irrefutable evidence that the eagle, feeding on a stone-cold carcass, could not have killed it and was actually aiding the rancher by disposing of carrion.

Sheep and goats in the Langtry region live a fairly wild though congested existence on most of the ranches, which are severely overgrazed and also offer slight shelter. There was little complaint about eagle predation until the federal government began clearing the juniper (locally called cedar) from the sheep and goat range. This deprived the domestic animals of shelter while supposedly improving the range, for it was claimed the tree poisoned the soil.

Wherever there is congested life of any kind, many deaths occur, and the young particularly die natural deaths. I still remember my first visit to one of the great bird colonies on an island off the coast of Maine. I was aghast at the number of spoiled eggs and even greater number of dead young gulls. Since then I have come to accept such losses as a natural part of any bird colony. There is a similar loss among domestic mammals, and this is greatest among those that run untended on open range; yet in the past practically all lamb and kid losses have been charged against the predators, particularly eagles and coyotes.

Annually our government spends millions for predator control. To me this is quite as wrong as the former paying out of tax dollars to catch and return human beings to slavery, a use of tax money that so incensed Thoreau that he refused to pay his taxes to support such a grave injustice and was willing to go to jail rather than betray his convictions. Tragically, predator control is a direct result of man's reckless injury to the land by putting on it more cattle, sheep, goats and so on than it can support.

The belief that eagles carry off human babies and attack men is still widespread. Yet the average weight of a golden eagle is a mere twelve pounds. It would be a rare mother who would leave an infant of that size untended in the open. A very hungry golden eagle will attack an animal that outweighs it by many pounds, but it is physically impossible for it to carry away a baby that equals or exceeds its own weight.

Frequently yarns appear about attacks on men by eagles. When these are investigated it is usually found that when an eagle fighs a man, it is because the eagle is injured and fighting for its life within a closed area from which it cannot escape.

Not long ago newspapers published an account of a golden eagle that attacked the Volkswagen in which two rabbit hunters were riding. Dr. Walter Spofford traced this story to its source. Actually the eagle had been feeding on a skunk, a highway kill, when the small car approached at high speed. The eagle started to cross the road and make its escape but it was too late. The Volkswagen hit it. The great bird came through the windshield and was hurt but not killed by the impact. The rabbit hunters, unable to dislodge the injured eagle, shot it.

Eagles are also accused of killing deer and antelope. Undoubtedly they do upon occasion. They probably take fawns and weak kids and even sick adults. But before passing judgment, it must be remembered that eagles and pronghorns existed and flourished together when the latter roamed the plains in numbers comparable to those of the bison. Only biological illiterates today do not appreciate the necessity of maintaining predatory species if game animals are to retain their health and vigor. When predators are removed, many species overmultiply until they deplete their habitat and starvation follows close on the heels of disease.

Golden eagles reproduce very slowly, each breeding pair averaging one young when nesting is successful. They are among our most magnificent birds yet one we may lose through the arrogance of those who are ready to destroy any life that has an adverse effect, even a very limited one, on their personal endeavors. Our land has been and still is terribly abused in many ways, and few areas show this more vividly than the once fertile grasslands in west Texas. Disastrous overgrazing has reduced much of it to a wretched scrubby thorny wasteland. It is easy to blame the eagles and coyotes for declining productivity in the region, but sooner or later men will be forced to face up to their limited vision and personal responsibilities to the land they occupy, or we will not survive as a race.

The eagles that nested for many a decade in the cave on the Rio Grande canyon wall at Langtry helped weed out unwary jackrabbits and other rodents. Occasionally they fed on weak or dying larger mammals. They took only what they needed for themselves and their young. In doing so they weeded out the unfit, the stupid and the diseased. They played a vital part in maintaining the vigor of mammals and birds in the area. The empty nest remains a mute testimony of a balanced ecology that has ceased to exist but one that man should ponder when forming plans for his own future. In understanding the place of the eagle in nature, man, the greatest predator of all, may come to understand some of the ecological principles that govern the survival of all species, including our own.

8

We Meet a Rock Hound

IT WAS COLD, nipping cold, that wakened us while Marathon was still indistinct in the fading night. Allan slammed down the window, touched a match to the fire laid last night by our host and then leaped back under the blankets with his teeth chattering. Crackling flames dancing over the wood soon drove frost from the cottage, and as the grayness paled we could rest no longer. We dressed hurriedly and had a quick breakfast at a counter shared with silent, tall-hatted, booted cowboys bent over coffee and eggs.

Rose and lemon now flamed in the east, and as the sun's rim flared on the horizon of a cloudless sky, we turned southward from Route 90 toward the basin of the Chisos Mountains eighty miles away in the Big Bend National Park. More than a thousand square miles of desert, canyon and mountain are enclosed within the boundaries of our only national park, sixth in size, that boasts an entire mountain range within its borders.

To us, accustomed to sea-level air, the thin, crisp dryness we breathed was as heady as the product of Champagne Province's finest year. Above us the sky vaulted up forever, and on the horizon, incredibly distant, serrated tops of mountains were etched sharply against it. Introduced though we had been to the desert yesterday as we drove west from the Pecos River, now we faced a world that was new and strange to us. Yesterday the hills had been pale as if fainting for want of water. Now the early sun flung gold across a wide valley and over folded hills and mountains piled range on range. This was a raw landscape and a harsh one. Bare rock ribs thrust through its tawny-colored skin. Earthy colors in great sweeps of red and ochre, of burnt umber and sienna, splashed the desert. Far from being barren it was well covered with desert plants, but each in its urgent need for water kept a careful distance from others. Most were armed with thorns, spines, barbs and other hooked or pointed appendages that demand and receive respect. Most of the odd prickly adaptations of plants to desert conditions are essentially for water conservation, not defense. Occasionally we saw a bright cerise cactus blossom. Many of the yuccas held tall flower stalks but the buds of those were still tightly furled and tinged with rose. Sometimes we saw a wandlike ocotillo tipped with a spike of fireman-red flowers. More than a thousand species of plants have been identified in the Big Bend and those growing along the approach to it were varied enough to have detained us all day if other sights had not drawn us on.

The intoxicating air, the strange dusty pungent desert smell, the queer shapes of rocks, the sounds of many new birds, the blazing lights and shifting colors and most of all the jagged bulk of mountains ahead of us suddenly rushed together into a piercing needle of magic, of happiness that struck like an arrow. The shock was so sudden that the joy was marked precisely and will forever be associated with the white track leading into a land new to us. This land looked as though man had never touched any of it excepting only our winding road first traced by unknown men called Pre-Basket-makers by archeologists. It was deepened by the feet of Comanches and Apaches and widened by conquistadores. Later it was smoothed for the mules and horses of settlers and finally made suitable for the wheels of modern man.

We were still dazed by the harsh but magnificent land rising before us when we came to a small screwbean literally alive with yellow-headed blackbirds, a species common in the West but which I had never seen before. All were males, and all sang boisterously but less musically than groups of redwings do in early spring in the Northeast. Like redwings, each sang his individual song without regard for those of his companions, so the result was more of a hullabaloo than a chorus. These birds are larger than redwings and, garbed in bright yellow helmets above silky jet bodies, they are strikingly handsome. As I walked closer to them the volume of song diminished, and suddenly in a compact flock they rose, displaying big white wing patches, and swirled away into the distance. A hundred feet beyond, a red-tailed hawk stood on a fencepost fluffing and shaking its feathers. It was either unaware of us or quite unconcerned, for it paid no attention when we stopped to shoot its picture from the car window.

A flock of mourning doves feeding beside the road hurried up on whistling wings and joined some white-winged doves in a mesquite. Now lark buntings in parties from a dozen to a hundred or more began to move. Some streamed toward the north, parallel to the car. Some crossed the road before us. Others, feeding intently, played a sort of hopscotch as those behind darted over the backs of the leaders and settled in front of the flock, so the troupe was in constant motion and appeared to roll along the ground.

Allan stopped when he saw a roadrunner. It was equally curious about us and hopped nimbly on top of a large rock, then swung about and gazed at us. It jerked and switched its tail erratically, staring as if surprised and not particularly pleased with what it saw. It bristled all over and raised a shaggy crest on its head. Behind its eyes the feathers parted to reveal a long streak of bare skin that first was white, then blue and finally turned fiery red. Having looked its fill, the roadrunner opened its wings, skimmed lightly to the ground and bounced across the road in front of the car, half running, half flying. It paused for a final disdainful look at us, flattened its feathers until it was thin and sleek, stiffened its tail, thrust forward its head and, streamlined as a racehorse on the final stretch, dashed away on some project of its own with its long legs working rhythmically.

Overhead white-necked ravens flipped by. Turkey vultures found rising air currents and began to circle up and up on rigid wings. Every mile or so we passed a mockingbird on a conspicuous perch. Swainson's hawks sailed low against the hills. Horned larks flushed from the roadside. Some of them towered until they became mere specks in the sky and there began their fine jingling trill that continued as they dropped lightly back toward the ground. Rosy house finches, oblivious of the fine sharp spines that would bring misery if touched by human feet, perched on prickly pears and sang joyously.

Though we advanced at a snail's pace, the hills began to close in and bigger and bigger grew the circling mountains. Directly before us the Santiago Range swept higher, blocking our southward passage, and as we came closer, it changed from blue to violet, then to rose and finally became yellow and red and the prevailing buff that we called desert color for want of a more specific name. We wondered if this primitive land resembled the world of prehistory or foreshadowed the look of the earth when it has grown old and is dying. At an altitude of 2,962 feet we reached Persimmon Gap, the northernmost boundary of the Big Bend National Park. Toward the south the Comanche Trail snaked downward to a broad flat that stretched on and on. The sun had put to rout the morning frost and now it poured blazing light over the flat until the heated air pulsed and quivered. Far beyond loomed the Chisos, the ghost or spirit mountains. Behind the pulsing air they wavered insubstantially against the horizon, a ghostly red and yellow cloud smudged with blue that appeared to float above the burning desert.

Allan, hearing the scold note of an unknown bird, threw off his coat, tossed it into the car and vanished in the direction of the sound. I, too, was glad to take off my coat, unbutton my sweater and open all the car windows. The pull-out where we stopped was bordered by large stones, some of them flat-topped. One of these, I thought, looked like a fine seat, and I put out my hand to see if it was uncomfortably hot only to have that thought wiped away. The rock was brightly colored red, brown and yellow. Looking more closely I could distinguish faint but definite rings. One blackish side was furrowed and had a scaly appearance. Surely it was a chunk of petrified wood with fossil bark still clinging to it, a part of a tree that grew long ago in a tropical forest that once thrived in this now desert land.

Geologists have discovered many strange events that happened in west Texas long before man appeared on the earth. More than a hundred million years ago a great sea rolled over this area. For a million years or so currents of this ocean sifted sand and the limy skeletons of marine life over its bed and piled some of this deposit into subterranean mountains. At last the ocean receded, and the mountains lay exposed to the blistering sun. In the ages that followed, rain and wind filed and scraped the lofty heights until only vestiges of the former peaks remained. Even as interstellar space is too great for most of us to comprehend so is the time that passed before those mountains became dust.

Then once more the ocean advanced and swallowed the ancient limestone. New deposits of marine skeletons and sediment buried it. Again mountains were fashioned beneath the sea. Then the bottom began to heave and tilt upward as pressures increased deep in the innermost recesses of the earth. Again the ocean drained away, and swamps overgrown with lush vegetation occupied its former bed. In this period dinosaurs became kings of the earth, and in their supremacy they grew bigger and more and more varied.

But the earth is never finished. Kings and nations rose only to be deposed and replaced by others. Ponderously and imperceptibly the land continued to change. Then ashes from great volcanoes were blown from far away and fell on the rank forest, smothering it. The existence of dinosaurs became difficult. As hazards multiplied, they began to die, and finally the domination of the great reptiles faded and the entire order of dinosaurs vanished forever from the earth.

Violent convulsions heaved and wracked the Big Bend country. Limestone covered for long, long ages was pushed once more to the surface and formed the beginnings of the mountains now bordering the Big Bend. A time of calm settled over the new mountains; but it was an ominous calm, for the earth was only waiting.

Millions upon millions of years passed while mountains were raised and lowered and some turned upside down. Our imagination falters before the span of time required for all the changes and the building of the present peaks of the Big Bend, and the eras that have drifted past since the topmost layer was added to the highest mountains and the last convulsive shudder set them on edge. So slowly do natural processes of reducing dizzy heights to dust go forward that in all the Age of Man few important changes can be detected. Though volcanos erupt and earthquakes shake the earth, it is rare that these cataclysms have a world-wide chain reaction. Probably this has been true since land and water first separated into definite blocks.

But if for many an age a kind of lethargy seems, deceptively, to have gripped the world of the Big Bend and transfixed it into immobility, nevertheless the changes go on and on, little regarded by man. Drop by drop and grain by grain, the earth is forever in a state of flux. On the desert and the rocky slopes of the mountains before me, wind and driven sand never cease to abrade all exposed surfaces. Alternating cold and heat chisel them, etching and sculpturing their forms. Rain, falling on the peaks, rushes toward the lowlands tearing and scouring the slopes, hurling down loose rocks and triggering avalanches. Now as I sat on my chunk of stone that had once been part of a living tree struggling to make and hold a place in the sun, I looked through the liquid shimmer of air toward the Chisos and saw on the flat before me dust devils pick up bits of mountain powder, whirl them into the air and deposit them somewhere else, sanding smoother a cliff here, and gouging deeper a crevice there as they gyrated this way and that, growing, diminishing, stretching toward the sky and then suddenly thickening into squat monsters that brooded restlessly before abruptly spinning off in a new direction.

Half dazed by the pitiless heat and blinded by the intense light, I stared over the haunted landscape toward the gaunt outlines of the Chisos, and it was not difficult to imagine rolling gray-green seas or tropical forests or dinosaurs wallowing in marshes. Slowly, as the heat waves lashed like colorless flames above the pale Comanche Trail that twisted and fell away to the flat, I seemed to see a string of heavily laden burros guided by dark Spaniards wearing conical hats and gaily striped serapes while a couple of brown-garbed, rope-girdled padres plodded behind them in a cloud of tawny dust. Surely behind that large rock crouched a party of fierce Apaches tensed and ready to ambush those intruders into their domain.

There was a loud bang and my heart leaped. I shot off my chunk of petrified wood as if the Apaches had struck. A shriveled little man with bristling hair and bright blue eyes in a sunburned face was advancing from the first car I had seen since we left Marathon.

"Hi!" he called with a wide smile. "Are you a rock-knocker? If you are you'd better lock up your collection while you are in the Big Bend. Its against the law to collect in a national park."

I must have looked bewildered as I assured him that my outdoor manners were perfectly in accord with national park regulations, for he looked at me incredulously.

"You don't know about rock-knocking? That's what we call ourselves, we rock hounds who collect rocks and minerals. There's nothing like rock collecting. You should see my collection in Los Angeles. It's a beauty," he boasted.

For a moment he hesitated. Discretion warred with enthusiasm on his mobile face. Enthusiasm won. He shot back to his car and unlocked the trunk. It was filled with rocks until the rear springs sagged from their weight. Just then Allan returned, and his eyes began to shine as he picked up a lovely stone banded with yellow and bright Chinese red.

"What a beauty this is!" he exclaimed.

"That's jasper," the rock hound told us. "It takes a beautiful polish but, see, it is already smooth and shiny when you break off a chunk of it. I've been collecting all around the park boundaries and have lots of good stuff. Most kinds of rocks in the park can be found outside, too. I'm on my way home now. I'm cutting through the park with my trunk locked and I won't stop to look at a single interesting rock anywhere along the way. It might tempt me. But I'll collect again when I get near Terlingua. Look at this."

He thrust a roundish stone into my hands. I thought it quite unappealing. It wasn't half as pretty as the water-smoothed stones that shingle the beaches of Maine islands.

"See anything queer about that?" he asked.

I shook my head and handed it to Allan.

"It is rather light for a stone of this size," Allan thought as he weighed it in his hand.

Our new friend laid it on a large rock, picked up a geology hammer, struck the round stone a sharp blow and it split apart. It was as if he had opened a casket of jewels. Inside was a cavity lined with glittering quartz crystals.

"That's a geode," the rock hound told us. "They are nodules formed in a cavity of a rock or in clay or sand. As water seeps through surrounding rock it is saturated with minerals, and when it reaches the cavity the minerals are deposited as crystals or in a smooth mass so you can have either a lining of crystals or a layer of colorful minerals such as jasper or chalcedony. Geodes as big as four feet in diameter have been found. You can tell them because they are far too light to be solid rock. I know a river up in Iowa—Mud River, it's called—near a little town named Lowell that used to be filled with geodes. But they are gone now. Too many people collected them, and you can hunt all day and maybe not find a single one. It's a good thing rock hounds can't collect in national parks or pretty soon all the rocks in them would be hacked to bits."

As the rock hound told us about geodes, I realized that Thoreau had once found one in Concord, for on May 14, 1858, he wrote in his *Journal:*

> I discovered this morning that a large rock three feet in diameter was partially hollow, and broke into it at length with a stone in order to reach some large black crystals which I could partly see. I found that it had been the retreat of a squirrel, and it had left many nuts there. It had entered a small hole bristling with crystals, and there found a chamber or grotto a foot long at least, surrounded on all sides by crystals.

But the rock hound was interested only in the present, and again he reached into his car and held out a geode that had been sawed carefully in half and polished. The hollow of this one was lined with chalcedony that felt rather waxy and was smooth and shining as New England milk glass. Looking closely we could see wavering lines that followed the irregular contours of the hollow as layer after thin layer had been deposited in the hidden cavity. It is true that under certain circumstances rocks do grow, even though they are lifeless.

"You find lots of amazing stuff when you prowl this country," his face glowed with fervor. "I come as often as I can. There are trees turned to beautiful agate. That happened under water. Queer to think of enough water to submerge a tree so it could turn to stone in this desert, isn't it? Queer to think of great tropical trees ever growing in this country, anyway. But I've found fossil trees five feet in diameter, and from some of them I've chipped off agate and jasper and amethyst." He held out a handful of colorful pieces of these minerals. "I'll split and polish some of these pieces and tumble some of them and they will be as beautiful as precious stones.

"I've found fossil clams almost four feet long and three feet wide. Some day I'll open one of those big babies and find a fossil pearl in it. A pearl as big as a baseball. Maybe bigger."

He fell silent, dreaming of the great discovery he would make one day. If he had ever read Bishop Joseph Hall, who wrote in sixteenth century: "There is many a rich stone laid up in the bowels of the earth, many a fair pearl laid up in the bosom of the sea, that never was seen, nor never will be." It is certain our rock hound had not been influenced by such negative thinking. He completely disdained Holmes's remark: "Our whitest pearl we never find," for he found treasures on all sides, not treasures men fight for, but treasures of beauty and treasures with a magic history. He never doubted that if rarities existed he could find them.

"I've found fossil oysters, too, and bones of dinosaurs and dinoaur gizzard stones—some of the biggest dinosaurs didn't have any teeth, you know, and they swallowed stones as chickens do gravel to help their gizzards grind up their food. I found one gizzard stone that weighed more than three pounds. And once I found a small meteorite—a star fallen to earth."

His words tumbled out impetuously as he strove to share

his adventures and infect us with the enchantment and endless discoveries possible in rock hunting. Again he reached into the trunk of his car and pulled out a blanket, which he unrolled carefully. In the middle was a large box. He unlocked it and then chuckled, "When the fellows in the club see these I'll have to fight them off."

Ignorant as we were about minerals, we were impressed by the rainbow beauty of the chunks of agate, turquoise, jasper, amethyst, opal and even quartz threaded with shining gold. To hold those bright stones and enjoy their colors and gleaming textures aroused our lively enthusiasm, and the small man beamed with satisfaction.

"There are lost gold mines and silver mines and all sorts of valuable minerals and metals in these mountains, but I don't care about such things or about tales of buried treasure. I just like to find rare or beautiful pieces of rocks and minerals," he told us.

The rock hound slowly closed the box, wrapped it lovingly in the blanket and replaced it in the trunk, which he slammed and locked.

"That trunk won't be opened again until I leave the Maverick Gate of the park. I'll be seeing you!" and he climbed behind the wheel, gunned his motor, shot onto the then unpaved road, heeled sharply as he swept around the curves of the twisting road leading from Persimmon Gap to the flat below and grew smaller and smaller in the distance. As if he were a genii returning to his magic jar, an eruption of dust rose around him and hid him from view as he sped along the lion-colored flat.

Now slowly we followed the rock hound down the hot serpentine road. We towed our own great cloud of dust as we advanced across the flat toward our goal, and as our eyes swiveled from side to side we saw lizards, motionless as small figurines watching us furtively from rocks, flicker away the instant we paused. Here a meadowlark singing in the middle of the dusty road rose before us. There a creosote bush was covered with small five-petaled yellow flowers and jackrabbits leaped from forms in their dainty shade and dashed away, skimming lightly with incredible leaps over sprawling prickly pears.

We crossed dead streams bedded with desiccated sand. Beside them stood gauges to warn travelers of danger when a flash flood awakened an empty arroyo to surging deadly life. The paint on gauges had been sanded away by past floods, and the wood itself was abraded by the grinding rocks they carried.

The colors of the Chisos grew richer and more varied as we drew nearer. Then the triple peaks: Pummel, Wright and Panther, rose before us and we began to climb, slowly at first and then more and more sharply. A small herd of mule deer grazing near the road lifted their heads and then burst away with a funny stiff-legged, bouncing gait for all the world like a group of lively boys on pogo sticks. We came to two water barrels provided for cars that overheat on the steep climb, and in the shade beneath them a lark sparrow sang its rich, varied song in comparative coolness.

We entered the woodland zone, and among the shiny dark leaves of smooth, red-barked madrone trees were clusters of white huckleberrylike flowers. As I buried my face in them and breathed their light fragrance I was transported for a moment to woodlands in the Northeast.

Above us reared rock stacks and pillars and massive cliffs, many of them red, some the same lion color as the desert and others tinged with bright yellow intensified by patches of yellow lichens, those lowly soilmakers that through the ages slowly break down lifeless rock into viable soil. Sweeping the mighty ramparts with our binoculars we discovered that small spots of green that looked like moss to our naked eyes were really pines and oaks anchored in small deposits of soil. By thrusting roots deep into crevices where water seeped, they supported a meager existence in lofty, lonely grandeur. Now and then we saw the black mouth of a cave that hinted of the mysterious and the unknown. Around one, white-throated swifts darted like erratic missiles, and later on we saw bats emerge from some of the caves.

Pinons and oaks were already in bloom. We saw many alligator junipers with their pale gray bark divided into neat squares. Mountain mahogany and serviceberry, both members of the rose family, added to the dramatic change from desert conditions that altitude and water can make. A canyon wind screeched by and suddenly we were poised on the top of Panther Pass almost six thousand feet above sea level. Far below in the roughly circular Basin huddled the park buildings, looking like dollhouses. To our left Casa Grande's massive buttresses thrust into the Basin, and the trees of an open woodland swirled around it as water swirls before the bow of a ship, then spread into a circular forest broken on the west by the great slash called The Window. Through this the sunset flames in spring. On our right rock stacks in weird shapes stood above the circling trees. The road fell away swiftly in hairpin turns that hugged the wall and then straightened in a steep decline down which we shot as if on a child's slide.

That evening we walked in the Basin with our coats buttoned tightly again, and our fingers ached with cold. Great stars flashed white fire and against the sable sky the lofty notched rim of the Basin loomed blacker. The snort of a startled white-tailed deer, the bark of a gray fox on the hunt, the long thin streak and triangular face of a ring-tailed cat caught in the beam of our flashlight, the scuttle of a silvery wood rat, the sobbing of a poor-will, the high-pitched chatter of a pair of tiny elf owls no bigger than sparrows and most of all the thin cold air bearing strange scents and an indefinable perfume that at the same time reminded us of snowflakes and spring flowers excited us so we were reluctant to return to our adobe cottage.

But at length the unaccustomed altitude and the chill air created a drowsiness no willpower could combat. With the draperies pulled wide to let in the night we went to sleep with flames from the fireplace casting flickering shadows on the walls. Later the waning moon lifted above the rim of the Basin, and though it was old and shrunken it shone in the clear air with exceptional brilliance, awakening us. But so sweet was the air and so haunting the sobbing of the poor-wills, so wild the signal of coyote to coyote across the Basin we could not shut out the night, and instead, we buried our faces in our pillows to shut out only the radiant moonlight.

It is about forty miles from the Basin to the mouth of Santa Elena Canyon. The road provides a constantly changing rugged mountain panorama of deep gullies, grotesque rock stacks and the strange peaks known as the Mule Ears. It drops into desert country where sotol, screw beans, cactus and dense stands of lechugilla—sometimes called shin-agave because of the damage it can inflict on the legs of people who walk through it—form a plant community that can resist prolonged heat and drought.

The morning chill quickly dissipated. When we reached the mouth of Santa Elena Canyon and walked across the dry bed of Terlingua Creek the rocks were already blistering hot.

We stared wide-eyed at the narrow fault and soaring walls through which the Rio Grande, called Rio Bravo by the Mexicans in this its middle section, had chiseled its way. From the northwesternmost point of Texas to the gulf the Rio Grande forms the boundary between the United States and Mexico. For 107 miles it is also the boundary of the Big Bend National Park, and in these many miles it flows for much of the way through desert country between low banks often densely overgrown with reeds and rushes. Behind these range thickets of screw bean, named for its strange seed pods that grow in a tight spiral and called *tornillo* by the Mexicans. Associated with the screw bean are desert willows, which are not willows at all but close relatives of catalpa. After each good rain, desert willow bursts into bloom, covering itself with delicate orchid-colored, deep-throated flowers spotted with brown and purple that are quickly replaced by long thin pods that cling for months.

In most of Texas the general movement of the Rio Grande is southeasterly, but the great massif of the Big Bend country forced a detour southward and then north before its general direction toward the gulf could be resumed. In spite of the detour, it was compelled to rasp its way through the mountains themselves, and it gnawed a twisting passage in the ancient rocks by following faults. It worked ever deeper until some of the narrow canyon walls rise as much as 1,750 feet and cast eternal shade on the river far below.

Many minor canyons and three major ones have been chiseled as the river worked its way around and through the Big Bend massif. While Santa Elena, known in the early days as the Grande Canyon de Santa Helena, is most often visited and is perhaps the most famous, Mariscal Canyon, originally called San Vincente, is even more spectacular and has the highest walls of any. When conditions are good, float-boat trips through this canyon are possible for hardy individuals. Boquillas Canyon, with walls a hundred feet lower than those of Mariscal, is more open, so its profile seems to carry above the actual walls to the five-thousand-foot peaks beyond. Of all the canyons, Boquillas is conceded to be the most colorful and most wildly sculptured.

Allan, astonished by the narrow river and towering walls of Santa Elena, promptly picked up a stone and with little effort threw it across the Rio Grande. He hit Mexico's Chihuahua State with a bang that echoed and reechoed. A pair of common ravens disturbed by the noise began to scold. Allan imitated them perfectly and threw them into a state of wild excitement, convinced that a strange raven had invaded their territory. So excited were the ravens that twice in quick succession one of them dashed to the mouth of the canyon, folded its wings with a snap and turned completely over in a perfect barrel roll. The dispute rose in volume, and the uproar, trapped so it reverberated between the sheer walls, disturbed a drowsing great horned owl. It, too, joined in the vocal fracas.

We climbed along a trail first worn by animals. No doubt it dated back to the time when ocelots hunted in the Big Bend and panthers were regular predators that kept the herds of deer within bounds so they did not overbrowse their habitat and become the prey of disease and starvation. In those days bighorn sheep nimbly walked along the narrow ledges. Though a bighorn was seen in Mariscal Canyon as late as 1899, today both it and the ocelot are gone and only a few panthers (more properly *cougar* though this name has a less wild and stealthy sound than panther) remain in the fastness of the Big Bend. To be sure, a few desert bighorns have been introduced into the Black Gap area, and if they accept their new home, the day may come when visitors to the Big Bend will occasionally see this former resident.

The heat was appalling. Allan, with rivulets of perspiration running down his face and his shirt darkened with wet patches, climbed to the top of the wall, which flattened into a mesa that stretched on for many miles. Below him the Rio Grande had shrunk to a silver thread. As for me, I proceeded along the trail that hugged the lower part of the canyon wall until at last the undercut palisade of the Chihuahua side towered over my head.

With a last look at the narrow band of deep blue sky, I slid under a shelving rock and in its pleasant shade, pulled a treasure from my pocket and began to read while the Rio Grande glided almost silently below me. From the Library of Congress I had obtained a photographic copy of an article in the

January, 1901, issue of *Century* Magazine entitled, "Running the Canyons of the Rio Grande, by Robert T. Hill, United States Geological Survey; an account of his trip made in 1899.

Hill launched his three specially made boats with two men in each in the river near Presidio on October fifth. He led a party of five including his nineteen-year-old nephew Prentice Hall; an extra boat hand; a Mexican cook; and two remarkable frontiersmen—James MacMahon, a trapper who had three times drifted through the canyons with his traps but looked only for beaver sign and possible ambushes and had seen nothing else, and Henry Ware, a man of great strength, inured to hardship, capable of doing anything needed on so wild and dangerous an expedition.

Away back in 1852–1853 when Colonel Emory, for whom the highest peak in the Chisos was named, was engaged in the Boundary Survey, he deemed the Rio Grande impassable in the Big Bend country, and though he occasionally viewed the river from a height, he was forced to leave that whole area without a good survey. For almost half a century these remained the least known of any of the great American canyons. Perhaps even today they are the most secret.

Scarcely was Hill's expedition under way than adventures began. A great roar deafened the party, and seething currents dashing around massive volcanic boulders, tumbled every which way, barred their passage. The long journey through the wild Big Bend country went on with one perilous episode following another so rapidly that the reader wonders at the recuperative powers of the human body and at the human spirit that sticks it out, no matter how threatening and exhausting the project.

Sudden floods; rock-falls that necessitated hauling the boats and equipment over them where the shifting of a single boulder could have been fatal; rapids; and temperatures that plunged to freezing at night, then soared to 136 degrees at

midday demanded incredible stamina. The explorers encountered Old Whitelip, charged with the murder of several
men, but this time he was incongruously holding an infant in
his arms.

They passed the hamlet of Polvo, appropriately meaning
dust and saw bloodspatters on both floor and walls of the
store from a gunfight in which several men had been killed a
couple years before. Later they encountered rustlers driving
stolen Texas cattle into Mexico: the leader of that gang of
rustlers was also an infamous killer.

But Hill's party made it. They mapped almost four hundred miles of the Rio Grande from Presidio to Langtry, made
careful notes of geological formations and listed the birds and
other animals they saw. In short they not only performed
heroically, but made a thoroughly professional scientific survey of the unknown canyons.

As I came to the last paragraph of the tale of a bold journey I realized a charming song was ringing from the sheer
rock wall before me. A canyon wren was engaged in a concert. As beautifully as the vast rounded dome of the Rucker
Cave, the towerng walls of Santa Elena echoed this vibrant
song. A canyon wren could never find a more perfect setting
for its silvery, bell-like melody. I put aside my tale of exploration and surrendered myself to the solo concert resounding between the narrowly separated precipices.

Monday, we were told, was the best day to go to Hot
Springs, because then the Mexicans came across the river to
get their mail. The nearest Mexican post office was seventy
miles distant. It is a wonder we ever reached Hot Springs, for
there were so many sights ranging from cactus wrens building
endless nests to whiptail lizards, bullsnakes, cactus flowers
and one yellow zephyrlily under a creosote bush to detain us.
Rock formations and just plain stones interested us keenly
since our talk with the rock hound, and when we came to a

strangely sculptured reddish rock that looked like the head of a great ferocious snake we stopped to examine it. We lingered again to examine the stone remains of ancient Indian dwellings and to look over the rimrock, on which the houses were placed, to see far below creosote bushes spaced as regularly as if they were the trees in a young orange grove. Behind them the dual tracks of the one-way road twisted between the rimrock and the green band that marked the bank of the Rio Grande and the high eroded cliff where Tornillo Creek entered it.

Making our way down the steep dusty road, we found the Mexicans had either gotten up late or they had come a long way, for the first arrival on a small yellow burro was just splashing into the Rio Grande. On the left we saw a file of horses and burros and men on foot irregularly spaced moving toward the Hot Springs ford and from the right came three more. The men on foot waited for a lift across the river, so most of the burros and small wiry mustangs arrived on our bank with an extra man clinging behind the saddle.

Hot Springs is gone as a post office, but the warm waters still gush from the earth. In the old days before the park was established, baths could be had for twenty-five cents. According to a yellowed, fly-specked handbill still pinned to the post office wall on our first trip, the therapeutic waters helped hiccups, asthma, boils, dropsy, kidney ailments, jaundice, stomach trouble, pellegra, rheumatism, sunburn and genitory diseases.

Allan with a deadpan face asked the postmistress if the baths were really that good. She stared at him a moment and then replied, "Can't say I'd promise anything, but if anybody comes this fur he can sure use a bath."

The slender lithe Mexicans dressed in tight blue jeans and bright shirts, with wide-brimmed sombreros tilted at rakish angles above dark faces, often with wide curled moustaches, looked more Indian than Spanish. All with one exception ignored us, studied their Sears catalogs and similar mail while they drank pop. Nobody appeared to have received a letter.

Pedro Gonzales, unlike his companions, was eager to chat with us. He was an official and proudly showed us his badge of office. He had walked to Hot Springs to investigate a shooting incident. A few days before, some Mexicans illegally driving a small herd of cattle across the river into the park where grazing was good had been intercepted by a border patrolman. He tried to turn the herd without success. It was vital to keep cattle from entering the United States; from adjacent Mexico a bad outbreak of highly contagious hoof and mouth disease could easily leap across the border. This was not understood by the Mexicans. Even when an entire herd suddenly died it was shrugged off as the will of God. Naturally the Mexicans knew they had no business driving their cattle across the river; but their animals were starving, so they attempted to smuggle the herd to a place of better forage.

Tempers flared. Finally the outnumbered patrolman shot the lead cow. For a while it looked as if more shooting would follow, but the patrolman finally chased the cattle south of the Rio Grande. Perhaps the shooting was responsible for the aloofness of the visiting Mexicans.

But Gonzales, having investigated to his satisfaction (though this was limited, so far as we could see, to drinking several bottles of cold pop) now wanted a lift to Boquillas. Though he was an important official he was without a horse, for his beast had thrown a shoe the day before and was lame.

Allan fell in with the idea, and after we had waded across the river to Mexico and back again to cool our own feet, we began the twisting dusty ascent above Hot Springs and turned toward Boquillas. Gonzales was eager for information about the number of Mexicans who lived in New York and what life there was like. He listened with pleased attention as we told him about crowded subways at rush hour, of ice skating on the plaza at Radio City and the precious jewels in

Tiffany's windows. Gonzales had never been farther than twenty-five miles from his birthplace; but he had thumbed through picture magazines until they fell apart, and he was well acquainted with bulky mail-order catalogs with their hundreds of pictured items. But when we described escalators and elevators he looked as if he distrusted us as much as the gauchos of Hudson's *The Purple Land* disbelieved the British narrator's account of a January snow in London (for wasn't Uruguay's summer heat most intense in January?) , a black London fog and a palace of glass. Ours was not the first car Gonzales had ridden in. He had a friend who drove a truck for the mining company, but he preferred horses.

For the first time we came to Deadman's Curve, one car wide and so abrupt the tail of the car swung quite frighteningly over the abyss. A high sheer cliff rose on the left and on the right the same cliff continued to fall away for hundreds of feet. Every time after that when we came to Deadman's Curve, where a man was killed in one of the many border clashes, the passenger scouted the far side of the sharp curve while the driver cautiously inched around the cliff. Now Deadman's Curve has been eliminated by a tunnel, and we regret it; though the road is infinitely safer some of the adventure is gone from the drive to Boquillas.

By the time we reached Boquillas it was furiously hot, so hot we could scarcely breathe. We ran our car under a corrugated metal shelter attached to the border patrol cabin. Allan remarked that Gonzales would get his feet wet when he crossed the river this time, because there was no one to give him a ride on his horse. Gonzales showed all his fine white teeth.

"Please to come with me. You will see."

He set off at a good clip, his sore feet apparently forgotten. We regretted following him almost at once. In spite of the dry air, perspiration drops rolled into our smarting eyes and behind our ears. Gonzales led us toward the top of a high cliff signaling the beginning of Boquillas Canyon. The rocks burned our hands as we grasped them in scrambling upward. Cautiously we picked our way to avoid all sorts of disagreeable thorns and spines. There we saw our first resurrection plants; spore-bearing selaginella, dried and rolled into tight nestlike balls. So it would remain until rain fell; then it would open into a lacy bright green rosette, only to shrivel again as it lost its moisture.

As we breathlessly arrived at the top of the cliff, Gonzales' grin stretched wider than ever. We saw ahead a small boxlike car suspended from a cable that sloped at a steep angle toward the Mexican side of the Rio Grande. This, we assumed, was some of the equipment used when the Puerto Rico lead and silver mine was in operation back in the 1890's.

"It is not permitted that anybody use this," Gonzales told us, and we realized that much is permitted an official that is denied lesser men.

Gonzales climbed into the car while we privately thought it would have been far easier to wade the cool waters of the Rio Grande than struggle up the steep hot slope we had negotiated with much effort. But after fiddling with the cable, Gonzales turned toward us, swept off his hat, held it against his chest, bowed low, returned his hat to his head with a dramatic gesture and sailed away in majestic if slightly jerky grandeur. We held our breath until we saw him disembark in triumph in Mexico. We suspected Gonzales had taken his life in his hands as he made his spectacular exit from the United States in order to avoid wading the shallow river. Later that afternoon we learned our concern had been unfounded. The car was safe. It provided the border patrolmen an easy crossing of the river whenever they had reason to go to Boquillas, even though the water was high. The elevated car was called a bucket, and similar ones at intervals in the canyon country provided, in a place where there were no bridges, a river crossing even when high water surged dangerously.

We looked down on a Mexican hamlet built of adobe that blended into the desert with but one exception; the water tower standing on stilts was painted dark maroon. Not a blade of grass poked its head through the baked earth. Only close to the sandy shore of the Rio Grande grew a small fringe of green where some screw beans and desert willows found sufficient water to support life. As we looked at the expanse of barren desert we wondered how a single cow, let alone a herd, could possibly survive in that desolation. Nowhere have I ever seen so lifeless an expanse of mountainous country.

Recess came and as the bell rang, children burst from the school and began to play a singing game. My hand brushed something hot, and I glanced down. I had touched a piece of red and yellow jasper, the first collector's rock we had seen since the rock hound had locked the trunk of his car. It looked as if it had been freshly broken from some secret horde. I often wonder if that six-inch piece of jasper still lies there under the hot sun in all its gleaming colors, or if dust settled on it and rain turned the dust to an encasing shell so it now looks like an ordinary piece of desert-colored stone.

One day as we explored a slope not far from Juniper Canyon, Allan noted some rocks heaped in an unnatural manner and climbed to investigate.

"It looks as if somebody had begun a mine and then abandoned the idea," he remarked.

The blinding light made it difficult to see into the shallow hole, and he got down on his knees to look more carefully. Suddenly he jerked back.

"There are two and maybe three big rattlers in there," he called. "One of them is really big, and its swollen jaws really gives its face an arrow shape."

For his hot climb he had found only rattlers and no strange or beautiful rocks.

One afternoon we were returning from the desert, and as

we neared the junction where the Basin road left the one leading to Maverick Gate, Allan jammed on the brakes.

"That's not a dog!" he exclaimed. "It's a coyote."

During our exploration of the Big Bend country we had looked in vain for either a panther or a coyote. Now at last one of the smaller predators was right before us. Just then the door of a low white house (it has since been torn down) opened and a woman called, "Won't you come in? Yes, it is a coyote."

We accepted with alacrity. Our hostess, Mrs. Wallace, was the wife of the Park engineer, and she was very fond of animals. Some weeks ago she had found the coyote not far from her house. It was badly wounded by shots. Daily she took food and water to it until it recovered. It had accepted her as a friend, though it remained extremely wary. Now it had pups in a den scraped from a bank or in a natural cave somewhere not far away. The coyote came daily for whatever suitable food she had to give. It appeared aware of strangers and refused to come for food until they left.

"I'm glad the coyote keeps its wariness," Mrs. Wallace said. "The crews of all the ranches ringing the park try to kill every predator whether it is a coyote, a cougar, a golden eagle or whatever. In fact, I suspect that somebody on one of the temporary work crews in the park itself may have shot this coyote, though the men are not supposed to bring guns into the park. There is still a lot of lawlessness in this wild country."

Mrs. Wallace led us into her living room. We both forgot the coyote and stared at the remarkable fireplace. It sparkled with crystals and glowed with rich gemlike colors.

"Now there is a story," Mrs. Wallace told us. "Before the park was established, the ranchman owning this area became interested in rocks and in tales of old treasure. Every day when he rode around the ranch, he carried a geology hammer and cowhide bag and kept his eyes open for beautiful stones.

Few areas in this country are richer in the beauty and variety of rocks and minerals than this one. Of course you have heard about Lost Nigger mine. Frank Dobie's exciting books have really stirred up the treasure hunters, and a small army has tramped these mountains in search of that mine, which was found, according to the tales, by a Seminole Indian who was murdered for it. Ever since, the mine has been under a curse. If anybody locates it he dies a horrible death before he can cash in on his discovery.

"Then there is Lost Mine. The wind has chiseled the shape of Alsate, a great Apache chief, on the top of Lost Mine Peak. There the dead chief's spirit guards all the hidden Apache treasures including the Lost Mine. But once a year he gives a clue to that particular treasure. You have to go to the door of the old San Vicente Mission across the river in Mexico on Easter morning and watch the very first shaft of light from the rising sun, for at that very instant it shines into the opening of the Lost Mine. So far nobody has been able to detect the place where the first Easter sunbeam hits the Chisos."

"The fireplace," we said. "Do tell us about the fireplace."

"The rancher was forever filling that cowhide bag with trophies that he brought home. He couldn't forget rocks and treasures even at night, and he spent his evenings reading everything he could lay his hands on that dealt with rocks, minerals and lost treasures of this country. One night he was reading about the coming and going of Spaniards along the Comanche Trail from Mexico City to the missions in Santa Fe and other places and how renegades and Indians sometimes attacked them and stole their freight, which was often gold and silver bars. There were even some photographs of such bars in the book, and as he studied the pictures, he suddenly remembered an odd rock, one that had not particularly interested him, that he passed almost daily. The rancher was so excited he could not sleep, and as soon as the first gray light of dawn came, he saddled up and was off to check that odd stone. It was in truth a silver bar darkened by time and weather. He sold it for enough to build this house and he used part of his rock collection to make this magnificent fireplace. He is dead now. They say he died of a broken heart because he had to give up his beloved ranch when the Park took over."

We were silent. In order to save some of America's great wonders for future generations we sometimes cause grief to individuals who have lived all their lives in a unique area that good planning for future generations demands should be set aside for the enjoyment of all. The poignant sacrifice made by those individuals should be honored through our appreciation of the remarkable locality, and through our protection of the values that have been preserved at the cost of individual ownership and perhaps heartbreak.

A few days after we saw the glittering fireplace made from pieces of beauty hidden in the rocks of the Big Bend country we began retracing our path. Not far from Langtry we came to an overturned truck that had been hauling flagstones from a nearby quarry. These lay shattered in a heap. A highway officer was using his radio to call for help. The driver of the truck, still dazed, told us, "The front tire blew and I thought I'd been shot."

The sheets of sandstone had been uniform in thickness and were beautifully banded with cream and rose.

"Sure, you can have all you want," the truck driver was generous. "Most of those stones are no good now."

Allan chose a couple of fairly small but very bright pieces and so began a collection that grows steadily larger.

The rock hound, whose name we do not know, really sent us off on a fascinating tangent. He added a new dimension to all our days in the field. Since time for this interest is limited, we have taken advantage of modern roadbuilding to show us where treasures may be found. A huge scraper working near Flaming Gorge in Utah uncovered wonderstones, those mysterious sandstones with blue-gray cores circled by bands of varied colors. After some blasting in the Black Hills, Allan found a fine chunk of rose quartz. In Colorado, where a cut was made through a vein of rock, he picked up some alabaster. Where the coastal road between Morro Bay and Monterey in California clings to the abrupt slope of the sea cliffs, he located a slab of serpentine newly shattered and smoothly shining. In southern Arizona he found a chunk of bright blue and green chalcocite.

To our constant field companions: Peterson's field guides to the birds, Pettingill's guides to bird finding and Palmer's mammal guide, we now added a fourth P; Pough's guide to rocks and minerals, as essential to our full enjoyment of our country. The story behind the formation of each kind of rock adds to our understanding of this varied world we live in and arouses a sense of wonder at the tales they tell us of the earth long before the first man set foot upon it.

9

Needle to the North

THE FIRST TIME we went to the Big Bend Allan was engaged in filming wildlife from the Chisos Mountains to the gulf and north to Aransas Refuge. Our days were strictly budgeted. By the third week in April we must be in the lower Rio Grande Valley where birds nest early and bring off their young before intense heat sets in. From the middle of May through early June we had to work in the great colonies of herons, spoonbills and ibises, of skimmers, pelicans and terns on the islands strung like beads in the shallow offshore waters from Galveston Bay to the southern end of Laguna Madre.

As we hurried toward the Big Bend flocks of birds everywhere were moving toward the north. Lark buntings, white-crowned sparrows, white-necked ravens: all were on the move. Sometimes the flocks actually colored the ground as they fed on last year's seeds.

"We are too early." Allan shivered in the bitter wind. "We see only birds that wintered here and they are only now beginning to move north. The summer birds haven't come yet."

When we arrived in the basin, Robert Gibbs, acting super-intendent, introduced us to the staff and asked them to give us all possible assistance. We shortly discovered that Mr.

Gibbs' remarks really impressed one of the men.

Rising from the floor of the basin is a steep bluff called Duffer's Peak, a favorite roost for vultures. Taking his camera and tripod, Allan climbed to the top and I scrambled up behind him. A fresh wind was blowing, and he soon had some fine shots of vultures riding the buoyant air.

We hurried back to our car, only to find it surrounded by wide-eyed tourists just arrived by bus. A grounds-keeper leaned on his rake and was holding forth about Allan's distinction among wildlife photographers in the entire country, in fact, in the whole world. His fascinated audience was clearly impressed by the fact that so great a photographer was shooting a film in the Big Bend.

"Now you look at that book," the grounds-keeper commanded, dramatically pointing to a thick book lying on the dash. "Nobody who wasn't crammed with brains would read such a big book, and he sure wouldn't tote such a big book all around the country."

Allan winked at me. The book about Texas was indeed a thick one, useful chiefly for bits of local history and information about industries, parks and so on. We had grave doubts about its value in the natural history field. One item about the Big Bend stated the walls of Santa Elena Canyon were so high that if birds dropped between them they died of starvation because they could not fly out again.

For some minutes the man propped himself upright with his rake and continued his extravagant discourse about Allan and his unique position among wildlife photographers, but finally, having repeated everything three times over with a slight additional embellishment each time, he dismissed the tourists.

"Well, I must get back to my work," and he began raking busily.

The tourists, told by their leader that they must return to the bus in half an hour, dispersed, and we dispersed with them. Not until the bus pulled away and the grounds-keeper had vanished did we claim our car, hurriedly move the big book to an inconspicuous place in the duffle and make our getaway.

We searched the Basin for birds. Ruby-crowned kinglets, blue-gray gnatcatchers and Bewick's wrens were some of our old friends. Many were new to me: black-eared titmice, Mexican jays and brown towhees. Again I heard the bell-like song of canyon wrens echo between rock walls and the clattering roll of roadrunners when they rattled their mandibles as a Spanish gypsy does her ivory castanets.

One day bright clouds filled the Basin. A sudden gust ripped them apart and set white tatters flying wildly. Revealed for a moment was a small bird perched upright on a dead twig. It was blue as a June sky, lightly touched with turquoise, the most exquisite color I had ever seen. We heard a gentle warble. Then a streamer of pale cloud hid the bird. It was a mountain bluebird.

Unlike the other bluebirds, mountain bluebirds lack the rusty flush across the breast. They belong in pale or snowy settings. One stormy May day in Wyoming, as we approached the Unita Mountains, a snow squall blinded us. Then out of the veil of snow we heard the mellow notes of mountain bluebirds and found ourselves in the midst of a flock of fifty or more. Some stood on fence posts plastered with wet snow, and others, scattered over the snowy ground, actively chased tiny insects that sprang along the surface. Nowhere could we see any color except white and the ethereal blue of the birds.

Again, high on Bald Mountain in an aspen grove as light and bright as a white birch woodland in New Hampshire, we found mountain bluebirds nesting in an abandoned woodpecker hole. The day was warm and sunny, yet we thought of snowfields and glittering white clouds as the male clung to the white bark by the nest.

One day we climbed on snowfields in the Olympics, and

each time we came to an ice cave we were enthralled by the
unearthly blue light inside. Then from a low conifer came
the song of a mountain bluebird. A small white insect rose
from the snow and the bluebird darted toward us as lightly as
a butterfly and hovered for a moment above the ice cave. It
was as if the spirits of the mountains and the snow and bright
clouds were suddenly focused in one small winged point of
blue.

There was no sign of nesting in the basin. In old century-
plant flower stalks Allan found holes made another spring by
small woodpeckers, perhaps ladder-backs. There were other
uninhabited holes in the trees. We found the pendulous
felted nest of a common bushtit lying on the ground. It was
tattered and forlorn. We wondered if a mouse had occupied
it during the winter, only to be eaten by some small hungry
mammal. A mass of stout sticks spilled from a large prickly
pear. Probably a pair of roadrunners had reared a family
there last summer.

Allan put a handful of grain on a stone by our cottage and
to it came rufous-crowned sparrows, a brown towhee and a
pale Chisos chipmunk. All of these were very plainly colored.
Allan loves bright colors, not only for his film but because he
reacts to gay colors as to a happy smile. Fortunately some
Mexican jays found the grain, and the soft blue color and vi-
vacious antics of these birds lifted his spirits.

The Park dump lay in a well-concealed hollow not far
from the Green Gulch road, and like most dumps from the
Atlantic to the Pacific provided a good birding place. Red-
tailed, Swainson's and occasionally a sparrow hawk gathered
there to seek the ever-present rodents. White-necked ravens
assembled to snatch anything edible while smaller birds
found that the rich shubbery nourished by decaying refuse
offered good protective cover and ample food. We seldom
failed to see scrub jays and chipping sparrows as well as some
of the lingering winter species such as Oregon juncos, green-

tailed towhees and Brewer's sparrows near the dump. It was there we saw our first black-headed grosbeak and hepatic tanager of the spring. One day we came across a flock of nine acorn woodpeckers exploring the trunks of trees around the dump. Some hammered acorns into holes they had drilled to receive them. These woodpeckers have black backs, and the black extends up to a red cap and forward around their eyes, which are startling snowy-white and remind me of the berries of white baneberry, which children often call doll's-eyes.

We climbed Lost Mine Trail between oak trees and past great rocks. At one point we looked down into Juniper Canyon, where a bluff rose steeply from the floor and was crowded by a massive sculptured rock. It looked like an enchanted castle straight out of a book of fairy tales. As we swung our binoculars across the rock castle, a golden eagle rose majestically from the highest turret and glided down the canyon on seven-foot wings with the tips spread and slightly upturned. It was the only one of these great raptores we saw in the Big Bend.

Among some oaks Allan located a small group of mixed warblers: Audubon's, Macgillivray's, black-and-white, and orange-crowned. In this group, busily feeding among the drying flower catkins and tiny pink leaves, he picked out two inconspicuous chestnut-capped, yellow-rumped Colima warblers, a species extremely rare in the United States, where it is known to nest only in the Chisos Mountains. But search though we did we could not find the other two Chisos warbler rareties: the red-faced warblers and the painted redstart, nor did we find those two handsome species until we spent a later spring in the Santa Catalina and Santa Rita mountains of southeastern Arizona. There they were not uncommon within the narrow range of altitude they demand. Red-faced warblers were fairly common above Bear Wallow and in Marshall Gulch on Mount Lemmon, and we found a painted redstart nest not fifty feet behind our Santa Rita Lodge cabin in Madera Canyon. The Colima warblers in the Big Bend not only showed no sign of nesting, but there was no indication they were a pair. Apparently they wait until May and then somewhere above six thousand feet they hide their nests under tufts of grass or beneath drifts of old oak leaves.

The desert drew us like a magnet. From a distance its shadeless expanse of radiating heat, of stiff and thorny plants, looked empty and lifeless. Nothing moved except whirling dust devils. When we entered that area and felt the full weight of the desert sun and smelled the sharp astringent scent of hot fleshy plants and resin-coated leaves, it seemed birds must be nesting. We came across verdins conversing with a peevish, whining *see-lip*. Horned larks squatting low and closely matching the desert floor rose reluctantly before us. Now and then a curve-billed thrasher perched on a cactus and stared at us with pale yellow eyes.

Many cactus wrens, big as wood thrushes, sang with loud voices to match their large size. Some of them trailed long pieces of tan grass as they flew, and we watched those weave the fibers into conspicuous flask-shaped nests. Most of these nests were barely started, and all were tucked into the spiny stems of opuntia. It is claimed that cactus wrens use their excessive energy to build nests that are never occupied. However, enemies can easily locate the bulky nests, conspicuously tan in the gray-green cactus; and it may be that once the nesting season is under way, the empty new nests simply indicate that the eggs or young have been taken by other birds, rodents or reptiles, so they are abandoned in favor of another location. Systematically we moved from one nest to another, examining each in our search for one that was occupied. Finally we admitted failure, and with our fingers bristling painfully with cactus spines, we headed toward a little group of cottonwoods that marked the site of an abandoned ranch.

As we approached, Allan stopped and then began to back away. I paused and stared into the pale quivering leaves. Finally in the densest shade of the tallest tree I saw five pale gray scaled quail with a faint yellowish-brown wash on their bellies. They were utterly motionless; statues that did not even blink their black eyes. By that time Allan was back with his camera, and I heard him mutter a hope that the pale desert behind the deeply shaded quail would not give him an unpleasant picture. He ground off several feet of film before the quail erupted, dropped to the ground and scattered in all directions, their whitish crests bobbing as if they were wads of cotton insecurely glued in place.

I managed to keep one of the swift birds in my binocular field, and laughed to see it run so fast yet as stiffly as if its legs were bound to splints. To tell the truth, all birds, even such strong runners as the ostrich, have their legs tied by nature, for they are encased within the body-covering all the way to the knee joint. Contrary to what many people believe, the knee that "turns the wrong way" is actually the ankle joint. Though birds occasionally rest with their feet flat, they walk on their toes.

All members of the quail family apparently share with the scaled quail an exaggerated stiffness of gait that is amusing to see. I had little time to watch that quail, once it shot off its perch. It sped away as erratically as a dust devil, a fit companion for those creations of the hot desert wind, and was lost among the cactus and needle-pointed agave.

As the quail vanished I caught sight of Allan engaged in a weird dance. He ran, turned, stooped and kept reaching for the ground. He was trying to catch something small. Once more he shifted his footing and pounced. Beaming now, he straightened. He was holding a horned lizard.

"Look at those two long horns in the center of its head," Allan said. He was rather out of breath. Perspiration ran down his red face. "It's a Texas horned lizard and surprisingly quick—nothing like the sluggish ones kept as pets."

A short horn on the top of its nose gave the lizard, regarding us with bright but tiny beadlike black eyes, an insouciant look. There was also a small horn above each eye; a row of them along the top of its head, with the middle two much longer than the others, made it look formidable: a shrunken dinosaur. Most of its scales, though they lay flat against the body, were pulled into points. Around the edge of its pan-cake body ran a double fringe of horns that looked sharp as cactus spines. Truly this was a fitting member of the bristling desert community.

Basically the lizard was rich brown, but it was mottled with yellow, red and tan. It was almost invisible when placed on the desert earth. As the days went by we occasionally found a round-tailed horned lizard. These lack the fringes around the body, and they have four long horns of equal length on the top of the head. Never again did we see another Texas horned lizard in the Big Bend. Fortunately Allan decided to photograph his catch.

While he arranged his camera I held the lizard in my cupped hands. It twisted about but the horns did not hurt, and it soon became quiet. Though these lizards can move swiftly as this one had already proved, more often they rely on their ability to hide in plain sight by becoming immobile. This characteristic enabled us to make excellent portraits of the small reptile, but either it remained stock-still or darted off in a flash. Finally Allan put it on an anthill, since ants are its favorite food, and hoped for a shot of it catching a meal. The flicking of its pink sticky tongue as it gathered in an ant was so quick that even when Allan speeded up the movie camera from a normal twenty-four frames to sixty-four frames per second, the action was too swift, and we left the lizard in the dazzling light to continue catching ants undisturbed.

Most species of horned lizards give birth to live young, but the Texas horned lizard is one of the few that lay creamy, pebbled, leathery-shelled eggs. These may number two dozen or more. When the female hides them in the sand each weighs $\frac{1}{18}$ as much as she does, and the total weight of all may be greater than her own. Each egg is stocked with food for the unborn lizard, but with that fabulous ability of desert creatures to extract water from an arid environment, she sometimes supplies more than her own weight in water alone in the egg whites.

These charming lizards hibernate deep enough in the ground in winter so true frost does not reach them. Once spring warmth arrives they emerge from their winter's sleep, but even then they feed only when it is truly hot. Oddly enough, forced exposure to the intense heat of the summer sun for half an hour in this dry and obdurate region will kill horned lizards as it will snakes.

It is quite true that horned lizards have the ability, unique among all the animals of this earth, of squirting a thin but well-aimed jet of blood as far as five feet right into the face of an attacker. However, it appears that this is seldom exercised except in late May and June when they are about to shed their skin or have just sloughed their old one. Snakes become irascible when they shed their skins, and horned lizards share this characteristic with their reptilian cousins. But the latter express their crabbed outlook on life and their bad temper in an original way. Since they shed at the time of year when mating also takes place, it may be that reproductive excitement plays a part in shooting blood from their eyes. Several springs may elapse when not a horned lizard we pick up shoots blood from its eyes; then, as if an epidemic of blood-shooting had burst forth in the desert, several in quick succession expel thin jets of blood.

In 1967 the Texas Legislature joined a few southwestern states in protecting horned lizards. It is now a misdemeanor to collect them, take them as pets or laminate them in paper weights. In spite of such protective laws, many horned lizards are sacrificed as pets and forced to endure for a time poor care and unsuitable temperatures so that they refuse to eat and fi-

Most species of horned lizards give birth to live young, but the Texas horned lizard is one of the few that lay creamy, pebbled, leathery-shelled eggs. (Chapter 9)

We came, on a moment of rare tranquility, to one of the strangest forests anywhere in all this diversified world, the yucca forest of Dagger Flat. (Chapter 10.)

These giant daggers grow nowhere else in the United States. Their species reaches a height of thirty feet . . . it is the giant among American yuccas. (Chapter 10)

A curve-billed thrasher flew straight toward us with caterpillars in its bill. (Chapter 10)

Looking towards the Chisos I saw the whole range was in the cloud's shadow. (Chapter 10)

Hard on the heels of the vanishing bison, pronghorns were reduced until close to extinction. Now they have recovered to a point where these beautiful and unique North American mammals will remain on the open lands of the West. (Chapter 11)

Prairie dogs dig shafts that drop almost perpendicularly down for an average of twelve feet. About two feet below the surface they build a barking platform to yelp a danger signal. (Chapter 12)

These small brown burrowing owls often occupy abandoned burrows of prairie dogs. Should their eggs or young be found by the prairie dogs, they would be eaten. (Chapter 12)

A grizzled animal somewhat more than two feet long entered a prairie dog burrow. It was a badger. Shortly the head reappeared at the mouth of the tunnel and remained there as if enjoying the sun. (Chapter 12)

A lark sparrow flushed from beside the road; the nest and young were there. (Chapter 12)

For the first time I saw avocets, large shore birds with long blue legs
and upcurved bills. (Chapter 13)

Willets fought and searched for food on the Loma de la Montuosa, displaying their lovely black and white wing patterns. (Chapter 13)

Of all the multitude of birds nesting on the loma, none is more closely associated with the harsh thorny deserts of the Southwest than verdins, members of the chickadee family. (Chapter 13)

One fairly common bird on Montuosa was the big greenish-olive sparrow which is found as far south as Yucatan and Costa Rica but barely enters the United States, seldom going farther north than the vicinity of Corpus Christi. Repeatedly we heard their cardinal-like *clink* around Montuosa's run. (Chapter 13)

The Mexicans call the vermilion flycatcher *Brasito de fuego*, little coals of fire, and to many people in our Southwest it is known as the firebird. Of the 365 members of the tyrant flycatcher family, this species is by far the brightest. (Chapter 14)

An emaciated horse with hanging head stood by Loma de la Montuosa Chica. On its back were five bronzed cowbirds. Once these were known as red-eyed cowbirds, a fitting name, for the red eyes of the males shine like rubies against black velvet. (Chapter 14)

nally die of starvation.

Though horned lizards are reptiles, they are incorrectly called horned toads by a majority of people. It happens that in the extensive flat flooded Chaco of Argentina there is a genuine horned toad, an amphibian that natives fear, believing it is dangerously poisonous. These genuine horned toads sometimes grow big enough to cover a large saucer. They are cream-colored with a bright pattern of emerald green, black and silver. Their mouths are so wide that it seems the toads must split apart if they open them fully. Over each eye the skin is drawn up into a sharp-pointed horn. They like to burrow in mud until only the horns and eyes stick above the surface, and there they squat in the wet. When alarmed they blow themselves up like balloons, yelp like furious prairie dogs and jump at anybody who digs them out of the mud. Their jaws are strong, and to have one of these genuine horned toads clamp on a finger is more painful than the pinch of a strong mousetrap. Though it is nonsense to believe as the natives do that the bite of these South American horned toads is poisonous, it is wisdom to leave them strictly alone. Knowing there actually are amphibians properly called horned toads should make it easier to remember that our small, flat, harmless southwestern reptiles with horns are lizards.

One day members of the Park staff invited us to join them on a fire-fighting drill. They planned to swing north of Mount Chilicotal, go as far as the mouth of Juniper Canyon and then return by way of Robber's Roost. If we wished, we could climb up the canyon to small but famous Juniper Spring regarded by Glen Evans as the best place in the Big Bend for observing hummingbirds and band-tailed pigeons. Delighted, we inserted ourselves into the already crowded truck with the young men, fire-fighting equipment, water and food, and were off trailing a great plume of dust.

We followed the Boquillas road until we approached

Nugent Mountain. There we branched to the west and were immediately thrown about as the truck jolted and lurched along the rough track. Wild and colorful country unrolled before us. It was a stony, barren land. We could see monstrous crags overhanging mysterious deeps. Overhead the sun pressed down with fierce heat. Now and then a squall of hot wind screeched by, filling our eyes with dust.

The trail roughed. The walls of Juniper Canyon began to close in. Then the truck rocked to a halt and we piled out. It was very hot, though we had reached about four thousand feet. The young men stopped long enough for a drink; but they were on serious business, and we were impressed by their efficiency in handling tools and attacking the problem that had been outlined for them.

We have occassionally seen a forest fire in our western mountains and have the deepest admiration for the preparations that are made to meet fire emergencies when they burst forth, always unexpectedly, and often in inaccessible places. Once in Madera Canyon we watched as fire-fighters hurried on horseback toward a lightning-set fire on the shoulder of Mount Wrightson where a plane soared over the blaze releasing a rosy cloud of borate, while helicopters dropped bundles of tools. Only by thorough preparation are men prepared to meet fire emergencies when they arise.

Leaving the men to their fire drill, we shouldered our cameras and toiled up the trail to Juniper Spring. This water is permanent, and through the centuries innumerable wild creatures have beaten trails to it. Perhaps the aboriginal pre-Basket Makers of arid Texas knew it. Certainly the Apaches did. Unlike most Indian tribes, who regarded mountains as the home of spirits, the source of many dangerous powers, and places to avoid, the Apaches knew the secret places of mountains and used them for refuge. The peaks and the pinnacles were their lookouts.

Spanish explorers may have lingered beside it. Border surveyers of the midnineteenth century located it and camped there. Later renegades and rustlers depended on the never-failing water so precious in this parched land. Cowboys and sheepherders stopped for cool drafts from the spring. But long before the first men drank from the spring, wild animals had etched faint trails to it for others to follow, and birds, leaving no trace of their passage through the air, came season after season to drink and to bathe. Except for the wavering trails and some smoke-blackened stones where campfires had burned, there was little trace of the living procession that had filed to the spring for water through the centuries.

Near the spring the abundant century plant was *Agave scabra,* its thick fleshy leaves edged with teeth and tipped with steel-strong points. For ten to twenty-five years this agave, a member of the amaryllis family, stores up food in its thick leaves until finally it produces the enormous flowering stalk that it is said at times grows as much as a foot in twenty-four hours. There are many side branches on this, and the panicles of yellow flowers are dense and quite flat. Only one flower stalk is ever produced, and by the time the seeds are ripe the mother plant dies. Occasionally offsets grow around the base of the mother plant, and in time one of these may reach maturity and bloom, having in the meantime choked to death all or nearly all other offsets. That dead stalk may stand for a long time after the seeds have ripened. Small woodpeckers chisel holes in them for nests, and these are often taken over later by other hole-nesting birds or by mice.

In one dead stalk Allan saw a well-worn hole. He scratched the stalk with his fingernails. A small face popped up at the opening. It was an elf owl. Wild yellow eyes below whitish eyebrows glared down at us. Of all the owls in North America, this is the smallest. In spite of its name the seven-inch pigmy owl is a full inch longer than the elf.

In hummingbird country, agave flowers attract great numbers of those tiny birds. In May and June, when the Big Bend agaves bloom and the panicles are filled with nectar, insects swarm to them. Then flycatchers perch close by and sally forth to snap up insects going to and from the flowers. Doves visit them, apparently eating both nectar and insects. Hummingbirds come to sip the sweet nectar, for their swift metabolism demands half their weight in sugars each day, and they boldly fight other hummers seeking a share of it.

That day we were too early for an agave bird-show. All the buds were still tightly furled. We heard a loud trilling rather like a distant roar. The strange sound was made by the wings of a broad-tailed hummingbird. It perched on one of the budded agave branches and became still except for a slight turn of its head. Its black gorget then burst into rosy-red fire as the sun touched it.

Perhaps it had just arrived at Juniper Spring from as far away as Guatemala. This species is widely known as the Rocky Mountain hummingbird, and perhaps was journeying to the pines of Grand Teton or the Yellowstone. Its attachment to pines is well known. Once Allan found a nest only thirty inches above the ground on a steep slope of the Uintas. It had been saddled on a fallen pine twig caught in a small shrub.

The quiet form of the broad-tail aroused speculation that it had arrived at the agave after a long journey. Following a torpid night in deep sleep not unlike hibernation, it had wakened, and almost instantly its metabolism had shot up to daytime power. Perhaps at dawn it had boxed its mysterious internal compass, and, its needle pointing to the north, it had taken aim at a dim mountain slope on the far horizon. Flying high, invisible to those in valleys far below, it had cleaved the air toward its distant goal like a bullet, its wings beating between fifty and seventy-five times a second.

Once the broad-tail darted a few feet from its perch, and we saw it catch a pale insect, tiny as a grain of pepper. Another time it went to an oak twig and floated beneath it apparently lapping up minute insects or insect eggs. It then returned to its perch and again became immobile.

Most hummingbirds, which occur only in the Western Hemisphere, are brilliantly irridescent, and their dazzling colors stir poetic thoughts. The Central American Indians called various species by such names as Rays of the Sun, Fiery Topaz, Golden Torch and Little Star. Comte de Buffon wrote that they were the "most elegant in form and brilliant in color" of all birds, and Audubon called them "glittering fragments of the rainbow." Thoreau wrote of the splendid metallic, fiery reflections on the throat, and once commented after watching a hummingbird feed in the midst of a shower that it was "unmindful of the rain," and he marveled that each drop that struck it was not a serious matter.

Scientists have proved to their satisfaction that hummingbirds can store only enough food to enable them to fly nonstop about 7.7 hours, during which, at 50 miles an hour, they could span 385 miles. This is not suffcient to permit a Gulf of Mexico crossing, which would require a passage of more than 500 miles over the shortest distance. Nevertheless people persist in claiming to have seen them take off on such over-water flights. It has been definitely established that one species of hummingbird leaves the coast of Chile and arrives at the Juan Fernandez Islands, the Robinson Crusoe islands where Alexander Selkirk was marooned for four years. There is no possible resting place between the mainland and the islands more than 400 miles distant. Repeatedly animal life, from microscopic plankton to man, exceeds the possible.

The 319 species of hummingbirds are placed in the order *Trochilidae,* which appropriately means "little bird." The Cuban bee hummingbird, about the size of a bumblebee and weighing scarcely as much as a dime, is the smallest. The largest of all is fittingly called giant hummingbird, yet it would take twenty of his fellows to make a pound. Some hummingbirds migrate at least two thousand miles, and one of these small creatures lives above twelve thousand feet in Ecuador. Scientists calculate that a hummingbird behaving in the ordinary manner of his kind if compared to a 170-pound man whose energy output is approximately 3,500 calories daily, would expend 155,000 calories in the same time.

Their feet are tiny, and their toes clasp their perches firmly. They rarely use them for locomotion; but may occasionally sidle along a twig for a short distance. They prefer, instead, to use their powerful wings whose muscles comprise a quarter or more of their weight. Some feed at the very edge of the Andes snowfields and nest as high as fifteen thousand feet above sea level. Tiny 3 ½-inch rufous hummingbirds that migrate through the United States breed as far north as Alaska and the Yukon, and most of them go south of the Rio Grande to spend the winter.

The broad-tailed hummingbird we watched by Juniper Spring was a medium-sized, four-inch bird. It was abruptly galvanized from its lethargy when a black-chinned humming-bird, scarcely larger than a rufous, charged it. Briefly we glimpsed the royal purple band beneath the black gorget of the attacking black-chin, and with a whirring of wings and clashing of bills, the two birds joined in combat. It was quickly broken off, and the broad-tail, as if aware other mountain slopes lay between Juniper Spring and his goal, straightened out, pointed his slender bill toward the north and quickly vanished from sight.

With his binoculars Allan scanned some oaks not far from the spring. Suddenly he stiffened.

"On the dead branch near the top are two band-tailed pigeons—and there are more below those."

The two pigeons stood close together, their black-nailed yellow toes grasping the branch firmly. They were as still as if carved of wood, as were those lower down. They faced us, and their plump gray breasts were lightly tinged with pink.

Their bills were yellow and tipped with black. Yellow eyes were circled with a narrow band of red skin. Even from the underside we could see the wide pale gray band on the square tail for which they were named. Finally one turned enough so we could see the white crescent on the back of the neck and, beneath that, delicate irrdescence so prevalent among the pigeons was pronounced. Though slightly larger than domestic pigeons, band-tails are quite like them in shape.

The terms *dove* and *pigeon* are interchangeable, but the smaller species are usually called doves and the larger ones pigeons. The terms are rather like mushroom and toadstool, which in everyday language are synonymous, but people persist in calling poisonous mushrooms toadstools, and only edible species mushrooms. Of all North American pigeons, the band-tail is the largest species living today.

Until slightly more than half a century ago it took second place to the passenger pigeon in size, but that species is now extinct. The population of passenger pigeons, one of the most spectacular of all time so far as we know, suddenly vanished before the combined actions of man—his ax, which destroyed the pigeon's habitat, and his gun. Biologists believe the passenger pigeon was doomed, and had not man's action sent it to sudden oblivion within the span of a few decades, it would have died out naturally in a few more centuries.

It appears that when a highly specialized species has an extraordinary upsurge in numbers it indicates a racial old age and approaching dissolution. The dinosaurs took the path of population explosion and ended in extinction. There are scientists today who regard the eruption of human population with misgivings, for we too, are highly specialized.

The last reliable record of a wild nesting of passenger pigeons was near Minneapolis in 1895. Even then market hunters were unable to believe their lucrative business in pigeon butchery was ended. Surely there were plenty of pigeons. They had merely moved to another secret nesting place.

When, in the winter of 1911–1912 mast failed in many parts of their winter range but was particularly good in Santa Barbara County, California, band-tailed pigeons concentrated there in tremendous numbers estimated to range from half a million to a million. Immediately a nationwide outburst of pigeon fever flared. Surely the passenger pigeons had moved west and again could be taken as of old.

Hunters converged from distant places upon the hapless flock of band-tails. One market gunner killed 280 pigeons in one tree in a single day. On a Sunday excursion 1,560 were taken to San Luis Obispo alone. The California ornithologist, William Leon Dawson, passed through the area in April after the great pigeon kill and reported papers from so many cartridge boxes tossed about that it reminded him of San Francisco's Chinatown after New Year's celebration. He saw only twenty-eight pigeons.

Fortunately the government had become somewhat wiser after the passenger pigeon disaster and called a five-year halt on all killing of band-tailed pigeons. So they were given a chance to recover from the bloody stupidity and callousness of the greedy killers who invaded Santa Barbara County. Now band-tailed pigeons are regular in many parts of the western mountains from southern British Columbia to Nicaragua. These largest of our pigeons are once more a prized game bird in the Pacific states and as such are taken under strict regulations that insure a strong breeding stock.

Never since the 1911–1912 concentration has there been another comparable to it. The Christmas Bird Counts give a good cross-section of our wintering bird population and the status of each species across the continent. Band-tailed pigeons are erratic in their winter movement, which take them where forage happens to be good. Acorns are a favorite food, and manzanita, elder, madrone and all other wild berries appear to be acceptable, so Bird Counts record them in large or small groups anywhere from Seattle to southern California, depending on available foods. The largest band-tailed pigeon count ever published in the Christmas Bird Count was made at Healdsburg, California, in 1925 when 1,743 were listed. Monterey, California, was not far behind that count in 1954 with a total of 1,167 band-tails, while the same year Santa Barbara, where the infamous slaughter took place, made the second highest count of 699.

Band-tails build a flat flimsy platform for their single large white thin-shelled egg. Apparently once the squab has left, the nest is occasionally used for a second egg. But of all game species in the United States, the reproduction rate of band-tails is the lowest with but one squab a year normal for the species. In contrast to the single egg of the band-tail, a carp lays up to 4 million in a season and a tapeworm 120,000 eggs in a single day. There is a record of two male and six female ring-necked pheasants, a popular gamebird, having been put on Protection Island off the coast of Washington. In six years those eight birds had increased to 1,898.

As we watched the pigeons standing so still and gazed at the shimmering iridescence across their shoulders, marveling that such large birds could remain almost invisible, we hoped they would come down to drink. As if to shatter our hopes the pigeons burst into the air with a loud clatter of wings and, flying rather like hawks, dashed up the canyon where they vanished among the towering crags.

It was very hot, and not far from the spring we noted a diminutive patch of shade and we settled in it, grateful for a light breeze sliding up the canyon. We still had about two hours to spend watching the spring of never-failing water.

"Desert animals usually visit water holes early in the morning and again toward sunset," Allan reminded me. "We may be wasting our time."

The gaunt outline of the savage ridge above us, the bright sun splintering on great jagged rocks and a herd of shining white cloud puffs moving toward the highest peak were proof enough that hours spent here could never be wasted.

There was a shadowy movement beneath a prickly pear. A rabbit hopped quickly to the spring, dipped its face in the water and drank deeply. From nowhere a MacGillivray's warbler: gray-hooded, black-throated and yellow-breasted, jumped about scolding impatiently, and no sooner did the rabbit withdraw than it jumped down, found a shallow place to its liking and surrounded itself with a spray of silver droplets. A Wilson's warbler, burning yellow and with a tiny black velvet cap on its head arrived and chattered excitedly.

A strange sound distracted me.

"It sounds almost like a great horned owl," Allan spoke softly. "Hollow-sounding, too."

It was the cooing of band-tails. They had returned to the oaks, and the males seemed to say *"Whoooo are you?"* The soft, often deep notes went on and on until suddenly we were startled by a loud clap. A male had leaped straight out from his open perch and clapped his wings above his back. Then with swift shallow wing beats he swept around and around in a large circle. A female joined him, and they circled together once and returned to their perch. More band-tails arrived, and their voices rose and fell on the slight breeze. Clapping wings over the back as each pigeon took off was a prelude to each circling flight.

Finally a pigeon dropped down to a rock not far from the spring, and there it stood for some time shifting its weight from one yellow foot to the other and looking nervously about. A second pigeon joined it and a third. At last one moved toward the water and the others followed slowly, warily. Cautiously one came to the water's edge and drank deeply, not like most birds, which fill their bills, then hold them high so the water can run down the throat, but like a mammal, its throat muscles working strongly as it drank. Now other pigeons crowded about, all trying to drink from the same place, and quarrels for position broke out. One wing and sometimes both were lifted and then snapped sharply when a companion came too close. Though doves are the symbol of peace, their reputation is undeserved. They fight savagely when feeding or drinking, though I have never seen one actually injure its fellows. They snap their wings at other pigeons, at other birds, and at squirrels, ground squirrels and even rabbits. At the nest, however, the pair is devoted, and their billing and cooing conforms to their reputation.

Almost subconsciously we heard the horn of a car far away. Allan looked at his watch and leaped to his feet, startling the pigeons into a loud clatter as they darted off up the canyon in a frantic rush. Snatching up our cameras, we hurried down the canyon.

Though the spring has been used by men through many centuries it remains wild. Except for stones blackened by campfires, little trace of their occupation remains. Man can, if he has sufficient respect for the wilderness, enjoy it to a considerable degree while leaving its fragile qualities intact.

Despite our difficulties in finding birds to pose for us, bit by bit Allan had collected films of a variety of wildlife ranging from mule deer bounding as if on pogo sticks down grassy mountain slopes, the brightest red racer I have ever seen, an angry vinegaroon lashing its forward-thrown, sting-tipped tail while surrounding itself with a strong smell of vinegar, and jackrabbits leaping over high cactus. But Allan felt a deep regret that he had come too early for nesting birds. Not once had the blinds been used except by the feeder on the rock.

He decided to make one last trip to Boquillas to see what action he could record of the blackbirds there: redwings, yellow-heads and Brewer's. These fed around the feet of border patrol horses within some old roofless adobe walls that served as a corral. On the walls the blackbirds often gathered to sing and occasionally perform some of their spring displays, once they had their fill of grain.

So down the hot road we went, with the sun beating the smell of dust from the parched desert. The rocks collected the fiery rays and cast them back at us like a blast. Across parched Tornillo Creek, once again bedded with dust and boulders, past the Hot Springs turnoff and around the great buttress from which Dead Man's Curve had been etched and on toward the band of green mesquite that bordered the Rio Grande we went. The blackbirds were gathered as usual in a noisy crowd, and among them Allan pointed out several with white patches. Albinistic patches are not rare in birds, and we have seen several completely white birds: a tree swallow, a robin and several white English sparrows. Once we saw a white Swainson's hawk and another time a turkey vulture that was not white but very pale silver-gray all over. Of all the white birds we have seen, the most beautiful was a red-wing Allan discovered in a large flock in the Duda cow pens in Florida. The red-wing was entirely white except for his flaming red shoulder patches. Near Lake Okeechobee I was once startled to see what I believed was a magpie standing on a fence post. Allan, less impulsive, took a good look at the bird. It was a male boat-tailed grackle with albinistic patches arranged in the characteristic pattern of white on a magpie. Had Allan not insisted that I check each feature of the bird I would probably be convinced to this day that I saw an out-of-range magpie from the West.

Allan made some shots of a few of the oddly marked red-wings, including one with a pinkish-white helmet of head feathers; then stopped when a couple of male Scott's orioles flew by. Perhaps a group of migrants had arrived during the night and were feeding and resting in the mesquites and desert willows by the river.

We soon plunged into the breathless, steaming thicket of bright green. It was alive with darting colors. Black-headed grosbeaks, male summer tanagers, one black phoebe and several plain flycatchers moved restlessly about. Yellow warblers and a Nashville flitted nervously. We caught sight of several Scott's orioles glittering yellow and black under the torrid sun. A male western tanager, his red head glowing like a hot coal, his yellow body shimmering like satin while the high contrast of black on its wings and tail startled me. It was the most colorful bird I saw in all the Big Bend country.

Just then a dragonfly, big as an eastern aeshnid, with a red-velvet body and large golden-brown spots in its transparent wings, diverted my attention. It was the most splendid dragonfly I had ever seen. I followed it as it moved erratically through the sweltering green tangle until it poised for a moment, hovering in place like a heliocopter making a drop, like a sparrow hawk poised above a mouse. Beneath the dazzling dragonfly was a small gray hanging basket. Sitting in it and regarding me with white-ringed dark eyes was a small pale-gray bird. It was a Bell's vireo. The red dragonfly had led me to the first nest we found in the Big Bend. It was not five feet above the ground. Allan joined me, and as we stared, surprised and delighted, we heard a husky song repeated again and again, always coming closer. The second vireo was approaching us. Finally it stood above us singing an unmusical *cheedle cheedle chee, cheedle cheedle churr.*

Neither vireo was concerned by our presence. The intense light filtering through the delicate green tangle was ample for color photography. Though the humidity was high in that green tangle of plants struggling to find and hold a place close to the life-giving Rio Grande and the heat pressed down, a palpable weight, we settled happily on folding stools and exposed much film on the vireos.

Allan's camera was grinding away when the vireo sheltering four small white eggs speckled with fine brown dots flew off and its mate hopped down to the rim of the nest. It inspected the nest carefully, turned the eggs, swung around to stare at the camera and then settled over the eggs. It shifted about until it was comfortable and then became immobile, one black eye staring quietly, fixedly, at the whirring camera.

10

The Strange Forest of Dagger Flat

DAY BY DAY the clouds gathered deeper and darker around the Chisos peaks. Robert Gibbs warned us to keep an eye on them while we photographed.

"If you see a heavy shower falling on the summit, stop work immediately and hurry toward the Basin," he urged.

One day we were photographing blackbirds perched around the corral at Boquillas when the border patrolman paused in grooming the horses and stared toward the mountains.

"That's a shower that may bring trouble," he remarked.

Within minutes we were in our car and racing toward the Basin. We swooped across Tornillo Creek only seconds ahead of an onrushing flood that cut off Boquillas from the rest of the world. Ours was the last car to cross the creek for two days!

That evening we walked to the little store in the concession area in the Basin for stamps and coffee. The narrow space was bursting with a crowd of about eight people. All were listening to some young members of the Park staff. They were grousing about the flood, a desert flood of all things, and coming as it had on Saturday night, they regarded it as a personal affront. They had planned an evening in

189

Marathon (population 741) at the movies, and there was a rumor that a dance would follow the showing of the film.

Rain was still falling when the young men passed Panther Junction, but they had continued merrily on their way. They heard the singular rumble of Tornillo Creek long before they reached the crossing of the Marathon road, but never having experienced a desert flood, they only joked about what might happen to their car in midstream. Midstream was mostly mythical as far as they were concerned, for they knew bone-dry Tornillo Creek very well. Even when they saw that water rose to a dangerous level around the roadside gauge they were optimistic. They simply did not believe in an impassable water barrier at Tornillo Creek. One took off his shoes, rolled up his pants and facetiously announced he was going to hike to Marathon, a mere fifty or sixty miles away.

His companions cheered him on as he waded in. Laughter was suddenly choked when he lost his footing in the powerful torrent. Only a strongly-rooted creosote bush, which he was able to seize, enabled him to struggle back to safety, bruised and choking from swallowed water. For a moment he had been face to face with death. For the first time he and his companions grasped the reality of danger inherent in desert floods, a danger respected by people accustomed to these periodic outbursts of violence.

Now safely back in the Basin store, with the resilience of youth they were already forgetting their disappointment over shattered plans for the evening and instead, pride and a little boasting was embellishing the incident at Tornillo Creek.

Next morning we went to look at the swollen monster snaking its way from the heights in what had been for many long months simply a dry depression angling off the mountain and across the flat. Then Tornillo Creek had been lined with sand and dotted with water-worn rocks. From a distance it had looked rather like the shed skin of a large snake. Certainly it had been as desiccated, wrung as dry of moisture, as such a sloughed skin. Now plunging water was hurtling down with stunning force that shook the air above it and beneath the turgid surface we heard rocks roll, clash and grind against one another as they were shoved downstream.

We swung about and turned toward the Maverick gate. From a high overlook we could see almost to the Rio Grande. In the distance broad expanses of water changed from silver to lead and back again with the intermittent sun and cloud. Both exits from the Rio Grande were locked. Though surrounded by desert, we were imprisoned by water.

Not only were stream beds distended by torrents gathered from the high peaks, but on the desert where a whole year's rainfall may total a meager ten inches, some of that annual rain was now turning dusty flats into mud and spreading the unpaved roads with a slippery paste. This would have been suitable for molding adobe bricks, but was decidedly unpleasant as a walking or driving surface.

The storm was most impressive when we were in our adobe cottage directly under Casa Grande. The clouds clung to the lofty peaks and traveled in an orbit around them. At intervals in its revolution of the peaks it attacked savagely. This was our first experience with the violence so characteristic of storms in western mountains. At times forked lightning clawed at the peaks with crooked, skeleton fingers and thunder crashed, rolled and bumped across the clouds, then reverberated through the canyons. Winds howled off the crags in vertical blasts carrying rain on their backs. We would hear a gust launch itself from Casa Grande and listen to the ominous cacophony of mingled shrieks as it brawled down the precipice, passed with a shout and then moaned on down the slope below us, finally dying away in the distance like the fading roar of a departing rocket. If we ventured out of our doors when such a gust was advancing toward us, it smote us with a blow that threatened to hurl us to our knees.

Rains in desert country, even when born high in mountain

crags, are soon ended. By morning the wind was still and by noon the clouds had vanished except for a drifting unstable wreath clinging about Casa Grande. The brightening sun flung a rainbow across that wreath so low we almost believed we could touch it with our fingertips if we stretched just a little higher on our toes. Hour after hour the luminous band hung suspended before the rugged lichen-encrusted promontory. Slowly, oh so slowly, as the sun lapsed westward the rainbow was lifted higher and higher by the oblique rays. As sunset approached, the rainbow's softly glowing colors soared above the summit of Casa Grande and framed it perfectly within the arch. The long-lasting arch turned out to be an auspicious portent. True to the ancient belief that a rainbow presages fine weather, this one was followed by sunny skies.

Swiftly now the torrents drained from the arroyos, and even Tornillo Creek was dry again. Between the stones in its bed, drying mud cracked into irregular blocks, and the topmost layer of each curled at its edges and finally disintegrated into powdery dust. Dust-devils resumed their whirling march across the flats.

Suddenly the desert burst into bloom. Where we had rejoiced at the sight of a single ocotillo waving its flame-tipped wand, now thousands blazed over the desert and tossed in the wind. Their formerly brown thorny stems were densely furred with small green leaves. Instead of a cactus flower here and another there, the entire desert was splashed with their brilliant flowers: yellow, salmon and orange and all hues of pink, cerise and red.

Cottontails stood on their hind legs with their front paws turned down and nibbled the bright petals. Jackrabbits, too, ate the gay petals, feasting on those too high for the cottontails to reach. Curious about this food which the rabbits were eating with evident enjoyment, I tasted a petal.

"Much like lettuce," I thought. "But the juice is slippery

on the tongue—rather like okra juice but not so abundant or thick."

Indian paintbrush and primroses mingled with the cactus. The creosote bushes were hung with small yellow disks. The flower stems of lechuguilla no longer looked like skinny stalks of asparagus; each bore on top a panicle of creamy flowers. We hurried from one display of blossoms to another, and always the finest were ahead of us and they pulled us on and on under the hot sun. There was no great carpet of a single species like those which have made the flower displays of the Mohave Desert famous. There when rain and temperature cooperate, carpets of gold poppies, or lupine, or coreopsis may extend unbroken for miles as the seeds of annuals awaken and with magical speed produce their flowers. In the Big Bend it was as though a giant had thrown handfuls of bright spangles that scattered, and each came to rest apart from its neighbors. Though less spectacular than a solid blanket of flowers, the Big Bend desert was more satisfying. Of abundance there was plenty, yet each plant remained an individual to be studied and enjoyed as the unique growth it was.

Old-timers on the park staff said the desert flowers were the finest they had ever seen. A ranger granted the glory of the desert generally, but said he had just returned from Dagger Flat and there the forest had put forth the greatest show in seventeen years. Displays like it seldom came more than once in a couple of decades.

Allan carefully noted the directions to Dagger Flat, for in those days only an indistinct, unmarked track and an obscure one, led to it. Rarely did anybody except a ranger on duty visit it. As Allan put away his notebook, the ranger tipped his head toward the peaks. Clouds were marshaling their forces above them once more.

"If you see rain falling on the mountains, leave Dagger

Flat at once," the ranger urged, already regretting his generous wish to have us see the beauty of the forest.

Having watched Tornillo Creek in full rage, we were prepared to respect the ranger. We had acquired some hard-earned knowledge of desert and mountain weather, and though that knowledge was still very limited, we already had a healthy regard for the gigantic force of heavy rains and cloudbursts in such places. We would take no chances, but on that sunny morning in mid-April we set off filled with joyous anticipation and confident that delightful adventures lay ahead.

So completely had the desert returned to its accustomed arid condition that again we towed a great billowing cloud of dust behind us. We crossed Tornillo Creek, where only the cracked earth remembered the recent flood, and continued northward toward Persimmon Gap until we came to a faint track angling eastward toward the Dead Horse Mountains. Here we left the unpaved road for a mere trail; and as we progressed we gave close attention to each small landmark, for equally dim vestiges of wheel marks ambled aimlessly away from the one we followed. In some places there was a veritable labyrinth of tangled tracks to bewilder us and make us unsure that we followed the correct one. We stopped to examine them on foot before we proceeded.

All around us was a great stillness. Even the restless wind was quiet. It was so silent our ears consciously reached farther and farther in search of sounds. Gradually tight muscles and nerves relaxed and we were bathed in a unique peace. As the number of people multiply, so do their machines until noise has become an ever-present condition of life. Rattling, throbbing, squeaking, buzzing, roaring and screaming machines and voices batter us day and night. Now along the track we followed were none of the everyday racket and man-made sights that we have come to accept until our senses are so blunted we are only unconsciously aware of them. Yet when those corroding elements that depreciate the quality of environment are absent, how swiftly the body and mind respond with an upsurge of well-being, of suddenly intensified delight in everything around us. Except for the machine transporting us, the trappings of the machine age were left behind. When Allan switched off the motor only the light sounds of nature reached us. Except for ourselves there was no evidence of man. Not even the contrail of a distant jet profaned the sunny sky. So it happened that we came, on a morning of rare tranquility, to one of the strangest forests anywhere in all this diversified world, the yucca forest of Dagger Flat.

Ask a hundred people how a forest looks to them and you will receive a hundred answers. The experience of each of us is unmatched, and the most profound impressions of a lifetime are as endlessly varied. One, lucky enough to have had a forest playground as a child, will see it as a place where games and imaginative adventures are woven around tall trunks and spreading branches. Another will see again his first giant sequoias, the oldest of living things with their feet in the snow and their crowns in the clouds and between, a drifting curtain of snowflakes that blurred his view of them. To Joseph Conrad it could have been a tangled, almost impenetrable mangrove forest with turgid water lapping sluggishly across its floor and to Humboldt a tropical rain forest where towering smooth-barked oaks and locusts bore on their lofty branches dense masses of orchids with long sprays of many-colored flowers. To some a forest would be an aromatic conifer forest of the north, where footfalls are muffled by deep mats of fallen needles and spongy moss. But whatever the kind of forest, or wherever that forest may lie, from the humid tropics to the chill north, most people remember the canopy of the forest top, a canopy of branches and leaves that dims the sun. Moreover, in all forests there is, year in and year out, a change of leaves, a replacement of those small liv-

ing factories that use sunlight and the chemicals of the air and
the earth to manufacture food for the trees. The leaves may
assume bright colors and then be cast away quickly by some
deciduous trees in the temperate zone. The process may be
protracted, as in many conifers that shed their leaves a few at
a time as new ones grow, so they are never bare. Some tropical trees retain their leaves until the flowers are well developed and then drop them suddenly, transforming themselves
almost overnight from mounds of green to gigantic bouquets
of flowers. Still other trees not only shed their leaves but
many twigs at the same time.

Now we looked at a forest some ten miles square, but its
outriders spread off in all directions as far as the eye could
see. These were more and more widely spaced as they became
distant from the forest itself, and finally they stood on the
shoulders of distant ridges like sentinels at attention, guarding the ramparts of the mountains. Each was crowned with a
tall cluster of white blossoms, many more than five feet high.
So it was that the tips of the flower stalks even on the shortest
yuccas were held high above our heads. The incredible
masses of blossoms released a delicate perfume making the air
redolent with a seductive scent.

These Giant Daggers, (*Yucca carnerosana*) grow nowhere
else in the United States, though some scattered colonies of a
large yucca puzzle botanists, who may finally decide they too
are *carnerosana*. This species reaches a height of at least
thirty feet, and as its name indicates, it is the giant among
American yuccas. Not from their height alone, but also because they have woody stems they are truly called trees.

In a state of delirious excitement we wandered through the
forest. Its great extent, the huge clusters of flowers and the
purity of the stand of yuccas were overwhelming. Though
other plants grew among the yucca trees they were so dom-
inated both by the size and number of the yuccas as to be
inconspicuous. Everywhere we looked, the crowning glory of

the daggers, their panicles of blossoms, went on and on like a white sea with sharply crested waves.

Yuccas belong to the lily family and the flowers have three sepals nearly equal in size and whiteness to the three petals. Both sepals and petals are glossy white faintly touched with cream on the outside. Inside, the petals have a thick, almost velvety texture. In the center rises a tall barrel-shaped pistil of creamy white. Furry stamens fold close around it, but the anthers, tipped with a spot of clear yellow, bend away from it. Perhaps this position of the anthers evolved to prevent self-fertilization.

I wondered how many flowers there actually were on a single giant dagger. Choosing a short one bearing a lovely panicle, I bent it down and began a systematic count. The panicle had forty-three branches. On each the flowers nearest the main stem were widest open, while those on the top were sometimes tightly folded, still-sleeping buds. Beginning with the lowest branch of the panicle I counted fifty-six flowers. Was this possible? I counted again. Fifty-six. I caught the next branch of the cluster. This one bore sixty-two flowers. Finally I came to the conclusion that my single giant dagger held at least fifteen hundred and perhaps as many as two thousand blossoms. To contemplate the number of flowers in that forest made me dizzzy. Their numbers were truly astronomical. Other forest trees, a tulip tree for instance, may have as many or even more blossoms, but they are scattered widely over a large surface instead of being gathered in one dramatic cluster borne aloft on the very summit of the tree.

Surfeited with the beauty and fragrance of the flowers, we turned from them really to look at the trees. Here was a forest that belied its name. It supported no shady canopy. It had no interlacing boughs and leaves to screen the sun and light from the earth beneath. Nor was there any evidence that these trees shed their leaves as other trees do. Apparently each kept every one of the leaves it produced throughout its entire life span. As a miser hordes his gold, the yuccas kept their leaves for life. Instead of falling to earth and disintegrating into leaf mold when its time of food production had ended, each leaf merely turned its pointed tip toward the ground and clung tightly against the trunk. There it and all the other old leaves formed a dense thatch around the trunk. They insulated it from the severe desert heat. During ephemeral desert rains, they trapped moisture to help the tree survive long periods of drought. Most of the old leaves had bleached to soft gray, but a circlet of those most recently added to the thatch were still yellow-brown.

The dark green, rather narrow leaves fanned out in a large bristling ball, a dense pompon, that made a theatrical holder for the flowers. Each leaf, as long as a fencing foil, terminated in a needle-sharp, steel-strong tip. For centuries desert people have seized a yucca leaf when bitten by a poisonous snake and driven the sharp tip repeatedly into the flesh around the bite until it was completely enclosed within the yucca punctures. It was believed a substance exuded by the yucca counteracted to some extent the venom injected by the snake. Probably this treatment was useful chiefly because it was a readily available tool, and punctures quickly made induced prolific bleeding that carried away part of the venom.

To most of us a forest is a source of lumber and firewood, of nuts and sweet sap that can be reduced to syrup and a place where birds nest and turkeys, doves, deer and bear grow fat in summer. It is a place for recreation and is vital to the future of our dwindling fresh water. It not only traps rain and snow and slows runoff so topsoil remains in place, but it helps some of the precious water to seep into our steadily lowering water table.

The strange yucca forest does not fit within this conventional picture of a forest. The yuccas may send down roots for forty feet or more, a depth considerably greater than the height of the very tallest individual, in their search for life-giving moisture. True, they may help to slow the runoff and evaporation after one of the infrequent desert rains, but they contribute little to the water economy of man. Nevertheless, in the lives of the desert Indians, the yucca held an important place. In early spring, when the flower stalks were still tender and juicy, they were boiled and eaten with relish. Little Indian boys experienced a less pleasant use of the yucca when they reached the age of our primary school boys. Then in their first initiation into the world of men they were beaten with whips made of yucca until they cried. In contrast, Indian women made use of yucca fibers to construct their jewelry. They strung bits of shell and pretty stones: turquoise, jasper and bright pebbles, on yucca fibers and hung them around their necks or made ear dangles of them. But the women had little time for such frivolity, and usually when they gathered yucca leaves, they softened them until the fibers could be removed from the flesh. These fibers were woven into cloth and used for sewing the cloth into garments. Ropes, too, were made of yucca fibers, which were rolled into thick strands and pulled as the rolling continued until the desired thickness and length were achieved. Baskets for carrying and storing were woven of yucca leaves. Sometimes the trunks of yuccas were used in building houses by the Big Bend Indians. The walls were made of stone; and then yuccas trunks were laid across the wall tops, though the lighter, more easily handled ocotillo wands were preferred. Over the yucca foundation, stones were laid and covered with mud, forming a weatherproof roof.

Our survey of the forest was broken when a curve-billed thrasher, intent on some business of its own, flew straight toward us, swerved when it saw us, and, taking the first available perch, clutched a yucca leaf. It held a large collection of soft caterpillars in its long curved bill, and it inspected us with bright pale orange eyes. About the size of a brown thrasher, it was as softly colored as the desert floor and had

only the faintest of spots on its breast. Having finished inspecting us, the thrasher continued on its way, and in a couple of minutes Allan had followed it to its nest.

This was a bulky mass of rather thick twigs tucked into the
daggers of a yucca. Three fully fledged young thrashers so big
they almost spilled out of the nest, were still dark-eyed but
alert and ready to explode away. Both adults began to scold
but not at us. Among the brown daggers hanging near the
ground coiled a brilliant red snake, a red racer. Until that
moment I had thought yellow-bellied green snakes the most
beautiful of American snakes, more beautiful than the brilliantly colored coral snakes, which many consider the epi-
tome of snake beauty. The red racer, slightly more than four
feet long and quite slim, regarded us with beady black
eyes.

"I want to photograph that snake and the thrashers, too,
but if I try to work on the snake, those young thrashers will
fly."

Allan was in the frustrated state common among wildlife
photographers when two desirable subjects appear at once
and a decision must be made between them. This time the
problem was solved by the adult thrashers. They dived at the
racer so furiously that it glided away. Allan went in hot pursuit. The young thrashers shifted restlessly but did not jump
from the nest.

In another moment Allan shouted, "Come quickly and
help me."

He put the lively red racer into my hands, cautioned me
not to let it escape, rescued his hat, which had been speared
and pulled from his head by a dagger, and dashed off for his
camera equipment. Soon he was back, breathing hard and
with perspiration streaming down his face. He had brought
my equipment as well as his own.

Having a genuine respect for the speed capability of the
racer, Allan used an old trick. Cuddling the snake in his

hands until it quieted down in a tight ball, he put it on the ground and put his hat over it before withdrawing his hand. Once everything was ready he called, "Now!" and I snatched the hat away. Long enough for the viewer to have a good look at the snake it remained quiet, then it flowed into motion and sinuously undulated over the bare ground to a small mesquite, which it climbed swiftly, its bright red form in the equally bright green leaves making us think of traditional Christmas colors. Then unhesitatingly it continued to the flattened stems of a prickly pear that bristled with clumps of fine spines. Around the yellow flowers it went, then slithered toward the ground and we lost it, but Allan had caught all the action in a beautiful sequence for his film.

Cautiously Allan now set up near the thrasher nest while the young birds, which already looked very much like their parents, though their breast spots were more distinct and they still had whitish baby skin at the gape of their long, sickle-shaped bills, watched him suspiciously. Unlike their parents they had dark eyes.

To me the change in the eye color found in many species of birds is far more magical than the change to breeding plumage in spring. The feathers are molted and replaced by new ones, or in some species (the indigo bunting for instance) the tips of the new feathers wear off to reveal the beauty of nuptial apparel. All birds, however, keep the same eyes throughout their lives, yet the colors in certain species undergo a startling change between the nest and maturity. The dark eyes of young brown pelicans become almost white by the time the birds are mature, and those of eared grebes turn as red as a stoplight. The majority of passerine birds have unremarkable dark eyes throughout their lives. Those of the Mexican junco, however, change from black to bright red-orange; white-eyed vireos' turn white; and those of the curve-billed thrasher pale yellow.

Leaving Allan at work on the thrashers, I slung my tripod

with the camera fixed in place over my shoulder and wandered first one way and then another through the forest. Rounding a dense clump of daggers, the tripod legs swung sharply against a snowy cluster of dagger flowers that hung half-open like bells. Instantly a cloud of white burst away. Dismay at my carelessness swept through me. It was a desecration to shake flowers from that exquisite spray. But what magic was this? The snowy petals were drifting in the still air. They were drifting upward, dancing lightly, and one after another they vanished into blossoms still half-closed. I had disturbed a party of sleeping yucca moths.

The strangely intertwined lives of creatures on this earth are many and varied, but none is stranger than that of the yucca and the yucca moth. The story of their relationship has been told over and over again and will be repeated as long as there are yuccas and people who keep their sense of wonder for the world around them. There are many species of yucca and many races of yucca moth, yet all follow the same complicated patterns of life. Since they also look almost alike, their races are important chiefly to scientists.

The dependency of yucca and yucca moth upon each other began so many aeons ago that the steps leading to the mysterious relationship will never be known. We can only marvel at the association between them, and their complicated annual development as each keeps pace with the other until on a single night of the year both flower and moth reach a transient maturity, a maturity that lasts but a few hours and fades with the coming of dawn. During the brief hours when flower and moth arrive at the moment of sexual perfection, through a series of complicated acts the fertilization of the yucca flower is accomplished. Its seeds are stirred to growth, and the yucca moth provides a nursery and food for her offspring.

The mouth of the little yucca moth has become as specialized as the bill of a hummingbird or a crossbill or a flamingo.

She feeds exclusively on nectar of the yucca flowers and as she feeds she uses long tentacles on her first maxillae to collect a large ball of pollen. When the ball is larger than her head, she flies to another yucca flower that has opened its petals for its single night of utter perfection. There she pushes the ball of pollen against the stigma and then pushes and rubs it with her head until a firm contact is made and the pollen can send its vital force down the style into the ovary and stir the seeds to life and growth.

Then the yucca moth moves down the pistil and inserts her ovipositor into the style and lays some eggs. I have read many accounts that say she lays several eggs: though I have checked many a yucca seed pod since that day in Dagger Flat I have never found more than three but usually only one or two. The moth, however, may fertilize and deposit eggs in more than a single flower.

In all the world no similar dependency between insect and plant is known. To be sure, flowers have evolved endlessly complicated methods for compelling insects to distribute their pollen. Usually this is insured by the position of the nectar, which can only be obtained after brushing against the pollen, but there are exceptions to this method. In Australia there are four species of *Cryptostylis* orchids that all resemble stylized females of a species of *Ichneumon* wasps. Though humans cannot detect any odor from the orchid, it must emanate a scent irresistible to the male wasps, which seek to mate with it rather than with the female wasps. This is an oddly one-sided relationship; for the orchid is fertilized, while the wasp ignores any nectar that may be present and gains nothing except unproductive physical gratification.

Only by yucca moths is pollen deliberately gathered from one perfect yucca blossom, transported to another freshly opened flower and there as if by premeditation forced into close contact with the pistil's stigma. The yucca flowers are pollinated in no other way, and the plant and the yucca moth have become mutually dependent.

Yucca seed pods look rather like those of iris. When young and green the outer covering is thick and spongy. Cut across the pod and you will see three petal-like divisions. Inside each of the three sections grow two rows of seeds separated by a membrane that thickens with age. Each row contains about fifty seeds; thus there are approximately 300 in a pod. Each seed is fastened to the shell by a tiny white "stem," and when the section is carefully opened the long way, it looks like black gums holding a row of white teeth. It is in these fleshy pods that the young yucca moth larvae hatch. They are whitish and have a pinkish-brown head. Safe within the thick walls they thrive and grow to full size on a diet of yucca seeds. They require from thirty to fifty seeds during their growing stage. Even if three larvae inhabit a single pod and eat fifty seeds each, half the seeds remain. Before the pod has matured and dried into a thin husk as tough as the shell of a Brazil nut, the full-grown larvae burrow holes in it, emerge for the first time into the open and, spinning silken threads, descend to the ground, form cocoons and lapse into a marvelous sleep that lasts for many months.

This sleep is scarcely suspended animation, for an amazing change is taking place in the creature cradled in the mummy-like cocoon. Its six legs grow longer and thinner, its several pairs of prolegs vanish, its mouthparts change from chewing to sucking organs useful only for drinking nectar, and those long tentacles mentioned before appear. Antennae shaped like delicate miniature ferns stand above the formerly shiny bald head. Wings are formed. Finally one spring day the yucca moth begins to stir. It opens the cocoon at one end and its cellophanelike covering splits. Its tightly folded parts slowly expand as the legs cling firmly to the stem of a small plant while the antennae dilate. The damp crumpled wings unfold and stretch, and blood courses through them as they are gently flexed and vibrated. In less than an hour the unattractive larva of last summer, the bundlelike pupa of the cold winter, is transformed into a fairylike creature of great beauty. The scales shingling the white wings are as perfect as snowflakes falling on a windless day.

The layman has endless cause to be grateful to scientists who patiently unravel the fantastic habits and lives of small creatures. Sometimes scientists go beyond facts, and with poetic imaginations, give names that tell stories of the creatures they study. Now the name of the yucca moth has been changed to *Tegeticula yuccasella*, but those who first learned the story of the yucca moth called it *Pronuba*. I deeply regret the elimination of that name, which so truly told of the habits of the yucca moth. In ancient Rome, Juno, consort of Jupiter, served many functions, and as Juno Pronuba she was goddess of marriage. At each Roman marriage a matron called Pronuba represented Juno and presided over the wedding. What a classical and appropriate name Pronuba was for the yucca moth. Not only does she fertilize several yucca flowers, but she also insures the perpetuation of her own race.

Those were the moths I had disturbed, highly specialized moths resting in flowers and waiting for night to fall when a new crop of blossoms would open fully for the first time. Because of their great delicacy, the wings of moths and butterflies quickly become tattered and shabby. All the moths in this group must have been newly emerged from their long months tightly wrapped in a chrysalis within a silken cocoon, for their wings were as perfect as the freshest yucca petal. Too surprised to observe carefully, I could not find a single moth once they vanished into new flowery bedrooms. So beautifully did they harmonize with the yucca flowers above my head that they became invisible as soon as they came to rest within them.

A shadow cut off the sunshine. A cloud was drifting by. Looking toward the Chisos I saw a big dark cloud standing on a column of rain. The whole range was in its shadow.

Forgotten now was my blithely contented circuitous ramble through the strange forest where each great cluster of snowy flowers deflected my passage. Snatching up my camera equipment, I paused for an instant to take bearings, to decide on the approximate location of the car and then dashed off on the most direct course toward it. Suddenly, as though I had hit an invisible wall, I was halted in midflight. Massive yucca bouquets lay at my feet. But no, they were reflected by the glassy surface of desert-colored water in a small artificial pond, a relic of the days before the Park was established and cattle still grazed the vanishing grasses of the flat. My vision of flowers was abruptly shattered as desert-colored frogs, squeaking with surprise, leaped from the steep bank into the water where each became the bull's-eye of a circle that quivered and collided with other circles in ever-expanding rings.

I stared, incredulous, for surely the desert was too inhospitable for these delicate amphibians, which have never truly become land animals. With rare exceptions, frogs today continue to lay their eggs without shells in still water as their ancestors did ten million years ago. Their tadpoles emerge into the water where they breathe oxygen through gills, and only when they develop legs do they also develop lungs. Even then they only gulp air instead of using an expanding thorax as we do. For every frog we encounter in a meadow or in the woods we see a hundred sticking their noses above the surface of a pond or poised beside the water ready to leap into it.

With smooth, moist, thin skin, frogs must find arid country a truly hostile environment. Yet here was a large congregation of frogs in the midst of the yucca forest. Far more than toads, frogs appear to cling to the element from which they first ventured as air-breathing animals so many millions of years ago.

We had been told there was no permanent water in the Big

Bend except in the Rio Grande and a few springs high in the mountains. Therefore the pond lying at my feet would soon give up its water to the thirsty air. What then would happen to these frogs? Would they burrow into the mud beneath the pond while it was still soft and then sleep through the dry months ahead? But how had they found their way across endless miles of desert country in the first place? I was so intent upon the frog ballet as the tawny amphibians with golden eyes leaped from the bank and back again that I jumped when Allan joined me and said, "Well what do you know! Frogs in the desert."

"What kind are they," I asked him, pleased that he, too, had found the frogs.

"They look rather like *Ranidae*," he said.

"*Ranidae?*"

"Leopard frogs," he elaborated. "But I can't see any spots, and who ever heard of a leopard frog without spots?"

We studied the frogs carefully. Not a spot could we see on those frogs that looked the color of the desert itself. But we have had enough experience to know that color can be every bit as deceptive as size when one is in the open on a brilliant day. Most of us have seen silvery crows and even sky-blue cowbirds until a change of position erased the unnatural hues. So we studied the frogs with questioning eyes. Finally Allan said, "I'll get that glass jar with the holes punched in the top and catch one of these to take back to headquarters for identification."

I went along, and as I put away my camera and was reaching under the picnic basket for the glass specimen jar I heard a loud groan.

"Flat tire," Allan grumbled. "Front left wheel. Flat as a flounder."

Dropping the jar I went around the car to give what encouragement and moral support I could to him in this depressing situation. Allan was already muttering about the miles between Dagger Flat and the basin. And could the tire be repaired at the basin service station? Those miles back to Marathon suddenly began to stretch and stretch.

It really did not take long to replace the wheel, and soon Allan kicked the hub cap into place, lifted the flat into the back of the station wagon, tossed the jack on top of it and wiped his hands. He reached for the specimen jar when a thunder bolt shook the air and rumbled away toward the Dead Horse Mountains. The Chisos had vanished behind a curtain of gray rain. With one accord we leaped into the car, slammed the doors and turned away from Dagger Flat.

It happened that the rain was not heavy enough to renew the floods of a few days ago. We crossed the arroyos and Tornillo Creek without dampening a tire. But time was running out, and we could not return to Dagger Flat. The road to that strange forest is now surfaced. A couple of times since we have returned in April, but never again have we seen that lovely forest of Dagger Flat repeat the glorious bloom of our first visit, nor have we seen a single desert-colored frog in one of the ephemeral ponds. They remain for us one of the mysteries of the strange forest of Dagger Flat.

11

On a High Plateau

WEST OF ALPINE we climbed almost a mile above sea level to the summit of Paisano Pass. A roadrunner, as if it knew the Spaniards had named the pass for it, stood on a rock, switched its tail and glared balefully at us. Below us stretched a barren, austere plateau about fifty miles long and rimmed by distant mountains. The flat treeless expanse with the sharp peaks of the Davis Mountains aloof on the far horizon to our right and the tumbled mass of the Cuesto Del Burro Mountains so far away they were crisp shadows against the southwestern sky only served to emphasize the monotonous flat, fading unchanged into the distance. Vultures sketched great lazy circles against the sky, and water mirages like splashes of silver shimmered enticingly and vanished, phantoms of the eyes and the heat.

It is true that the eye sees a level monotony that is apparent rather than actual. As any child knows, when you stand on a high bluff above the ocean, the infinitely distant horizon is obscured by sea mist. But when you run down the bluff and stand with your toes in the lacy fringe of the tide, the horizon has advanced toward you until the crisp blue sky meets the tumbling waves less than three miles away. So when you look across endless miles of seemingly featureless level plains, the entire land not only must be tilted (though this is imperceptible to the eye), but deceptive folds deep enough to screen herds of cattle lie there. Even the town of Marfa was concealed from us until suddenly we were upon it. In spite of a railroad, fences, Marfa, cattle and an abandoned air station, the hand of man was inconspicuous in the vastness of the plain.

Cold lingers far beyond the calendar end of winter on this high pleateau. Spring is an ephemeral greening of the dun-colored earth that lasts but a few days following some unpredictable rain. Then intense summer heat sears the transient growth, and all is again pale dull yellow. For a short time in June dark yuccas sprinkled across the pleateau hold aloft towering white candelabras of flowers. Miscalculate the time they will bloom any spring and you will miss the flowers and see only furled buds or stalks holding already swelling seed pods.

One cold day in early April when we sped along the highway, a clear whistle pierced the leaden sky. We stopped in the icy wind to listen. Wild and free and beautiful, the song rose and fell, infinitely mellow and sweet. It was the song of an upland plover. I had a sudden vision of a sunny May morning on the Hempstead Plains of New York and of Allan in a blind beside a nest set among bird's foot violets. Four large greenish eggs darkly speckled with brown lay with their points touching. As I watched through binoculars, I heard that same liquid melody like a distant gale, and two slender grayish birds with narrow pointed wings set and slightly cupped plummeted to earth behind the nest. For a while they stood motionless with their heads held high as they studied the blind. Then one lowered its head, ran toward the nest, stood for a moment among the violets, teetered nervously and settled on its eggs.

Now those Hempstead Plains are lost, buried beneath housing develpments and industrial plants. The vast array of

violets is gone, and few remember their former flowery profusion. The upland plovers have vanished. It had been a long
time since I heard their haunting cry.

Once these Bartramian sandpipers with ploverlike habits
and name were abundant birds of open treeless country all
across our northern states and central Canada almost to the
sub-Arctic. Overshooting brought them to the very brink of
extinction. Though hunting pressures have been lifted in
North America, our agricultural and land-use methods coupled with continued shooting on the pampas of Patagonia
may still spell the end of this beautiful, mysterious bird that
spans the hemisphere on its migrations, traveling almost to
the windy tip of South America to spend our winter. Now on
its swift seven-thousand-mile flight from the bleak pampas of
Argentina, the upland plover had looked down at a great
plain that must have recalled not only the flat land it had left
behind, but the grassy montony of its nesting grounds. Its
joyful song drifted ahead as it settled to rest and feed. Oddly
enough Texas ornithologists appear not to have recorded the
upland plover on this high plateau, yet we have seen it there
in spring, and one August we saw five as they moved southward after nesting.

Once I heard a recording of the song of an upland plover.
To my ear it no more resembled the wild sweet whistle of
this bird of the vast open spaces than the bray of a donkey
sounds like a Strauss horn concerto. Recorded on tape, the
song may be studied and analyzed, but the magic is not
there.

Though a sandpiper, the upland plover rarely flocks.
Buoyant, swift, borne on long wings, the solitary bird ranges
the continents alone. By day and night it arrows across the
heavens, and its strangely haunting song floats down to the
listening ear, a song that should be heard under the vast
dome of the sky. It brings with it the mystery of fragile life.
Indomitable, facing danger unafraid, spanning great dis-

tances in the night, guided by some accurate internal compass, subject to ancient laws man has forgotten and yet adap-
table enough to accept newly built airfields for rest and food
and golf courses as nesting places, the upland plover is the
facing voice of once wild vast plains of the Americas before
they were changed forever by the hand of man.

We gazed across the plain long after the elusive song had
died away and then quietly turned to find five pronghorns on
the far side of the railroad tracks staring at us. They moved
restlessly and then were off in a group that soon strung out
into a line. They were wary but not frightened by us, and
their easy gait of about thirty miles an hour could be maintained for many miles. As they ran their rump patches of
long white hairs were puffed so each looked as if it had two
pillows strapped on behind. These fleetest of American mammals have been clocked up to sixty miles an hour; and they
cover the ground in spectacular leaps and bounds. However,
they begin to tire after going at full speed for three or four
miles.

Once pronghorns were about as numerous as the bison
whose range they shared. Hard on the heels of the vanishing
bison, pronghorns were reduced by overshooting until perilously close to extinction. Now they have recovered to a point
where we may be confident that these beautiful and unique
North American mammals with no close relatives will remain
on the open lands of the West.

Unlike the deer family, the pronghorn does not shed its
horns, yet it does not keep them as bighorns and bison do. Instead it annually sheds a sheath or cover on the horns more or
less as a puffin sheds the great colorful sheath on its bill, and
for some winter months has only an ordinary thick dark bill.
Both sexes have horns, but those of the buck are much larger
than the doe's. While they curve backward, a prong points
forward, and from this it receives its name.

"This is a wonderful plain," I sighed happily when the

pronghorns stopped far off to look at us.

"It's a plateau," Allan corrected me that April day.

We returned in May. The wind was strong and cold, but with a rapid tinkling melody a horned lark sang happily of spring. Its delicate notes remind me of oriental glass wind chimes shaken rapidly. They have a ventriloquistic quality, so I looked here and there before discovering the lark had mounted high into the sky and hovered as if tethered, spilling its wiry twittering notes around us. Then it plunged down like a tiny missile. After Allan watched the small brown bird repeat its flight song several times he went straight to some bare ground, bent down, then motioned to me. Four naked baby horned larks opened their yellow mouths, expecting to be fed. They were neatly packed in a small grass-lined nest sunk into a slight depression.

In the meantime meadowlarks scolded us. Beyond the bare ground grew some tufts of sun-browned grass. One of the meadowlarks stood on a grass clump, holding a mouthful of caterpillars. It turned this way and that so we saw its plain brown back and flickering white outer tail feathers, and then its burning yellow breast banded with a black velvet V.

We backed away and watched. Soon the meadowlark went into a tuft of grass and flew off, its bill empty. Quickly then Allan found its nest tucked into grass that bent over it. Five gaping mouths of bright red, yellow and blue begged for worms. With two prairie-country species so close together, Allan decided we must photograph them. Soon our blinds were in position, Allan's by the meadowlark and mine by the horned lark's nest.

We had photographed young horned larks in March on Long Island when snow was piled high around the nest and our fingers were stiff with cold; also on a patch of sandy ground at the Aransas Refuge in April when the temperature soared toward ninety, and in May on a rolling prairie in Montana where swarms of mosquitoes attacked us. While we were photographing horned larks on the Bear River flats of Utah, cattle crowded around the blind, disturbing the birds and me. But horned larks charmed us sufficiently to compensate for physical misery and unexpected difficulties. They never lose their fascination. They like barren country, and wherever they find it they are at home in this country and in Europe and Asia. They are one of the most abundant land birds in the entire world. While we have but one species of horned lark, their variations have interested many scientists, who have divided them into races. Bent lists sixteen of these and some of the names are both descriptive and poetic: Montezuma, pallid, ruddy, scorched, desert and prairie, to name several.

Once, when the male lark was feeding the young birds, I heard a strange sneezing snort. A buck pronghorn was striding up and down behind Allan's blind, now and again stamping with a front foot and loudly protesting the presence of something unusual in his territory. Pronghorns have a reputation for being unusually curious, and old-time hunters learned from the Indians to hide and wave a hat or a handkerchief until they had coaxed the inquisitive pronghorns within gunshot range.

Time passed and both larks fed, though the male with velvety upstanding feather "horns" came twice for each visit by the plainer female. Then a couple of pronghorn does, grazing slowly, approached Allan's blind, and I photographed them as they munched and stared curiously at the blind and the camera. Allan was using flash; his Speed Graphic was placed close to the meadowlark nest and the trigger set off by remote control.

Away in the distance I saw what I first thought were some large pointed leaves standing above the low vegetation. But they moved oddly. I looked more closely. They were the very long ears of young kids. Seven of them all alone sat quietly except for their ears, which were constantly in motion as if testing the air for sounds. Occasionally I could see a pair of large alert eyes as a kid stretched just a little higher for a good look.

That was a great day, for we recorded one of the discoveries people are forever making when they watch wildlife. This is not necessarily anything new to science, though it may be, but something we happen never to have heard of or read about. We found that the kids are gathered into what we called kindergartens for want of a better term and either left alone for a few hours each day or with a single doe on watch not far away. Apparently the does and their kids—which may be singles, twins and occasionally triplets—spend the night in a group and feed and water together early in the morning and again in the afternoon.

But for a while each day the kids were left in kindergartens, and then they sat tranquilly together in the meager vegetation of the plateau where it was high enough to conceal their bodies but low enough so their eats were above it; by stretching a little they could see over it. Unlike fawns, the kids were not spotted but had rather long silky tan coats and white erectile patches on the rump which they flash while still very young. Several times we tried to steal close enough to a kindergarten to photograph the group of kids, but long before we had narrowed the distance sufficiently for a shot, they leaped to their feet and bounded away. Since a four-day-old pronghorn can outrun a man, we simply had to give up that project. Each time we attempted to stalk a kindergarten we first studied the plain, and seldom in the solitude could we see a doe. But with astonishing speed a doe or several of them appeared when the kids burst away and soon led them from our sight.

Whenever we come to that plateau between the Davis and the Cuesto Del Burro mountains we see pronghorns, sometimes only a single one or a small group of them, sometimes group after group of the beautiful plains mammals. Nowhere south of Wyoming do we know of a place where we will so surely encounter them. And we listen for the plains birds; migrating lark buntings, many species of sparrows, flycatchers and white-necked ravens. Later the nesting birds, the meadowlarks, horned larks and lark sparrows fill the air with songs. Always we wait hopefully for the wild melodic whistle of a migrating upland plover whose numbers remain perilously low and whose nesting habitat continues to shrink.

12

Llano Estacado, the Staked Plains

NOBODY KNOWS for sure how the short grass plain of Texas received its name of staked plains. Some say that since it lacked trees for tying horses, it was necessary to stake them at night to keep them from straying. In 1818 Francisco Amangual described the Llano as a place where, "There was nothing but grass and a few small pools of rainwater with very little water, and some dry holes; on the plains where we camped it was necessary to drive stakes for the guard and reserve horses."

Some claim it was named for the stockaded effect as if the Cap Rock—an escarpment that extends across the Panhandle to the Pecos Valley and the Edwards Plateau, then west to the New Mexico line—held the short grass prairie above the mesquite and mixed-grass low plains of east central Texas. The Peterson *Field Guide to the Birds of Texas* divides this area into the Panhandle, Staked Plains, and South Plains; but geologically it is not only a unit sloping from about 3,000 feet in the south up to 4,700 feet in the northwest corner of the Panhandle but actually is an extension of the Great Plains of Kansas and Oklahoma. Thomas Falconer, an Englishman who accompanied the Texas Santa Fe Expedition of 1841, wrote: "We commenced the ascent of the grand prairie . . . looking, as the name denotes, as if staked from the lower ground and as if boldly lifted up, or else as if the ground about it had at some former time sunk around it."

I prefer to think the Llano Estacado was named for the prairie dogs that surely stood high in their hind legs to stare inquisitively at the first Spanish explorers on horseback to penetrate that great plains country. Then the prairie dogs must have looked like thousands of small stakes driven into the ground at regular intervals of fifteen to twenty feet across the level land.

The early explorers saw a dry land without trees. Here the plain was level as a slightly tilted table top with an infinitely distant horizon; there it rolled gently like low frozen waves of the sea. The Llano had no strong features though the Canadian and Red Rivers flow through it and Palo Duro, the deepest of its arroyos, is gouged out of it. Palo Duro is invisible until one comes to the brink and looks down into the wildly sculptured channel below the level of the Llano Estacado.

Change, forever going forward on this planet, was so gradual that time seemed to stand still on the plain. Violent winds swept over it. Bitter cold was replaced by burning summer heat. Occasional great droughts parched the thirsty land. But usually the hungry found food. Death, when it came, was swift. The plants tied down the soil, and certain creatures fed upon them. In turn, the predators fed on those that ate the vegetation. All life was linked together in mutual dependence. Each had adjusted through aeons of time to the climate and to each other.

Massive dark bison grazed on the grama and buffalo grass but, harried by packs of wolves, they never remained in one place long enough to damage the long tangled roots that not only lived on after the grass blades were cropped but held the light soil in place when fierce winds swept over it. At one time the bison may have numbered 60 million and among them grazed almost as many pronghorns, smaller and pale as the seared grass. Jackrabbits bounded away from hunting coyotes and foxes. All the predatory mammals, large and small, sought food in the easiest way and therefore usually attacked the injured, sick or otherwise weakened creatures to satisfy their hunger, so they actually strengthened the races they preyed upon. The Indians (the Kiowas, Comanches and other plains tribes) depended particularly upon the bison. From it they obtained food. Its skin was used for food and clothing and its dried chips for fuel. The effect of the Indians upon the plain was no more destructive to its health and balance than the predation by furred and feathered predators.

In the sky, hawks, eagles and vultures circled, on the hunt for remnants left by some large carnivore after it had feasted and for small rodents and other mammals and birds they could attack and conquer. Prairie birds leaped into the air to sing their tinkling songs, then dropped back to search for insects and caterpillars to satisfy their hunger and that of their young.

This was the land of the prairie dogs. They gave to it. They took from it. For countless centuries the land of the prairie dogs remained virtually unchanged. Here a colony of plants advanced. There some died out. Certain species of animals became more numerous but others faded away. In early spring the prairie dogs gave birth to litters containing an average of five but sometimes as many as ten. They were a staple food for the plains predators that might stoop from the sky, pounce from the concealment of a purple lupine or slither into their burrows. The species was first described by Clark on the Lewis and Clark Expedition when they entered what is now South Dakota on September 7, 1804. On June 5, 1805, Lewis wrote: "as we had not killed or eat anything today we each killed a burrowing squirrel as we passed them in order to make sure of our suppers. . . . I had the burrowing squirrel roasted . . . and found the flesh well flavored and

tender . . ." Indians also must have eaten these fat little
mammals that are to a large extent vegetarians.

Then in less than half a century the timeless adjustment of
the plains life was ruptured. The first cattle drives across the
high plains country of Texas in the 1870's broke the surface
and clouds of dust began to fly.

The Indians had lived and hunted there for untold centuries. They believed the plains belonged to them. Oddly
enough they wanted to stay, and they fought to keep their
land and their hunting grounds. The new Texans demanded
the Indians be ejected from the plains. So it came about that
the economy of the Indians was disrupted. The elimination
of the great bison population that gave the Indians their
necessities of life became our governmental policy. The bison
that had numbered in the tens of millions were reduced to
541 individuals by 1889. The Indians vanished. So did the
other predators, both furred and feathered. One by one the
plains animals fell away, and some reached the verge of extinction. All, that is, except the rodents. With the disap-
pearance of birds and mammals that had preyed upon them
and kept down their numbers, the rodents exuberantly multiplied and ate heartily of plants man wanted for his stock or
for himself.

When people of European descent claimed the Llano Estacado, the Staked Plains, for themselves, they transferred familiar names to the animals native to the area. But the American buffalo is really a bison. The American antelope is not a
true antelope but a pronghorn. Jackrabbits are not rabbits
but hares. And prairie dogs are not dogs. They are rodents, at
present placed by zoologists between the marmots and
ground squirrels. They are energetic diggers and burrowers
that prefer to live in sociable groups called towns. These may
vary from a few dozen to thousands of inhabitants.

The prairie dogs dig shafts that drop almost perpendicularly downward for an average of twelve feet. About two feet

below the surface they build a barking platform to which they drop when an enemy appears, and there they pause long enough in their flight to yelp a danger signal to the colony. Between the burrows runs a vast network of connecting tunnels so the prairie dogs can visit neighbors or escape into the maze of channels or race again to the surface through another shaft when the enemy pursues them underground. When excavations are made for gleaming new buildings that continue to sprout upward in Lubbock and Amarillo, faint traces are found of long disused prairie dog burrows. These are usually filled with earth that sifted back into them when the prairie dogs vanished.

These small tan rodents were a primary food for plains predators. One of these, the black-footed ferret, was so dependent upon them that it is now very near extinction. Only a single individual was sighted in Texas between 1955 and 1966.

Aside from their role as food for many predators, the prairie dogs contributed to the well-being of the plains by supplying water-conservation conduits to that land of light rainfall. At Muleshoe the average annual precipitation is about seventeen inches in contrast to Port Arthur's average of more than fifty-six inches a year. Usually much of the precipitation of the high plain is deposited in sudden storms during the hottest months of the year. Such rain, falling abruptly on the plain, is subject to quick evaporation as high winds sweep over it and the intense sun sucks it back into the air.

But the prairie dogs' burrows and interconnecting tunnels once formed a network that, multiplied over and over again in town after town, added up toward a million miles of underground chambers that collected the precious moisture. In digging their burrows, the prairie dogs used their noses to form the excavated soil into spongy volcano-shaped mounds that soaked up the rain and funneled it into the tunnels. Moisture was absorbed into the soil and slowly released to the water-seeking roots of the grasses that once tied the soil firmly in place from the Rio Grande to Canada. More water, prevented from evaporation in the cool underground tunnels, slowly seeped downward to recharge the vital water table so springs continued to flow in times of great drought, which were a normal part of the weather cycle of the plains.

Inveterate diggers that they were, the prairie dogs brought endless quantities of lifeless earth to the surface. There it was changed into living, viable soil by the sun and air and the plants that broke down its mineral components and realigned them. Finally the soil was pushed back into the burrows by the winds and rains to make the rich topsoil deeper.

Unlike the bison, cattle and sheep were held in restricted areas where they grubbed the plants to their roots, which finally died. Barren areas began to expand, and with each high wind, soil was lifted up and deposited on living plants, suffocating them. Rains were no longer trapped by the tangled grasses and began to run off in swift eroding streams. Windmills continually drew from the underground water that fell lower and lower until never-failing springs became dry. The bison and Indians were gone. The wolves, coyotes and foxes were few in number, killed off because they occasionally took some stock. So were the eagles and the hawks, for had they not been seen eating young lambs? Of course the predatory birds had killed the lambs and it was nonsense to claim they were only eating carrion, that the lambs had died natural deaths! Meanwhile the rodents had a happy life, for the majority of their deadly enemies were gone. They multiplied, for their checks were gone.

There is little doubt that the population of prairie dogs was enormous during the colonial period of the high Texas plains, late in the nineteenth century. As the once rich verdure became spare and poor because of overgrazing, bare areas spread. The plump little prairie dogs found the new barrenness much to their liking and their towns expanded.

Moreover, without their enemies more lived to reproduce themselves.

Sheep and cattle began to die of hunger and thirst. Incomes plummeted as the depleted prairie failed to sustain the domestic animals that grazed upon it. It did not occur to the sheep- and cattlemen that their overuse of the prairie was responsible for the deterioration of the range. Of course not! The prairie dogs were responsible! Horses and cattle, less agile than the bison, broke their legs in the burrows. Moreover, the prairie dogs ate grass meant for domestic stock. A scientist had found that it took only 256 prairie dogs to eat as much as a cow, and 32 ate as much as a sheep. The wolves, bison, Indians and other varmints were gone. Most of the hawks were gone. Now the prairie dog must go.

In 1905 Vernon Bailey wrote a report entitled *Biological Survey of Texas*. In it he described an almost continuous prairie dog town 250 miles long and 100 miles wide along the Prairie Dog Town Fork of the Red River. It had an estimated population of 400 million individuals. Poison must be used to exterminate those prairie dogs, claimed the ranchers when traps and guns failed to accomplish the job. Thereupon the government, using our tax money, began a program of systematic poisoning of the prairie dogs.

By 1928 H. E. Anthony wrote that there were many regions where the prairie dog was a conspicuous part of plains life and some large towns still existed.

Soon after this, new and terrible poisons came into use. One of these in popular use, set up a deadly chain reaction. Poison a prairie dog and whatever ate its carcass died, and so did whatever ate the second victim, ad infinitum, be it one of the extremely rare black-footed ferrets or our national symbol, the bald eagle.

In 1966 the United States Bureau of Sports Fisheries and Wildlife prepared a report called *Rare and Endangered Fish and Wildlife*. Included in the list is the black-tailed prairie dog and comments "Status: Rare. Numbers, colonies, and distribution greatly reduced."

From some source I do not recall, I acquired a long time ago a print probably dating back to the 1870's or 1880's when Colonel Charles Goodnight established the first great ranch in the Texas Panhandle, when longhorn cattle drives stirred the dust from Texas to Dodge City, when General Custer fought on the Little Big Horn and Theodore Roosevelt was ranching in the wilds of North Dakota. The print showed a great town of prairie dogs, and on each mound stood one of the inhabitants; all watched a man in frontier dress on horseback. The man and the horse were as still as the rodents. Each time I looked at the print I longed to see a similar prairie dog town. At the time it did not occur to me to wonder if the horseman shared my delight in the multitude of mammals arrayed before him, that he might instead consider their burrows a deadly hazard to the safety of his horse's legs and thus a danger barring his way westward. Each time we went to Texas I looked in vain for a prairie dog town, one undisturbed in the wilds, until I dispaired of ever seeing one.

In the meantime we saw a couple of prairie dog towns under protection, one noteworthy because a part of an ancient town has been preserved and is now completely surrounded by a rapidly growing city, and the second because of the prairie associates congregated in it.

One wild afternoon when tornadoes rampaged across Texas and surface winds were high we came to Lubbock. Now Lubbock lies on land where prairie dogs once had a large town. Back in the thirties, MacKenzie State Park was established in what was then the outskirts of the city. Soon after, the directors met to discuss a problem. Some prairie dogs had been found within the park area. How should they be exterminated?

The directors were persuaded instead to save the prairie dogs which after all had lived in the area long before the white men took it over. By saving the prairie dogs children of the future who otherwise might never know what a prairie dog town was really like could glimpse a fragment of old-time Texas.

In 1938 a trench three feet deep was dug around several acres and surrounded by wire netting that extended about thirty inches above the surface, while on the side where visitors come to watch the antics of the prairie dogs and to feed them, a stone wall was built. A sprinkler system was installed and the enclosure planted to rye and grass, the only food provided for the rodents other than that given to them by visitors.

In Lubbock, a city of almost 160,000 people, a few hundred prairie dogs are visited by more than a million people each year. A few rabbits have moved into the prairie dog town and usually a burrowing owl or two may be seen somewhere in the enclosure.

The school day had ended, and children arrived with their parents and scout leaders. The prairie dogs received the children enthusiastically. Like puppies they scurried about switching their tails, wagging their rumps and competing for cookies, candy and pieces of lettuce. When successful they ran to their mounds, stood upright and holding their morsels in their front paws, enjoyed their treats.

Suddenly one of the children shouted.

"He's going to fish! He's going to fish!"

All the children surged forward eagerly. Startled, for there was not a drop of water in sight, we saw the children had surrounded an evident hero. It was an attendant who carried a fishing line baited with a carrot. Amid excited shrieks, he tossed the bait close to a prairie dog. It snatched the carrot and ran swiftly into a burrow. Pull though he did, the attendant could not dislodge the two-pound rodent. Presently the line went slack. Sharp teeth had severed it. The children groaned. Again the attendant baited his line.

Curious, we edged forward.

"The number of prairie dogs that can live comfortably in this enclosure is limited," the attendant told us. "So whenever an accredited institution wants some prairie dogs we catch some and ship them off if the proper papers have been signed. They must promise to keep the prairie dogs on open ground without a floor, because they are natural diggers and don't stay healthy and happy unless they can dig. Now some are wanted in Philadelphia. Once I caught some for the king of Saudi Arabia and they were flown across the ocean in a jet," he added proudly.

Meanwhile the children were leaping and shouting with excitement, each suggesting which prairie dog would be the best catch. Surveying the mammals carefully, the attendant cast the carrot in front of a fat eager fellow. As it snatched the carrot, the attendant threw a loop around its front legs and began pulling it in. The prairie dog struggled but kept hold of the carrot. Soon it was in a boxlike cage, a creel for prairie dogs.

Abruptly the shouting and excitement died away as mothers and scout leaders hurriedly propelled their reluctant charges toward cars. We heard the blare of a loudspeaker. A funnel cloud had been spotted near the city. A plane was following its movements. A police car tracked it from the ground. Citizens were advised to remain calm but seek shelter and keep radios turned on for further information. The attendant looked at the boiling clouds, shrugged his shoulders and hastened away with the prairie dog in the creel contentedly munching on its carrot.

Above us dark clouds rumbled. West of us a curtain of red-brown dust, sucked from soil stripped of its natural cover, was advancing toward us. The city was already concealed behind it. The curtain, muffling the wind, moved forward with ominous quiet except for a strange hiss. Suddenly it was upon us. It closed over the prairie dog town. Blinded, we raced toward the station wagon, then cautiously groped toward our motel through an opaque half-light. The streets were filled with slow-moving cars, and their headlights burned round holes in the dense curtain. Then lightning flashes blinded us and the crack and roll of thunder deafened us.

Until darkness was complete, planes continued to follow the twisters and report their positions. Then only police cars continued surveillance of the unpredictable tornadoes. The city that night was not touched by any of the funnel clouds spawned when warm humid air from the gulf clashed with cold dry air from the north; but a brief heavy shower pushed the dust back to earth, and next morning our blue station wagon was filmed with a clinging brown coat. Many people, knowing that a twister can shatter in a moment strongly built modern buildings, spent the night in storm cellars. Long before plains people learned to dig such refuges from wild storms, prairie dogs remained snug and safe when savage storms swept over their mounds.

Since national monuments, parks and refuges protect all natural features within their boundaries, most of those within former range of sociable prairie dogs now exhibit one of their towns. Muleshoe, the first federal wildlife refuge in Texas, is no exception, though it was set aside primarily as a wintering place for sandhill cranes and waterfowl.

One May morning we swung into the gravel road leading to this refuge headquarters. Many weeks had passed since the wintering birds left for their nesting grounds. When their number is greatest, usually in December, Muleshoe provides one of the finest shows in all America. As the sun slides toward the horizon the sky is filled with thousands upon thousands of lesser sandhill cranes in majestic flight. Their long, broad wings stroke powerfully downward and then move up with a quick flick of the tips. Their bugling, loud, slightly harsh, and resonant, rings with the voice of all wilderness and wild creatures. To me it is one of the most impressive sounds in all nature. Usually birders like to keep their backs to the sun so birds receive flat light making it easy to see the colors. But when the stately cranes in long lines, wavering skeins and massed ranks sweep into the refuge, they should be watched silhouetted against a flaring sunset sky. In *Wandering Through Winter,* Edwin Way Teale brings to life the coming of the cranes to Bitter Lake in New Mexico.

At the peak of concentration it has been estimated that as many as 100,000 lesser sandhill cranes congregate at Muleshoe. This is the greatest concentration of these birds in North America. In addition, as many as 700,000 waterfowl may settle on the three sink-type lakes or playas, which depend entirely on runoff from the meager rains so they are often dry for part of the year.

Our chief reason for visiting Muleshoe out of season was to see the prarie dog town overlooking White Lake, which in winter is stippled with ducks. In winter the prairie dogs, which become very fat in autumn, are quite inactive and go into a heavy sleep during most of the cold weather. This town lies on as irregular prairie as any in the Texas high plain except for Palo Duro and the larger river channels, for not only does the surface roll in high billows, but it is broken by a rimrock of caliche and several deeply gouged draws lead into the elastic ponds.

After we had towed a great whitish cloud of dust for about two miles, White Lake came into view, and between it and the road lay the prairie dog town. Unlike the prairie dogs in Lubbock's MacKenzie State Park, which are accustomed to people, these were very wild and timid. All except those on the farthest rim of the town ran to their burrows, and their excited yelps rang out on all sides. We sat quietly. Soon wriggling noses and quivering whiskers appeared at the burrow mouths. Here and then there a prairie dog resumed its place on its mound, standing upright and barking sharply, its short tail jerking with each outburst. Most amusing were those that stood on all fours and suddenly hurled their foreparts upward throwing their front legs above their heads as they shrieked *wheee* and then dropped back to the mound.

Soon the rodents forgot about us and began to visit neighbors. They greeted each other by rubbing noses. Now and then a small head peeped above the mound only to be chased in again by its watchful mother. Often there was conflict, whether caused by anger or for play we could not tell, but several times when two or three prairie dogs congregated on a single mound, the meeting was quickly adjourned with loud yips and what looked like unfriendly biting.

Alan caught my hand. "Look at the burrowing owls. . . . three, four, five—there are eleven standing round the far edge of the town."

These small brown owls are frequently called prairie owls, and once it was believed they lived, along with rattlers, in harmony with the prairie dogs. It is true they often occupy abandoned burrows of the prairie dogs instead of digging their own, but should their eggs or young be found by the prairie dogs they would be eaten. The young prairie dogs in turn are eaten on occasion by the owls. As for the rattlers, they eat both young prairie dogs and young owls.

Like all prairie dog towns, this one was free of all vegetation more than about six inches in height. The prairie dogs seldom venture beyond the edge of their town and in fact, rarely go very far from the immediate surroundings of their burrows. It is surprising they remain so fat on the limited plant life available to them. An advantage in the low vegetation is the clear view the rodents have of their entire town and the approach of a predator.

The yelping and barking of the dogs rose in volume, and most of them plunged into their burrows, only to poke their heads out again. We followed their gaze. There was a motion in the short yellow grass. A grizzled mammal somewhat more than two feet long was making its way quickly toward the town. It was a badger. Its loose coat waved and flapped at the sides as if it were only attached to its backbone. To our surprise it entered a burrow that looked too small for its bulk. Shortly its head reappeared at the mouth, and the badger remained there, turning its head this way and that as if enjoying the sun, though it is quite nocturnal in its habits. Its long-nailed forepaws rested on the mound. It is said that if danger threatens, a badger can dig itself from sight with amazing speed and plug the hole behind it. Badgers were once an important control of the plains rodents. This one had apparently claimed an abandoned prairie dog burrow, perhaps having first eaten the original owners of it.

All we could see were the round ears of the badger, which moved slightly at each sound, and a white stripe that ran from the top of its head to its round black nose. Except on the opposite side of the town, not a prairie dog remained above ground. Allan decided to photograph the badger.

"You won't be able to get anywhere near it," I said, recalling the shy habits of Badger in *The Wind in the Willows,* but Allan paid no attention. The badger watched as he came closer, turned suddenly as if it meant to hurry into the burrow, then remained still. Triumphantly, Allan shot exposure after exposure until all the film in the pack was used. He returned to the station wagon grinning happily.

"You never can tell!" he exclaimed. "You may make a thousand futile tries for photographs of some rare or shy species, and then you come across one like this fellow that pays no attention to you and you simply walk up and click the shutter."

While Allan was putting another pack of film in his camera I saw a movement near one of the burrows. I lifted my binoculars. It was a stocky snake.

"I think it is a rattler," I told Allan.

Allan took a look. "It is a western diamondback," and he was off again.

A truck with a great billow of dust behind approached. It was the manager of Muleshoe.

"Well, it's a little warmer than the last time you were here," he grinned. "What is Allan photographing?"

"A rattler," I responded. "Maybe I had better try for some shots, too."

The manager went with me to look at the snake.

"A fine coon-tailed rattler," he remarked. "That's what a lot of people here call western diamondback rattlesnakes because of the rings next to the rattles. These are clear black and white when the snake has just shed. This fellow is bulging so much it must have found a nest of young prairie dogs. Between the hawks, coyotes, badgers, foxes and snakes, this town is kept lively and healthy."

The rattler was sluggish from having recently gorged itself on a large meal. It posed quietly for a few minutes. Then the hot sun proved too much for it. Turning abruptly, it defied our efforts to control it with a stick and glided into the nearest burrow and out of sight.

We went north to photograph some of the national grasslands. Texas has about 300,000 acres of these, divided into five areas. All are located on overgrazed, badly eroded ranges, but now under intelligent management their quality is being restored. Some of the wildlife is returning to them. We saw pronghorns grazing with cattle. A coyote trotted in the distance. It paused to look at us, then sat on its haunches. The day was hot and its pink tongue hung from its slightly open mouth. We took a couple of steps toward it, and that was enough to send it on its way. A jackrabbit leaped up and bounded off with erratic changes of direction, but the coyote, perhaps already well fed, trotted on its way and out of sight.

If the officials stand firm against the tremendous pressure of those who demand that greater numbers of cattle be grazed on the national grassland than the range can support and still maintain its excellence, it will again be covered with luxuriant grasses that will tie down the soil so the eternal winds cannot blow it away or sudden rains erode it. We looked in vain for prairie dogs: if any have returned to the national grassland, they are in an area we did not visit.

East of Canyon we drove across gently rolling prairie country. Allan spotted mounds of a deserted prairie dog town and we stopped to examine the abandoned burrows. To our surprise the prairie dropped away without warning. Below us was Palo Duro Canyon where Kiowas and Comanches once camped and where they took refuge from blizzards. A strong wind was blowing, and as Allan stood on the brink, I was afraid it would hurl him from the rim into the depths below.

We continued along the highway and soon were twisting and winding our way down the steep canyon wall into the state park below. In the bottom of the gorge it was calm, but we could hear the wind howling across the top of the canyon.

We were shut in by walls of red Permian sandstone 250 million years old. Sheer palisades and towers with caverns etched in them rose above us. We crossed the Prairie Dog Town Fork five times, splashing in shallow water at each ford. We saw no mammals except a tame deer with one antler, and a jackrabbit crouched under a bush where it looked like a rounded boulder covered with brownish gray lichens until it moved its long ears.

There were birds everywhere. Lesser goldfinches made bright drops fly as they splashed in the edge of the stream. Ash-throated flycatchers and a golden-fronted woodpecker were fighting over a cavity in a cottonwood. Allan found a blue-gray gnatcatcher's nest, as beautifully made as a hummingbird's though considerably larger, saddled on a branch of a dead hackberry. It was extremely hot in the still canyon, and we wondered that the gnatcatcher had chosen to nest where it had no protection from the ardent sun. Mockingbirds and both canyon and rock wrens sang continuously and their songs echoed and reechoed between the vertical crags. A prairie falcon looking much like an extremely pale peregrine and every bit as slim and elegant as that majestic species perched on one of the soaring rock minarets.

Falcons have been the darlings of royalty for many centuries. In fact, ancient manuscripts indicate that a prehistoric Persian king originated the sport of falconry. We wish falconry had remained a sport restricted to kings, since those rulers are now almost as rare as whooping cranes and therefore would have had little effect on the sadly diminished population of falcons. If falconry were carried on by experts or under the supervision of experts, the sport would only add a valuable dimension to man's relationship to birds. Unfortunately many people, particularly energetic boys and young men, become fired with the beauty and excitement of falconry, though they know nothing about the falcons or their habits and the care and training they must undergo. So it has come about that the ignorant enthusiasts have sought out and unintentionally destroyed so many falcon eyries and caused the death of so many of these birds that they stand accused to a considerable degree of the present dangerously reduced population of American falcons. Three species, including the handsome prairie falcon, are rare and threatened by extinction.

Like a meteor, the falcon stooped into a flock of cliff swallows. The twittering throng scattered as if they were pellets fired from a shotgun. Thousands of their jug-shaped nests, each made of hundreds of little mud spitballs, were clustered on the highly colored cliff faces. The heads of young swallows plugged the entrances, and their open bills pleaded for food. Darting up and down between the lofty wall, the adults scooped into their wide mouths small airborne insects, then darted to their nests, hovered before the opening, their wings blurred like whirring propellers, stuffed their catch into the gaping mouths of the young and were off to make another catch of ephemera.

But once more I was disappointed by the absence of prairie dogs, for surely, I thought, some of those millions of prairie dogs that once lived along the Prairie Dog Fork must still be there. All we saw were deserted sites of former towns, genuine ghost towns of the old West.

Allan was not satisfied with shots he had made of lark sparrows. He recalled having seen, during a lecture trip, an area northwest of Amarillo where he was confident he would find them nesting. Soon we really were in great open plains country. The plain reached from yesterday into tomorrow. There was no shade anywhere to temper the bright glare. The grass was seared yellow, and everything shimmered as heat waves danced. A lark sparrow flushed from beside the road. It carried a billful of caterpillars. Allan said to watch closely. When it vanished into a clump of grass and came out without the food we marked the spot well, for the nest and young were there.

Now our highway had paralleled a railroad, and between lay some very depressed land with half-dead lupines, sad-looking grass and bare areas. My eyes left the lark sparrow when I heard a familiar yelp. Had the intense heat and the shimmering air conspired to deceive me? But no, there were about twenty mounds, and on several were the stakelike forms of prairie dogs. In spite of the parching sun, they yipped shrilly and some barked, all jerking their tails as they objected to our presence. Some prepared to dart into their burrows if we came nearer. At long last I had located a wild prairie dog town in Texas.

That day Allan made the photographs he wanted of lark sparrows, with white rims on their tails and chestnut "ear muffs." These charming birds sing melodiously throughout the summer on much of our great central plains country. While he worked, I watched the prairie dogs. It was almost intolerably hot; the land was so desiccated that most of the plants were yellow and all drooped, yet the prairie dogs looked in perfect condition, their tan coats shining, their bodies plump. They rubbed noses, nibbled dead grass, whistled challenges to neighbors, repaired mounds, and kicked clouds of dust out of their burrows. Though most of the prairie dogs are gone from their former range except those that are wards of the state, here was indisputable proof that not all their towns are ghost towns and some still live in the wild places on the high plains of Texas.

13

Loma de la Montuosa

A HIGHWAY RUNS east from Brownsville to Boca Chica on the gulf, where the Rio Grande finally loses itself in the sea. Except for fishermen, few people use this highway in spring and then only when wind and water conditions combine to lure the optimistic.

This highway lies like a backbone down the middle of a very irregular peninsula known locally as Jackass Prairie. The entire plain is without strong features, and its soft desert colors blur it and the harsh yuccas, catclaw and other viciously armed plants that cling to precarious life on the dry mounds above flood tides. Shimmering heat waves set in motion by the merciless sun, haze born of gulf waters, and dust continually stirred by the ever-active wind from the east further veil the plain, so a car half a mile away appears incredibly distant as if seen through the wrong optics of a binocular. A horse grazing on the sparse vegetation seems in perfect scale with the mounts of a set of toy soldiers.

The last ten or twelve miles of the twenty-five-mile highway lie across a plain that barely rises above high tide. As if the extreme flatness of the land made the waters of San Martin Lake and Laguna Madre uncertain of their domain, the shoreline swings so wildly in elongated points and exaggerated indentations that it spans a fantastic number of miles, though the ship's channel dug from just south of Port Isabel to Port of Brownsville is only twenty miles long.

Along the southern edge of the peninsula, the Rio Grande meanders aimlessly, tired and old after its journey of more than two thousand miles from the chill cloud-shrouded peaks of the San Juans in Colorado to the sea. Its once crystal waters begin their search for the sea by plunging wildly down snowy precipitous slopes. Then the river begins to pick up more and more earth and gravel until it turns into a powerful cutting force in the Big Bend. Always accumulating more silt as it travels, the great river finally becomes sluggish and heavy. Reluctant at last to lose itself in the mother sea, it twists, turns and almost curls back upon itself.

Often storms send sheets of salt water over the plain, so the few plants existing there are tolerant of briny conditions. But the plain was largely built and is still being built grain by grain as the Rio Grande in its frequent floods spills from its channel and spreads its burden widely.

A bird-watcher with little time at his disposal but attracted eastward by the end of land and a great river, might quickly decide he was wasting his energy, that the area was worthless as a birding place, and turn back to Brownsville. Close to that city are rich resacas teeming with aquatic life where he might find cinnamon teal, least grebes, black-bellied tree ducks and even a jaçana. Jaçanas have fantastically long toes and run over the water hyacinths as easily as a duck swims in water. If he hiked along the dikes he would surely find land birds strayed across the river from Mexico, species found nowhere else in the United States, and he would regret those minutes wasted on the featureless coastal plain.

We were fortunate the first time we followed that highway, for the Rio Grande had been in flood and only recently shrunk back within its channel, but its murky waters still colored the gulf to the horizon. As we approached Boca Chica, the sky, bending toward illimitable distance, covered a boundless tawny universe shining with great spreading lakes that we quickly found were only films of water left behind as the flood receded, so shorebirds a quarter of a mile from their shores stood less than ankle deep.

Companies of wading birds fed in the shallow water. Others crying loudly chased their neighbors. Many rested in compact groups. These tucked their bills into the feathers of their shoulders, and most stood on one leg but all regarded us steadily from one open eye. Allan systematically examined the throng and soon identified the majority of species regularly seen on migration along the Texas coast. Black-bellied plovers, whimbrel, both yellowlegs, dowitchers and bands of smaller shorebirds loomed large on the featureless plain.

For the first time I saw avocets, large shorebirds with long blue legs and thin up-curved bills. They had a striking pattern of black and white, while their head and shoulders looked as if an artist had brushed them with cinnamon mixed in dry sherry. When they spread their wings and darted about excitedly, then paused to lower their heads until their bills lay close to the water, they reminded me of playful kittens about to spring at a ball. When we came too close, they leaped into the air, circled, plunged about us and yapped loudly. Allan said they behaved as avocets do on their breeding territories, but these birds must merely have been practicing spring behavior, for in Texas they nest only on the high plains country of the western part of the state.

The hour we spent that afternoon near Boca Chica slipped quickly away but not before the charm of that flat and lonely plain silvered by flood waters and alive with moving waders and their haunting cries was firmly fixed in our thoughts. We looked forward to the day when we could return to that flat land with its quivering heat waves and its loneliness, for surely when the northbound migrants moved on, black-

necked stilts and snowy plovers and willets would stay behind and nest.

Another April we returned to Brownsville, this time to
stay for several weeks. We went straight to the dikes by the
Custom House to look at the Rio Grande and were stunned
by its contrast to the last time we saw it Then the powerful
brown current thrusting large trees toward the gulf had
swirled just inches below the top of the dike. This time the
river had shrunk to an aimless narrow creek shining in the
middle of a wide channel bordered by high banks. From
south of the river boys came to splash in it, and girls waded to
the center of the stream where they stood waist-deep to wash
their black hair. Men came out of adobe cottages, made their
way down the steep side of the dike and arroyo to the stream's
edge, dipped up buckets of water and then toiled carefully up
again with their precious loads.

The change in the river at Brownsville did not prepare us
for the change on the peninsula. Eagerly we drove once more
along the Boca Chica highway, anticipating the discovery of
many shorebird nests. But not a drop of water was visible
except where the lacy-edged gulf, now clear and blue, lapped
the shore. Everywhere it was dry as Sahara sand dunes usually
pictured in geography books as typical of desert country. Far
in the distance the lonely cry of a shorebird was carried on
the strong easterly wind, but we saw no sign of life. Where we
had splashed in broad sheets of water populated by innumerable shorebirds, dust gritted between our teeth and was swept
upward in a dense curtain that reached for the clouds.

Disappointed, we turned back toward Brownsville. For the
first time we noticed that the plain was less level than we
remembered. Pulling out our United States Geological maps
of the area, we found that the well-defined mounds called
lomas each had a name. They looked quite like islands, for

their borders were sharply defined and each was covered with a low tangle of yuccas and small thorny shrubs while the level plain resembled a tidal flat.

Soon we came to Loma de la Juaja and stopped to read the inscription on a monument. It commemorated the Battle of Palmito Hill, which had taken place just south and slightly east of the loma. This battle, the last of the Civil War, was fought on May 13, 1865, thirty-four days after the peace treaty was signed.

A golden-fronted woodpecker looked out of a hole in a telephone pole, and a few feet away a ladder-backed wood-pecker swooped to a cavity in a weather-beaten post, turned so we saw a mouthful of brown caterpillars and then vanished inside. Just then a mockingbird, flashing its white tail feathers, darted into a bristling yucca in the steep, eroded windward side of the loma. We followed and found the mocker's half-built nest deep among the bayonets.

"The lomas must be ancient sand dunes anchored by vegetation," I suggested, reaching down to pick up a handful of sand. Instead, I found the earth was baked as hard as cement. Curious about the strange islandlike mounds, we pursued the matter and found that geologists are not agreed as to how they were formed, but it is generally accepted that they were built very slowly, doubtless begun thousands of years ago when the sea reached its present level. Then the winds blew as they do today with an average during the spring months above twelve miles an hour, with gusty periods of forty miles or more. The wind blowing across the tidal flats was aided by the blazing sun, and together they dried the mixture of clay, salt and marl exposed there. As the surface dried, it cracked, and the upper layer of broken sections curled. The driving wind seized the raised edges and tore them loose. It rolled them until they were broken into pellets no larger than grains of sand. These were pushed about until at last they were trapped by some obstruction; salicornia perhaps, or a

trash line left by a receding flood. Crystallizing salt broke
more clay into pellets. These were added to the piles by the
restless wind. Slowly the piles grew into dunes; clay dunes.
Almost always the dunes rise in the lea of a depression where
conditions may be marshy. Sometimes these depressions are
deep enough to hold shallow temporary ponds, a haven for
swarming fiddler crabs and birds that feed on them. Many
geologists believe that most of the material in each clay dune
came from the depression on its windward side. As centuries
passed the dunes were eroded by tides and then by the wind,
which took away as well as added to them. Slowly the dunes
were anchored by grasses and then by larger salt- and drought-
resistant plants.

As we stood beside the mocker's half-finished nest, curious
now about the lomas scattered at intervals across the plain,
there was a sudden movement above us.

A flock of sheep and six dirty white goats that looked at us
with evil yellow eyes spilled over the edge of the dune and
scrambled away toward the west. They were herded into a
compact group by a small blackish dog with a brown spot
over each eye. Allan spoke to the dog. It only pulled its
shaggy tail closer to its haunches, and its short legs flew faster
as it circled the flock; but it would not look at him. Then,
like an apparition from the Old Testament, a shepherd, tall
and extremely thin and carrying a long stick, appeared on the
rim of the loma. Like the dog, he did not glance our way, and
his deep-set dark eyes looked into the distance. Lanky white
hair and a scraggly beard blew about his bare head and
swarthy weathered face. Whipping about him was a dingy
blanket with a hole torn in the middle so that the shepherd
had pulled it over his head poncho-fashion. His horny feet
were bare except for sandals made from an automobile tire.

In spite of his obvious age the shepherd ran nimbly down
the eroded slope, and the small group went off across the
plain at a good clip, obviously with a goal in view. We

watched them through our binoculars and finally saw the shepherd and the small black dog herd the flock into a corral made of upright sticks driven close together into the hard-baked earth on the north end of a loma densely covered with brush.

Scanning our map we found the Loma was called de la Montuosa, that it was about a quarter of a mile from the highway, was shaped roughly like a section of an orange and rose to a surprising height of 27.5 feet. It was about a mile long from tip to tip.

"Let's see if there are any birds on that loma." Allan was already starting the motor. "It's close to the highway but far enough from it so we could work there without being disturbed."

So it happened that a shepherd and his flock led us to Loma de la Montuosa and one of the finest places for land-bird photography we have ever found. Close to the loma, its resemblance to an island was even more pronounced. Its rim was as sharply defined as if water lapped against it, and on the flat land surrounding it shore birds were abundant. Willets fought and searched for food and courted there, displaying their lovely black and white wing patterns. Black-bellied plovers in rich breeding plumage moved restlessly, and the cry of curlews rang across miles of emptiness. Ring-billed gulls and laughing gulls cackled by. Occasionally a flock of Franklin's gulls, so similar to laughing gulls in looks but so unlike them in voice, in their close flight formations and swift fluttery wing-beats, swooped low in their passage over the loma.

From the loma came a loud chorus of passerine birds, and eagerly we turned from the plain to examine it. For a moment our enthusiasm was dampened. We faced a veritable gnome forest. All the trees were stunted, dwarfed to bush size, and the lichen furred branches were so tightly inter-twined that the thicket was virtually impenetrable. In addition, every branch and twig was armed with long straight thorns ready to pierce like steel needles or hooked like cat claws to seize and hold. Almost invisible spines detached themselves and clung tenaciously to skin and clothing.

After a few ineffective attempts to enter the pigmy forest, we made our way along the edge, following the "shoreline." Immediately our spirits soared. Not only did the songs of many passerine birds ring in our ears, but we found nest after nest, more land-bird nests than we have ever found in an area of equal size elsewhere. Mockingbirds, cardinals, curve-billed thrashers, mourning and ground doves, black-throated sparrows, and an occasional lark sparrow—one after another we found nests of all these birds, and often five, ten or more of a given species. Boat-tailed grackles were abundant, and redwings, those denizens of wetlands, were incongruous nesting birds in that arid thicket.

We found scissor-tailed flycatcher nests that looked as if they were built of the white waste blown around a Brownsville plant where compresses were made. We found a couple of Bewick's wren nests in cavities in small mesquites and a nighthawk nest on the bare ground beyond the rim of the gnome forest. Verdins nested in the thicket, and so did a pair of roadrunners. We saw a pair of vermilion flycatchers feeding young already out of the nest.

Added to the nesting birds were migrants. Dickcissels swarmed over small bushes to perform their staccato buzzing choruses. Cassin's sparrows leaped into the air trilling their brief songs. Orioles piped their joyous melodies. We saw tiny buff-bellied and ruby-throated hummingbirds dart into huge yellow opuntia blossoms that dwarfed them to sip nectar or eat tiny insects. We decided we had stumbled on a bird photographer's paradise, easily accessible yet removed from human disturbance.

In spite of the abundant and varied nests, Montuosa was not quite the utopia we first thought. The intense drought had dried every fresh-water pool on the plain. Much of the always meager forage was dead. The miserable cattle pastured there grew thinner until their ribs stood high above deep hollows. The skeletonlike horses hung their heads, formed lines and wandered aimlessly behind the leader. At first three foals on long unsteady legs stayed close to the flanks of the mares that bore them, but over a period of a couple of weeks all disappeared. Daily a cluster of vultures circled above a new carcass of a horse or cow that had succumbed to hunger and thirst.

Each day we brought two gallon jugs of cool water; but in spite of this we were always thirsty, and our lips dried and cracked. We were tormented by swarms of flies. These avidly sought moisture from our lips and eyes. They did not bite. They simply clung, and though we killed them by the dozen, as many immediately took their places. They were as wild for water as the cattle and horses. When we drew a cup of water, the flies made it difficult to drink, for they pressed around the rim and even fell into it in their urgency. The constant high wind failed to dislodge them, and as the heat mounted the numbers of thirst-maddened insects swelled. We had to accept them as we did the killing heat and desiccating wind that seared us and shook the nests we tried to photograph.

A pair of white-necked ravens about the size of common crows often drifted over the loma. Their movements were light and aimless as sheets of paper charred black and riding air currents above a fire. Their persistent attachment to the loma led Allan to believe they nested somewhere on it. One day he saw one of the ravens leave a mesquite on the summit of the loma and join its mate circling overhead. In the central crotch of the mesquite was wedged a mass of large sticks woven into an upright funnel.

Armed with clippers and a machete, we worked our way along a sheep trail, and when that failed us we hacked a passage to the mesquite, which Allan climbed. Five greenish eggs with pale brown spots lay on a bed of wool and cow hair. From then on we watched the ravens closely. One day their behavior told us the eggs had hatched, and again Allan climbed the mesquite. Five naked, blind bits of life wriggled there begging for food. Allan said we would wait until the birds were eight days old and then we would photograph them.

Our hopes collapsed when the ravens, gathering food a mile from the loma, were shot and hung on a fence. By the time we discovered this the young ravens were already dead from hunger or the broiling sun, and ants were eating them.

Ants played a part in another disappointment. For days we watched a pair of hooded orioles weave their exquisite nest of plant fibers in one of the few yuccas on the loma. Then the orioles vanished, and we never saw them again. Allan waited a couple of days and then investigated the nest. The orioles had abandoned two white eggs blotched and scrawled with a dark design. Winding up the yucca, across the nest and on toward the top of the plant was a line of marching ants. Whether they forced the orioles to leave or something else caused them to desert the nest we have no way of knowing.

No doubt ants do considerable damage to birds. Once we found a bushtit's foot-long nest not far from Alpine. Five lively young looked from the top opening, but they appeared abnormally restless. Allan noted ants running about the nest. That afternoon we again passed the nest. The eyes of the young birds had grown dull. The adults had torn a hole in the side of the nest and were feeding them through it instead of the large top opening. Two days later the young birds no longer opened their eyes when the adults offered them food. In a burst of sentiment we carefully lifted the young birds from the nest. Sure enough, there were several ants on each bird. Gently we removed all the ants and made a snug little nest for them and hung it a short distance away. The adults quickly found their young, and when we left they were feed-

ing them regularly. The next morning we checked the
bushtits again. All the young were dead, and ants made a
seething dark cover over them.

One fairly common bird on Montuosa was the big greenish
olive sparrow, which is found as far south as Yucatan and
Costa Rica but barely enters the United States, seldom going
farther north than the vicinity of Corpus Christi. It resembles
a green-tailed towhee far more than a sparrow. Repeatedly
we heard their cardinal-like *clink* around Montuosa's rim,
and hour after hour we attempted to track them to a nest.
The olive sparrows sang their loud songs beginning with a
series of evenly spaced notes all on the same pitch, then gradually increasing the tempo until the notes became a buzz.
Then they fell silent and vanished.

One day while I was crawling under the thorns at the
loma's rim my face almost touched a nest. It was just inches
off the ground and securely bound to a couple of upright
twigs of catclaw, a large round nest of grasses with the opening at the side giving it a domed appearance. Two wide
mouths, one big, one tiny, gaped at me. It was an olive sparrow's nest, but the larger bird was a cowbird. Quickly we put
a blind beside the nest and soon had photographs of the
adults feeding the cowbird. The small sparrow went hungry.

The solicitousness that attacks even realistic people when
the underdog is suffering through no fault of its own seized
us. For a few days we brought bits of chopped beef and
dropped them into the mouth of the undernourished sparrow. We may have kept the miserable creature alive a few
hours beyond its fated span, but the vigorous, demanding
cowbird shoved and pushed its nest-mate until the small sparrow was lifted and tossed out. We found the naked olive sparrow on the ground already being eaten by ants while the
cowbird thrived as the devotion of both adult olive sparrows
was lavished upon it alone.

Of all the multitude of birds nesting on the loma, none is

more closely associated with the harsh, thorny deserts of the Southwest than verdins, members of the chickadee family. They are found in the driest, most inhospitable prickly desert scrub. There they weave their large intricate nests of tough, bristling twigs of catclaw, buckhorn, acacia and other viciously armed bushes of the arid country. They actually appear able to survive without any water beyond what they find in their food and in dew. To man the verdins seem to have chosen the most comfortless, repelling environment possible, a place where searing heat, thirst and drying winds prevail for much of the year. Yet verdins are slim delicate birds scarcely more than four inches long. Their bodies are garbed in a suitable desert olive-gray, but this is relieved by a softly yellow head and a Chinese-red streak on each shoulder. They were not described until 1864, and in the early years were called goldtits.

Day in and day out we heard their weak little songs and plaintive, rather complaining *tseee seeseee* as pairs seeking food kept in touch with their mates. Their nests were positively abundant on Montuosa. It is believed that verdins, like some wrens, build nests that they never use. Moreover, once the breeding season is finished, they build "winter" nests in which they sleep during the hottest time of the day and at night for the remainder of the year.

The nests are remarkable structures for such small birds to build. Some are nearly as large as a football and may contain up to or even more than a thousand sticks. These coarse prickly twigs are woven so tightly into globular shape with the opening at one side that they withstand the storms of several years before at last they disintegrate. They are strapped so securely to the branch that it is virtually impossible to dislodge them except by cutting away the lashings. Though there were few long flexible twigs in the gray gnome forest, the verdins all managed to find one on which to hang, near the tip, their beautifully formed nests. This created a problem for us, as the constant high wind rocked the cradles without ceasing.

Of all the verdin nests I have seen, those on Montuosa were not only the largest, often measuring eight inches or more in length, but they were the most carefully woven. In neither Arizona nor California have I seen a verdin nest that showed any particular form to the entrance hole. Those on Montuosa invariably flared slightly at the entrance, so they truly resembled jugs hung on the side while the outside bristled like a curled hedgehog. Inside, the thorny nest was padded so densely with felted plant material and, I believe hair from the red-brown cows that grazed on the arid plain, that it looked quite like a camp blanket. Only a few feathers surrounded the pale greenish eggs. The incredible labor demanded of so small a bird first to break off the necessary twigs, then weave them into the armored nest hung so carefully from a thin flexible branch won our admiration.

We finally located a verdin nest suspended about five feet above the ground and containing four half-grown young. We dragged a blind through the latticed tangle and shoved it into the thicket until it was the right distance from the nest for photography. After Allan had recorded the activity he needed, I spent several days watching and listening to the lively verdins.

There are many advantages for a person hiding in a blind. Birds, unaware of the watcher, go about their activites quite naturally and unafraid. Usually the view is severely limited, so attention is securely confined within a small frame. Never was this more true than when I sat in the blind by the verdin nest; for the dense tangle of prickly shrubs pressed tightly against the fabric, and a narrow tunnel through them opened on the nest. Within those few feet I saw some astonishing sights.

Once I stared in surprise at a twig on which I counted twenty-five insect pupa cases standing upright. Scarcely had I thought that never before had I seen a twig so parasitized than a slight movement sharpened my eyes. No wonder I thought the pupa cases were on a twig. A caterpillar almost perfectly matching the twig had about reached the end of its life as it came to the end of the twig. Soon a new crop of insects would emerge from those upright pupa cases on the back of the dying caterpillar on which they had dined and grown to larval maturity. But how, I wondered, had the insect that laid its eggs in the body of the doomed caterpillar managed to see a nursery and larder that so precisely matched the twigs on which it lived? In this instance a protective color and pattern had not saved the vulnerable caterpillar.

Not long after, a green anole clung to the same twig. It was quite the palest anole I had ever seen. In fact, as I watched, it turned from its abnormally pale green to almost white. Suddenly the anole's long delicate toes released their grip, and the lizard dropped to the ground. It twisted and thrashed about in agony. Then I saw a small hole near the back of its abdomen, and from that were emerging small insects. Like the caterpillar it had been parasitized, and its body had provided both food and shelter for the ravenous vampires it harbored.

A commotion of bird voices grew in volume and came closer and closer. A roadrunner strode jauntily into view, its shaggy crest lifted, a red streak of skin behind its glowing eye and its bill open as if it were laughing. It stalked past the blind switching its mobile tail, and all the noisy birds followed after it. They were so oblivious to everything but the roadrunner that some of them settled momentarily on the blind to chatter and scold. Probably the roadrunner had just made a good meal of the babies of one of the angry crowd that mobbed it.

Scarcely had the agitated, complaining birds moved on down the loma than I heard something heavy scrambling behind the lattice of branches. Was it a coyote? Or was it the big rattler that last evening at dusk had startled Allan so he rose straight into the air and reversed his direction as perfectly as if he had been on a high springboard executing an impeccable half-twist dive? I strained my eyes toward the rattling, thumping sounds.

A desert tortoise, one of the gopher family, lumbered toward the blind, its brown eyes questing from side to side. It stopped to nibble daintily on a green leaf. Then behind it came another tortoise. Its neck was arched and its beaked mouth was open as it wheezed and hissed with springtime passion. So primitive, so savage, was the sound that I was transported back in time for a hundred million years. The ancestors of these very tortoises had conducted similar hissing courtship rites in Texas as far back as the Permian era.

Occasionally we had found one of the normally sluggish tortoises hiding in the shade of a creosote bush or an opuntia. Rarely did we see one stumping along on its short, stocky, heavily scaled legs. Unlike their eastern relatives, which often dig long burrows, these desert tortoises found the earth baked too hard and took shelter instead under rocks or debris. There they sleep through cold weather and very dry periods, seldom emerging except after a rain has jolted the desert vegetation into sudden growth. Then the tortoises feast and extract liquid from the succulent plants, storing the excess in sacs lying under the carapace, sometimes reserving as much as a pint of it for use during drought periods.

Both sexes have an odd extension of their plastrons, or under shells, which look rather like chin rests. The extension is considerably enlarged in the male, who uses it in fighting to turn over his opponent.

Now the usually sluggish tortoises were suddenly fevered by spring into a frenzied primordial courtship so fierce I was abashed. Oblivious of their surroundings, the female, followed by the hissing male, entered the front of the blind, made her clumsy way between my feet and went out the back. Hearing a particularly frantic scraping and hissing, I saw the female had thrust forward her neck until it was stretched out long and thin. The male now clearly showed his reptilian relationship, as his head held by his arched, taut neck looked exactly like a snake. The female, not yet ready to accept him, went on, and the male hissing on and on, standing high on his elephantlike legs, vanished into the dense chaparral after the smaller female, and the sound of their passage died away in the distance. The primitive mating of the desert tortoise, I decided, could only be regarded as rape made acceptable through millions of years of successful perpetuation of the race. What a contrast it was to the exquisite airy courtship dances of butterflies and the extravagantly varied wooing of birds. Even the running-on-the-water dances of western grebes exhibit a restrained yet ardent charm, though they make us laugh.

I was jolted back to the present when a bird landed on my camera lens and another on top of the blind. Then they thrust their heads into the opening around the lens. It was a pair of great crested flycatchers hunting for a nesting cavity. But no, their bills were completely dark, and their calls had a staccato quality, "Come *here!*" They were Weid's crested flycatchers, the largest of their genus. For a long time they were known as Mexican flycatchers, for few of them spill north of the Rio Grande into the United States except in southern Texas, Arizona, California and a few accidentals on the Florida Keys. For several hours the Weid's crested flycatchers tried to enter the blind; and a couple of times the tail of one hung over my lens when the verdins came to their nest, and I was unable to photograph the visit. The next day the flycatchers or another pair came back and again they spent several hours in a fruitless attempt to enter the blind. They ignored my unfriendly urging to go away. After a couple of days they disappeared, probably going on to a more suitable habitat, for they prefer larger trees than those on the loma and are found most often in Texas where groves border streams or ponds.

Many species of birds approach their nests so quietly, so warily, that a photographer hiding in a blind must be constantly alert or the visit will be missed. The verdins, however, announced their coming well in advance. Long before I saw them, I heard the pair conversing in their light whistles. Usually they arrived together, and the slightly paler female clung briefly to the entrance and then went inside to feed the young birds. Often she returned to the entrance, took the food held by the male and fed it to the small verdins. Then off went the adults to gather more food, calling as they went. Beyond imagining that the verdins called *see, see* to each other I never managed to put words to their calls, though I have found this helps to fix a bird song or call in my mind—as the song of a Scott's oriole approaching a nest with food seems to sing "Eat! Oh now you're going to eat!"

Days flew by and soon in spite of our disappointment over the white-necked raven's nest, we had photographed seventeen species of birds on Loma de la Montuosa. Though we had searched diligently we found only one pair of vermilion flycatchers on the loma, and they were feeding young out of a nest we never located. This brilliant species we longed to photograph above all others in the area, but failure stared us in the face. Our gnome forest had permitted repeated sightings of the vivid flycatcher, but it was too elusive for our cameras.

14

The Loma of the Coals of Fire

THE MEXICANS CALL the vermilion flycatcher *Brasita de fuego,* the little coals of fire, and to many people in our Southwest it is known as the firebird. To the layman many names given to birds by scientists appear both inaccurate and inappropriate, but surely none could be more fitting than *Pyrocephalus* (firehead) , the name of this fiery species.

Of the 365 members of the tyrant flycatcher family, this species is by far the brightest. Moreover, it is one of the few in this large family where the male and female have markedly different plumage. It is the only tyrant flycatcher in the Peterson field guides for the United States that required a separate illustration and description for each sex.

In our country the vermilion flycatcher breeds in Texas and the arid Southwest but frequently strays far from its breeding limits, to the delight of birders. It has been observed in Colorado, Louisiana, and has even surprised birders in Ontario, Canada. One winter a male spent several weeks near Flamingo in Everglades National Park, where thousands delighted in its brilliant plumage. This tropical-looking species is found all the way to central Argentina and has established itself on the Galapagos Islands, five hundred miles west of the coast of South America. No wildlife photographer can see one of these glowing males without longing to capture its beauty on film.

The first time we were in Texas we watched briefly the courtship flight of a vermilion flycatcher. Fresh young mesquite leaves made a tender spring backdrop for its brilliant performance. The male leaped up from a small twig with his feathers so puffed he looked round: a ball of fire. Perhaps fifty feet up he began to drift lightly with butterfly bounds and then hover like a kingfisher above a pond. His wings quivered and his glowing feathers vibrated delicately. All the time his sharp tinkling voice accompanied the airy flight. Suddenly, as if all vitality had drained away, he dropped vertically to the perch from which he had risen and resumed his upright, motionless pose typical of all the flycatcher family.

Whenever we worked on the southern end of Montuosa, we were tantalized by the pair of vermilion flycatchers that had already brought off their young and were kept busy feeding them. We could come close enough to enjoy their beauty, but it was impossible to approach near enough for a good photograph.

Now it happened that we had noted Loma de la Montuosa Chica on our map. It was scarcely a quarter of a mile west of Montuosa, and it was clear that unlike the larger loma, it was covered by an open grove of mesquite and ebony trees. Preoccupied by the wealth of photographic material on Montuosa, we gave no thought to the smaller loma, though it, too, rose from the plain like a small island, less than half a mile long and perhaps a hundred yards across at its widest point.

Late one afternoon when the sun threw a sheet of golden light across the plain, small flocks of migrating sparrows hurtled before the wind like handfuls of brown leaves. Each little flock dropped to the plain, then rose again for a few feet, and so leaped swiftly ahead in spurts as a skillfully thrown flat stone skips across a pond. Snatching our binoculars we followed the rapidly moving mixed flocks, but the strong wind made it difficult to identify the darting birds. Suddenly we were in an open grove of trees. The wind, deflected by the trees, swept across the dense canopy of leaves with a murmur of a thousand distant voices. The low sun thrust long banners of light into the delicate shadows, gliding the earth and the trunks of the slender trees. It touched the fragrant pale yellow catkins with gold. Migrating yellow warblers turned burning yellow, brighter flowers among the mesquites and ebonys. Painted buntings flared into flying jewels.

The searing boisterous wind no longer tugged at us, and in the sudden hush the open, almost lacy glade of Chica beckoned gently. It was like a fairyland after the thorny, almost impregnable gnome forest of Montuosa. In those magic moments before the sun slipped behind the horizon, nighthawks wakened from their day-long sleep on the ground or parallel to some branch and dashed about with gusto, some rising sharply toward the scudding clouds and then plunging earthward at tremendous speeds. When a crash seemed inevitable, they pulled out of the dive with a strange boom, as air rushed through their wing feathers, and they scaled up with merry exuberance.

Just then we heard the sharp call of a vermilion flycatcher, and Allan hurriedly searched for it. Not far from the performing flycatcher, his keen eyes discovered a flat gray nest scarcely as large as a silver dollar plastered on a horizontal limb. The female edged away as Allan went close. Two warm white eggs belted with bold dark spots and scrawls lay in the nest. If we could not find a vermilion flycatcher nest with young in it, at least we could photograph a female as she incubated her beautiful eggs.

The following morning we turned off the Boca Chica highway toward the little hill and almost immediately heard the short call of a vermilion flycatcher. To me it seemed to say *"Boca Chic', Boca Chic' "* sometimes stammering the first part to *"Boc', Boc', Boca Chic'."* The accent was on the final syllable, which rose slightly in pitch with a questioning inflection. Since then I never hear a vermilion flycatcher, whether in Texas, Arizona or California without a sudden vision of the lonely plain, its islandlike lomas and the road leading to Boca Chica.

An emaciated horse with hanging head stood by Loma de la Montuosa Chica. On its back were five bronzed cowbirds. Once these were known as red-eyed cowbirds, a fitting name, for the red eyes of the males shine like rubies against black velvet. The gunmetal gray females, too, have red eyes, though they are lighter and tinged with orange. Allan promptly sprinkled grain for the cowbirds. Since they do not build their own nests but parasitize other species, he hoped they would pose for us when they came to eat the grain. This happened with surprising success. We had always known brown-headed cowbirds fairly well but they had never captured our imaginations. So we were surprised when a male bronzed cowbird that claimed the territory near the grain turned out to be a tireless clown. From dawn until dark this male cowbird put on an astonishing display. He trembled and shook so constantly that Allan quickly named him Admiral Palsy.

Even when Admiral Palsy paused to snatch a few grains he did not entirely forgo his unquenchable urge to display, and his wings continued to droop and quiver as he ate. Around the back of his neck ran a feather ruff that when fully raised, as it was most of the time, reminded me of the rolled sealskin collars often appearing on winter coats of foreign diplomats.

The females that aroused such fervor were darkish gray with a touch of brown blended in it. Whenever one appeared, Admiral Palsy's drooped wings vibrated wildly, and he sprang into the air with his bill pointed downward and his tail bent slightly forward. With rattling primaries he held himself motionless ten or fifteen feet above the female until at last he dropped down in front of her and stood as tall as possible with his spread wings arched forward and the quivering tips resting on the ground. Then he began to bow, doing push-ups at the same time. If she so much as glanced his way, he leaped impetuously into the air with his primaries rattling and all his feathers puffed until he was round, and flew in a circle perhaps fifty feet in diameter. Undoubtedly the fluttery sound of his primaries helped to compensate for his insignificant voice.

Often when the circle flight ended, the cowbird was so exhausted he fell forward with his bill touching the ground. Usually, too, he was frustrated, for by that time the unreceptive female had gone away. Then momentarily the vibration of his wings diminished, only to increase once more when another female came in sight.

Whenever another male sidled toward the grain, Admiral Palsy went into a frenzy until he had chased it away. He ignored all male brown-headed cowbirds, allowing them to eat the grain with impunity, but once we saw him perform before an indifferent female brown-headed cowbird, which is considerably smaller and lighter gray than her bronzed cousin.

Whenever we had a few moments we watched the bronzed cowbird comedy, which continued as long as we worked on Chica. The amazing endurance of that bird was surely comparable to that of bull seals on their breeding islands, where for weeks without food or rest they defend their territories and the females in it. Bent quotes Friedmann (1929) as finding certain males each day in the same tree in southern Texas. While Admiral Palsy occasionally flew into a mesquite, most of his time was spent on the ground, except when he was making a display flight.

We pulled ourselves away from the comic show, and while Allan searched the southern border of Chica, I examined the trees on the opposite side. The ardent sun was tempered by the dense canopy of leaves, and best of all, no flies clung to us.

By keeping well within the grove, I avoided the gusts of wind sweeping across the plain. The chorus of bird song was every bit as vociferous as on Montuosa, and soon I found nest after nest without any entanglement with thorns or spines. As I stopped by a half-built, pale soft nest, the pair of scissor-tailed flycatchers scolded me and hovered in the air above my head. They spread into wide scissor-splits their fantastic tails, which are much longer than their white bodies. Both had bright salmon patches under their wings.

Then my ear caught the alarm note of a vermilion fly-catcher, and looking around I saw a male fluttering slowly downward, its body feathers puffed and its movements almost as quick and shallow as those of a recently emerged cecropia moth engaged in expanding and drying its crumpled wings. He perched briefly and once more performed his butterfly flight and then repeated it a third time. Hearing a note directly above me I looked up. It was the female. Withdrawing a few yards I was erased from her attention, and she moved down several branches, then inched along one of the lowest limbs and began to tug at a small twig. It broke off, and she carried it away.

Later we found an abandoned nest. It was formed chiefly of grass and horsehair. A half dozen small feathers lay in the middle. Around the outside, apparently held in place with spider silk, were some tiny gray catkins and small lichen-covered twigs. Most of the twigs were under an inch in length. While hummingbirds use similar gray lichens to decorate and camouflage their nests, they pull the lichens from the twigs and paste them on the nest with spider silk.

Allan called that he had found a flycatcher nest with two eggs in it. The female was already incubating them. All the nests we found on Chica were very small, and Irby Davis, the distinguished bird expert of the valley, told us that sometimes when three eggs are hatched, one young bird falls from the overcrowded nest. Later in Arizona we invariably found three young birds in each vermilion flycatcher nest. The nests there appeared definitely larger than those on Loma de la Montuosa Chica. Certainly we never had the experience in Arizona of finding a young vermilion flycatcher crowded from its nest. Hudson wrote in *Birds of La Plata* that in Argentina vermilion flycatchers have a normal clutch of four eggs. The same species, it appears, varies its habits in different places.

We now knew the location of three pairs of vermilion flycatchers, but we were still not satisfied. We wanted to photograph the gorgeous male, and it is not his habit to come to the nest until the young hatch. We had come to the end of Chica, but we noted that an irregular line of mesquites and ebony tree continued rather like the tail of a woodrat or the handle of a camp frypan. We decided to examine those trees, though the wind seized and shook us as soon as we left the loma. Almost immediately Allan signaled me to stop. A male vermilion flashed by with something in its bill. It darted into a mesquite that was tossing wildly in the gale. A female stood above a nest, took the insect and fed it to two small birds that looked for all the world like puffs of pepper-and-salt candlewick.

It required our combined efforts to set the blind by the nest. When Allan attempted to throw the cover over the framework the wind caught it. It billowed like a sail and almost pushed him over. Finally we wrestled it into place and I held on while Allan stretched guyropes from each corner and fastened them with tent pegs. The tiny flat nest was saddled on a branch that swayed in a wide arc, so Allan tied ropes to it. These he pulled taut, fastening them also with tent pegs.

While we struggled with the blind, the male flycatcher repeatedly bounced lightly in aerial flight with his bright feathers gleaming. Before we were finished he was joined by a second male. As Allan prepared to go inside the blind he said there must be another nest close by. He did not have to suggest I search for it. No sooner was the blind closed than I proceeded along the row of windswept trees.

Not two hundred feet from the nest where Allan was photographing I caught sight of a glint of red in a mesquite. A male vermilion flycatcher was sitting low on a nest shaken by the gale. Surely that meant the eggs had hatched. I heard a bobwhite sing his piercingly sweet song from the top of a broken stump. From the plain came the clear poignant whistle of a white-crowned sparrow on its way north, perhaps to nest below the snowfields of Mount McKinley in far-off Alaska. A mockingbird burst into a resonant, endlessly varied improvised melody with grace and passion, and then spreading its wings and tail to their fullest to display the white, it darted high above its perch and returned in a great loop. I wished my voice could soar with equal enthusiasm, for I had found a vermilion flycatcher nest with a male in attendance.

Now I could really appreciate his exquisite beauty, for he was only seven feet from my watchful eyes. The short feathers on top of his head were soft and dense as plush, and he flattened them at will or lifted them into a downy pompon. His breast was brilliant red that shaded slightly toward red-orange near the tail. This lighter color curved up beneath the wings and showed only when they were raised in preening or flight. The slightly forked tail, the upper surface of the wings and the back were black lightened by deep rich olive green, a color sometimes used either in nature painting or background draperies by artists in the twelfth and thirteenth centuries. This dark mantle was pulled up to the nape, and slim points were drawn around to the eyes and shining black bill as if the bird were draped with some soft delicate material whose corners were long and crushed almost to nothing as they were pulled forward.

The female, apparently concerned about the strong wind, spent much of her time sheltering the young. When powerful gusts made the sturdy branch sway dangerously she crouched lower and lower until she was almost invisible. Between blasts she relaxed and sat comfortably over her young. During periods of comparative quiet she left to hunt for food. But on that windy day most of the food was brought by the male, who fluttered above the nest until the female reached up, took it and crushed it before feeding it to the young birds. On the few occasions when the female was absent, the male had difficulty in feeding the young. Apparently this was not one of his regular tasks. He did not bother to crush the insects that were too large for the tiny gape of the little birds. Sometimes after struggling to push food too large into their yellow mouths, he ate it himself. Once in a while he dropped the food and did not bother to recover it. Whenever the two birds arrived at the same time, they stood on either side of the nest, their heads close together and their wings fluttering gently.

At first the dull female scarcely seemed to warrant color film. But slowly I came to appreciate her more subtle colors. The slight upward tilt of a light line above her eyes gave her an alert, lively expression. Strong gray-buff lines streaked her breast and back. She had a salmon-pink wash under her wings and tail. In this respect there is great variation among female vermilion flycatchers. Apparently the young ones are yellow where my bird was salmon-pink. The colors and streaks deepen and darken with age, so older females are more beautiful than the young ones.

Though the wind was forever troublesome, the flycatchers presented varied and interesting activities for our cameras, and we could not bring ourselves to take away the blinds. The young birds grew quickly, and soon small feathers began to push through the down. One morning the nest was empty, and the adults darted about feeding the young, which soon managed flights of a few yards.

Perhaps it was exuberance over the successful rearing of

the brood, perhaps a resurgence of sexual enthusiasm or only concern because we were so close to the nest where the young birds had been tended, but twice while we untied guy ropes and folded the blind, the male shot high with excitement. His tail swung forward, his fiery feathers were lifted and his glowing crown expanded. Vibrating his wings, he bounded ecstatically, rising, falling, until finally his strength was exhausted and he fluttered down, a radiant vermilion ball shouting "Boca Chic', Boca Chic'."

In the fairylike forest of Chica, we had watched the bronzed cowbird's courtship performance, and it was a hilarious sight. It made us laugh as ludicrous behavior of people does.

The flycatcher puffed himself until he was every bit as round, as ball-like, as the cowbird. Yet the sky dance of the flycatcher as he bounded lightly as a butterfly held us breathless. It was ethereal and poetic.

The end sought by each was the same. Perhaps it was the somber black coat of the cowbird with its implication of night and the unknown, while the flycatcher is perhaps the most brilliant of all birds in the United States and actually appears lighted with an inner glow, that triggered the contrasting response to the courtship of the two Chica species.

Aldo Leopold, in his *Sand County Almanac,* warned that it is not wise to return to a wilderness once loved, but his wisdom did not enter our thoughts three years later when we turned toward Loma de la Montuosa Chica with happy anticipation. Had we remembered, we would have ignored the thought as not applicable in Chica. Chica was a very small place, and though shunned by people, it was very close to a city. There we would watch once more, we thought, the comic performance of bronzed cowbirds seeking mates and the ethereal beauty of vermilion flycatchers fluttering like flaming balls.

A barbed wire fence now bordered the Boca Chica road.

Signs posted on it warned of danger from packs of rabid dogs. Dismayed, we looked across the plain toward Chica. It was gone. Dead. Dead as sunken Atlantis. Dead as Pompeii. Dead as the legendary hanging gardens of Babylon.

I rolled under the barbed wire and walked toward the site of the loma. Baked hard and bleached white, the loma was only a gently mounded skeleton. Where a lacy canopy had sheltered a host of birds and lesser creatures, there was nothing. The mesquite, which burns with the greatest fragrance of any Texas tree, may have been used for firewood, but what possible explanation could there be for removing every vestige of life from the once fairylike grove?

Tomlinson wrote in *The Sea and the Jungle* that "I begin to think the commercial mind is the most dull, wasteful, and ignorant of all the sad wonders in the pageant of humanity." Perhaps some misguided cotton grower thought he could add an acre to his field and so killed the loma and its gentle beauty and all its complicated life community.

Bleached shells of the long thin snails that once contentedly marched over the flattened stems of opuntia eating as they progressed, lay in windrows. All bird life went when the trees and plants were destroyed. Of animal life only ants remained on the hot cracked earth.

Thought, feeling and tears were frozen by the total destruction, and I could only echo William Henry Hudson's "The beautiful has vanished and returns not."

15

Vingtune

HAVING UNCEREMONIOUSLY declined a presidential pardon shortly after the War of 1812, the pirate Jean Laffite with a gang of his followers left Louisiana and set up a ribald, roistering, unholy nest of brigands, smugglers and riffraff where Galveston now stands. In the midst of gambling halls, saloons, slavemarkets and other unsavory establishments, swashbuckling cutthroats thrived and died prosperously. Then in 1821 some members of this brawling roost with very bad judgement fired on ships of the United States. Forthwith the nest was cleaned out but not before the Indians revenged at least one of the injuries they had suffered at the hands of the pirates. Four of Laffite's thugs on a hunting trip stole a squaw and abused her so she died. The enraged Karankawas promptly caught four of Laffite's men, roasted and ate them.

According to persistent folklore, Laffite knew the Vingtune Islands in Trinity Bay very well. Some say, in spite of the very slight tidal movement around them, that his ships were careened there. Others claim that Laffite, a compulsive gambler, loved to play twenty-one. When he wished to play undisturbed he would withdraw with some favored cronies to the Vingtunes. Those who support this version say there never were twenty-one islands in the group, and *Vingtune* is merely a corruption of the French name for Laffite's favorite game, *vingt-et-un.*

All along our eastern seaboard legends of visits by pirates cling to the majority of islands. Naturally no self-respecting buccaneer ever left an island without burying a fortune for the lucky one who can uncover it. Probably Laffite was as well supplied with gold and jewels as any other nineteenth-century pirate, yet no legend suggests he buried treasure on the Vingtunes. This lends a certain authenticity to the tales of his association with the islands. To have buried treasure on them would have been the height of folly. The first severe storm would have flung the glittering booty about, exposing part to the greedy eyes of the first comer and washing the rest into the bottom of Trinity Bay to lie helter-skelter among the oyster shells and become encrusted with stonelike skeletons of sea creatures.

Yet though no lingering tale connects Laffite's ill-gotten plunder with the Vingtunes, today they hold a treasure of enormous value. No American with the slightest appreciation of our wildlife heritage or with even a primitive sense of beauty can remain unmoved by the stunning variety and splendor of the birds that nest on the two larger islands of the Vingtunes. During the breeding season they are protected by a warden of the National Audubon Society and the added watchful care of Joe Whitehead of Smith Point.

While Joe was still a schoolboy, his interest in animal life impressed John Baker, then president of the National Audubon Society, who enlisted his help in guarding the treasure of the Vingtunes. This Joe continued to do until he left to study engineering at Texas A. and M. Having earned his degree, he decided that engineering was not really his field and returned to study veterinary medicine. Now a practicing veterinarian at Smith Point, his interest in the birds of the Vingtunes continues. Over the years the colony has flourished, and its numbers have increased almost to the total capacity of the islands.

Actual protection of the nesting birds has been easier than maintaining a good habitat and ample feeding grounds around the islands. The colony is located not far from the busy, rapidly growing cities of Galveston and Houston. It is in the midst of oil-rich waters. Seismograph crews constantly test the depths in their search for new pools of oil beneath the waters of the bay. Dredges scoop oyster shells from the bottom to use in cement and road building. Sometimes they come too close to the islands, and occasionally their excavations have made the loosely mounded islands shift. Fishing skiffs and shrimpers dot the waters. Thus there have been repeated problems in persuading various business interests of the value of protecting the islands and of keeping as a safe distance from them during the nesting season. That the colony continues to flourish is due to the effective diplomacy of many Texas organizations interested in good conservation practices. The National Audubon Society, in addition, financed the protection of the islands so neither well-meaning or merely curious people can interfere with the birds by visiting them. Moreover, it has a continuing program for awakening Americans to the fragile quality of the wildlife treasure we still possess in easily destroyed places such as the Vingtune Islands.

Discovery by oyster shell dredgers not long ago of a ninety-foot ship of Civil War age indicates the water around the Vingtunes was deeper in the past. Now it is difficult to approach them except in small boats. The islands are almost wholly built of loosely heaped oyster shell, some of it broken as fine as sand. Hurricanes rip the islands apart and rebuild them in new shapes and sizes. Occasionally a great tempest builds a new island or erases an old one. A recent War Department map shows five islands, where an older Coast and Geodetic map shows only four. Two of the islands hold spectacular concentrations of large wading birds during the nesting season.

Except on a fairly detailed map of Galveston Bay, it is seldom possible to locate the Vingtunes. Many maps fail to show them at all. Sometimes they appear as a small unnamed peppering of tiny dots. But if a map explorer studies a large-scale map of Galveston Bay he can locate, fingering into the bay from the northeast shore, a good-sized peninsula shaped like a wave with its crest curling slightly backward toward the east. This peninsula, Smith Point, creates two subsidiary bays: East Bay between Smith Point and Bolivar Peninsula, and Trinity Bay reaching toward Anahuac and swinging westward to Houston Point. The Vingtunes lie on the inside curve of the wave off the swampy tip of Smith Point, which swarms with a stinging plague of mosquitoes.

In the comparatively short time we have known the Vingtunes they have changed greatly. The first time we were sent to photograph the colony, the largest island was covered with a dense low thicket of opuntia and thorny bushes so close together that herons skipped over their tops as easily as they ran on the beach. Hundreds of herons nested on it, and a few spoonbills added bright color to the colony.

Then a hurricane swept away practically all vegetation. The Houston Outdoor Nature Club members, foreseeing disaster ahead for their favorite bird colony, energetically swarmed over the island almost as soon as the hurricane died away. They planted salt-tolerant, quick-growing tamerisk and oleanders. Soon these shrubs formed a dense band of irregular depth just above the beach all around the island. Herons and spoonbills nested in a bouquet of pink and white oleander flowers and filmy sprays of rosy tamerisk.

For a few years the swampy interior of the island was an open cane field. Glossy ibis built their nests in the wetter parts, and when the bushes were entirely filled with nests, the overflow population of herons occupied the drier parts of the

cane. When nutria moved into Texas some of them swam out
to the Vingtunes. They ate the cane until its roots no longer
bound together the interior of the largest island. The next
hurricane tore out its center, which then became a pond. Finally during a storm the ring of shell on which the tamerisk
and oleander grew was broached on the south, and the tide
washed in and out of the former pond. Gradually the shore of
this pond was enlarged and the bottom lowered as the tide
scoured it.

Since the behavior of wild animals has changed little for
countless centuries and will remain little changed for countless years to come, a wildlife photographer can glimpse time,
past and future, as he works. Because comparatively few people have reason to visit undeveloped areas preferred by wildlife, a photographer working in the field sometimes steps
back in time as lodging, too, is concerned. On our first trip to
the Vingtunes, we existed in a minute dreary room. There
was no plumbing; only primitive outdoor facilities. We
cooked outside over an open fire, slapping mosquitoes and
fanning smoke from our eyes as we heated something from a
can. We learned to respect redbugs then, for both of us were
covered with great red welts where they burrowed under our
skin. We were doubly uncomfortable, since we had no place
to bathe. We tried the bay, but sand flies attacked us there
and the water was so shallow we had scarcely reached knee
depth by the time we were exhausted from wading away from
shore.

We returned in 1954 to stay about a week. Then we lodged
at a camp near the mosquito swamp of Smith Point. The
manager was frank enough to say the camp was set up for
fishermen. He claimed fishermen did not care what kind of
shelter they had so long as fishing was good. When we paid
our bill we wondered if the manager was a blood brother of
Laffite. The cost of the wretched cabin was somewhat above
that of first-class accommodations elsewhere in Texas.

Indoors and out mosquitoes tormented us. Our screens were in wretched disrepair, so the mosquitoes roamed freely through them. Each evening when my hands were busy in the changing bag preparing Allan's film holders for the next day's photography, he stood alongside swatting the insects as they settled on me.

This time we had plumbing, not in our cabin, but in a central washhouse. Clouds of mosquitoes mustered for attack as we dashed toward it, and swarmed over us inside. They even bit us as we stood under the shower.

The central washhouse presented other hazards. One evening we returned to find the seismograph crew who parked their explosives truck between our cabins, standing over a forty-two-inch rattler they had just killed a few feet from the door. Cattle grazed freely about the camp grounds; regrettably they were not lawn-broken. One morning we opened our door to find our way barred by about two hundred cattle including many huge, short-tempered Brahma bulls. They held us prisoners until the manager rolled out his truck, loaded it with grain and disappeared down the track sounding his soft, mooing cattlecall.

The water at the camp was salty and the nearest available drinking water was two miles away. In those days the road to Smith Point was dusty and unpaved. The nearest telephone was fastened to a pole some fifteen miles away. The store was about twenty-five miles distant in Anahuac.

Anahuac is a very old village whose history goes back to the earliest days of Americans in Texas. For a while after the fall of the Alamo it was the only open port on the entire Texas coast. Its name, Aztec in origin, means country-of-the-waters. When our larder was low, the trip to replenish our supplies was a long dusty one, but I enjoyed the step back into early Texas history. A traveler from New York reached Anahuac in March, 1831, and was much struck by the boundless uniformity of the prairie and the multitudes of water fowl clustered together. They were not shy, those thousands of ducks, geese and other fowl including one he had never met before. It was of great size and "must have weighed forty or fifty pounds but it spread its great wings at the click of the gunlock and was soon out of reach." Most early explorers, impressed by unfamiliar wildlife, overestimated size und numbers. The New Yorker may have seen a swan, a whooping crane or a white pelican. Of these large birds, the trumpeter swan that once migrated as far south as the gulf coast weighed as much as thirty pounds.

In 1961 Carl W. Buchheister, then president of the National Audubon Society, needed new films of the Audubon sanctuaries on the Texas coast, and again we returned to Smith Point. We rented an airy cottage behind the new Vanta-un store, which stocked fruits, salad materials and had a frozen food locker with TV dinners and ice cream. Conditions for photographers on assignment at the Vingtunes had changed radically. The primitive days had ended for anyone fortunate enough to rent the single available cottage.

Each morning we followed a twisted channel that almost doubled the actual distance from Smith Point to Vingtune. In the shallow bay miscalculation of the channel means being stuck on a mud bar. Each morning the spray soaked us to the skin, and I was grateful to the chemists who had developed nylon, a positive godsend to wildlife photographers. Though dripping with salt water when we reached the island, my clothes were dried in minutes by the same wind that had flung water over me.

Arriving at the larger bird island, we stepped into warm greenish water and pulled the boat against the shore. In a short time Allan and I were settled for the day in our blinds, usually at opposite ends of the island. The warden patrolled the area to make sure no boat came close enough to disturb the birds, and then went home. There was no danger of illegal landings with our blinds standing conspicuously on the island.

My favorite post was close to the edge of a water-filled depression scooped out of the wide west beach that spring. This storm-hollowed pool was about twenty feet long and ten wide. It was shallow enough so the smallest herons—Louisianas and snowys—could wade anywhere in it without wetting their feathers except at periods of highest water when wind-driven tides increased the depth several inches as bay water seeped through the loose shell.

Through the back window of my blind I could see a long sweep of brilliant beach lapped by sparkling bay waters. This beach swung in a semicircle around the west end of the island on my left. From the front window and the one on my right I watched the little pool bordered with bleached and broken oyster shells. In the background a tangle of feathery tamerisk brushed with delicate rosy clusters of small flowers curved to the right until they met the glaring beach. Allan dragged a large twisted piece of silvery driftwood to the right extremity of the pool. The birds welcomed this as a convenient perch and often posed on it.

The first day I spent in the blind I learned the birds lacked nest materials. They worked feverishly to break twigs from the living tamerisk, leaping repeatedly from the ground, seizing a twig in the bill and settling back as if to use the weight of their bodies as well as their bills to snap off the desirable stick. They stole twigs when incubating birds drowsed in the heat. I formed a habit each evening of gathering a large bundle of stiff grasses and small sticks on the mainland and heaping them on the shells near the pool for the birds.

The grasses and sticks were rapidly carried away. Louisiana herons and white ibis carefully weighed each stick and, having made a choice, went off with it. Several times a spoonbill jumped down from its nest to join in the competition, but after balancing and discarding one stick after another, went back to its nest empty-billed. Probably the sticks were too small; spoonbills built their nests of heavier material than the other species near the blind.

The snowy egrets were most active of all and carried away the bulk of the sticks. They were delightful to watch as they ran about picking up and discarding sticks before choosing from the pile. They spread their wings and ran with a dip and swoop, turning stick-gathering into a lovely dance. Having made a choice, a snowy egret raised its snow-flake plumes in a filmy cloud and ran to the nest to present it to its mate. Of all the heron tribe, the snowy egret is the most animated, lively and graceful. With profound gratitude we can thank earlier generations who saved them from extinction at a time when the fragile plumes were worth twice their weight in gold and entire colonies were being exterminated for fashion and profit.

Conger Hagar, that amazing bird-watcher of Rockport who through her intensive and precise knowledge of the birds has changed the whole picture of bird migration in that area, once told me a story of her childhood. She accompanied her mother to an elegant formal tea. One lady in a Paris gown wore a hat with a small fortune in egret plumes perched on top. As she bent over the tea table, a candle flame touched the plumes and they blazed instantly and as quickly became a charred ruin. While the ladies commiserated with the fashionplate for the loss of her costly plumes, little Connie hugged herself with joy. She had been taught to think rather than conform blindly, and as far as she was concerned, egret plumes belonged only on the birds that grew them.

Though most Americans have a civilized conviction that wild bird plumes should not be used for decoration, there is a constant threat to this belief by fashionable couturiers who not only use in their collections the feathers of rare birds but the pelts of rare mammals, particularly some of the close-to-extinction felines.

Daily the temperature rose into the upper nineties though a strong southeast wind usually tempered the heat slightly. So many birds had died in a big spring storm that a miasma of putrefaction had settled over the island. I thought the birds fortunate in having an underdeveloped sense of smell. From I blind I had a clear view of nests of Louisiana herons, snowy and common egrets, white ibis and roseatte spoonbills while half concealed in the thicket I glimpsed a hundred and fifty or more. There was constant noise and motion in the colony. Overhead, laughing gulls cackled. I watched a diamond-backed terrapin lay its eggs in a hole it excavated in the shells with its hind legs and then cover them with alternate sweeps of its hind feet. As it swept, it moved slowly forward as if to confuse with extra disturbance any predator that might hunt for the eggs. Even as the terrapin entered the water the strong wind was erasing the faint marks it had made. It swam away without a backward glance. Its responsibility for the next generation had been fulfilled. The future of the eggs, unprotected and forgotten, was in the hands of nature.

A clinking of shells made me turn. One hundred and twenty-three spoonbills had gathered on the beach behind the blind. Half a dozen left the company and strode off the beach into my pool. Their bills, shaped like a Ubangi belle's lips, were strange and primitive. Their eyes were cherry red. For a period during the breeding cycle, the bare head of an adult spoonbill becomes apple green, but these birds had only a small greenish area around the eyes. Black skin reached from the throat over the ears and across the nape. An odd little pouch, oblong in shape, was slung beneath the base of the lower mandible. Their upper legs were rosy pink but this flush of color was lost in black toward the feet.

Their plumage was glorious. The neck, upper breast and shoulders were white with a suffusion of ochre near the wings. Most of the body and wings were bright yet delicate rose-petal pink. On the upper breast was a badge of curly stiffened carmine feathers surrounded by a flush of pink and pale ochre. The same rich carmine dripped over the wings and there was a touch of the deep color on the throat.

The spoonbills opened their wings and laid them flat on the surface of the pond, and spread their vivid orange-ochre tails. As they turned I saw the short dense feathers surrounding the tail were as bright carmine as the wing coverts.

There was a hiss of wings followed by the rattle and clink of shells. Several young spoonbills had come to bathe. Black-tipped primaries gave character to their otherwise too delicate pink and white plumage. Their dark eyes were surrounded by blue skin so they looked blue-eyed at a distance. Downy feathers covered the entire head which is naked in the adults. Each time an adult came to the pond, four or five young birds would string out behind it, jerking their heads up and down comically and pleading for food which they were quite old enough to find for themselves. The adults ignored the young birds and their pleading.

Some spoonbills were still incubating eggs. As the temperature climbed, these birds turned their backs to the sun and at once assumed a most ferocious appearance, one fierce enough to halt a predator and give momentary pause to the stoutest heart. The drooping tail resembled a wide flat nose. Around this, rich carmine glowed almost blood-red. The wings were held slightly away from the body so deep shadows lay between like enormous dark frowning eyes.

The heat was almost too much for a Louisiana heron incubating its eggs under the full blast of the sun. Twice it darted off the nest into the pond, almost diving as it reached the surface; but flattening out there, it slid its head and neck under the water. With a single splash of its wings it sent beads of water over its back and then flashed back to its nest in a matter of seconds.

With a rustle of many wings, a large band of white ibis swept down to the pond. They were in the full beauty and vigor of breeding time, quite unlike the faded ones that had taken sticks earlier or now were incubating their eggs. In manner they were confident, almost arrogant. Their plumage was glossy and their legs were vivid red.

Blue eyes glistened in their flaming frames of red and their bills were brilliant red about half way from the face where glossy black replaced it. The tip was yellow. The skin on their bare faces was finely wrinkled but gave no impression of age. These birds were at the very peak of beauty and virility.

Some of the ibises had flaming bubbles about the size of golf balls under their bills. These they expanded at will and let collapse to nothing very much as tree frogs expand and contract their throat membranes when they sing.

A few of the ibises splashed energetically in the pond and then withdrew to the beach where they lay with their wings spread wide and their eyes closed. It is likely most birds enjoy sun-bathing, and I have photographed many species engaged in it. Always the birds looked sick or dead so I stopped using film on sun-bathing bids. An activity obviously enjoyed by a subject does not necessarily make an attractive photograph.

One day I noted a pair of spoonbills, one still immature with fuzz lingering on its head and only a tinge of yellow in its tail and little carmine on its shoulders, building a nest on my right. How they did clap their bills as they arrived at the slight platform with additional sticks! Each time they approached, they perched on top of the blind before going to the partly-built nest.

A pair of common egrets busily incubating eggs near the new nest resented it. Perhaps they sensed the immature spoonbill was not old enough for parental responsibilities. Several times when the spoonbills departed to collect nest materials, one of the common egrets with very green lores stole a stick and presented it to its incubating mate who accepted it with guttural notes and tucked it under the eggs.

Finally the spoonbills, returning with sticks in their bills, caught the thieving egret in the act of removing a twig. Standing side by side on their nest platform, the spoonbills jabbed noisily at the egret. The egret persisted, pulling more sticks from beneath the spoonbills' feet. Quickly other herons gathered and snatched sticks amid great confusion. Wings beat wildly and bills flashed. In a short time the nest was a ruin. The spoonbills made no further attempt to build anywhere within range of my vision.

Each day late in the afternoon there was a rush of air as if a whirlwind approached. The sky was filled with spoonbills, deeply carmine and rose, shining in the late sunlight that emphasized every shade and tint. Twice around the island in close-massed flight they raced in an explosion of pink. Then the show was over. No doubt the spoonbills had fed well in some distant marsh, and then, homeward-bound, they had gathered other feeding groups into their ranks, and returned to relieve their mates that had incubated the eggs or sheltered young birds for many hours, and free them for their turn in shallow waters where killifish swarm.

The exuberance of the spoonbills as the speeding cloud swept around the island was a visible emotion. It aroused drowsing birds on the nest. Herons and ibises in the pool stirred and became restless. As if the arrival of the spoonbills had broken a spell of idle tedium cast by the feverish sun, the colony became animated. Though devoid of music, squawks, grunts and clacks filled the air as young cried for food and battles between neighbors broke out. After a somnolent afternoon noise and agitated movement were everywhere.

The flight of the spoonbills may have been a signal to all birds belonging to the colony, for lines of herons and ibises converged on Vingtune from all directions. Sometimes three or four flew together. Sometimes half a hundred swept toward the island in swift, airy masses. The lapsing flight of herons was direct in its course, and the swiftly beating black-tipped wings of the white ibises was undeviating as the flight of an arrow. All came toward the island guided unerringly by an accurate internal compass across miles of empty skies.

Long before Carla smashed into the Vingtunes on September 11, 1961, more than two thousand ibises, herons and spoonbills had dispersed in various directions, some of the young herons venturing as far north as Canada. The older herons and the spoonbills formed small bands and wandered through coastal Texas and bordering states, lingering wherever they found good feeding conditions. Most found a place of safety during the great hurricane and suffered little from it.

Though Carla's devastating winds did little harm to the Vingtune birds, they severely damaged the vegetation. They reduced the size of the larger island considerably. The smaller colony island lost about a a quarter of its area. Because of the impairment to the islands, the population was surveyed the following spring with deep concern. The number of bird nesting there actually increased despite crowded conditions. More than twice as many spoonfuls nested there as in 1950.

By 1967, the population of spoonbills, believed threatened by extinction in the United States in the 1930's, has recovered most satisfactorily, not only in Texas but in Florida. The coastal islands of Texas now support many of their colonies under the protection of the National Audubon Society and others interested in the welfare of our wildlife. It is no longer included in the list of rare and endangered species published by the United States Bureau of Sports Fisheries and Wildlife.

If, as some scientists believe, roseate spoonfuls as a race are declining from old age, it appears that the steps taken to protect them and their nesting places have been so effective that Americans for many, many generations to come may be able to see them in their natural surroundings. This rosy picture is dependent on continued interest in their protection.

Though spoonbills look exactly as they did in the Pleistocene when shambling, beetle-browed creatures only faintly resembling modern man hunted saber-toothed tigers, they will continue to fly like fragments of sunset clouds for centuries to come if we care enough to save the islands and the marshes they require for life.

16

Joe's Henry

JOE WHITEHEAD, on his hands and knees by a lumber pile in a shed on his parents' ranch near Smith Point, puffed out his cheeks and with his lips closed directed moaning, gulping sounds toward a hole larger than those made by woodchucks. In a few minutes something deep in the hole answered.

A quiver of bushy yellowish-gray whiskers blocked the entrance to the hole, and then a short nose above long incurved red-orange incisors as prominent as those of Bugs Bunny came forward. Small dark-brown eyes with round pupils that shrunk quickly to narrow vertical lines looked blindly at us.

"Nutrias are mostly nocturnal," Joe said. "Probably he can see little more than motion. But he can stay under water up to seven minutes and close his ears when he is under the surface," he added as little round ears came into view.

For a moment the dim-sighted eyes looked our way, and round ears moved as if zeroing in on sounds. Then a bulky rodent body emerged, dragging a long round tail, naked except for coarse black hairs that were fairly dense near the body but very scattered toward the tip.

"This is Henry," Joe introduced his pet as he picked up the thirty-pound mammal, which straddled his arm contentedly. "Nutrias are generally considered an ecological nui-

279

sance, but Henry is a fine pet. I've had him since I found him, a quarter-grown kit."

Henry's overcoat was dark reddish-brown except across the shoulders, where the fur was tipped with yellow.

"I can understand why nutria fur isn't very popular," I commented. "It is too coarse, and the color isn't pretty."

"Don't judge Henry's fur potential by its unprocessed appearance," Joe said. "Remember the guard hairs must be removed from beaver and otter pelts before the fur is ready for use."

He ran his fingers through Henry's long fur and lifted it. Underneath was a short dense bluish-gray inner coat. I touched it gingerly, for Henry's teeth were formidable and I had heard that nutrias, if cornered by a dog, fight savagely and frequently kill their attackers. I was not sure how Henry might react to the touch of a stranger. But he did not object when I put my hand on his fur. It was soft as moleskin, soft as eiderdown.

Joe lowered Henry to the ground and shook his arm.

"Henry is too heavy to hold that way. Wild nutria average twenty pounds or less and are under thirty inches long. Henry is about twenty-five inches long, not counting his tail."

Joe reached into a plum tree beside us and picked one of the ripe purple fruits. He handed it to Henry, who took it in his four-fingered, unwebbed front feet and turned it as dexterously as a raccoon. Using his long tail as a prop, he sat upright on his heavy five-toed, webbed hind feet. Only those powerful hind legs are used in swimming, and the shorter, more delicate front legs then lie close to the body. Apparently nutrias have sensitive tactile corpuscles in their paws, and their sense of touch is far more important than their sight. Their hearing comes second in usefulness and their sense of smell is poorly developed.

In no time Henry had finished his plum and begged for another. Before he was satisfied, he had eaten nine of them. Then he groomed himself meticulously as a cat. Replete and clean at last, he set off for a pond shaded by a fine stand of cypress planted by Joe's grandfather. Henry walked into the dark water under the trees and swam up and down with a long silver V trailing behind.

"Henry is almost as large as a beaver," Allan remarked. "It would be difficult to tell whether you were seeing a beaver or a nutria swimming along if you couldn't see the tail, wouldn't it?"

"Beavers don't have such a crop of whiskers," Joe said. "There are definite records of beavers in only nine Texas counties, but nutrias have been recorded in at least 100 of our 254 counties in the state. Most Texas beavers are found along the Rio Grande in the Big Bend country, and some of their holes are so big a man can crawl into them and are 30 feet long. Some men have claimed to find beaver holes 150 feet long but that sounds to me like a tall story—or a long one! When you see a big rodent swimming in coastal waters or marshes of Texas you can be quite sure it is a nutria."

Henry came out of the pond and again groomed himself.

"Nutria always take excellent care of themselves and are clean and dry before they go into their burrows or piled-up nests if they live where burrows aren't feasible. Their nest platforms look almost like swan nests and are put close to the edge of open water. You can see a lot of them along the canals and tidal fingers in the Smith Point marsh."

Henry, now thoroughly clean and dry, was going back to his hole under the lumber pile and would sleep there until sunset.

"See how the body almost drags on the ground?" Joe asked. "Of course he is too fat, but all nutrias are low-slung like otters."

The introduction of nutrias into the wilds of this country was unintentional. In the early 1930's the late Edward A.

McIlhenny of Avery Island, Louisiana, (where fiery tabasco sauce is made) imported a few pairs from South America and kept them in "escape-proof" enclosures. Along came a hurricane that flooded the area and boosted the imprisoned mammals over their confining walls, whereupon they made a successful flight from captivity. Once free in the Louisiana marshes they multiplied with all the prodigious fecundity of the guinea pigs in Ellis Parker Butler's hilarious story, *Pigs Is Pigs*. Soon they were so numerous it was almost impossible to walk in the marshes without stepping on their tracks. The situation was far from funny to trappers, who depended for their livelihood on the great Louisiana muskrat population.

Muskrat traps proved too small to hold mature nutria while those too young to be of commercial value repeatedly sprung the traps. Also nutria cut down to some extent the muskrat population by literally eating them out of home and food. Soon farmers were aroused to wrath when nutria, forced from the marshes by over-crowding and hunger invaded agricultural fields and irrigation channels where they ate the crops and perforated the dikes. Food normally available for wintering waterfowl was devoured. Hitherto abundant sport provided by hunting clubs declined abruptly.

After our introduction to Henry, we hurried to Smith Point, hoping to see a wild nutria. An amazing change had taken place since our last visit to the area for then we had never heard of nor seen a nutria there. See a wild nutria we did, and his brothers, sisters, aunts and uncles. They crisscrossed the canal. They splashed off the banks. We heard others moaning and gulping back in the marsh grasses. Excited by their abundance we squelched through the marsh surrounded by a cloud of mosquitoes whining with high thin voices. Everywhere we went we saw nutrias until we had counted no less than two hundred before darkness hid them from sight. Their moaning and gulping with occasional cries like a wounded man in agony continued, and so did splashes as their heavy bodies dropped into the water.

The nutria continue to multiply. A female is mature in six or seven months and has three litters annually. These average five to the litter, though there may be as many as thirteen. Though they live only an average of four years, in that time a pair of nutria multiplies enormously.

At Smith Point we sometimes watched a female swim across the canal with kits on her back. This mammal has made a surprising adaptation to her aquatic habitat. Her milk glands are on her back, four or five on a side, so the young can swim beside her or cling to her back as she swims and help themselves to her milk bar as they travel. Then they must impede her almost as much as a sea anchor slows a boat, but she plows right on through the water.

Whenever plants or animals are introduced deliberately or by accident into a completely new habitat, trouble often follows. Without the controls developed through millenniums of time the displaced plant or animal often runs wild.

The whisper of tumbleweed rolling before prairie winds is now a part of the arid West. Tumbleweed was inadvertently introduced on this continent in gold-rush days when bales of Manchurian-grown hay for horses could be purchased more cheaply from the Orient than from the eastern United States. Bounding before prairie winds and dropping its seeds a few at a time it established colonies over all the arid western plains. Now it clogs drainage ditches. It lodges against fences where it drops many of its seeds and then may shove over the fence itself as, piled high, it makes a wide interlaced surface that howling winds can push violently. It forms a tinderbox for wild prairie fires.

Endless insects including the Japanese beetle brought accidentally into this country have become terrible pests, for they lack the controls present in their native environment. One such pest, the *Aedes aegypti* mosquito, arrived in the Americas from Africa in the fresh-water supply of slave ships and carried with it the dread diseases, yellow fever and dengue. It has caused untold misery and death. For decades it held up the Panama Canal, causing the French to abandon the deadly project later completed by the United States. Yet the deaths caused by that small mosquito in Panama were but a fraction of the total in the Americas. Now that mosquito, at a cost of billions to taxpayers, is being exterminated in the West Indies and both North and South America.

Domestic plants and animals almost universally require the care and protection of man and do not easily escape into the wild. But unwanted wildlife that follows man wherever he goes has often proved to be an enemy. The Norway rat, a carrier of bubonic plague and a destroyer of products valued in tens of millions of dollars annually, has made himself at home here. No sooner had canals bypassed the hitherto impassable Niagara Falls than conger eels swarmed into the Great Lakes and did incalculable injury to the fishing industry there.

Innumerable instances of unfortunate introductions of plants and animals may be recalled and should be sufficient to make us all cautious about bringing any species into a new habitat. Yet recently newspapers carried a story about an irresponsible person who tired of caring for some piranha fish and dumped them into a southern stream. Should they begin to multiply those waters would become dangerous to swimmers and boatmen.

Joe's Henry is by now dead from old age. He was an interesting pet, a gentle mammal with exotic long red-orange teeth, and was immaculate at all times. His kind made trouble for many people and for the wildlife of the gulf marshes. They did not choose to come here, but once happily chewing their way across the vast wetlands, they found a congenial home and abundant food. They settled in and are probably here to stay. At first the hand of man was universally turned against them, but gradually the trappers are finding they can obtain a stable million dollars annually from the nutria pelts and from the carcasses which are sold chiefly to mink ranchers.

About 1598 Shakespeare wrote, "the evil that men do lives after them" and this is particularly true in relation to our environment. When good men deliberately or inadvertently introduce a strange form of life from a distant place so its natural controls are lacking, it may burst forth as wildly as a forest fire before a high wind and modify all other life endlessly. We may learn to control with it or live with it, but its effect is endless.

17

Colonists from a Far Country

THE PITILESS SUN approached the zenith and a burning shaft probed through a hole in the dense mangrove canopy on my right. It lighted two white birds so that they glowed as if suddenly incandescent, pulling my eyes from the spoonbill incubating three greenish-white, chocolate-splashed eggs on a bulky nest before my blind in the little Vingtune colony.

The spotlighted birds were cattle egrets, motionless as graven images, their necks thrust forward at a slight angle as they stared at my blind. I had not seen them arrive, and my astonishment grew as I returned their frozen gaze. For the first time I saw cattle egrets at close range in the full glory of their breeding colors.

On their heads, down their backs, and over their breasts fell delicate threadlike plumes the color of aged bourbon. Their stout bills, pale in winter, were tipped with lively yellow that merged into bright rose suffused with blue near the face and continued more intensely over the lores. Their orange-yellow eyes were edged by a thin streak of black and their legs, so anemic in winter, were bright yellow.

Suddenly there was a commotion. A small company of Louisiana herons and snowy egrets swept into the mangrove cavern. The cattle egrets erupted into small tornadoes, whirl-

ing this way and that in tight little circles, jabbing fiercely
with flashing bills at the intruders. Their plumes were lifted,
and raised feathers gave their usually slender necks a thick,
almost massive look. From frozen statues the egrets had exploded into noisy darting furies.

Grumbling pettishly among themselves the intruders withdrew, and silence fell in the green cavern. The cattle egrets
returned to their former perch and, side by side, again became immobile. Suddenly their feathers contracted, and they
appeared to shrink. They slumped into an obsequious cringe.
One, advancing in a crouch, sidled along the limb and to my
astonishment settled on a nest I had not noticed before. The
second egret crept warily to the side of its mate and lowered
its head submissively as if in obeisance before a superior
when a great blue heron swooped into the mangrove and
poised on the rim of a large nest a couple of feet from the cattle egrets.

Instantly five half-grown great blue herons shot upright,
their long skinny necks began to sway and with loud begging
cries they demanded food. While the feeding proceeded the
cattle egrets preserved their humble pose and maintained it
after all the food had been devoured and the young settled
down to sleep. The adult heron stood quietly on the nest for
some time, but no sooner had it gone off, presumably to collect more food, than the egrets stood erect and diligently, arrogantly, chased away every small heron that ventured into
the green arbor.

The arrival of cattle egrets in our country from the Old
World, where ornithologists call them buff-backed herons, is
unique in our history. Recently Willard H. Dilley, chief
naturalist of Grand Teton National Park, told me that he
identified a cattle egret near his former home in Clewiston,
Florida, in May, 1942. He dismissed the bird as an escape
from one of the many exotic bird farms in south Florida. A
full decade passed, and no more was heard of the species in

the United States.

Then in 1952 excitement broke out among birders. An Old World species of bird for the first time in recorded history had arrived on our shores and established a firm beachhead. Nothing like it had taken place before. It all began quietly enough. On April 23, 1952, one of these herons was shot at Wayland in the Sudbury Valley of Massachusetts. This bird had been observed feeding in pastures close to the feet of dairy cattle and many birders were dismayed when it was shot. Perhaps it was an escape from a zoo, but there was a chance that it had arrived in North America under its own power. It was an interesting bird to watch, and what service to science could one stray heron, dead, contribute? The debate went on until about a month later Richard Borden projected some movies he had made on March 12, 1952, in Florida at Eagle Bay on the northwest side of Lake Okeechobee. There was a burst of excitement. Feeding among a herd of cattle with some snowy egrets and immature little blue herons was a cattle egret. It was in full breeding plumage.

Expecting only the usual species of white herons, the photographer had concentrated on composition and action and had not noted the stranger in the white flock. Following on the heels of the Borden record, the Louis J. Stimsons saw a flock of about ten cattle egrets not far from Lakeport, Florida, on June 1.

Early in 1953 came reports of increased numbers of cattle egrets in many places, some as far north as Virginia, Maryland and Cape May, New Jersey. One was collected in Florida. Sam Grimes located four of their nests on an island in Lake Okeechobee and photographed one of them.

By 1955 their nests had been located in widely scattered places. On May 2 of that year Allan and I made a trip on the St. John's River all the way to its source in Lake Helen Blazes, and not far north of this, on Saw Grass Island, Allan found four pairs nesting. By this time it was clear that a genuine invasion by cattle egrets was under way, and when their nests were found in 1957 as far north as New Jersey, a suspicion that they might occupy suitable habitat across the continent began to grow.

In August, 1961, a roost of short duration in mangroves on Merritt Island, Florida, was estimated to contain, at its height, more than thirty thousand cattle egrets. The numbers reported through its expanding range were so great that surely the increase could not result from reproduction alone but followed the feeding-in of birds from other places. From merely locating breeding places and noting the expansion of its range, interest turned toward the source of the influx, and steps were taken to document this mysterious invasion and occupation as well as any physical changes and alteration in breeding habits that might evolve in a completely new habitat.

Ten years after the first cattle egret was collected in Massachusetts, signaling the voluntary arrival of the species to this continent, they were nesting as far north as Ontario, inland to Tennessee and Oklahoma and along the Texas coast.

In Europe these egrets nest only in Spain and Portugal, but they occur elsewhere on the continent as stragglers. They also breed from northwest Africa and Egypt into the Middle East. Another race is found in southern Asia. In all the world there are fifty-nine species of *Ardeidae* (Welty) ranging in size from our own least bittern, barely ten inches long with his neck fully stretched, to the huge goliath heron of Africa, which stands almost five feet tall. Suddenly one member of this family has, in the past century, undergone a mysterious change. Not only are its numbers increasing fast, but its range is extending explosively.

Though it was reported several years earlier, the first cattle egret collected in the New World was shot on May 27, 1937, near the Demarara River in British Guiana. One was collected in the state of Guarico, Venezuela, on January 27,

1945. They were observed in Surinam, Dutch Guiana, in 1946. On January 3, 1951, another was collected on the lower Rio San Juan, Colombia, and the species followed that river downstream to the Pacific Ocean the same year while another specimen was collected high in the Andes Mountains on the Bogota Plateau more than 8,500 feet above sea level. They have been reported in California, and on the other side of the world they have appeared in Australia.

In 1958 Allan and I saw cattle egrets in St. Croix and in Puerto Rico where they were particularly abundant around the airport at Mayaguez. There they numbered in the hundreds, and we wondered then, if having moved to the northwestern part of Puerto Rico, they were poised for yet another leap across the open ocean.

If we disregard the Willard Dilley report, designating it as he did at the time an escape from an aviary, it was less than four years after the first cattle egret in North America was definitely recorded that the first authentic record of the species in Texas was established. On November 25, 1955, members of the Texas Ornithological Society on its annual field trip to Rockport identified a cattle egret on Mustang Island five miles south of Port Aransas. Three days later at least thirty members of the same distinguished society certified the identification. From then on there was a scattering of observations; the largest numbers observed in the early years were on Galveston Island. On May 7, 1958, Luther Goldman, the distinguished biologist with the United States Bureau of Sports Fisheries and Wildlife, recorded the first cattle egret in extreme south Texas at Laguna Atascosa.

On May 10, 1959, Sandy Sprunt, research director for the National Audubon Society, and Joe Whitehead, while checking the various colonies in Galveston Bay, confirmed a suspicion that cattle egrets were already nesting in Texas when on North Deer Island in the West Bay they discovered eight cattle egret nests. The same year there was evidence that the species was nesting on Green Island far south in the Laguna Madre, but the actual nests were not located. On that island the thorny tangled vegetation prevents movement except along the few trails.

The following year cattle egrets began to nest on the Ving-tune Islands in late June and July after the spoonbills and native herons had completed their nest duties and left the islands. Assuming that if the cattle egrets nested it would again be late in the season, my surprise to find a pair already engaged in nest activities in May was keen and exultant.

In other parts of the world some cattle egrets are sedentary while others are migratory. In Africa migration hinges on seasonal rain and drought periods. Cattle egrets from the Sudan and from South Africa both move into the equatorial region when the dry season approaches in those areas. So it happens that the Sudan cattle egrets move into the equatorial region in September while the South African population moves out at the same time. To some ornithologists this contrasting movement by populations controlled by the dry season suggests a reason for the migration of all birds that move to and from the tropics.

Cattle egrets eat a variety of animal food, but here their chief item is grasshoppers. Since insects vanish with the cold in the north, our growing population of cattle egrets will surely become migratory. Even in Florida the great masses of that species move from the northern and central part of the state in winter, and apparently many leave Florida for the West Indies and South America.

No sooner had cattle egrets begun to increase both their numbers and range spectacularly than questions arose about their influence on our native birds and effect on man's interests. Many, perhaps the majority of people, regard wildlife in a narrow way and evaluate it solely on its obvious relationship to their own plans. Since in this country the chief food of cattle egrets is insects, with grasshoppers favored above

other species, farmers and ranchers look with approbation on
this heron, which stays so close to the hooves of their cattle
and catches the insects that the big ruminants flush from the
pasture. Probably they take young and eggs of such grassland
species as meadowlarks and vesper sparrows when they find
them. We have seen one eat a five-inch lizard and once
watched while a cattle egret caught a toad and then shook
and pounded it for more than twenty minutes before it could
swallow it. One of their popular names in Africa is "tick
bird," but apparently they take comparatively few of these in
this country. They do occasionally run up and down the back
of a cow or horse, but they appear to pick off only flies.

Those egrets which in Spain may feed at the feet of brave
bulls destined to hear the roar of thousands as they face gaud-
ily dressed matadors in Seville are found with goats in North
Africa, and they also run beside dromedary camels led by
bearded Moors dressed in burnooses.

In equatorial Africa they often feed in company with herds
of hippopotamuses. Fearlessly, too, they accompany rhinocer-
oses, short-tempered monsters that armed men approach with
the greatest caution. On these mammals photographers use
their longest lenses and are usually backed by bearers with
powerful guns. Even then the photographers usually work
while standing in a truck with the motor running and ready
for a quick getaway.

The late Dr. James P. Chapin of the American Museum of
Natural History once told us of watching, in central Africa, a
herd of elephants accompanied by a large flock of cattle
egrets. The egrets stayed close to the heads of the hulking
beasts, though a single misjudgment would have meant death
under the mighty feet. The herd, moving slowly but steadily
forward, came to a dense band of cane. At once the egrets circled into the air and settled on the backs of the elephants, five
or six on each. They hitched a ride through the thicket rather
than fly over it, but as soon as they reached short grass on the

far side, all the egrets dropped down to feed once more among the feet of the elephants.

While cattle egrets associate with all kinds of mammals, they are most frequently seen with large ruminants. In parts of Africa, however, they sometimes flock around the largest living species of bird, the ostrich, to catch insects put to flight as these birds stride through the grass.

In most parts of central and South Africa, cattle egrets have increased tremendously within the past twenty-five years. At the same time they have appeared where they were never seen before often in places thousands of miles from their known habitat a century ago. As we ponder their movements, it is clear they fanned out in many directions. They have appeared on Madagascar, Ceylon, the Philippine Islands, Bali and Australia. They moved into the Americas. Still expanding swiftly, they have been recorded in many places over a large portion of the United States. The mystery of how they traveled so far intrigues us each time we see one of these birds or one of their great flocks.

The shortest distance between Africa and South America is somewhat under two thousand miles. This appears to be a prohibitive barrier to the movements of egrets across it. Yet in 1959 bands were placed on the legs of nestlings of some cattle egrets in Spain. In 1960 one of these birds was recovered in Trinidad. Proof of a transoceanic journey by a cattle egret was established.

Herons have been clocked in normal flight at speeds up to twenty-eight miles an hour. Assuming cattle egrets maintained that speed it would require about seventy hours to make the shortest crossing from Africa to South America. It is a known fact that the speed of birds is tremendously increased if they have a good but not overpowering tail wind. Migrants by the tens of thousands make a routine nonstop flight of more than five hundred miles across the Gulf of Mexico twice annually. Roger Tory Peterson states that golden plovers can made the twenty-four-hundred-mile non-stop flight from eastern Canada to South America with only a two-ounce loss of weight. The more we examine regular bird movements across the sky, voluntary flights by cattle egrets across the Atlantic seem less fantastic and less dependent on accidental storms sweeping flocks irresistibly to distant shores Certainly the arrival of cattle egrets on our shores is completely unlike the arrival of windblown waifs cast upon our continent by tremendous storms.

In 1927 a lapwing, a species that frequents English farm-lands, was banded in the Lake District and then shot in Newfoundland after a vast low swept it across the Atlantic. We have seen a ruff on Westhampton Beach, Long Island, and once after a hurricane screamed over Cuba and then turned northward, a Cuban emerald hummingbird was deposited in our garden and stayed for several days, to the joy of all the local birders who came to see it. Allan has identified a European black-headed gull in several places along the Atlantic coast and once in the Gulf of Mexico not far from St. Petersburg.

Scarcely a year passes without some strange bird from distant places appearing unexpectedly and causing great excitement among the vast bird-watching public. Such strays, jettisoned so far from their normal range, are almost always solitary. If they do not fall before a collector's gun, they vanish into the unknown, lost among the swarming birds of the continent. Perhaps strong fliers such as ruffs and black-headed gulls make their way home once more, but most probably die in a strange environment far from their kind.

Birds cross the Atlantic from west to east also, and more than thirty species of American birds have been recorded in the British Isles. Oddly enough the most often sighted has been the yellow-billed cuckoo. Robins, myrtle warblers, slate-colored juncos, eastern goshawks and swallow-tailed kites are other unlikely oceanic travelers to Britain. Allan once identified a pectoral sandpiper at the Slough Sewage Farms near London, one of less than half a dozen records of that species in England.

That pair of cattle egrets on the small Vingtune was the first pair we ever photographed and we believe the first photographed by anybody in Texas. Until the fifth and final pale blue egg was laid, they were covered only when the great blue heron came to its nest. Once the clutch was complete, both shared incubation duties, and for a member of the heron tribe, the exchange was made with little fanfare. The returning bird alighted on the limb and walked along it to the nest. The incubating bird extended its neck full length, and the arriving bird laid its neck across that of its mate. They held that position for a few seconds while both softly croaked *rick rack*. Then as the incubating bird slowly gave way, the newcomer sidled under it and wriggled until the eggs were comfortably adjusted. As with many herons, the intensity of flesh colors reached during the culmination of pairing was of short duration. By the time incubation was under way, the blue flush had faded from the lores and bills of the birds and most of the rose was gone.

We could not stay long enough to witness the hatching of the eggs, which apparently takes place in from twenty-two to twenty-four days after incubation begins. We had not expected to find any cattle egret nests so early in spring anywhere along the Texas coast, so we considered ourselves fortunate to have been able to make the first nest photographs of the species in the state.

There are no precise figures for the breeding pairs of cattle egrets in Texas that spring of 1961, but probably they did not exceed a dozen or so. Experienced field scientists estimated that more than twenty thousand pairs nested there in the 1966 season. The tide of colonists from the Old World is sweeping westward in the twentieth century more rapidly than did the human settlers during the eighteenth century.

Though eventually they may compete with native herons for nesting places, as far as their feeding habits go they are filling a vacuum by eating chiefly insects avoided by most native birds. Their arrival on our shores was unannounced and is shrouded in mystery, but so far they are most welcome wherever they appear.

18

Safe Haven after a Thousand Perils

A STRONG LOW-PRESSURE area advanced across Texas during the night. Small craft warnings were hoisted. A weather bureau alert urged watchfulness, for a severe band of turbulence lay along the forward edge of the disturbance. Thunderstorms, rain squalls, high winds and even tornadoes were anticipated.

The front hit Smith Point at dawn. Wind, underscored by the rumble of thunder, howled through our cabin. It slammed doors, shook window shades and opened Peterson's *Guide to the Birds of Texas* and shuffled its pages. A roll of paper towels blew off the table and snaked into a wild tangle as it spun across the floor.

As we dashed about securing doors and closing windows on the windward side, we knew we could not go that day to the bird islands. At long last we could spare the time to explore Galveston Island where that heroic Spaniard, Nunez Cabeza de Vaca, had endured cold, hunger, sickness and slavery while held captive by the Karankawas. Little did we realize that henceforth De Vaca's travels of so long ago would be inextricably bound in our thoughts to other travelers from far-off lands who, after facing a thousand perils over vast distances, also found a temporary haven on Galveston Island.

Buttoning our raincoats, we bent low before the early May gale and raced to the car. As we drove down Bolivar Peninsula the sun thrust a shaft through dark tumbling clouds, and like a searchlight, it brushed the tossing waters of the gulf, sped across a wide beach and over mudflats to the land where a few wind-sheared trees swayed and marsh grasses were molded into long shifting furrows by the tempest.

We passed a black lighthouse and boarded the free ferry for the three-mile crossing to Galveston Island. Ahead of us white froth edged racing waves, and above them black terns, laughing gulls and brown pelicans faced the storm and hung motionless as if tethered below the scudding clouds. As we approached, they swerved, and the wind tore them from their invisible moorings. Careering wildly, they hurtled away like thistledown.

A sudden burst of rain rattled against the windshield as we drove from the ferry onto the island where De Vaca had survived the wreck of his clumsy, badly made boat and struggled above the reach of the grasping waves. That was late in the year 1528. To be sure, after four hundred years and more, historians still wrangle about his landfall. Some claim it was San Luis Island southwest of Galveston Island. But since historians do not agree, the layman, after reading available evidence, it justified in making his choice, and ours is Galveston.

We drove along the sea wall, a formidable gray shield against storms, which rises above a normally wide smooth beach. That morning most of the sand was covered by a wild swirl of froth-edged gray-green water. This sea wall in recent years has saved the city of Galveston many times from major disasters during severe hurricanes.

Allan remarked that the wind was losing some of its fury. It was easier, he said, to hold the car against the battering gusts. I scarcely heard him, for I was far away in another century when the only human inhabitants of this narrow, twenty eight-mile long island were Karankawas, cannibals who ate their enemies and tossed their bones on trash heaps that we call kitchen middens. Instead of pale sanderlings running like rolling pebbles in the windblown spume at the edge of the waves, I saw De Vaca fighting the pull of an undertow and slowly, staggering with weariness, escape the clutch of the waves and reach the safety of dry sand. Cars, streets, houses almost smothered by gay oleanders, and all the man-made changes vanished, and the low island with the gulf on one side and West Bay on the other was a lonely tangle of shrubs and oaks, of sand dunes, shallow ponds, marshes and mudflats. This was the haven De Vaca found after many fearful days on the treacherous gulf.

Nunez Cabeza de Vaca was the son of one of the noble families of Spain. He was a conquistador in sharp contrast to most of them, for he was just, honest and a truly great man. To naturalists he has a particular appeal, for instead of indulging, as did his companions, in miragelike dreams of golden cities, he really saw the country, the plants and the animals, and he studied the habits of the Indians and learned to speak their language. He had no means for keeping notes, yet his memory retained such vivid images of places and sights that when he wrote about his wanderings his exact account, published in 1542, enables readers to trace his course from Texas to the Pacific and to identify plants and animals he described. He was the first to call sweet gum liquidambar. This tree grows near many east Texas rivers. He was also the first to describe mesquite and at one time was kept alive by the sweet beans of this tree, which are eaten today by many country people in Mexico. He was also the first to describe bison, which he called wild cattle.

In June, 1527, De Vaca joined as treasurer an expedition led by Panfilo de Narvaez, a Spanish adventurer who, after many rash exploits in the New World, was commissioned by Charles V to discover and conquer the people between Florida and Rio de las Palmas. They set out with five ships and six hundred men from San Lucas. A pleasant landing was made on the shore of Old Tampa Bay near St. John's Pass north of St. Petersburg on the tenth of April, 1528, only fifteen years after Ponce de Leon discovered and named Florida, Cape Canaveral and the Tortugas. This landing in no way presaged the awful fate in store for the expedition, which divided at that place.

A skeleton crew was assigned to each of the five ships. They were to sail to Apalache Bay. There the explorers, having journeyed overland, would rejoin them. Gaily the land party set forth afoot and on horseback. Surely gold was ahead for the taking, and they would all become rich. They quickly discovered they had not engaged in a picnic. They were tormented by mosquitoes and other insects. Their horses mired down in swamps. Tangled vegetation hampered their movements. Food was scarce. In the Suwannee River, then without a name, one of the Narvaez soldiers in full armor was drowned.

Having suffered severe hardships, they finally reached Apalache Bay near St. Mark's. The golden city they expected to find on its shore was only a tiny huddle of open huts, and the only gold was yellow corn in woven baskets. The frightened Indians hid from the Spaniards and were soon turned into bitter enemies when the soldiers, after luring them from hiding places by holding out trinkets, killed some and wounded others.

The ships did not come. Their destination was Davy Jones's locker; a storm destroyed them all. The Narvaez expedition was in a dangerous situation. The men were growing weak and rebellious; the Indians, so treacherously used by the Spaniards, were in an ugly, vengeful temper and ambushed their tormentors whenever possible.

In desperation, the almost naked Spaniards set about building boats without either tools or knowledge of shipbuilding. They turned their stirrups into nails. Crossbows were formed into saws. Stones were used as hammers. Their once glittering swords were used as axes. They ate the horses, one each day. As they labored, the Indians lurked in the underbrush and with arrows and spears picked off one Spaniard after another.

After incredible toil three boats, each about thirty-three feet long, were finished and launched. How we wish De Vaca had sketched those rude vessels that must have been more raft than boat. The conquistadores, reduced to 247, crowded aboard and set sail for Mexico. Some were in rags, some were naked and a few were wrapped in redolent raw skins.

The hardships endured as their unstable crafts lumbered sluggishly westward were beyond our comprehension. Thirst tortured them. Hunger gnawed their vitals. Indians were a constant threat, for they were without supplies and had to stay close to shore. The unrelenting pressure of body against body must have been almost unbearable; so closely were they packed that even the simple pleasure of a deep, free breath was denied them.

Somewhere off the mouth of the Mississippi River a storm separated the boats. On November sixth, 1528, Cabeza de Vaca's boat slammed against the shore of Galveston Island and overturned in the surf. Later that night a second boat capsized in the breaking waves. The third boat, with Narvaez aboard, was never heard of again.

The torment of the survivors was increased rather than alleviated. The Texas winter, cold and bleak on Galveston Island, was intensifying, and the naked men had no protection against it. They were always hungry. Sickness felled them. De Vaca later spoke of the Karankawas as tender-hearted and "when they beheld the sad plight of the Spaniards they sat among them howling like brutes over the misfortunes of the white men." But sympathy was soon turned to hatred as the castaways insolently took whatever they wanted of the simple belongings of the Indians. In retaliation, the Karankawas made slaves of the Spaniards and compelled them to do many difficult tasks and killed a few whenever the impulse seized them.

Eventually most of the surviving conquistadores escaped and set out toward Mexico City, but at the time De Vaca was ill, perhaps with malaria. Seven long years as a prisoner followed. Bearded, naked and burned dark brown, De Vaca was first a slave and then a trader of trinkets he made from shells. He traded so successfully that at last his captors sent him to deal with other tribes. Thus he learned various Indian dialects, studied the landscape and acquired information about the country and the tribes to the west and south. Finally the Indians decided De Vaca was a healer with magic powers.

After eight years he left Galvestion Island and began his remarkable journey to the Pacific. He was passed from tribe to tribe and the Indians believed he cured the sick. For his healing powers he was given food, guides and respect. After years as a slave of one of the most primitive tribes, De Vaca now approached the stature of a god in the eyes of the Indians.

As he advanced across Texas, sometimes subsisting on tunas, fruits of prickly pear cactus, and again on mesquite beans, he took such careful note of the country that we can follow his trail over the Edwards Plateau and around the Big Bend to the crossing of the Rio Grande. His was the first transcontinental crossing of North America by a European, and the marvel is that he survived the incredible hardships and remembered so many details and so much of the beauty of the country through which he passed. His photographic memory served him well and enabled him long afterward to write an account, with forty-eight words in the title, of his fantastic journey and to preserve for readers today wonderful details of his adventure.

The final episode of Cabeza de Vaca's epic journey when at

Of all the heron tribe, the snowy egrets are the most animated,
lively and graceful. With profound gratitude we can thank earlier
generations who saved them at a time when the fragile plumes were
worth twice their weight in gold. (Chapter 15)

The roseate spoonbill's body and wings were bright yet delicate rose petal pink. (Chapter 15)

The roseate spoonbills' eyes were cherry red; their bills like a Ubangi belle's lips. (Chapter 15)

The heat was almost too much for a Louisiana heron incubating
its eggs under the full blast of the sun. (Chapter 15)

The blue eyes of the white ibis glistened in their flaming frames of red. (Chapter 15)

The nutria's overcoat was dark reddish-brown except across the shoulders where the fur was tipped with yellow. Underneath was a short, dense bluish-gray inner coat. Wild nutria average twenty pounds or less and are under thirty inches long. (Chapter 16)

On the cattle egrets' heads, down their backs, and over their breasts
fell delicate threadlike plumes the color of aged bourbon. Their
stout bills were tipped with lively yellow that merged into bright
rose suffused with blue. Their legs were bright yellow. (Chapter 17)

We heard the frantic wild *yip, yip, yip* of black-necked stilts. Of all the birds in the world, except only flamingos, stilts have the longest legs in proportion to their body size. And of all the shore birds that nest in Texas, they are the most charming. (Chapter 18)

A pair of great blue herons had used one of the cactus plants as a base for its nest and now one of them stood on the side of its bulky pile of sticks. In that flat expanse the cactus and the heron joined in a unit. They looked like a giraffe towering above all else on a vast plain. (Chapter 19)

As we approached, the colony of royal terns leaped into the air and now whirled overhead wildly as snowflakes in a gale, a blizzard of wings. (Chapter 19)

The terns settled down but they did not quiet down. These second largest of American terns landed, held their heads high and shrieked in shattering decibels without ceasing. Never have I heard such an ear-shattering racket. (Chapter 19)

Though the pelican is a symbol of charity, the species receives no charity in many places. Brown pelicans have all but vanished from Louisiana, though they appear on the seal and the flag of that state. They have become rare in Texas where they were once common and nested in many areas. (Chapter 20)

Pelicans on the ground are grotesque; on the water they are buoyant as small racing ketches poised for the starting signal; but in the air the white pelicans are beautiful beyond compare. Their wingbeats may be the slowest of any birds in the world, and this clothes them with dignity and grace. (Chapter 20)

"I see an oystercatcher and it looks as if it is on eggs," Allan cried. (Chapter 19)

Whenever a reddish egret assumed a graceful pose we caught it on film. Long soft feathers lay close as shingles on the neck until an intruder came too near to the nest. Then those feathers were lifted until they resembled an old-fashioned boa. (Chapter 21)

A handsome male pyrrhuloxia darted into the mesquite. Allan shouted he had found the nest with three young. The difficult name means crooked-billed redbird. The short thick bill is not crooked except at the closing edges of the mandibles, but it is extremely thick, almost parrotlike. (Chapter 22)

last he rejoined the Spaniards is a revelation of the character
and spirit of the man. He had crossed the continent, climbed
mountains, traversed deserts and finally approached the
Spanish holdings. The first Spaniards he met were on horseback and chasing terrified Indians. Their mission was to either convert the Indians to Christianity or kill those who refused to abandon their ancient beliefs. If converted, the Indians were permitted to live on as slaves. De Vaca, naked and
unkempt though he was, flashed at them in anger and, with
all the commanding presence of a high-born Castilian, ordered them to stop their treacherous chase and to free all Indians pressed into "Christian" slavery.

This nobleman, who left a castle in Spain to add one of the
few pages of true glory to the early exploration of the Americas called Galveston Island *Isla de Mal Hado*—Island of Mis-
fortune. Several times since De Vaca passed from the scene,
his name for the island has seemed a fitting one. It was there
Laffite established his rowdy Campeachy in 1817. Wild,
bloody times followed. After the settlement was burned, the
few people who remained suffered repeated depredations by
the cannibalistic Indians, who had good reason to hate the
white people who had robbed them of their land and mis-
used and killed them. Nevertheless, in 1825 Galveston came
into being as a port and quickly grew in size and gained
importance as a deep-water shipping center.

Then in 1900 came The Storm. It killed an estimated six
thousand people and left eight thousand homeless as storm-
driven water from the gulf swept over the island, which was
then nowhere as much as nine feet above high tide. A four-
thousand-ton British steamer was torn from its moorings and
finally stranded on a thirty-foot bank in Chambers County
twenty-two miles from deep water.

Few places in our land have had as violent and gaudy a history as the small island where Cabeza de Vaca was cast ashore.
Now Galveston is made beautiful by a profusion of bright

flowers, particularly oleanders, and by lovely homes and open spaces. Repeatedly during fearful storms of recent years the great gray sea wall has saved the city from major hurricane disasters.

As we made our way slowly southward that day, greenish waters of the gulf gnawed angrily at the sand but the tide was ebbing. Allan said he no longer had to fight the wind. We went past Sweetwater Lake dotted with blue-winged teal, shovelers and coots. Herons fished in the shallows.

We continued past Laffite's Grove, where the pirate had his headquarters, and glimpsed several tranquil wood thrushes in the oaks. Nervously active Wilson's warblers, male Baltimore orioles bright as streaks of flame, many dickcissels and dozens of indigo buntings moved through the shrubs and live oaks. We were in an area where, on certain spectacular days, bird-watchers have seen the bushes, trees and power lines crowded with weary travelers exhausted by adverse winds. But that day land birds were not present in exceptional numbers, though all around we heard their querulous voices eloquent of fatigue, hunger and a restless desire to be once more on their way to still distant goals.

From the scudding clouds came wind songs of traveling shorebirds. There is a haunting magic in their voices. Not considered song-birds, their songs are among the most melodious and beautiful of any birds.

Moving down the narrow island where it faded into low sand dunes and grassy reaches, we came to many pools left by recent rains. On our left the tossing gulf rolled landward in white-edged furrows. On our right shimmered the quieter waters of West Bay, where the ebbing tide had bared extensive flats. As we looked, the clouds split apart and the wind abated. Instead of thick gloom we were flooded with radiant light. Marine life, dashed about by the winds and stranded by the retreating tide, was already mingling its effluvium with drying salt and the mud.

The flat was swarming with shorebirds, big ones, small ones and in-between ones. Wild cries of curlews, whimbrels, yellowlegs and plovers rang across the wet meadows and the flats, and their piping blended with the drying gusts. Probing in the ooze, oblivious of our presence, were hundreds of little "peep." Their thin dark bills darted in and out of the sand and mud, and their legs twinkled in perpetual motion.

Allan systematically scanned the flat, and among the peep he found least, western, semipalmated and even some white-rumped sandpipers. The latter particularly are great travelers and journey up to nine thousand miles from the Straits of Magellan to Baffinland to nest. As they fed, the plain little birds twittered sweetly.

Willets, with their startling black and white wings flickering, circled up from the flat and settled farther away. A black-bellied plover, still gray beneath, looked at us with a large black eye, teetered uncertainly, then winged away whistling its plaintive cry. A compact flock of dunlin swept in at great speed, accompanied by an impressive rushing of wings, all beating in perfect time as they swiftly changed their flight, first this way and then that, until finally with ineffable butterfly airiness they settled, arching their slender pointed wings above their backs so I glimpsed the delicate silkiness of their undersurface. Then the flock broke apart and each dunlin began stabbing the water with its one-and-a-half-inch bill.

A speeding flight of semipalmated sandpipers circled in, their feet moving even before they touched the sand, and immediately they, too, began to feed urgently as if half starved. Harlequin-plumaged ruddy turnstones advanced along a line of drift, turning the seaweed energetically but always ready to abandon this activity to charge semipalmated plovers that sought food under the same sargassum.

Allan located a group of five knots already decked out in brick-red breasts, so they justified their popular name of robin snipe until they wheeled so that we only saw their gray backs. Chunky dowitchers with astonishingly long bills had lost their winter gray and were bright rust on the breast while their backs were warmly mottled with brown.

"Almost all the shorebirds that occur in Texas are here." Allan's eyes lighted with enthusiasm. "Look—there is a buff-breasted sandpiper, a very rare bird in the East. Probably a lot of these waders have simply dropped on the first land they have seen since leaving the far side of the gulf yesterday."

We swung around when we heard the frantic wild *yip, yip, yip* of black-necked stilts. Their clamor rang across a meadow that apparently had been overgrown with rank canes, but these had been burned, leaving stiff sharply pointed stubble behind. Between this unpleasant bristle new green was shooting up. In its midst lay a thin sheet of water perhaps forty feet long and half that wide. Four stilts were running about pugnaciously challenging each other in water that extended only an inch or two up their extremely long legs.

Stilts of all the birds in the world, excepting only flamingos, have the longest legs in proportion to their body size. No wonder they are popularly called the daddy-long-legs of the bird world. As we came near all four stilts flew up excitedly but continued to circle the pond. We quickly discovered the reason.

There was a stilt nest on either end of the shallow pool. Both were slight depressions with a half dozen grasses twined around, while a few small fragments of broken shell suggested a lining. In each nest lay four large honey-colored eggs with conspicuous brown and purple spots. The larger ends of the exquisitely pear-shaped eggs fanned around the outside, making a pattern like some exotic flower.

"It is a bit early for stilt eggs," Allan remarked. "Usually their clutches aren't complete before the end of the first week in May."

Our blinds, each facing north, were soon in position beside

a stilt nest. The morning clouds vanished, and for the remainder of the day the blinding glare of a fierce sun beat down. As we arranged the blinds the stilts had flown over us, long and thin as horizontal exclamation points, their needle-like black bills thrust straight forward and their skinny red legs trailing straight behind. In their excitement and dismay, they hovered above us yipping, and sometimes they dived with a speed that made us duck.

We were scarcely concealed in the blinds before they settled in the shallow pool. There they teetered as if uncertain of their balance and spread their wings. They stared at the blinds with more curiosity than fear. Now and again they fluttered their wings feebly, putting on a vague sort of broken-wing act so characteristic of shorebirds when they suspect danger is near their nest or young. Each spreading of the wings brought my pair closer to its nest. Each time they paused, they folded one leg and held it high so droplets fell from the half-webbed toes.

Satisfied at last, they walked toward the nest, setting their feet carefully at each step. The birds looked almost alike; black above and shining white beneath. The female, slightly larger than her mate, had a brownish tinge on her scapulars while the male was lightly brushed with a greenish sheen, and on his throat was a very faint flush of pink.

Both stilts inspected the eggs carefully, and there was an air of confiding softness, a gentle tenderness, about them that was charming. Then the male folded his long legs on either side of the skimpy nest, squirmed about to move the eggs into a comfortable position and became immobile. The female strolled off, indolently groomed herself, picked a few bits of food from the water and flew away. She was not gone long and repeatedly came back to visit the incubating male and to inspect the eggs.

The nearly motionless stilt incubated the eggs with one large soft eye fixed on the blind. In spite of the now dazzling sun its pupil was so expanded that I thought for some time the eye was black, and only careful study revealed its reddish-brown iris. Above the eye a white patch like a very short, wide eyebrow gave the stilt an expression compounded of innocence and astonishment.

About two hours passed, and again the female approached in a dilatory way, but this time she meant to take her place on the eggs. Arriving at the nest, she placed her neck across that of her mate, and there was some low conversation. The male was reluctant to surrender the care of the eggs, but finally the female pushed herself beneath him and he relented and went off. His unwillingness to leave the eggs shed a new light on the exclusive incubation of the eggs by male phalaropes. We tend to sympathize with the hard-working male whose brightly dressed mate takes no part in building the nest and as soon as the eggs are deposited in the cradle built by him goes off happily to mingle with her carefree sisters. He assumes sole responsibility for the eggs and for the young phalaropes when they hatch. Far from having these parental duties thrust upon him, he may have demanded and assumed them until finally the female became so conditioned to his care of the eggs and young that she lost all instinct to challenge his authority over them. It would appear that stilts are moving toward the same family convention. Like the female, the male returned to the nest at frequent intervals, and then in an hour and fifteen minutes, with repeated affectionate motions and low-pitched notes, he forced her from the eggs.

The majority of the fifty-three species of shorebirds that nest on our continent north of the Rio Grande do so in the far north close to or beyond the Arctic Circle. Only a score nest south of Canada. Nine of these have nested in Texas. This number includes the gallinulelike jaçana, the shorebird with enormously long toes suited to leaf-trotting over water. Jaçanas occasionally enter the Rio Grande Delta and have been known to lay their four brown-scrawled eggs in leafy cups on floating vegetation near Brownsville. But of all the shorebirds that nest in Texas, the black-necked stilt is the most charming. A few winter in the delta country but most go on to Central or South America.

The photography of these birds while they incubate seldom provides much variety of action, yet when they hatch, the young shorebirds, being precocial, run about almost as soon as they are dry. They abandon the nest and do not return to it. Therefore we sacrifice action for portrait studies of the adults when we find a shorebird nest. Knowing that once the stilts settled down on the nest there would be little excitement, we looked forward to uneventful hours in the steaming blind with time passing langorously as we waited for the birds to exchange places. We were unprepared for the drama of that day, which began when the wild front stormed across Galveston Island and raged out over the gulf. For a time the wind died and the clouds parted to let the hot sun shine down. We had been in our blinds about four hours when we heard the first murmur of returning wind.

The average tide fall at Galveston is about a foot and a half, and even this slight movement is often negated by strong winds. So shallow is the water along the island shore of West Bay that a rise or fall of an inch or so covers or reveals wide flats. Now the wind was rising again, and the tide crept implacably over the flats. Perhaps many of the shorebirds, being well-fed, now sought the shelter of the greening meadows, and others, simply weary, settled away from direct assault by the wind. Steadily as the wind increased, our shallow pool welcomed a growing host of the birds that range our hemisphere. Others settled in the stubble and among the new green shoots.

Flocks circled the pond, dipping, flaring, merging and flashing white, then almost vanished as they wheeled and presented their dark backs. Their numbers and their simultaneous movements stole my interest away from the stilt so

close to my blind. So perfectly coordinated were their movements that it was as if a body had parted into separate units
but all remained controlled by a single brain. They reminded me of a legend told by Loren Eiseley of a scientist
grown old who persisted in wearing enormous padded boots
so he would not fall between the molecules. To walk across a
floor had become for him a horrendous journey from particle
to particle across a bottomless abyss. For a moment I had the
illusion that I was actually seeing the old scientist's world of
whirling electrons materialize before my eyes, and then the
flock landed and broke into unrelated individuals, each bent
on satisfying his own desire for food or rest.

From whichever window of my blind I looked, I saw shorebirds in swift and complex evolutions. Some of them dropped
in a compact mass from the clouds and scatttered like tossed
confetti. Others rose from the pool or the meadow to turn
and swoop with the exactitude of West Point cadets on parade but at speeds between forty and fifty miles an hour.
Many believe the dashing precision of shorebird flocks is possible because of their high metabolism, which permits swift
reactions, and their extraordinary visual acuity and alert-
ness.

Twice a year shorebirds set forth on a dangerous journey.
Some of them travel from islands north of our continent to
the stormy islands off the tip of South America. Some may
have traveled a thousand miles from the previous resting
place before dropping down on Galveston Island. Banded
golden plovers have made a twenty-four-hundred mile unin-
terrupted flight from Nova Scotia to South America expend-
ing almost a third of their weight. A banded turnstone has
traveled more than 450 miles in a single day and a lesser yellowlegs averaged 385 miles in a trip from Cape Cod to Mar-
tinique. Baird's sandpipers travel from Tierra del Fuego by
way of the high Andes and the Rockies to the Arctic. White-
rumped sandpipers take an equally long journey, usually

keeping close to the sea. Many of the sandpipers I watched from my blind travel almost from polar circle to polar circle, yet never endure winter. Annually they have two summers, each spent at opposite ends of our hemisphere.

It was on Galveston Island that the Eskimo curlew was sighted on four consecutive springs from 1959 to 1962. One was shot in Barbados in the autumn of 1963. It may have been the last of its race; and if it was another species is forever lost to this earth because of excessive shooting. Eskimo curlew were slaughtered by the thousands during the last century. Sometimes when "sport" was especially keen, carts were emptied and the curlew carcasses left to rot while the hunters refilled their wagons with fresh kills. A single shot of an old muzzle-loading shotgun brought down twenty-eight curlews at once, for their flocks were extremely compact. There were tremendous numbers of these small curlews in Texas until about 1875. The gunner's name for them was doughbird, for in the autumn they were so fat the breast often burst open when they hit the ground.

All through the grass and brittle pinkish salicornia, small earth-colored sandpipers ran about until the surface so slightly raised above the gulf and the bay seemed to heave and quiver. I heard hoarse guttural sounds from the pool. A pair of avocets teetered on long blue legs. They were white with black splashes on their wings, and a wash of ochre on their heads faded onto their shoulders. They towered like giants over the least and semipalmated sandpipers and the dunlin. The avocets looked very saucy and confident with their long up-curved bills. They in turn were overshadowed when a group of long-billed curlew, wild and roving spirits, dropped down beside them. At that the avocets changed their tune to a high-pitched chime almost like sleigh bells, and off they went. With a hoarse barking, a flock of Wilson's phalaropes settled on the water and began to spin and dip. The females were large and bright with a broad black face and neck stripe that changed to reddish cinnamon low on the neck and then split into two streaks that continued almost to the tail. The smaller males were plain gray with white breasts.

Turnstones with bright orange legs and head, their shoulders and breast boldly pattterned with black and white, contrasting strongly with their bright brown backs, moved in constantly shifting formations. Once a sharp-shinned hawk stooped at the flock, and it burst into a poetry of motion, darting like a single organism in swiftest flight, appearing and disappearing like magic as they swerved, dipped and climbed to escape the marauder in search of a meal. The sound of their wings as they rushed through the air was like the brisk shaking of a stiff dry palm frond.

As the afternoon lengthened, the wind continued to rise, and thunderclouds climbed out of the gulf. The small sandpipers clung to the ground, only now and then taking wing where they were at the mercy of the wind.

At the other end of the pool I saw Allan shaking the side of his blind. Whenever it is possible we have somebody walk-away from our blinds when we enter them so the birds will think all humans are gone, and we like our walkaway to return before we emerge so the birds will not leave in a panic, perhaps injuring the eggs or young. But when a walkaway is not available, a gentle shaking of the blind cover will cause the bird at the nest to stand and then move away without hysteria. The stilt lifted its head sharply, then stood up and edged off the nest and away. Then out dashed Allan and ran quickly toward the bay. I heard willets screaming loudly. A pair of them dipped strangely over the water. Allan splashed right in. Through the narrow slit in my blind I saw four gray baby willets were being blown steadily farther from shore by the strong wind. Allan reached the willets, mere balls of fluff, and one after another he caught them. By this time my stilt had left its nest, too, and I ran to join Allan as he waded ashore.

"Something, maybe a snake or perhaps a rabbit, must have scared the little willets and once they were in the water they couldn't get back to shore in the teeth of this wind."

Allan carried the little willets into the grass and placed them in the shelter of a driftwood log. Half a dozen adults attracted by the calls of the frightened parents screamed excitedly above him and darted threateningly at his head.

We took down our blinds and packed them away. A vivid rainbow arched over the gulf. We sat on the beach to count off the shorebirds we had noted that day. As we marked our check list, Wilson's plovers piped their soft whistles. Sanderlings ran in the froth as waves tumbled headlong against the beach and swung in wide arcs across the sand like the swirling skirts of a Spanish dancer.

Flock after flock of shorebirds continued to drop from the stormy sky. Pushed by the strong wind, they ranged themselves in narrowing wedges behind scattered clumps of grass and even large knobbed whelks. I had tossed my beach shoes on the sand, and these, too, soon had a trailing wedge of sandpipers sheltered behind them. There they slept, comet tails of weary travelers.

Of all the bird families in the world, the shorebirds are the greatest travelers. No wonder their flight muscles make up half their total weight. Their dramatic travels across trackless skies challenge the imagination above those of any other birds. Bird-watching pilots have reported lapwings and golden plovers migrating over Britian above six thousand feet, and over the Americas yellowlegs and black-bellied plovers have been observed at eight thousand feet. Members of Mount Everest Expeditions have noted godwits and curlews at twenty thousand feet. But birds generally migrate at low altitudes. As the clouds darkened and the wind increased the flocks came in lower and lower, their speed undiminished until they swung about and faced into the wind. Then they cupped their wings sharply and plunged down to join their resting fellows.

When we left the beach, weary travelers from far-off continents were still arriving on the island where De Vaca spent seven years as a captive of the Karankawas. The birds would sleep briefly and then feed. Soon they would be off again, arrowing toward the north, where shortly their eggs would be laid and hatched beneath the midnight sun. Not many weeks would pass before Galveston Island would again offer food and rest to shorebirds on their journey toward a southern continent.

19

The Day the Tern Eggs Hatched

WHO WOULD THINK I would say "never again" to a day in a bird colony? But never again will I stay in a blind in a colony of royal terns when their eggs are hatching. Once was enough, and the very thought of it revives the torment I suffered that day. There was no escape. I had not arranged any signal for help with Salty Johns, and to come out of a blind in the midst of a congested colony would mean disaster to the eggs and young. I was forced to endure the torture and wait for Salty to come for me. Then his conspicuous approach would alert the jittery terns so they would take off in as restrained a manner as hysterical terns ever do.

I have endured killing heat on the desert and on Texas islands, cold that not only stiffened my fingers but froze my camera shutter, stood with my feet in foul ooze, been assailed by the stench of bat caves and clung to sheer cliffs with pounding surf flinging itself up at my heels, all for the sake of wildlife photographs. I can think of many an unpleasant situation and some quite hazardous ones where we have photographed, and if given the opportunity to return under the same conditions, I would do so with actual delight. But stay in a royal tern colony when the eggs are hatching? Never.

I have a navigation map of the Texas coast, and on it the

National Audubon Society sanctuaries have been circled with a blue pencil. In three areas there are so many circles that they overlap. One of these is Galveston Bay, another is San Antonio Bay adjacent to the Aransas Refuge and the third is the Corpus Christi–Aransas–Redfish Bay complex of waterways. We had spent little time in the latter area and had never visited Lydia Ann, which had improved under Audubon protection and developed into an outstanding sanctuary. Reaching Lydia Ann was rather complicated. We drove from Aransas Pass across a causeway until it ended by a ship channel. We were transported by ferry to Mustang Island and Port Aransas. There we hurried to the yacht basin near the coast guard station and looked over the boats tied up in it. No blue-fiber-glass boat with red trimming was berthed there. Allan, swinging his binoculars up the inland waterway saw such a boat approaching, pushing a V of white foam aside from its bow. It swung in next to us, and a tall, very straight, brown-as-an-Indian man with a sweeping, wild western type of moustache and a shock of graying hair leaped up with his hand extended.

"I've been expecting you," he said. "The New York office wrote me you would be here this afternoon. My name is Salty; Salty Johns. I'll take you where the birds are. I'll show them to you, but I only know five kinds of birds: pink birds, herons, pelicans, big gulls and little gulls, so you'll have to name what you see. There are lots of birds on Lydia Ann and lots more on Hog Island, too. Pink birds nest there with a lot of other birds, and I think it should be a sanctuary, too. I'll take you there someday. What do you want to do first?"

He looked at us expectantly. Allan told him he wanted to take our photography equipment to Lydia Ann next day, leaving Port Aransas very early and coming home late.

"Fine. I fish around there all the time and keep an eye on the birds, and so do all my friends. Nobody is allowed to land on the island. I take good care of the birds, so don't you disturb them."

Allan assured him that we had had much experience in bird colonies, and the safety of the birds was always his foremost consideration, more important to him than any photograph.

"That is one reason why we always go out very early to bird colonies," Allan told Salty. "Then our blinds are in place and we are hidden in them before the sun is high and hot. The birds are not afraid of the blind and come back quickly to protect their eggs and young from the killing sun. We stay until the sun is low in the afternoon for the same reason."

While Allan made the arrangements. I stared at this unusual man who was acting as an Audubon warden. Usually wardens dress in suntans with their Audubon warden insignia sewn on the left sleeve near the shoulder. But not Salty Johns. He was barefooted and wore levis sawed off above the knees and then tattered at the bottom like those of Hollywood pirates. Above the waist he was naked, and no wonder he reminded me of an Indian, for his mother was a Choctaw. On his head he wore a dashing copy of a foreign legionnaire's cap with his insignia above the visor.

Salty grinned at me. "That's the only place I have to wear my badge, at least while it is so hot."

Salty invited us to see his house, but we turned back toward the yacht basin when a commotion arose. A man, frisky as a colt, pranced out of a wharfside bar and leaped gaily into a boat. With a giddy flourish he gunned the motor to full speed ahead, shot into the middle of the channel and began cutting fancy circles. These grew smaller and smaller until the inner gunwale was skimming the water and the other stood straight toward the sky. Then the careening boat and its speed pitched the tipsy man into the water. Even before the splash, Salty, who fortunately had left the key in the switch, turned on the motor, while Allan leaped aboard and threw off the line. Salty brought his boat close to the sinking man, and Allan grabbed hold of him. It took both Allan and Salty to haul the waterlogged man aboard, now subdued and chastened. His wallet had sunk to the depths of the waterway. His eyeglasses were gone. He still had his watch, for it was strapped to his wrist; but it was not improved by its plunge into the salt water.

Salty's house was an arresting one, though it was tiny. Bleached driftwood held dozens of bottles on many branches. Inside, the walls were covered with pictures of the greats and near-greats of many worlds: sports, theater, aviation and the sea. All bore friendly inscriptions to Salty and many referred to adventures and experiences they had shared. He had flown in the First World War, piloted commercial planes for American Airlines, barnstormed all across North America, had been successful as a racer of motorcycles, had circled the world twice as a sailor, had been a ticket scalper on Forty-second Street in New York, made three films with Gene Autry and married two movie actresses, one quite famous. Salty picked up a script that lay on his desk.

"Gene Autry wants me to go back to Hollywood to make another film, but I'm not going. The last time I went back, I had another heart attack. Now I am going to stay right here in Port Aransas and fish and watch the birds. I have a good time here, and I like staying alive."

We left rather breathless from our introduction to Port Aransas and Salty Johns, but more was to come. We had scarcely entered our motel when great clouds plunged westward like a herd of elephants charging over a plain and broke into a crashing thunderstorm that flooded the streets until they were racing muddy streams. Then the electricity went off and darkness obscured Port Aransas, except when shattered by livid bolts like sudden torches flung across the sky.

The next day was the most fatiguing I ever spent in a blind, though I sat on my folding stool on level ground. At the end of the day I was almost prostrate, and my nerves were pulled so taut I was on the brink of tears from sheer exhaustion. I was ready to believe that a human locked in a closed bell tower while a great carillon pealed would be killed by the sound waves. Too much sound is genuine torture.

The day began well enough. When we wakened, the sky alternated between livid sunshine and sudden shadow. A rainbow arched across the deep bruised blue in the west but was quickly wiped away when a great cloud with a halo of crepuscular rays boiled rapidly toward the zenith from the east. The wind blew in erratic puffs. Allan and Salty studied the sky. They decided to risk showers and go to Lydia Ann.

"I'll be fishing nearby and will get you in a hurry if a shower comes our way," Salty promised.

The foredeck of Salty's boat was roofed over, and under this we stowed as much equipment as possible.

"It has the best chance to stay dry there," Salty said. "The water kicks up in a hurry and wets everything fast."

We sailed past a sunken, rusted oil tanker, torpedoed scarcely a mile from Port Aransas by a German submarine in the forties. Two seismograph-equipped boats sailed ahead of us on their way to search the bottom of the gulf for oil deposits. We saw a row of posts, all that was left of a large hotel destroyed by a hurricane. Farther along stood a tiny tin shack where an eighty-year-old oyster- and-crab man lived a hermit life.

"See that island?" Salty pointed to long low Harbor Island on our left, its grassy surface interrupted only by an old lighthouse tower and its attendant buildings.

"That light is automatic now," Salty told us. "Nobody lives in the buildings any more. There are lots of rattlesnakes on the island. I killed a couple this spring. Before the birds came I turned over all the logs and planks that have drifted onto Lydia Ann but I couldn't find a single snake there."

The wind grew steadily stronger, and spray flew. I tried to

hold my flapping slicker over the cameras while watching flocks of laughing gulls, herons and spoonbills that overtook and passed us.

Presently we came abreast of Lydia Ann, and I studied it eagerly. Every sanctuary island is unique, different from all others. About a mile long, this island was never more than half a mile wide. It lay very low and flat, and thin sheets of water shone here and there on it. In fact, it looked as if the land and water were reluctant to part. On the east side of the island the water is so shallow one had to wade a thousand feet from a boat to reach dry land. On the west side where we were, in places a small boat could approach within fifteen feet of the shore.

Except for grass there was little vegetation, though two clumps of prickly pear cactus stood perhaps three feet above the ground. On that flat surface these immediately attracted the eye, for they were the only break on the level land. A pair of great blue herons had used one of the cactus plants as a base for its nest, and now one of them stood on the side of its bulky pile of sticks. In that flat expanse the cactus and heron joined in a unit. Together they looked like a giraffe towering above all else on a vast plain. Though I examined them through my binoculars, I was ready to disbelieve my eyes, for surely no heron could appear so tall. It may be that a mirage gave it and its cactus perch additional stature, for later low posts stretched upward until they seemed as tall as the Harbor Island lighthouse we had just passed. Laughing gulls cackled over the island, and we heard the animated whistle of yellowlegs. In the distance a cloud of terns burst upward, swirled about and settled again.

"On April twenty-fifth we had a bad storm," Salty told us. Green water swept over the island, so the nests that had been started were destroyed. But the birds are nesting again and even more than in late April."

We cruised slowly now with the motor throttled down, and

Allan studied the island carefully. As we came near the north tip, he was suddenly excited.

"I see an oystercatcher and it looks as if it is on eggs," he rejoiced. "It is very late but maybe the April storm destroyed its first clutch and it is on a second set. This would be great luck. You seldom see really good photographs of oystercatchers. Not long ago the Audubon needed such a photograph and wrote to several wildlife photographers without being able to locate a single one they liked."

He was out of the boat while it was still in motion and splashing through the warm choppy water. Leaving deep imprints in the soft mud of the shore he hurried to a slightly raised mound of broken shells, then waved exultantly. Two eggs, darkly spotted with brown and purple, lay in a slight depression. The pair of oystercatchers trotted together some distance away, often pausing in a half-squat with spread wings, then running on again. Often as they ran toward each other they hunched their shoulders and piped a loud, far-reaching, whistled *wheee-oooo* while their wide-spread tails were lifted and their wings drooped. Their blazing eyes were set so far forward both could be seen at once, and their stout red bills were carried like lances poised for a deadly thrust.

Leaving Allan in a blind beside the oystercatchers' nest, Salty and I sailed on to the royal tern colony nearest the north end of Lydia Ann. There I worked rapidly, for it is vital to the safety of birds in a colony, or at a single nest for that matter, to hide quickly so the adult birds will return to their eggs or young before they are harmed.

As we approached, all the terns had leaped frantically into the air and now whirled overhead wildly as snowflakes in a gale, a blizzard of wings. Within three minutes the blind was zipped shut and my camera in place. Then as Salty made his way back to the boat the terns funneled down behind his retreating figure, and soon the ground before the blind and on either side of it was covered by a seething white and silver blanket. Terns were so closely crowded together that they averaged fourteen to a square yard. Those twenty-inch-long, slim, fork-tailed birds literally squeezed together as tightly as they could, though plenty of space that looked equally good to me fringed the colony.

The terns settled down into a compact group, but they did not quiet down. These second largest of American terns landed, held their heads high and shrieked in shattering decibels without ceasing. Never have I heard such an ear-shattering racket.

On lighthouse islands off the Maine coast I have occasionally walked directly in front of a diaphone fog signal when it began blaring out warnings to ships at sea. The sound actually shook me, but it was only necessary to move a few yards out of the direct line for it to become bearable. In the Lydia Ann colony there was no escape from the tern pandemonium. I wished I had arranged a signal with Salty. Had I done so, I would have used it in order to quit that royal tern colony as fast as I could.

We have worked in colonies of arctic and common terns, and with least, roseate, gull-billed and Forster's terns along our eastern seaboard and among noddy and sooty terns, the wide-awakes, on the Dry Tortugas. Sooty terns have a reputation as constant noisy chatterers. Inland we have worked in colonies of Caspian terns, the largest of all our tern species, and with black terns where leaches sucked blood from our legs and the terns attacked us with their pointed bills until they, too, drew blood. But never, in any tern colony had I heard anything comparable to the high, strident, incessant uproar of the royal tern colony that day.

As if a signal had been given, a whole section of the colony would erupt into the air with a roar of wings to fly around excitedly screaming for a moment or two and then settle back, and another block would erupt for no apparent reason. Sometimes they rose in such close formation I was sure they would collide, yet so miraculous was their precision of flight and so swift their maneuverability that I never saw anything closer than a near brush of primaries. In contrast, as they landed they often grazed a tern standing over its single whitish, black-spotted egg and then a frantic squabble followed with yellow-orange bills sparing like rapiers in a duel.

Minutes and even hours blurred as the painful screeching went on. The din soon frayed my nerves until I was quivering. I tore some strips from a paper tissue, rolled them tightly and pushed them into my ears. The shrill sounds were slightly dulled, but I was still made acutely uncomfortable by the racket. Yet I was fascinated by the sudden inexplicable charges into the air and the equally sudden return. With nests jammed close together so they were less than peck-distance apart, the terns constantly bickered, jabbing to right and left and sometimes actually seizing a neighbor's bill and pulling mightily.

The terns did not settle on their eggs. They stood over them. Suddenly I became aware of a movement within the shadows of some of the terns. The eggs were hatching. Here was one downy young, and there another, until I could count dozens of pale gray balls of down that shortly turned whitish with gray speckles and then soft tawny gold. If possible the screaming voices grew shriller and higher pitched with the opening of each egg.

Other voices chimed in. I heard the soft *whoop whoop whoop* of laughing gulls. They were giving a note I have heard only when these gulls nest among terns. Why these pairs decided to nest in the confusion of the royal tern colony instead of far down the island where most of their species built in the low grasses I do not know.

I was surprised to see only three royal terns with black foreheads, for most guides tell us their foreheads are white in winter but black in summer. Except for those three individuals the forehead of all the terns within range of my eyes was either white or variously speckled with black. They had shaggy crests rather like unkempt inverted Vandyke beards. These were erect as the birds screeched.

A different note attracted me. A pair of royal terns, both with speckled foreheads, was mating. The female stood docilely calling in a soft but high *wheep wheep* while the male mounted her with his wings flapping rapidly. This voice was deep bass *kik kik kik*. How I did wish the entire colony would forsake its egg-hatching shrillness for less painful courtship calls.

Throughout most of the morning, the empty eggshells remained in the nests. Later they were pushed out of the slight nest depressions or carried away.

Again I heard a different sound and discovered on the left of my blind a Sandwich tern standing over two pinkish, brown-spotted eggs; but even as I watched, one egg split apart, and a tiny wet and very limp young tern lay in its parent's shadow. I could clearly see the small egg tooth—that filing tool used by the embyro to weaken the shell enough so it can hatch. The "tooth" falls off a few days afterward.

The Sandwich tern was four or five inches shorter than the royal terns. Its crest was short and trim, and its forehead was black, but a narrow band of white separated the black of the forehead from the black, yellow-tipped bill. Its wings extended well beyond its deeply forked tail. It added its voice to the vociferous screaming of the royals, throwing back its head and opening its bill widely so the white feathers at the gape made a dramatic constrast to the black bill and black forehead. I was delighted, for I had never photographed this species and I almost forgave its sharp voice.

Scarcely had I finished writing a description of the Sandwich tern than its mate arrived. It had a speckled forehead. Examining the crowd of terns, I located ten Sandwich terns shading their eggs, and of those only two individuals had completely black foreheads; all the others were speckled.

Lunch time came, but there was no lull in the screaming of the terns. My sandwich and banana stayed in their box. The soft ground was fouled with excrement, and though there was a covering of shells and shell fragments, gradually my stool, tripod and feet sank deeper and deeper into the malodorous mess.

Trying to forget my unpleasant surroundings and the strident clamor of the terns, I looked across the water, which was now sparkling under a bright hot sun and ruffled by a fresh wind. Quite a few royal terns were sitting on the water as lightly as gulls. This was a surprise, for I had seen terns perch only on some floating object; a drifting plank, a lobster buoy or a floating island of seaweed. When fishing off the Florida coast we have watched several species of terns suddenly hover with a peculiar wing beat close to the surface of the water and have learned to associate this flight with the surfacing of a loggerhead or other large sea turtle. No sooner is the turtle's back above the water than the tern settles on the temporary island. Some of the royal terns were bathing, flapping their wings to splash water over their backs. Still farther out I saw terns circle, then plummet to the water after a fish and rise again, shaking the drops from their silvery plumage.

Nothing, though, could shut out the piercing bedlam of the colony. The day dragged on, and instead of joy in so great a bird colony I wished only to get away, to leave the babel behind. With intense relief I watched the boat return much earlier than I had expected it and saw Allan and Salty wading toward the shore. Gratefully I packed away the cameras and slung the cases over my shoulder. Allan and Salty picked up the blind and other equipment. Allan was happy, for his day by the oyster catcher nest had been a most rewarding one.

Salty told us, "Small craft warnings are out, and the wind is picking up. So I thought I'd better not wait until the usual time to get you. Even now we are going to be pretty wet before we get back to Port Aransas. Cover everything as well as you can."

Concern was replacing jubilation in Allan's face. Could the cameras be sufficiently protected? Films, cameras and water are not compatible.

As for me, I was happy to escape from the terns and their shrieking screams. Happy, too, that a couple of trips from the beach, where the waves were already slapping hard against the shore, to the boat had washed some of the filth from my sneakers. How good the clean fresh air smelled. How lovely the hiss of water as the boat sliced through it. Just then a wave dumped a lapful of water on me. I realized we really did have a wet trip ahead of us. Suddenly the waves were plunging monsters as wind and tide bucked each other.

Then luck came our way in the shape of the tugboat *Yucca* from Port Arthur. She was snorting down the waterway with a huge empty oil barge in tow. Salty maneuvered his small blue boat until it was in the very middle of the slick behind the barge. We sailed in dry comfort until the tug turned right on the Aransas Pass Channel.

I'll happily follow Allan into any situation where he believes we will find good prospects for wildlife photography. I'll even venture into a royal tern colony. I'll go back if the birds are incubating, but never again will I spend a day in a colony of royal terns when their eggs are hatching.

20

Island of Silent Birds

FROM A GROUP of boats lying higgledy-piggledy on the shore of Padre Island almost in the shadow of the bridge from Corpus Christi, Louis Rawalt, Audubon warden and guard of South Bird for nearly forty years, selected an eighteen-footer of light weight alloy and attached an outboard motor to its stern. Shoving it into the water, we were off down the inland waterway of Laguna Madre like a silvery flying fish, hitting every wave with a sharp jarring slap. We felt as if caged without any padding in the head of an air drill. Spray flew, and we wrapped our slickers snugly around the cameras and held them on our laps to cushion the bumps.

The high wind threw water into our faces and soaked our clothes, but it also fanned us and tempered the scorching sun. Never had we enjoyed a brighter, more glittering spring day along the Texas coast. The waves, agitated by the wind, added their sparkles to the exuberant morning. Cormorants, standing on channel markers with their wings spread, hurried away as we approached. Laughing gulls facing the wind on bent wings cackled overhead. Herons, very tall as they stood in shallow water, rose with unhurried grace, folded their long necks between their shoulders and drifted away on slowly flapping wings. Terns waited until we were abreast of them before rising in compact noisy flocks from spoil banks. An osprey poised in midair when it located a fish near the surface, then plunged, raising a great fountain, and came up shaking the water from its feathers. It held a fish in its talons. This it dexterously reversed so the fish could be carried head forward; then the osprey straightened out and, unswerving as the flight of an arrow, headed for the mainland. Shorebirds bound for arctic tundra whistled plaintively. They still had a thousand miles and more to travel before ending their spring flight to their nesting places.

On our left the high dunes of Padre Island lifted in tawny magnificence accented by sharp dark shadows. Far away on our right the mainland lay flat as table, except for uncertain hazy blue shapes of trees wavering indistinctly in the shimmering light. Between Padre and the mainland, level expanses of sand barely rose above the waves. Lion-colored water covered, by only a few inches, equally vast reaches of submerged sand.

The silting of Laguna Madre throughout its length is going forward at an appalling rate but most rapidly in the north. Now except for the artificially dug waterway channel, it is completely cut off from Corpus Christi Bay as far as navigation is concerned. In recent decades the laguna has produced a fabulous take of fish. This will decline seriously as silting and greater concentration of salts make the water less suitable as a habitat for edible fish and shrimp.

Ahead we saw a white sailboat floating lightly on the water; it resolved itself into a white pelican. The unique nesting island of these silent birds was our goal. The colony is remarkable, for it is the only coastal nesting place of white pelicans. All others are on islands in inland lakes, some as far north as Canada's Northwest Territories.

Fossils of pelicans that must have looked very much as pelicans do today have been found in deposits almost forty million years old. Within the span of human history pelicans have been known so long that the very origin of their name is lost in the fog of time. An ancient belief held that parental love for their young was so great the pelicans pierced their breasts with their bills to draw blood for them to sip. This belief must have been in the thoughts of the author of the 102nd Psalm, which is a prayer of the afflicted and aging, when he wrote: "I am like a Pelican in the wilderness. . . ."

In Christian religion the pelican has come to symbolize Christ's sacrifice on the cross, and in the Middle Ages artists sometimes painted nesting pelicans on top of the cross. I find a thirteenth-century mosaic in St. Mark's of Venice particularly charming. It shows pairs of birds marching toward the ark. Storks lead the parade, and behind them come the pelicans, awkward walkers on their huge webbed feet. They look very grave and responsible as if they recognized the seriousness of the situation, but then, who ever saw a pelican that did not look grave, even lugubrious?

There are six species of pelicans in the world today. Only two of these, brown pelicans and white pelicans, live in the Americas, while four live in the Old World. There are ten known fossil species. To the early Spanish explorers, pelicans were *alcatraz.* When it was discovered, brown pelicans nested on an island in San Francisco Bay, and hence its name Alcratraz Island.

The brown pelican, state bird of Louisiana, is a coastal and marine species that occurs from islands as far north as British Columbia southward around South America and up the Atlantic coast as far as South Carolina and occasionally to North Carolina. Some actually breed on the Galapagos Islands, more than six hundred miles from the coast of South America. Ornithologists assume they were blown there by storm winds. With the single exception of the brown pelican, all pelicans are regarded as inland nesters, laying their eggs on islands of inland lakes or seas whether fresh or as salty as the Red Sea of the Near East or our own Great Salt Lake. Except for our brown pelican, white is the dominant color of living species, though some are tinged with gray or pink.

White pelicans have very short yellow legs and really tremendous webbed feet, so, standing on shore, they look squat and comical. Their fifteen- to twenty-pound bodies are five feet long from the tip of their foot-long bill to the end of their stubby tail. They have beautiful broad wings, black-tipped and black along the trailing edge, that span almost ten feet. During the winter their flesh colors fade, but with the approach of breeding time, these become brightly flushed. The feet and bill turn bright yellow, and a reddish tinge appears on the latter. The bare skin around the eyes becomes bright yellow with a touch of red in it. A yellow wash suffuses the wings and breast. Lengthened occiput feathers are sometimes nearly white, but usually either gray or yellow colors them. An odd courting-season growth on the top of the bill stands up like an open fan. This becomes almost three inches high. By the time the eggs are laid most birds have lost this decoration. I have searched the ground in white pelican colonies but never have found one of the discarded horny plates. Perhaps the abundant insects that occur in bird colonies eat them immediately as rodents eat the majority of antlers shed by deer.

When we had skipped over the waves for about seventeen miles, Louis, tall and thin as a black-necked stilt, pointed to a green streak slightly to port.

"South Bird Island," he shouted over the roar of the motor and flying water. "Everybody here calls it Big Bird Island in spite of what the map says."

The island was barely discernible above the leaping waves. It lay on the east side of the waterway about halfway between Corpus Christi Bay and Baffin Bay. It was nearly a mile long but less than half that wide and so low that bad storms completely inundate it.

As we rapidly drew closer we saw scattered at intervals

compact patches of white that looked like dense clusters of huge flowers. These were the villages of white pelicans. Then loud screeching attracted our eyes to a dense colony of royal terns on the south end of the island. Great blue herons and all three egrets: common, snowy and reddish, stood quietly on their nests. Laughing gulls sat on nests, each several feet from its neighbors. Willets scolded us, and black skimmers patrolled the shallows near the beach, skimming with their lower mandibles cutting the water. There was noise everywhere. The pelicans alone watched our approach without a sound. Few birds in all the world are more silent than adult pelicans. While vocal birds nested here, it was primarily the island of silent birds.

Soon we were close enough to identify conspicuous plants. Of these, prickly pear bearing still-green fruit called tunas around the edges of their flattened stems were most conspicuous. A few slender sprays of taller tamerisk whipped in the wind. Some short sunflowers already bore a few yellow discs. Various low beach plants added to the green covering, which was broken only where knots of pelican nests and excrement combined to kill the vegetation.

Louis cut the motor and slowly we drifted closer and closer to the beach. Directly before us rose a cluster of white pelicans backed by a thicket of prickly pear. Allan muttered that he hoped he had not made a serious mistake by leaving the blinds behind. When he had started to put them in the boat that morning, Louis persuaded him not to take them. The blinds might scare the pelicans more than our visible presence, he said.

"If you don't get the shots you want without blinds today, I'll bring you back tomorrow," he promised.

Now the boat bumped on the bottom, swung off and bumped again firmly aground this time.

The two dozen or so pelicans were now less than thirty feet from us. We had watched white pelicans from Florida to the

Salton Sea and north to Canada, but this was the first time we had been close to them while they incubated their whitish eggs. They regarded us solemnly from eyes of varied shades. As with brown pelicans all the young have dark eyes that become progressivly lighter until they mature when three or four years old. Some of the incubating pelicans still retained dark eyes, but most were pearly white with jet irises and ringed with a narrow thread of red.

Each held its bill, which was more than a foot long, against its neck so it looked dignified and thoughtful. A really tremendous pouch that could stretch to hold almost three gallons was slung beneath the lower mandible. This was deepest in color near the face and varied from orange-yellow to almost white when relaxed and flapping like a sail that has lost the wind. When expanded with its catch and the weight of water scooped up with the fish, it tends toward pink rather than orange.

Practically all the pelicans we could see either with our naked eyes or the binoculars had lost their strange horny growths. So far as we could tell, incubating pelicans sheltered two eggs each. These were chalky white when laid, but now most were darkened with stains and dirt. Most of the nests were nothing more than slight unadorned depressions, but one of those near us was built up into a low tower with a hollowed summit rather like a flamingo nest.

Two or three pelicans stood up and moved their feet restlessly when our boat touched shore but shortly settled back over their eggs. Their silence was dramatic, for most bird colonies are noisy places. Even here we heard the distant racket of the royal terns. Laughing gulls cackled and cried hysterically. Willets hurrying by, flashing their bold black and white pattern, clamored loudly between more musical pill-o-will-o-willet songs. Like an undertone came the throaty bark of skimmers. Occasionally a heron squawked. But not a sound came from the pelicans. While it is true young pelicans can be very noisy, particularly when hungry, even these are quiet until they become aware of the approach of parents with food. What vocal powers an adult pelican may retain must degenerate from disuse.

After watching the silent pelicans for some time, we ventured to move and slowly stepped into the warm shallow water. The pelicans did not stir. Smoothly and quietly we set up our tripods and mounted cameras. We were as close to the big birds as we wanted to be, yet the pelicans showed no alarm. We gave our concentrated attention to photographing them.

Something nipped the back of my leg. I gave an involuntary start and looked down. A fat young pelican that looked woolly as a three-week-old lamb and was as big as a full-grown Canada goose stood behind me. It looked for all the world as if dressed in too tight, too short balbriggan winter underwear. My eyes bulged as they moved from the young pelican taking liberties with my legs. Behind it on the bank and streaming down into the water were at least fifty others of the same age. All regarded us with interest. Their curiosity was as evident as that of children examining a weird custom-built car parked in their neighborhood. Just as the curiosity of children soon lags, so did that of the inquisitive young pelicans, and they wandered away.

Oddly enough white pelicans at the same stage in the breeding cycle group together in separate nesting areas. The ones closest to us were incubating eggs, but we could see villages where pink, blind, helpless birds must have emerged only hours earlier. These were sheltered carefully by the adults, for the fervent heat would quickly kill the delicate newborn young. Young pelicans begin to wander when still quite young, but we did see some groups where the young birds were strong enough to stand and had fair coats of down, yet they remained within the shade cast by the parent.

Several pelican villages were deserted by both young and

adults. The band of young that visited us probably all belonged to one village, for they were of equal size. Sometimes the tendency to wander as soon as they are clothed with down leads to cannibalism. Large young pelicans eat small ones they find unprotected.

Whenever adults approached an empty village, it was quickly filled with youngsters eager to be fed. In the middle of the day practically every village was crowded. By eleven o'clock pelicans that had spent the morning fishing at inland lakes began to return with their catch, and even the most adventurous young birds were more interested in food than in exploring. The throng continued to grow for about two hours; and then a slow thinning out of adults was evident, until finally only those either incubating eggs or sheltering young remained in the villages.

As adults settled in a village, a crowd of youngsters mobbed them, but each parent appeared to know its own children and unerringly picked them from the throng of beggars. Once child and parent came together, the child entreated until at last the parent opened its massive bill and the ravenous youngster plunged its head through the gaping cavity to the gullet opening at the back. Sometimes it even pushed its bill into the crop itself as it frantically reached for food carried there. All the time its still small wings waved up and down, eloquent first of hunger as it beseeched the adult, then contentment as it was satisfied. Sometimes when a newly arrived pelican was besieged by too many youngsters, it struck them sharply on the head. They retreated quickly, momentarily subdued by the punishment, but ready to try again when the next adult dropped into the village.

Adults feeding the tiny pelicans were gentle, even solicitous. It was marvelous that blind, helpless, three-inch babies could be fed from those long heavy parental bills. But the parents regurgitated partly digested food almost souplike in consistency and at first this was dribbled into the gaping bill.

When the baby could stand, it took food from the adult's bill for a few days. But baby pelicans grow fast, and shortly they ravenously plunged their entire heads into the food basket. Food is not carried in the bill, the famous limerick to the contrary, but must be regurgitated into it when the pelican is ready to feed the young. By the time pelicans are two months old, they weigh from about twenty-four to thirty pounds. In another month they have lost approximately a third of their greatest weight.

One summer we accompanied the manager of Lake Bowdoin National Wildlife Refuge in Montana to an island where white pelicans nested. The young were fairly large and covered with a dense coat of gray woolly down. While we counted nests, the young birds all took to the water where the adults appeared to herd them into a compact raft, and they floated several yards offshore. I was concerned by the mass exodus from the island, but the manager assured me they would come back as soon as we left. To prove his point, he stopped the airboat some distance off when we had finished the nest count, and sure enough, the woolly pelicans swam to the island and streamed ashore, looking like a flock of sheep on the move under the watchful eye of the shepherd.

Suddenly the pelicans we were photographing became restless. They stood up, and we saw their eggs were hatching. Fat and helpless, the infant pelicans lay wet and exhausted after their struggle to leave the egg. Quietly we shoved off, and Louis suggested we go to the opposite shore of the island. There we would be under the flight lines of pelicans returning from their morning expedition in search of food.

From our observations we judge that white pelicans have two feeding periods daily when nesting. Half the colony members depart early in the morning and return well fed and with food for the young birds sometime during the middle of the day. Upon the arrival of a partner, there is a brief recognition ceremony in which both birds of the pair point their bills straight upward. Shortly the nest guardian takes off to have its turn at feeding and gathering food for the young. Since the sexes look alike, I do not know if there is a sexual division in the feeding program. Once the young birds can be safely left unsheltered and unprotected, both adults then make two long flights to feeding places daily.

In Great Salt Lake white pelicans nest on Gunnison and Hat Islands. The water around the islands is so salty fish cannot live in it. So the pelicans must find other places to fish. They often go to the Bear River marshes, where they feed largely on carp, introduced from the Orient. Carp muddy the water until few other species of fish can live in it, so wherever there are carp-infested waters, white pelicans should be particularly welcomed by all who fish for edible species. Sometimes the pelicans go even farther to fish, and we have watched great flocks circle up and up until they were almost invisible except when the sun glinted on their snowy breasts and they looked like stars twinkling in the daytime. Then when they reached the height they sought, they straightened out and crossed the Wasatch Range to drop down to Bear Lake. It is claimed that the Gunnison and Hat pelicans make twice-daily flights to fishing waters seventy-five miles away. Probably the pelicans sometimes go as far from South Bird Island to fish.

The fact that pelicans eat only fish has aroused the ire of many fishermen. It is estimated that an adult white pelican eats about 4 pounds of fish daily. In the two months before it can fly, a young pelican is fed about 150 pounds of fish. Though this is chiefly trash fish despised by man, fishermen, particularly commercial fishermen, are blind to the truth about pelicans. Yet pelicans play an important part in the control of trash fish, and by eating them enhance the chances of game and food fish to survive. Like many biologically illiterate people, some fishermen see one fact only: that pelicans eat fish.

Human spleen is easily vented on the sociable pelicans, which are gregarious throughout the year. Since the places where they can nest are strictly limited, it is easy to locate their colonies and destroy them. Though the pelican is a symbol of charity, the species receives no charity in many places. Brown pelicans have all but vanished from Louisiana, though they appear on the seal and flag of that state. They have become rare in Texas, where they once were common and nested in many areas. The white pelican that nests on inland lakes and therefore is rather less in contact with commercial fishermen has fared slightly better.

It is true that in many places where fishing once flourished the take has decreased alarmingly. But too few people recall that when fishing was most productive, birds, including fish-eating pelicans, were most numerous. Fish and pelicans got along well for millions of years. They would still flourish side by side were it not for human activities, which include over-fishing and destruction of qualities required for abundant fish production.

In Laguna Madre where South Bird Island lies, the take of fish surpassed for many years that of any other area along the Texas coast. It is declining now, not because of pelicans, but from overfishing and, even more importantly, from the rapid silting in of the waters. This has resulted chiefly from diversion of water that formerly flowed into it. This diversion has also increased the salinity of the laguna. Already the Laguna Madre is one of the saltiest bodies of ocean water in the world. Once the salt is sufficiently concentrated, the water can no longer support fish, and it will become as dead as the Dead Sea and Great Salt Lake.

Quietly we drifted away from our post by the hatching eggs, started the motor and swung to the west shore. We chose a place apart from any nests to watch the flight that was already well under way. Pelicans on the ground are grotesque; on the water they are buoyant as small racing ketches poised for the starting signal; but in the air they are beautiful beyond compare. Their wingbeats may be the slowest of any birds in the world, and this clothes them with dignity and grace.

Now well-fed pelicans swept toward the island, some in long strings, some in V formation and some in wide echelons perfectly spaced with wing strokes so synchronized that each was a mere breath behind the bird on its left. The whole sky glittered as the sun touched the snowy birds. They converged over the island by the dozen, by hundreds, perhaps by thousands. Most were very high when we first saw them away off above the mainland shore, but they began to drop, gradually at first and then sharply as they neared the island. A few groups approached at high speed, and only when they were almost above their target did they suddenly brake their progress. Then we heard a rush of air like distant thunder as their powerful wings beat hard and they dropped abruptly as if spilled from the sky.

Some pelicans apparently freed from both incubation and feeding duties wandered away from the nesting areas and began to bathe and preen not far from where we were sitting. On the beach behind them was a large Audubon Sanctuary sign. In huge letters NO LANDING warned fishermen while still some distance away that the island was off limits to visitors. We were amused by the steady parade of pelicans from the water to the beach directly under the sign. Allan took the movie camera and waded far out and then swung in a semicircle toward the beach. The pelicans paid no attention to him and continued their bathing and loafing, so he recorded the pelicans confidently landing where no landing was permitted.

Half a dozen pelicans discovered a school of fish near the beach. Immediately they formed a fishing line and began to chase the fish closer and closer to the shore. Finally the pursuers began to dip them into their pouches. Unlike brown pelicans, which most often dive for fish, sometimes from a height as great as seventy feet, white pelicans never plunge into the water. Sometimes they fish alone, but far more often communal parties form an arc, and by kicking their feet and beating the water with their wings, they drive the fish close to shore. Then the fish are scooped into their pouches, the water is expelled and the catch is swallowed.

Propped comfortably against the beached skiff, I watched the great white birds fly in fluid lines and flocks, making an ever-changing pattern, a kaleidoscope of white and black against the bright blue. This was a day of satisfaction, for we had finally reached this unique pelican colony and successfully photographed the great white birds. It was not the first time we had tried to come, however.

I remembered an earlier attempt when we had planned to photograph here. The road down Mustang Island was still in the planning stage. We were told quite airily that it was easy to locate Louis Rawalt, who lived on the southern tip of Mustang Island. Just go down the beach from Port Aransas, we were told. It was just like driving on Daytona Beach.

If Mustang's beach is sometimes as smooth and hard as the famous racing sand of Daytona, it was not that day. It was so rough that the sixteen miles was one long series of jolts and jars. The wheels squealed in the sand, the motor overheated; but being hardy ourselves we tolerated it until the horn was shaken loose and began to blare. Finally Allan jerked away the wires and stopped that racket. Our only pleasure were the thousands and thousands of terns, chiefly black and royal, lining the beach and flying up in clouds as we approached them.

Hot and tired we reached the end of Mustang Island, then separated from Padre by a narrow shallow pass. Louis was in Corpus Christi. He had expected us but had been called to court to testify in an illegal hunting case.

In the meantime the tide began to rise and flow swiftly

through the pass. Laughing and ring-billed bulls and several species of terns dived excitedly. Time went fast for us. The hysterical birds were too intent on the feast swept into the channel to notice us. Almost as excited as the birds we made shot after shot of them individually and in groups. It was a torrid day, and splashing around under the birds invested our photography with gaiety. Some of the festive spirit evaporated when I discovered the bottom was positively alive with large crabs also feasting on whatever the tide carried close to them. Some crabs had formidable claws, and I became cautious as I moved barefooted among them.

Once our photography was interrupted when a jeep arrived and the driver asked to be ferried across the channel. A couple of men appeared from nowhere, and with the driver they began to shove what looked like a gargantuan child's raft off the sand into the water. It was built of great planks salvaged from a wreck. Once it was in the water two lighter planks were stretched from shore to raft, and the jeep rolled over them to the curious ferry. The two men began to push the ferry across the channel. This looked like fun, and we quickly put our cameras in the shade cast by a large box, plunged in and helped shove the ferry to Padre. It was rather more difficult than I had expected, for the ferry had a tendency to act like a crab and go sidewise. In the deepest place the water came to my waist, and how delightfully cool it felt under the blazing sun.

On the far side the planks once more provided a track for the jeep, which soon vanished down Padre as we shoved the raft back to Mustang.

The wind began to rise and clouds billowed across the sun. Louis returned, pleased with a conviction in the shooting affair, and said we would go to South Bird Island next day. Then he looked at the sky and qualified his words.

"The sky and the wind don't look good. A norther may be coming."

By late afternoon it was clear that Louis' concern was justified. The wind was howling. The clouds steadily thickened and darkened. We turned toward Port Aransas, only to find we were trapped. Waves were sweeping all the way across the wide beach and slapping the dunes. We weren't particularly disturbed. We had some simple camping equipment: sleeping bags, a boy scout cooking kit, a picnic basket equipped with essential tools and a small store of food. This was fortunate, for among the handful of beach cabins no food was available.

We searched for the most sheltered place as the wind increased steadily. Cooking over the driftwood fire was an ordeal. The wind sifted sand over the flames, nearly suffocating them one minute and then fanning long streamers into the pot of Dinty Moore canned stew the next. We finally decided to eat the stew lukewarm, but so much sand gritted between our teeth that any palatable flavor was lost. More sand clung to our clothes and cut our faces and hands.

Dispiritedly we hauled our sleeping bags from the car and had them unrolled when we saw a dark rain cloud coming up behind us, accompanied by a vivid play of lightning. Our sleeping bags were far from storm-proof, so we decided to drive back to the cabin area. In the sudden darkness, Allan switched on the lights. Nothing happened. The severe shaking suffered on the long drive down the beach had done something drastic to the electrical system. The car crept back through the dark. By the time we reached the cabin area the storm was upon us with slashing rain and screaming winds. We closed the windows and prepared to spend the night sitting upright in the front seat of the car, which was too crowded with photography equipment to allow space for stretching out in it. The car shook and quivered. Lightning revealed glimpses of rearing, white-edged waves in a turmoil and then left us blinded.

In a momentary lull the Rawalts came out of their tiny one-room cabin, and we shouted to them. They said it was the worst storm in months. Mrs. Rawalt's teeth chattered more from nervousness than cold, and the shawl she held about her shoulders snapped in the wind.

"I'm sure it's a hurricane," she said with a note of hysteria in her voice. "I know it's a hurricane. I can't understand why the coast guard didn't fly over to warn us so we could go to a safe place on the mainland. It wasn't right to leave us stranded in this low area in such a storm."

We heard the hissing roar of a new onslaught of rain and wind, and the Rawalts ran for shelter, shouting as they went that they were afraid the sweepers—long, windswept waves— would roll right over the point. We heard Mrs. Rawalt wail that we might all drown before morning.

The storm, having renewed itself, hurled wind, surf and rain at the point. Lightning's fiery claws darting downward glared on waves that drew steadily closer. We became so apprehensive that at first we did not realize when they stopped their apparently inexorable advance. Gradually the storm receded; though wind, rain and lightning continued, and thunder rolled across the sky. Probably we slept, but when morning came reluctantly with a dull sky and fitful winds, we felt no refreshment.

Sweepers flung their white-fringed edges all the way to the dunes, but less violently than the night before. There was no hope of making the long trip to South Bird Island. In fact, Louis said it might be days before the journey would be feasible. By afternoon the waves had subsided enough so they no longer swept the upper beach, and we made our way back to Port Aransas. So ended our first abortive attempt to reach the island of silent birds.

Our second attempt to reach South Bird began easily, for a smooth road had been built down the center of Mustang Island. To our surprise Mustang and Padre were now joined together. Silt had completely clogged the channel where we had waded among the crabs to photograph terns and gulls and had helped push the ferry. It was a windy day and gulf waves thundered ashore. Corpus Christi Bay was leaping, and spindrift flew from the peaks of lively chop.

Plans had been made long in advance, but weather has a way of circumventing arrangements made by wildlife photographers. Louis said a trip to South Bird was out of the question. He suggested we go with him down Padre Island instead. Enthusiastically we fell in with that idea. Few islands along the coast of the United States have a more exciting history. Its wild beauty is unique and it will be regarded in years to come as one of our greatest national treasures preserved under the National Parks system.

Padre, varied in width from a few hundred yards to about three miles, is compressed between the gulf and Laguna Madre. It is doubtless the narrowest island for its length, about 115 miles, in the entire world. Most of this threadlike area looks as untouched, as wild and natural, as it was when only Karankawas knew it. Endless ranks of waves break on the beach, packing it hard and depositing flotsam in an irregular band at the uppermost reach of flood tide. Behind the beach rise high graceful dunes, endlessly varied and forever changing. It is an enchanting place to hunt for treasure whether driftwood, pretty bottles or bleached shells that tinkle musically as the surging waves shift them up the beach and then suck them back again.

In 1804 King Charles of Spain gave Padre Island together with other lands to Father Nicolas Ball. Long before that a Spanish treasure fleet had been caught by a violent hurricane in 1553. Three ships went down, four made it to the Bahamas, but thirteen, driven off course by treacherous winds and great waves, were broken on Padre's shore. Three hundred men, women and children are said to have survived the shipwrecks, only to be attacked by the cannibalistic Karankawas. They fled down the beach before the savage onslaught; of them all, only two men survived to tell of the terrible ordeal.

A remarkable amount of booty from twelve of those wrecks was recovered by salvage crews dispatched by the king of Spain. According to old records, one ship's treasure remains untapped.

In the centuries since, innumerable ships have gone down in the western gulf, and parts of their cargo have been beached by the east winds on Padre's shore. In 1847 a schooner belonging to John Singer, brother of the inventor of the famous sewing machine, was wrecked, and many believe a treasure of $62,000 was buried in the dunes for safekeeping. Singer spent considerable time on Padre, where he had a trading post of sorts, but the legend persists that he never recovered his treasure. This is not as unlikely as it seems at first glance. Buildings of many kinds and for varied purposes have been built on Padre Island in the past, and storms have smashed them. Soon drifting sand has obliterated all trace of them. The dunes move and change shape as the strong winds and restless waves whittle and carve them.

By hunters of Spanish treasures Padre is considered the richest of all beaches. Pirates, smugglers, sailors, cowboys and fishermen have all found themselves willingly or accidentally on this long beach. Laffite and Morgan are said to have visited it. And who knows? They surely left treasure buried in the sands.

We wandered down the beach with Louis Rawalt with dreams in our heads. We picked up treasures of shells and driftwood that could be turned into bird feeders. Louis regarded the expedition more seriously. He is a genuine treasure hunter and has found nearly fifty thousand Indian artifacts during several decades of intermittent search. Some of these date back to the La Venta Horizan culture of about A.D. 300. One of his best discoveries was a Mayan clay figurine. He has uncovered almost a hundred Spanish coins, and of these the oldest is a 1556 Charles and Joanna piece.

He has found more modern treasure of genuine value. Once he collected a small fortune in raw rubber. Drums of kerosene, gasoline, diesel fuel and oil have all floated ashore and been rescued by him. Sometimes kegs of cucumber pickles, tins of lard and buckets of jam have been lifted, intact, from the edge of the surf. During the years of Prohibition he was richer by a total of sixty-five cases of whiskey.

Anything is likely to turn up on the shores of Padre. To most people the tragedies of World War II were removed by the breadth of the Atlantic and Pacific. This was not true along Padre Island. Dozens of ships were sunk by submarines in the gulf, and quantities of war materials came ashore. Life jackets, large lifeboats, beautifully made boxes sealed with heavy grease and containing deadly detonators and rations enough to supply a small army were thrust ashore by the endless procession of waves. Nobody combing the beach in those days could forget the grim calamity of war and death.

An enormous flotilla of Portuguese men-of-war had been cast ashore, and their pink-crested blue floats were shrinking under the hot sun. We found these beautiful sailors were venomous even in death, for when we touched some of the tentacles we were stung painfully. These creatures of warm seas are really very complicated colonies in which separate individuals are submerged and a sort of supercreature is formed. Their poisonous tentacles are sometimes very long. They quickly kill many kinds of sea life on which they feed, yet some fish are immune to the poison and swim freely among the stinging tentacles. An accidental touching of a tentacle causes brief discomfort, but application of vinegar wipes it away. A bad stinging demands instant attention by a doctor, for pain and fatal shock may follow. Their odd name was given them by the British long ago when fighting ships were under sail and for the first time they saw in the Portuguese seas, massed fleets of the strange and potentially deadly oceanic animals. From a distance their compact armadas with pink-edged blue sails look like squadrons of sailing ships. Great concentrations are seen only in the warm seas. Individually or in little groups, however, they occur as far north on our Atlantic coast as Cape Cod.

We left Padre Island richer by far than when we approached it though we carried with us only half a dozen bright shells and a few pieces of driftwood found by its restless surf. The blazing white sands, the high dunes insecurely anchored by salt-tolerant plants, the abundant and varied bird life, ghost crabs looking at us with stalked eyes, and most of all the uninhabited solitude, the wild serenity and the romantic history of Padre combined in a treasured memory.

Today there is a rising wave of interest in our wildlife. Perhaps an appreciation of its irreplaceable values will grow in time to save the big species that suffer gravest danger from mankind. But in spite of a growing awareness of the value of big birds such as white pelicans, new problems arise that may defeat our hope. We watched thousands of pelicans arrive and depart from South Bird Island that day. It was crowded with healthy young.

In 1966 many dead birds were found in the Corpus Christi area. White pelicans particularly fell off sharply in numbers. Only four hundred young were produced. Sick and dead birds that were examined contained a high concentration of DDT. Now when millions recognize the need for preserving our wildlife heritage, human activities involving no malice toward birds or mammals may defeat us. The island of silent birds and all the colonies of birds that feed on marine life may become islands of the dead.

21

Listen! The Wind Is Rising!

ON OUR FIRST spring trip to Texas, we were particularly eager
to reach Green Island, which lies in Laguna Madre about
twenty-five miles north of Port Isabel as a homing heron flies.
When John Baker, then president of the National Audubon
Society, outlined the schedule he wished us to follow, he
really whetted our desire to photograph the reddish egrets
nesting on Green Island. He said he considered that colony
one of the most successful of heron colonies in the entire
country. Moreover the birds nesting in it appeared far less
timid than the same species elsewhere.

"Perhaps," he conjectured, "they are less shy because John
Larson has watched over them since the late 1920's when the
island became the first Audubon Sanctuary in Texas."

To insure an early start from Brownsville, in the evening
we packed the car with food for a couple of days, sleeping
bags, blinds and the camera equipment. Everything was
made ready for our departure. When we closed the motel
door behind us and went out into the fading night, we could
leave immediately.

All night long the wind rattled the blinds, and the massive
branches of the tepeguajes above the motel tossed wildly. It
was still dark when we hurried toward the car, but my foot-

steps were abruptly arrested. Those tepeguajes looked radically different from the way they had last evening. Then the canopy of lacy compound leaves was so deep and dense they hid the branches and the sky. Now the trees looked as bare as winter maples in New England, and the naked limbs were outlined against the blanching sky.

"Look, Allan!" I seized his arm and pointed up to the bewildering transformation. "Those millions of leaves have all folded into thin strings."

For the first time we had come upon trees that go to sleep by furling their leaves at night. They react to light and dark much as animals do. *Tepeguajes* belong to the enormous *Leguminosae* order, the second largest among seed plants in the entire world, whose varied members range from tiny vines to towering trees. They are found in almost every habitat from desert to jungle and from the Equator north and south almost to the limits of seed-plant life. Like ourselves, the *tepeguajes* had slept through the night, but it would be the rising sun, not an alarm clock, that would waken them, triggering the spreading of their leaves.

We had left the *tepeguajes* far behind when dawn came. That morning the sky was a polished, colorless dome, and the rising sun showed neither rose nor gold but was a pallid and glassy spotlight focusing killing heat upon us. The temperature leaped to midday intensity soon after the sun cleared the horizon.

It was about thirty miles from Brownsville to Horsehead Island, which is joined to the mainland by a fill. Following a map, we soon left the pavement behind and drove along a rutted lane running between thickets of tangled prickly shrubs. Finally the lane petered out into a maze of tracks at the tip of Horsehead. We stopped by a tall flagpole with a green box nailed to it. Allan unhooked the cover. It was empty. Somebody had taken away the white flag we had been told to hoist as a signal to Mr. Larson, the Audubon warden, on Green Island about three miles offshore. What now, I wondered?

Allan was already rummaging in the station wagon and pulled out a black rubber poncho with grommets along the sides. He snapped this to the lanyard, and as he raised his black flag he laughed.

"If I had some chalk I'd draw a skull and crossbones on my pirate signal. Mr. Larson would be startled to see a Jolly Roger flying where he expected a peaceful white flag."

Even as Allan wrapped the lanyard around some cleats, the wind seized his flag and ripped a ribbon all the way across it, and then a second one. Mr. Larson must have been watching for our signal from his motor launch, for immediately Allan, staring through his binoculars, saw a puff of smoke and some lines tossed off the pilings. Then the boat pulled away from the dock. Allan ran to the pole and hauled down his flag before the wind could shred the entire poncho. It was fortunate he did so. We were going to need that poncho.

But now, with the poncho tossed carelessly on our duffle, we sat on the end of Horsehead and waited impatiently for the small launch to cross those three miles of Laguna Madre. Already heat waves quivered and trembled above the gray-green water, and behind them dim and hazy Green Island looked like a flat gray pancake. The small boat crept first to the north and then south again in a fantastic zigzag. Soon we were pacing up and down as the minutes fled. The forward motion of the boat was less than a snail's pace. Was the steering gear out of order, we wondered?

Gradually the boat inched closer, and feverish with the knowledge of flying time, we waded out to meet it. Allan carried the line ashore and tied it to a stake. Then back and forth we splashed through warm cloudy water until all the equipment was stowed. We pulled ourselves aboard backward and let our legs dangle over the gunwales so we drained off into the laguna and not into the boat.

We soon understood the reason for the erratic movements of the launch. Even though it drew little water, a muddy plume fanned out in our wake. Never more than three feet deep between the mainland and island, the water often shoaled, forcing long detours around mud bars.

"In spite of my caution I sometimes hang up on a bar. They change size and shape and even their location with every storm," Mr. Larson told us. "This shallow water is a challenge to people with more enthusiasm than sense, so every year or so somebody tries to wade to the island. The soft bottom makes wading particularly exhausting, and the hot sun adds to the difficulties. Finally I have to go haul the waders out of the mess they have gotten into."

Swinging one direction and then reversing again, we pulled away from Horsehead by slow degrees, and with equal sluggishness we crawled closer to Green Island, which we examined eagerly while our hearts beat fast with anticipation. The island was low and almost round with attenuated beaches reaching to the north and even farther to the south. We saw a few reddish egrets dancing along the water's edge and a couple of solitary great blue herons as motionless as stakes driven into the sand. Nothing indicated the presence of a great bird colony.

At last we flung ourselves forward to seize posts when the boat pulled alongside a primitive dock. This was simply a file of low stakes driven into the shallow water with a double row of narrow planks swaying drunkenly from them. Carrying the equipment ashore was a lively undertaking as the crude landing stage reacted to our marching feet like a trampoline and threatened to bounce us into the water with every step. Incandescent light poured down, and half-blinded by it and by perspiration rolling down our cheeks, we crossed the shifting sand. There least terns attacked us.

"We'll look for their nests later," Allan said. "And for snowy plover nests, too. Look at that plover injury-feign."

The plover resembled a whitened piping plover. It dragged its wings and spread tail on the sand, uttering pitiful cries of distress, but when we kept right on across the beach, it stopped, shook its feathers into place and with black legs twinkling dashed back to its nest.

We could see a corner of the cabin roof barely rising above the thicket of chaparral brush and near it a tower perhaps twenty-five feet high from which Mr. Larson could survey the entire island and the waters around it. Ahead an irregular path led up a gentle hard-baked slope to the cabin where Mr. Larson stayed while guarding the birds from the time they arrived in late March until the young were on the wing and the colony began to disperse in late summer.

Transfering our duffle from the beach to the tower under the blazing sun and being hampered by thorns that grabbed at it when we passed did not dampen our exhilaration. As soon as the final load was deposited on the bottom level of the tower, we climbed to its top and looked over the thirty-acre island.

Almost imperceptibly the island sloped up from the long south beach until it reached a height of almost twenty feet, then dropped with wall-like abruptness to the north beach. The vegetation above the glaring white beach was a muted gray-green tangle of chaparral so tightly intertwined that had it not been for the forbidding thorns, I believe I could have scrambled over the top as Darwin climbed over the impenetrable forest of San Pedro. Occasionally a yellow-green mesquite towered over the brush, and here and there a dark-green bayonet-leaved yucca accented the pale desert green. A boisterous wind made it difficult to hold our binoculars steady and even to hear each other, but its lively flow made the heat more bearable.

Scarcely a bird could be seen, and though we heard an occasional squawk and cackle, none of the usual sounds of a great bird colony reached us. My spirits were on the verge of collapse when Mr. Larson reassured us.

"They are there by the thousand," he said. "But they don't like this wind so they stay low in the bushes. Let's go down to the trail. The brush is impenetrable except along the trail. I hacked that out years ago so we could count nests and keep track of the production of young birds. Now I only need to come over sometime during the winter when the birds are away and clip the summer's growth to keep it open. That isn't much work, because desert plants don't grow very fast."

Swiftly then we followed Mr. Larson down the tower steps to the narrow path between straight walls of brush from twelve to twenty feet high. A blast of heat as from a hot oven when the door is unlatched met us. Overhead the white-hot sky pressed down, and we stewed in the breathless pour of the sun. Between the canyonlike intertwined thorny branches bordering the trail we could hear the romping wind scurry along the top only a couple of yards above our heads, but not an eddy reached down to cool us.

Suddenly we were surrounded by birds. In that furnace-like heat they were gathered by the thousands. Reddish egrets, snowy egrets, common egrets, great blue herons of the pale-headed Ward's subspecies, Louisiana herons and black-crowned night herons as well as white ibises, were packed together in a concentration of about three hundred to the acre. Each species had its own subdivision in the chaparral, though occasionally a heron or an egret nested among those of a different species. With the thorny catclaw, crossthorn, buckthorn and all the other bristling shrubs and cactus dulling the roar of the wind, the noise of the colony erupted around us. Clucks, squawks, grunts and cackles melted into the begging cries of young birds, parents saluting each other, quarrelsome birds defending territories, while occasionally impassioned croaks of late-courting couples rose above the level of the colony's clamor.

The birds paid little attention to us. Many of the adults

held eggs against their warm brooding spots, others with half-spread wings sheltered downy young. Reddish egrets whose young were a couple of weeks old climbed a few feet above them and turned to stare at us with aquamarine eyes surrounded by blue skin. Many of the large young were alone. Both their parents were seeking food for the rapidly developing offspring.

These birds were extraordinarily unafraid. Yet there was no air of tameness about them. They wanted no handouts from us as some wild ducks do that during the winter months, join wing-clipped captives on park ponds. These herons watched us alertly, yet with no more fear than if we had been deer or rabbits strayed unexpectedly into their domain. Here on semidesert Green Island, William Henry Hudson's imaginary Rioloma had become a reality.

"They know me, I think," Mr. Larson confided. "When the children were small they spent many a summer week here with me, and the birds accepted them as they do my guests and me."

By every posture and expression the birds retained the remoteness, the strangeness of untamed wildness, yet within the boundaries of this small island world they accepted man as a friendly part of their environment. To walk so close to the birds, to see their colorful plumes, watch the wild glowing eyes and listen to the unceasing chatter of the colony was an exceptional experience. We have a semblance of this when we are concealed in blinds in a bird colony, but nowhere else have we strolled so leisurely among wild nesting birds.

"We really would not need blinds here," Allan said, "but I think we can work more comfortably if we use them, because they will give us a little protection from the sun, and perhaps even these birds will be more at ease if they cannot see us."

The chaparral was so dense we could see only a foot or two inside the border of the trail. Quickly we chose locations for our blinds, which would have to be placed in the middle of the trail. Each of us selected an area where we could keep several nests under surveillance and where two or three nests were at different stages of development.

Hot wearisome labor followed as we dragged blind frames along the narrow path and then struggled with the covers which were hooked by thorns at every step. In spite of caution we frequently had to stop to pull a ball of cactus spines from our sneakers or blot a stream of blood from an arm ripped by one of the clawlike thorns. At last Allan was satisfied that everything was properly arranged so that the next day could be devoted exclusively to the photography of reddish egrets. Then we returned to the tower.

Mr. Larson was ready to run through his activities as a warden for Allan's camera, and they went to work while I unrolled sleeping bags, blew up air mattresses, arranged insect netting and then stowed the food in Mr. Larson's tiny cupboard. Finally Allan and Mr. Larson returned, well pleased with the footage they had made. Sometimes weeks go by when nobody tries to land on the island, but at that moment a boatload of holiday fishermen-picnickers pulled close to shore. When Mr. Larson explained they could neither picnic nor land on Green Island, they good-naturedly posed as would-be trespassers while Allan filmed a little sequence about that facet of the life of a warden on a lonely sanctuary island.

No sooner had the fishermen, delighted with their performance before the camera, pulled away than a Mexican fishing boat approached the dock. The Mexicans needed help. One of the men had badly burned his hand on the exhaust pipe. Mr. Larson got his first aid kit, and after doing the best he could, urged them to take the man to a doctor right away.

"I'm afraid they won't, though," he said. "They just go on the theory that I did enough and now either the hand will get bettter—or it won't."

The Mexicans were picturesque in huge hats, and their dark unshaven faces were decked with magnificent wide-spreading curled moustaches. They added a foreign touch to Allan's sanctuary film.

"When I first came here after the island was made a sanctuary I had trouble with the Mexican fishermen. They were accustomed to come ashore whenever they wished. They took birds and eggs as a change from fish. But I was patient, and they soon learned to accept the new situation, though I don't believe they understand what it is all about. Today they never come ashore if they want something, but stay in their boat by the dock until I come down to ask about their problem."

After eating some sandwiches and drinking an astounding amount of tepid pop, we took cameras and set out to walk the glaring beach around the island. The dazzling light and searing heat in no way affected the energy of the least terns. They circled frantically and darted at us, some actually hitting us on the head. Their shrill, sharp *kip kip kip* further protested our nearness to their eggs. These, usually two in a nest, were buff spotted with brown and so closely matched the sand that had the terns been less noisy and aggressive, they might have been overlooked. The eggs were laid in shallow scoops on the burning sand, sometimes with bits of shell added as if for decoration. We hurried away knowing they would be killed if left unsheltered from the sun.

Soon Allan found four newly hatched snowy plovers, and they also closely matched the sand. He quickly put his hat over them, for these are precocial birds, able to run about as soon as they dry off after hatching. Once his camera was focused, I picked up the hat, and the little plovers were quiet for a moment or two. Then they stood up and scampered off in response to their parents' calls. The nest scoop, having held the eggs during incubation, had served its purpose and was now abandoned to the wind, which would soon fill and level the slight depression.

On the east side of the island, grass ran all the way from the bluff into the water. We dragged ourselves through the saw-edged greenery with our shoes squelching in the mud and water and were glad to regain the sand in spite of the renewed glare and heat. Oddly enough, the herons feeding along the shore were as timid as herons usually are. Repeatedly we stalked an individual or a little flock feeding intently only to have them fly away before we were close enough to film the graceful swinging of opened wings and the quick darting steps of the reddish egrets. Over the years they had learned to accept men as harmless within the bounds of their colony on Green Island, but once away from the thicket, they knew him as an enemy.

Our cameras grew heavier, and our steps plodded more and more wearily. Once in a while a heron flying overhead was worth a shot, and whenever we came to a rivulet where water fingered deep into the beach, we usually flushed a group of feeding herons that also provided flight shots. But we were very tired, and the cabin was very far away. The day before we had hurried up and down the Rio Grande Valley, guided by Irby Davis, who knows where every species found in the valley can be seen. With him, we ran up the biggest list of birds that Allan had ever seen in a single day. As for me, I was stunned by the great numbers of strange birds. Even the names were new to me: verdins, pyrrhuloxias, pauraques, seed-eaters, groove-billed anis and chachalacas had been pointed out until my head reeled. Even the orioles and hummingbirds we saw were species unknown to me, and their identification was very complex after the simplicity of two orioles: the orchard and Baltimore, and a single hummingbird, the ruby-throated, in the east. My confidence sank to a low level, and I was afraid I would never learn the queer names, let alone acquire the ability to identify the valley birds, many of them never coming farther north than this semitropical corner of Texas.

We had seen the Rio Grande running brown and swift almost level with the top of the levees. Great trees ripped from some upstream bank charged like frantic horses down its racing opaque midstream. On the far slope was a foreign land, and the only buildings I had seen were low adobe huts the color of the earth.

Last night had been muggy and hot. Now the sun was low, but its heat was still unabated as we completed the island circuit and trudged wearily up the trail to the cabin.

Mr. Larson was sitting on the top level of the tower, scanning the laguna with his binoculars.

"My evening show is beginning," he called. "Come on up."

A show it was. Herons of all kinds were converging on the island from every point of the compass. Robbed of color by the pale light, they were all white or gray, though the Louisianas and great blues looked very dark. The white ibis darted toward the island as swiftly as arrows and dropped abruptly to their chosen corner of the thicket. Great blue herons, slow and stately with deliberate lapsing of the broad wings, made solitary punctuations over the water. The smaller herons and egrets arrived in whirling clouds; their long necks folded neatly between their shoulders and their long legs trailed until they neared their perches. Then they thrust forward their heads and dropped their skinny legs in a variety of awkward angles. Many spun out of their flock to circle the tower and settle near it where they inspected us with remote unfathomable eyes and then moved on to join the noisy multitude gathering on the southeast part of the island. As more and more birds joined the throng, the nucleus grew and spread wider and wider over the island.

Each new platoon was welcomed with an upsurge of many voices in an infinite number of keys until the croaks, squawks and laments shook the air. Our eyes swiveled from side to side as a flock appeared here and another there. They came from Padre Island, from the mainland, from the north and south of Laguna Madre. Nowhere was there idle wheeling. Nowhere did a bird soar and drift. As if pulled by a powerful magnet, they hurled themselves impetuously toward the growing tumult created by thousands upon thousands of birds packed so close together on top of the chaparral that the desert green vanished beneath the crowd of white and gray.

The sun dipped behind the horizon and the parade of birds became invisible. In the west were fitful explosions of lightning too far away for the sound of thunder to reach us, and we went down to the cabin. While we ate dinner, Mr. Larson told us of finding a rattler sunning itself on his door-step one winter day when he came to clear the trails. Before the rush of settlers pushed wildlife farther from the coast, he occasionally had trouble with coyotes. Always when one swam to the island and gorged itself on the birds, it would call until its fellows answered and then it would coax them, too, to swim to the island. It was essential to stop this invasion, for the sanctuary was meant to protect the reddish egrets. Coyotes would have forced the egrets to desert the safety of Green Island, and then man's predation would have been an even greater calamity to the species.

"One night," Mr. Larson continued, "I was returning from Harlingin with supplies when the motor broke down. I couldn't see to repair it so I threw the anchor overboard, made myself as comfortable as possible and went to sleep. Early the next morning along came a fish and game warden in his patrol plane. He spotted me and dropped his pontoons lightly beside the stalled boat.

" 'Shall I send somebody to help you?' he yelled over the roar of his motor.

" 'Certainly not,' I retorted. 'Just let me fasten a line to your seaplane and you can tow me to the island. I'll soon put the motor in order.' "

So Mr. Larson became one of the few people ever towed to port by a plane.

We were weary enough to crawl early into our sleeping bags, but we slept lightly under the starless sky. The birds were restless, and their voices rose and fell but never became quiet. Twice during the night we saw Mr. Larson's lantern dance down the trail. The first time Allan called to ask if he could help.

"Thank you, no," Mr. Larson answered. "The wind has changed and I want to check the mooring of the boat."

Though drugged with sleep at dawn, I was snapped to instant wakefulness by an urgent note in Allan's voice.

"This is the strangest sight I have ever seen! Look!"

Pushing aside the netting, I sat up. Sea and sky were lost in each other. The mainland was invisible. The very edges of the island blended insensibly into the atmosphere. Everywhere there was a golden radiance as impalpable as a dream, with far less substance than a thin fog, yet more concealing. Bathed in the diffused flood of light we had a curious sensation of floating within a luminous cloud, as if we had been caught up and trapped in the yellow band of a rainbow. Quickly the glory faded. Ashen light, heavy and depressing, erased the buoyant flush of color.

Slowly, lethargically, we prepared for the day. Thunder muttered and died as if choked by the dull air. The sky whitened and heat blasted the island. Allan was worried about the thunder that might sound the advance of rain, but perhaps the pewter-colored sky disturbed him even more. He feels strongly that the quality of light has a profound effect on photographs. On a bright blue day he can capture the animated lightness and vigor so much a part of birds, while the heavy light of impending storm gives a feeling of dull lassitude quite foreign to their usual airy vitality. This day was an important link in the sequence of photography planned for that brief trip. It was the only day to be devoted exclusively to the photography of reddish egrets.

Mr. Larson shook his head regretfully when he heard Allan wish for a blue sky. He had listened to the morning weather report. The air was unstable. A strong front was advancing, shoving turbulence ahead of it. Small craft warnings were flying along the laguna and people were urged to listen for tornado alerts. Such weather patterns were normal for spring in Texas and almost invariably pale skies preceded the disturbances.

By eight o'clock the temperature had climbed to ninety-eight degrees and we trudged to our blinds between the congestion of pale leaves and stiff thorns with hot beads falling from our foreheads.

I zipped shut my blind cover, and the faint sibilant notes of insects rose around me. They sounded like a bombardment of sharp sun rays pinging as they struck the hard ground. Inside the blind the moist heat curled around me in a smothering blanket. Even the reddish egrets looked listless, and a melancholy weight pressed them low on their nests.

Though the reddish egrets had been little concerned when we walked through their colony the day before, now Allan in his blind and I in mine could watch them without their being aware of our presence. Whenever one assumed a graceful pose or displayed interesting behavior we caught it on film. These herons, which had looked dark gray as they swept to the island last evening were actually garbed with great subtlety of color. Delicate reddish brown plumes fell down their backs. The bills, dark toward the tip and light near the face, varied greatly. Those nearest courtship stage had the brightest bills, and some of these were bluish-black at the tip and bright rosy red near the face while the bare skin around the aquamarine eyes was vivid blue. Long soft feathers lay close as shingles on the neck until an intruder came too close to the nest or a mate arrived with food. Then those feathers were lifted until they resembled an old-fashioned boa. Those on the head were fanned out around the face in a shaggy circle. In full display I thought they looked quite like quills of a porcupine in defensive posture.

The very young birds were sheltered throughout the day, but the juveniles were left alone while both parents sought food to fill their hungry maws. This was a time-consuming task, for they demanded almost their weight in food each day. When we entered our blinds many of the adults had already left in search of food, so the colony was as quiet as it ever becomes during the nesting season. One by one the parents returned, and as each arrived, begging cries rose urgently, each youngster calling for attention. On my left three tall juveniles stood quietly on their nest until they sensed the coming of a parent before I saw it. All three birds began to bow with tails high and heads jerking up and down to the accompaniment of high-pitched entreaties for food. They literally mobbed their parent, and finally one succeeded in taking a scissor-hold across the bill of the adult. It pulled fiercely until a fish was regurgitated, which it gulped greedily. The feeding process was so violent that each time a youngster demanded and took food, I thought if I were their parent I would surely desert such rough offspring. But the egrets were faithful, and not an hour passed when food was not delivered to the insatiable fledglings.

In spite of our satisfaction as picture after picture was shot, the oppressive heat made the hours drag by. Insensibly the white sky darkened, and by four o'clock it was so dull that I shook the sides of the blind so the egrets would not be startled when I came into the open. I carried the camera equipment back to the tower. Then, hampered by clutching thorns, I took down the blind and carried it back to camp. There I packed everything so we could make an early departure next morning when we would hurry toward Corpus Christi and another Audubon Sanctuary. Before I had finished Allan, looking as weary as I felt, joined me and completed the packing.

Mr. Larson was again on top of the tower. He was looking intently toward the southeast. We joined him and swung our binoculars in that direction.

"I've never known frigate-birds to land on this island except when a severe storm is brewing," he said, and even as he spoke five of the black, angular birds that had seemed to hang motionless as if anchored in midair began to drop down and soon perched among the herons.

It is always a thrilling sight to watch a flock or even just one of these extremely slender birds with narrow angled wings reaching out seven or eight feet. Its flight is airy and effortless as thistledown borne on autumn winds, and the frigate-bird drifts as it will or floats among the clouds on motionless wings, occasionally scissoring its long forked tail. It can, particularly in courtship, display startling antics as it twists, dives and plunges like a jet fighter. Once in Florida Bay I watched a frigate-bird skim low over a row of pilings, each capped by a royal tern, and force every resting bird to leave its perch. It looked like mischievous play on the part of the frigate-bird, but probably the bird was merely keeping in practice, for it regularly robs terns of fish they catch. Its skeleton, we are told, weights less than its feathers. Oddly enough frigate-birds do not dive or swim, though we think of them as oceanic birds. If by mischance they enter the water, their feathers become so waterlogged that it is difficult or even impossible for them to take off again. They are sometimes seen far from land, and scientists have put forth the theory that frigate-birds actually sleep in the air where they find a strong rising current and then simply rest upon it.

Above us ponderous tumbling clouds sank ominously lower. Mr. Larson stopped watching the frigate-birds and turned toward the west, froze for an instant, then raced down the stairs shouting as he went.

"Take your stuff into the cabin!"

A gust of wind hit us and whirled me about. It picked up a galvanized bucket standing under the cistern faucet, banged it against the cabin, then bounced it down the trail with a racket that receded in the distance. Clinging to the guard rail, I followed Allan down the steps and we snatched up cameras and sprinted for the cabin, dumped them on the floor and sped back for another load. We had grabbed the last bundles when a burst of rain smashed down. Instead of hitting the earth with a splattering of round marks, the drops skidded along the thirsty surface, penciling long thin streaks before the parched earth could catch and suck them to itself. Lightning, flame-clawed, straddled the lurid sky and thunder reverberated in the great cloud caverns.

A solid sheet of rain drenched us before we could reach the cabin. Tossing his load inside, Allan dashed off to help with the boat. Then as suddenly as it had come the rain squall ended, and the wind slammed across the island with renewed violence. In another few minutes it too died away as abruptly as the forced current in the wind tunnel when the switch is pulled.

Allan and Mr. Larson, breathing fast, hurried toward the cabin, and I laughed when I saw them. The wind had cemented sand all over their rain-soaked bodies until they looked like sandmen. Even their ears were stuffed with sand. Brushing themselves off as best they could, both suddenly stopped and they, too, began to laugh.

"Turn around and look at that cabin," Allan said.

In those few wild moments after the rain stopped the cabin had been plastered with sand until it resembled an adobe hut.

Everything was still, ominously still. We climbed back up the tower. A turmoil of waves raced every which way tossing foam about the laguna and piling it along the island shore. An appalling green light spread over the usually pale island and water. Purple and black clouds boiled portentously, yet the air around us hung limp and dead. My head throbbed. Lightning crackled across the sky, and webs of flame flickered, expanded and contracted but never vanished. A greater flash sheeted the clouds, and its glare extinguished sight like an explosion. In the blackness I heard Allan yell, "Listen! The wind is coming!" and there followed a sound like a freight train approaching under full throttle.

With one accord we ran for shelter, but before we could reach the cabin the wind caught us. Bending before its fury, we gasped for breath and then plunged through the door. Both men had to put their shoulders against it to push it shut. We had one brief glimpse of the tangled chaparral in convulsion. Then a solid wall of rain hid everything and the roar was like a cataclysm. Waterspouts shot through cracks in the walls, and we shoved the cameras and films under the cots. Then water squeezed under the door and washed over the floor. Deeply concerned for the safety of our cameras and irreplaceable films, we piled them on top of the cots. Scarcely was this done than thin jets sprayed down from the roof. Allan snatched the tattered black poncho that had served as a flag only yesterday and tucked it carefully around the precious items.

The cabin was shaking. Vibrating.

"It's partly the wind motor on the roof." Mr. Larson had to shout above the howling wind and pounding rain. "It charges the battery for my radio. It is made to withstand eighty-mile-an-hour winds."

Then came a confused rumpus and a great crash. The vibrating of the cabin lessened. The blades of the wind motor had been torn away, and they racketed down the roof and crashed onto the cistern with a tremendous thud. There was another monstrous buffet and the lantern flame flickered and smoked. The thundering storm battered the tiny cabin until we could not hear each other, and repeated onslaughts rocked it. Eyes did not meet as the storm's fury reached a shrieking crescendo.

"They wonder as I do if the cabin can stand the force of the wind," I thought, and recalled unpleasant pictures of wreckage left in the wake of great winds.

Gradually the storm blew itself to exhaustion and the rain lessened. Lightning began to fade and thunder rumbled rather than cracked and blasted. Finally we curled up and made ourselves as comfortable in the soggy cabin as possible. One by one we dropped into fitful sleep that deepened into placid oblivion.

I doubt if Noah and his family emerged from the ark with a greater sense of wonder than ours when we came out of the small sodden cabin at dawn. Beneficent calm lay on the island and above it the sky was serenely blue except in the east where a flush of apricot prepared the world for sunrise.

Every leaf, every thorny twig, was hung with trembling water-diamonds that burst into sparkles as the sun swept above the horizon. The whole island was fresh as the first day of creation and an intangible wild perfume lay over it. Everywhere there were land birds on migration that had found refuge in the dense chaparral from the storm that had rocketed across their path. These birds that had found sanctuary in time crowded every bush, and as if in thanksgiving their joyful songs blended into a great chorus scattering delightful music over an island where most nesting birds conversed in coarse guttural and discordant voices.

Concerned with the fate of the nesting birds, we hurried along the crystal-decked trail. Relief swept over us as we saw nest after nest intact, and herons and ibises going about their usual business as if nothing unusual had happened. Protected by the dense vegetation, most of the birds had clung to their rocking nests and provided sufficient shelter for the fragile life beneath their breasts.

Only when we reached the northern limit of the trail did our hearts sink. Disaster had struck many of the nests, for there they had been exposed to the full brunt of the storm. Broken eggs and lifeless young had already attracted the clearnup squad and both turkey and black vultures were circling above and preparing to land in the wrecked nesting area.

Pellucid water gently lapped against the beach, which had completely changed during the night. Here it was enlarged, there it had been ripped away. Calamity to the beach birds was complete.

The least terns had dispersed. Their nest scoops were filled with sand, erased by wind and water until no trace of them remained. Here and there a half-buried egg, its life and luster gone, lay in the flotsam left behind when the surging laguna water swept across the beach. We saw a solitary snowy plover but no trace of the young that opened their lively black eyes on the world only yesterday.

We climbed the tower and were amazed again by the changed appearance of the encircling beach. Mud bars had slipped beneath the surface of the laguna and new ones had been built overnight. Mr. Larson joined us and said there had been enough life in the battery so that he heard a weather report. Tornadoes had cut a great swath across south central Texas and left several damaged communities in their wake. Deep in the tight thorny tangle we had survived a storm that killed and destroyed in its mad rampage.

We began to count the land birds on the island. Mourning doves by the dozens, white-winged and white-fronted doves, too, were there, and so were yellow-billed cuckoos hiding silently in the thicket. Barn swallows by the hundreds and bank swallows began to rise and circle over the island in search of insects for breakfast. Bright little warblers were everywhere: black-and-white, yellow, palm, chestnut-sided and Canada warblers. We saw several male Wilson's warblers, burning yellow with black velvet caps on top of their heads, and redstarts flashing their wings and fanning their tails.

Two golden-winged warblers were a surprise but no more so than thirty-odd meadowlarks completely out of habitat in the dense chaparral. Another surprise was a flock of about twenty bobolinks, which normally are not seen along the Texas coast in spring, for they take a far eastern route north to their breeding grounds. Scarlet and summer tanagers made brave splashes of color in the subdued green of the island. More than half a hundred orioles: Baltimore, orchard and a few vivid hooded orioles startled us with their vibrant hues. We saw at least six male rose-breasted grosbeaks, their thick white bills as striking as their black and white plumage with the big rose triangle on the breast. Among the storm waifs we found several hummingbirds; most were ruby-throats but one was a buff-bellied male with a bright red bill and a shining green throat. It was a marvel that so tiny, so fragile bits of life had survived the violent pounding of the rain, for each wind-driven drop must have delivered a painful blow.

Vireos were there in abundance and so were flycatchers. A couple of dozen scissor-tails delighted me, but Allan was impressed by the numbers of yellow-bellied flycatchers and eastern and western kingbirds. To our astonishment we saw an olive-sided flycatcher, and characteristically it claimed the highest twig on the island for its perch. By the end of the morning we had counted 106 species of birds from the tower.

According to plan we should have left the island soon after dawn, but Mr. Larson said we would only mire down in the mud. The road from Horsehead would be impassable. Though we could have happily and profitably spent the entire breeding season on the island, on this trip our time was limited and our schedule tight. A delay in one place meant cancellation of some important segment of material we had come so far to photograph. Allan, worried about the hitch in the plan, took his blind and cameras and resumed work in the colony. At least he could take advantage of unexpected time to make some of the shots denied him yesterday.

It was but a matter of hours before the heat was back as fiery as ever, and a pewter film brushed across the sky. On the third day a new storm rumbled in the west and the film thickened swiftly into menacing clouds. We decided to brave the mudholes, and Mr. Larson took us to the mainland charting a new course as he did so.

Since the first trip to Green Island and the reddish egret colony we have returned many times. The old cabin has been replaced by a snug new one quite as small as the leaky old building. An intercoastal waterway that extends the length of the Texas coast now lies down the Laguna Madre. Except for the navigable channel, the laguna between Horsehead and Green Island is so silted it is impossible to float anything larger than a canoe on it. In recent years we have gone to Green Island by way of the Arroyo Colorado in a very shallow-draft boat. After Mr. Larson's death, his son John, Jr. left his own business and assumed his father's splendid work. The Green Island sanctuary today is a monument to the vision of the National Audubon Society and to the Larsons, who played a vital part in preserving an irreplaceable wildlife treasure.

That morning when we took leave of Mr. Larson and looked down the road, our spirits soared. With intense relief we saw that the hot sun and strong wind had dried it well. Little swirls of dust actually rose from it.

We were too optimistic. The storms had not yet finished with us.

22

Broza, Adobe, Tarantulas, and Pyrrhuloxias

WE WERE CONCERNED by Mr. Larson's prediction of road trouble ahead, but we reached and passed without incident the fill joining Horsehead Island to the mainland. Now, briefly, we had a sense of triumph. Surely we had crossed the place where mud danger was greatest.

We entered the brush country, the *broza*, a mixed thorny tangle of catclaw, mesquite, huisache, and granjeno with some cactus and dark yucca added in the less congested areas. All were armed with vicious thorns, and most had small sensitive leaves, an adaptation to the dry conditions under which they normally existed.

Our ebullient spirits plummeted abruptly. There was mud in the road ahead. Our muscles were tense and we held our breath as we approached the sticky area. The wheels churned. We were on the far side. We sloshed and skidded through another mudhole and still another. Then ahead lay a truly formidable stretch of mud with pools here and there on its surface. It was at least an eighth of a mile from end to end.

Allan stepped on the brake and studied the situation. Since the storm no wheeled vehicle had entered the quagmire to suggest a possible route through it.

"Let's go," Allan said tersely, and we moved forward at a good clip. The back end no longer obeyed the front of the car. There was a sickening skid. Wheels spun. Allan pressed harder on the gas muttering that he must keep the wheels turning. Mud spewed in twin fans behind us. We slowed. And stopped. Allan tried to back. The car would not budge. We got out. Mud, sticky abode mud, was packed so firmly around the front end of the car that we could not scrape it away with the stoutist sticks we could find. The mud had snared us, and we were hopelessly trapped.

Our eyes searched the road ahead for a clue to help. The land was without habitation as far as we could see. An empty dirt road went on and on through endless *broza*.

"I'll have to find help somewhere," Allan cast a worried look at the dark cloud on the horizon. "If I can walk far enough," he added, for in a dozen steps mud had caked on his shoes so he teetered insecurely on a high platform. Soon he had passed the worst section of mud and stopped to scrape it off as best he could with his pocketknife. Then he proceeded on his way. He grew smaller and smaller in the distance and finally vanished around a curve in the road.

The *broza* pushed close to the muddy road, and I could see brown water washing around the slender stems, an incongruous sight in an arid land. That the brush made a deep imprint on early settlers is evident from their names for various gradations of height and density. They engaged in warfare with the *broza*. Each time they chopped off a main stem, a dozen new ones shot up. It was a Hydra-headed monster. To clear a patch of land they found it necessary to grub out the roots that were often far larger than the tops of the *broza*.

The very worst *broza*, the densest and thorniest, was called chaparral. Cowboys detested riding through such tangles, but longhorns congregated in them and had to be driven out for branding and selection of those ready to be herded to markets. In desperation, the cowboys invented chaps (shortened from chaparral) made of cowhide or whole skins of sheep to protect their legs from needle-sharp barbs. While the brush country is shrinking before agricultural expansion in southeast Texas, large areas of it may still be found.

Desolated by my helplessness, I stared at the car wedged immovably in the mud. We were trapped by the same kind of earth used by prehistoric Indians to build such pueblos as Casa Grande in Arizona and others scattered through that state and in New Mexico and western Texas. It is still used by Mexicans for plastering mud-and-wattle huts and for the hand-molded, sun-dried bricks of more pretentious homes. Adobe bricks make beautifully textured walls, and on them the sun casts delightful shadows. They are durable, too, so long as the roof is tight. Moreover, they make an effective insulation against both heat and cold.

Scientists prefer the term *caliche* for the clay used in making adobe bricks. It is actually clay with calcium carbonate, one of the ingredients of cement, in it. Such caliche is found throughout the Southwest where arid conditions prevail. It was used by the Spaniards in building early missions, for the materials were abundant and close at hand. Moreover, the Indians who did much of the labor had long made packed walls of it and were familiar with it.

Today there are hamlets in Mexico where neither plaster nor whitewash is used on abode walls, so the buildings look as if they were a part of the earth and are beautiful because of it. Occasionally unplastered adobe walls may be seen north of the Rio Grande. Abandoned in 1891, Old Fort Davis in the Davis Mountains was built partly of adobe, and those crumbling sepia walls against a background of jagged red cliffs and swimming in a sea of light look as ancient as the earth they stand on. The ghosts of long-gone soldiers enter the bodies of visitors to the forsaken fort. I wander among the broken walls and I feel soft wet adobe between my hands and search the haunted cliffs for parties of Apaches bent on raiding the fort.

Time dragged, and I poked vainly at the mud trap but accomplished nothing. I stared down the empty road. Allan had been gone a very long time. Presently I caught sight of a big, hairy, dark-chocolate tarantula. It walked deliberately out of the *broza* and advanced along the roadside, avoiding the wetter places. No doubt it had been forced from its burrow by the heavy rains, for they are seldom abroad in daylight, except late in the summer and autumn when males search for mates.

This was the first Texas tarantula I had ever seen, and I was impressed by its bulk. It was a bear of a spider, stout and densely covered with long hair. Its body was fully an inch and a half long. Its eight heavily furred legs were extremely flexible. Every one had seven segments. Its walk was a marvel of synchronization. On the left side of its body, legs Number One and Number Three marched in time with Number Two and Number Four on the right side. Unlike insects, which have only six legs, all arachnids, whether ticks, chiggers, scorpions, mites or daddy-long-legs have eight legs.

When I held my hand above the tarantula, it halted and reared up on its hind sets of legs, swinging its front sets into a defensive attitude. Its mouth parts—a pair of palpus and two chelicera tipped with fangs—palpitated ferociously. Oddly enough, when I removed my hand and pushed a stiff blade of grass against its side, it paid no attention and continued on it way.

A dashing polished bluish-black wasp, a tarantula hawk, darted in on red-gold wings fully three inches from tip to tip. I jumped away, afraid of its sheathed stinger, for it is capable of inflicting acute pain. The tarantula hawk and tarantula are deadly enemies, and each is a Goliath of its family. Both are armed with venom. The spider injects this through the fang-tipped chelicera beside its tiny mouth while the far more potent wasp venom is introduced through a hypodermic-type tail stinger.

A tarantula wasp is protected by a sort of coat-of-mail, for a skeleton of chitin completely surrounds its body with a hard shell. The spider has a soft body and is extremely vulnerable to the sting of its enemy. The wasp settled on the ground near the tarantula, which had reared defensively once more. I expected a fight to the death, but for some reason the wasp went off without any overt threat. Perhaps it was not yet ready to lay its eggs. Perhaps it had not prepared a burrow for its young. When a tarantula hawk encounters a tarantula abroad in the daytime as this one had, it has little difficulty in winning the battle that normally follows. Its venom quickly paralyzes its larger victim, which very rarely succeeds in either driving the wasp away or giving it a fatal bite. Once the wasp inserts its stinger into the soft body of its victim, the battle is ended. But the wasp must bring considerable strength and ingenuity to the next step, for the heavy spider must be dragged into a previously dug burrow. When this is done, the wasp lays its egg on the abdomen of the helpless but living spider, which may remain paralyzed for months. As the wasp larva emerges it is amply supplied with fresh meat that lasts until it goes into the sleep from which it awakens an adult wasp. These wasps have been known to stuff their victims back into their own burrows if they overcome a tarantula near its home.

Though spiders belong to the order of arthropods that includes such succulent items of human food as crayfish, crabs, lobsters and shrimp, they are widely feared, sometimes to the point of hysteria. Nevertheless, except for black widow spiders, species north of the Rio Grande are all practically harmless to man. In addition to their innocuous position among the teeming life of the planet, they actively give man great assistance in his unending battle to control insects. While the larger tarantulas near the equator eat many small creatures such as snakes, lizards, frogs, mice and even small birds, our spiders are insect-eaters. Why deep-seated fear of spiders is so prevalent is puzzling, since these predatious animals are not only harmless but actually helpful to us. Yet there is a fear on a par with that of snakes. Doctors and nurses who care for psychiatric patients under the influence of certain drugs say these patients suffered hallucinations of spiders as often as snakes. In contrast, those who lack this baseless fear have found tarantulas are easily tamed and good pets. Small Navajo and Hopi boys in the Southwest frequently lead their pet tarantulas about, using light thread as a leash.

Since tarantulas are popularly associated with the tropics and banana plantations, it surprises most people to discover we have about thirty species in the United States. Knowing that, we still expect them to stay close to the Mexican border. In reality they spread east to the Mississippi River and north to a line extending from Missouri to San Francisco. Of all these, the tarantula that distracted me from our unfortunate predicament was one of the largest.

Our tarantulas belong to a large family called *Theraphosidae*. To this family belong the largest spiders in the entire world, and the South American giants mentioned before hold the world's record for size. The name is a carry-over from a European wolf spider, which gave rise to many superstitious notions, and is now too deeply embedded in our vocabulary to dislodge. The true tarantulas are common in the Taranto region of Italy. Their venom attacks the nervous system as does black widow venom but much less dangerously.

"What's in a name?" asked Shakespeare.

Plenty, we think. When the name of the superstitiously dreaded tarantula of Europe was wrongly attached to our largest spider, all the unreasoning fears and apprehensions connected with the Old World spider were transferred bodily to our species.

Spiders as a whole have very short lives. In fact, few species have a life span of longer than a year, quite aside from the high mortality they suffer, for they are eaten be many animals from insects to fish, birds and even men who relish certain species.

Tarantulas are an exception to the general rule of short life. Captive females have lived as long as thirty years. The species does not mature until it is about ten years old. During all those years of youth it is impossible in most instances to determine sex. Then suddenly, as tarantulas mature, the sexes become distinct.

Late in summer and early autumn, when mating takes place, males that have seldom left their burrows except on hunting expeditions or when forced out by heavy rains, wander about in considerable numbers.

As for the female, she finally accepts a mate after a ritualized courtship. The successful wooing is followed by the induction of sperm from the palpi of the male in the epigynum of the female. Popular conviction to the contrary, the male is not always eaten after mating. In fact, the male tarantula goes his way more often than not, but he has finished his usefulness and seldom lives beyond the year when he matures. The long-lived female has a new and young mate each year, no matter how ancient, according to tarantula standards, she may be.

When the female is ready to lay her eggs, she spins a sheet of tightly meshed silk and places on it anywhere from six hundred to more than a thousand large eggs. This big clutch of eggs is surpassed by some of the larger South American species that lay up to three thousand. After the laying, the female spins a covering sheet for her eggs and then fastens the edges together as a cook would fasten the layers of a two-crust pie. It takes up to seven weeks for the eggs to hatch, and in the meantime the tarantula watches over her treasure and sometimes drags the egg case to the mouth of the burrow for a good sunning.

The burrow is usually a large one and sometimes actually

roomy when a rodent hole is used, and this is made luxurious with a lining of silk. Though the young tarantulas remain for some time in the burrow, eventually the spiderlings leave home and mother and disperse by walking away. Not for them is one of the most exciting dispersal flights I know of. They are too heavy for it.

Once I witnessed an aerial dispersal of spiders on Washington's Birthday. It was clear and windy, and the Indian River danced and tossed sparkles about. Suddenly there appeared to be a snow squall drifting upriver. A snow squall in Florida? I dashed outside to look, wondering if tiny migrating butterflies were moving northward.

It was a great ballooning of spiderlings so tiny three could have stood on the head of a common pin. Each was borne along on a ball of gleaming silk or on long trailing strands of it. Some touched the water and floated there. Thousands upon thousands were blown ashore, and they covered leaves, twigs, grass and even clung to me. Their numbers were so incredible that tiny as they were, gossamer was spread everywhere.

Over the river, the multitude was most dense within thirty feet of the surface and thinned rapidly above that height. It was pure magic, this sudden appearance of incredible numbers of spiderlings floating away to new homes. We sometimes watch films of men dropping by parachutes to fighting lines and we know they face a serious condition. So, too, is the migration of spiderlings a serious, even deadly, business. It is part of life among the little known animals that share our world.

Many species of birds use spider silk when nest-building. It is odd that it has not been used more by men. So great is both its strength and elasticity that surely, if chemists had not developed many good synthetic threads, we would now be wearing dresses reminiscent of Rima's chemiselike gown of whitish color with a faint luster. Surely Hudson imagined a fabric made of spider silk when he wrote that description.

No book yet published about spiders is more interesting to the layman than Willis J. Gertch's *American Spiders*. This book opens our eyes on a strange and fascinating world, then sends us into the field to watch spiders with the same curiosity and amazement that will grip earth astronauts when they first set foot on another planet where life exists. We share this earth with spiders, but to borrow a term from Thoreau, they belong to a different nation, a nation so unlike our own that they are almost incomprehensible. We know some facts about them, and scientists steadily add to our superficial knowledge of spiders; yet their reality eludes us.

How do they hear? No ears have yet been found, though they respond to sound. Is each and every hair on their bodies an auditory receiver? What do their eyes see? We can understand why cave spiders have lost their eyes or retain only vestiges of them, for unused parts of the body deteriorate. But why do some spiders, living above the surface where sunlight falls, have only one eye while others have two, three or anywhere up to eight eyes? Their sense of touch is thought to be extraordinarily perceptive. Can they smell? Taste? They rarely accept dead insects but live on freshly caught ones. These they suck dry with their tiny mouth parts.

More than seventy-five thousand species of spiders have been identified. The biggest is about a hundred thousand times larger than the smallest. This span in size is roughly comparable to a man and the ocean liner *Queen Elizabeth*. Spiders are remarkably swift. One can cover about three hundred body lengths in ten seconds. If a track man could do as well he would run a hundred yard dash in less than two seconds.

Spiders occur wherever men live. We can touch them if we wish. Yet they are incredibly remote from us. No matter how long we watch them, or how many truths we accumulate about them we continue to look upon them as Tennyson reports Ulysses looked upon an unknown world, "an arch wherethrough / gleams that untraveled world whose margin fades / forever and forever as I move."

My attention was distracted from the tarantula when a male pyrrhuloxia landed on a mesquite and turned to look at me. It held a fat green worm in its bill, and I started toward it hoping it would lead me to a nest, only to find myself clutched by the sticky mud. I had just extricated myself when Allan trudged around the bend. He was alone and fatigue showed in his dragging steps.

I hurried to meet him. He had found a farmhouse about two miles ahead but the menfolk were all away. Rains had damaged the roads and they were helping to repair them. They would not be home before half-past five or perhaps six o'clock. There was no telephone. Allan had turned away, discouraged, when the farm woman told him that if he would continue about a mile he would come to a lane turning off to the right. A Mexican family lived down that lane. Perhaps somebody there could lend a hand.

So Allan toiled on. He turned down the straggling lane. Mud clung and built up on his shoes, so every few yards he was forced to stop and scrape it off.

The cabin stood in a thicket of mesquite. On the porch sat a handsome young Mexican in field clothes. He did not understand a word Allan said, not even when he changed from English to his college Spanish. The Mexican shouted. Two small boys about six and eight came running. They had gone to a local school and knew some English. They translated Allan's appeal for help. Grasping the situation at long last, the Mexican said he would come in one hour.

"Why not right now?" Allan urged.

The Mexican was adamant. One hour. He would come in one hour. Discouraged, Allan turned back but had to laugh when he saw the hens. The Mexican's yard was quite wet, and all the hens looked both comic and wretched. Mud had glued to their feet and at every step more mud was added until all were encased in huge mud-balls. They could scarcely move.

We could only wait. The tarantula that had entertained me was gone. Once a male pyrrhuloxia, soft gray with a tall crest of flame, and more red on its breast and a flush of it on wings and tail flew over. Excitedly Allan started after the lovely bird of the *broza*, but he sank into the mud and quickly gave up, too weary after his long walk to continue battling the wet caliche.

"How I would like to photograph that male." He gazed longingly after the bird, slimmer and more elegant than its brighter cardinal cousins.

Insensibly the long narrow shadows facing west when we left Horsehead had shrunk until they nearly vanished, but now they were lengthening and swinging east by north. Solitude hemmed us in and the road was empty of all life.

Solitude, which normally delights us, was now oppressive. We were impatient with our helpless situation and irritated by the long delay in escaping from it. Then a high-stepping, spirited horse rounded the bend. The rider of the glossy chestnut had dressed for the rescue, and we stared at him speechless. Gone were his worn, faded field clothes. A hat with a sweeping brim shaded his long oval face. His velvet jacket was embroidered down the front and along the lower edge with large red and pink flowers similar to those painted on tin trays by native artisans in Mexico. Smaller flowers, also beautifully worked in silk, edged the sleeves. His tight black pants were tucked into boots that were a marvel of complicated tooled design polished until they shone obsidian.

The handsome young man led a second horse. That was a horse of a different color. Its head hung low, its coat was dull and it plodded stoically down the sticky road. Two small bright-eyed boys rode bareback on the patient nag. They slid quickly to the ground when they reached the muddy section and ran excitedly to the car, exclaiming about the mud in which it was trapped. Mud squeezed between their bare toes as they explored the situation.

Their father remained on his horse. Like a movie hero gazing on the face of a fallen companion, the Mexican stared sadly at the mud. He was lost in thought for some time, and then his face cleared. He swung sidewise in the saddle, pulled his gleaming boots from bare feet and dropped into the mud. Leading his mount to the fence, he tied it to a post and fastened the boots to his saddle. The boys handed him a coiled rope that they had carried on the nag, and he tied it to the rear bumper.

The boys asked Allan to start the motor and reverse when the signal was given. It was apparent the old nag was to do all the work. Fortunately it still had strength and energy in spite of its apathy. In no time the car was out of the mud but on the end where we had entered it hours ago. The rope was transferred to the front bumper, and now the car with the engine and the nag pulling hard went forward. Wheels spun, mud flew, the car bucked and the boys yelled. I held my breath, but suddenly the car was on quite dry, firm track. Gratefully Allan placed some bills in the hand that was reluctant to take them, but finally the Mexican smiled his thanks.

The two boys told us wistfully that they did not have a car, so we asked them to ride back to the cottage with us. Cakes of mud flew from the wheels and underparts of the car as we sped along. The hens were still standing forlornly by the cottage, anchored by balls of mud. This time Allan had no desire to watch the hens, for a handsome male pyrrhuloxia darted into a mesquite behind the cottage.

"I think it had food in its bill," Allan was already racing toward the mesquite. The small boys got out, and the minute they opened the car door a white goat with yellow eyes crowded past them and began to chew the strap on my camera bag. Shoving and pushing the unwelcome goat, I managed to expel it from the car just as Allan shouted he had found the pyrrhuloxia nest with three young in it. We were far behind schedule, but Allan said this was too good a find to pass up. We were near the paved highway, so road troubles were all behind us. By that time the Mexican arrived, again leading the nag, and his white teeth gleamed as he gave his consent to bird photography in his yard.

Quickly Allan set up his blind and vanished inside with his camera. On that day when adobe mud trapped us and I saw my first tarantula, Allan made his first photographs of pyrrhuloxias, a species that belongs to the *broza*, the thorny dry brush country.

Now the *broza* has been pushed far up the Rio Grande Valley before expanding cities and intensive agriculture. To a great extent pyrrhuloxias have been pushed up the valley, too, though there is a scattering of them even in city gardens. The difficult name means crooked-billed red-bird. The short thick bill is not crooked except at the closing edges of the mandibles, but it is extremely thick, almost parrotlike.

Whenever I am in *broza* or chaparral and hear the cardinal-like song of the bird of the brush country, I remember the day when Allan first photographed the species. I remember the long hours before we were rescued by the elaborately dressed young Mexican and I was led into a world as strange as any Gulliver found in his travels when the tarantula stalked out of the *broza*.

23

The Song Has Ended

THE DAYS OF SPRING when birds are most active fled by. Song diminished and we found more empty nests than occupied ones. A hundred miles from our quarters in El Paso on June 20 Allan found a late rock wren nest. The wren, its bill crammed with fat worms, led him to a crevice where five large, well-feathered young crowded to the entrance and noisily competed for the food. It was a lucky discovery for we had despaired of finding an active nest in the short time remaining for bird photography.

The rock wrens, as wrens sometimes behave, were almost oblivious of our presence, so we did not use our blinds as we photographed them. The adults delivered food boldly, stuffed it into the youngster that opened its mouth widest and shouted the loudest, then walked away along a little path of neatly arranged stone chips before taking flight to collect another batch of insects.

The nest was not far from the ruins of the old Butterfield Fort at the mouth of Pine Spring Canyon. This canyon cuts a steep-walled slash just behind 8,751-foot Guadalupe Peak, the highest point in Texas. Back in 1858 the fort was a link in the Butterfield Overland Stage Line from St. Louis to San Francisco. The coaches traveled at a spanking speed that covered the distance between the cities in twenty-five days, provided a thoroughbrace did not break or a horse throw a shoe or a wheel come off. Then the Guadalupe Range country was considered so dangerous that a small military detachment was stationed at Butterfield Fort. When Apaches were hostile or a gang of desperadoes moved in, soliders escorted the stage through this particularly dangerous region.

By the time we finished photographing the rock wrens in that place where the romance of old Texas lingers, and our cameras were put away, the sun was setting below bright cloud banners. We faced the flaming west as we turned toward El Paso. Below us an ocean of darkness rose like a flood tide higher and higher on the slopes of the massive Guadalupe Mountains, blotting out their feet. More than 77,000 acres of this wild, canyon-rent, pine-topped range whose scored and eroded flanks reveal strange geological phenomena were recently added to our national park system. Its rugged crags are a fit home for eagles, bighorns and wheeling vultures, for the hunted and the maligned. The Park area includes Guadalupe Peak, beautiful McKittrick Canyon and El Capitan, long a landmark to westbound travelers, trail herders, and stagecoach drivers. As Americans moved westward the tide of migration split around the massive inhospitable range, leaving the fragile ecological community of wildlife in that harsh country relatively intact and unchanged.

In spite of modern scientific knowledge there remains vast ignorance concerning our environment. As our population skyrockets it becomes increasingly vital to human welfare that we do come to a genuine understanding of our world ecology and man's place in it. To this end, the protection of large blocks of habitats in their natural state is urgent as never before. On the approximately 200 species of animals that have become extinct since the birth of Christ, 38 per cent have been sent into oblivion in the last half century and presently at least 250 more species are in danger of extinc-

tion. Nobody knows for sure what indispensible part each of
these may play in the health of the earth and mankind, for
life on this planet has become enormously complicated and
very strenuous. It is hoped that this new Park will be developed so its irreplaceable wilderness will remain. If care is not
exercised, the fragile region will be overrun by multitudes
seeking only recreation until the wilderness value is trampled
beneath uncaring feet.

Hurrying toward food and rest, we dipped into a swift
decline below Guadalupe Pass, and only chance led us to look
backward. El Capitan, the thousand-foot majestic pillar-like
remnant of a once great Permian fossil reef appeared to float
above the sea of night. It soared over the gathering darkness
as luminous as if made of polished tigereye, fire opal and carnelian. It looked like the beginning of the world or its end as
it hung detached above the blackness of the lower elevations.
Aloof, withdrawn, its austere splendor knifed into our hearts,
filling us with awe and carried in its waiting stillness a bene-
diction and a promise. A few minutes ticked by. The primitive colors faded into dusk, but the wonder that struck deep
into us remained.

Next morning the sun rose early to shine on the longest
day of the year. By the time films were prepared for shipping
to the processors, notes completed and the car packed for the
trip homeward, the last spring day was already slipping
downhill. Heat pressed on us, a palpable blanket. Merciless,
illimitable light radiated from the burning sky. El Paso receives an annual average of 82 per cent of the possible sunshine, and that day not even a hawk hung beneath the polished heavens. On that June 21 the temperature soared to a
record-breaking 109 degrees, and inside the furnace-like car
the mercury in my thermometer burst its glass tube.

Though weighted by lethargy, we determined to take a
final look at Texas as spring ended. We drove to the farthest
west corner of the state, keeping to the old road through

Canutillo and Anthony. Their hot glaring streets were deserted.

Soon we sank wearily on the bank of the Rio Grande. The river in early spring, well fed by melting snows on distant mountains, had lapped the top of its banks. Now it had shrunk to a sluggish trickle threading its way through the middle of its parched bed. I walked across the hot gravel and thrust my fevered hands into the shallow water. There was no coolness in it, and I was blinded by the reflection of the glaring sky from its surface. Above our heads the leaves of a cottonwood hissed dryly as heat waves rose from the baked earth and stirred them. Across the river on a pale lifeless slope, unshaded adobe houses stood like floury loaves just thrust into a clear plastic-domed oven.

Something stirred at our feet. Goats had recently passed that way, and their passage had lured a dung beetle from its burrow. With infinite labor he had rolled some goat dung into a perfectly formed ball larger than himself. Now traveling backward he patiently shoved it with his hindfeet toward his underground home. As the ball was inched forward the sand gave way and the ball spun backward. Bracing himself with his front legs, the dung beetle braked the rolling ball and slowly, still using his hind feet, pushed it forward again. As he moved, his folded membranous flight wings were hidden as if in a hanger by his hard forewings. These were iridescent as those of his scarab cousins, regarded by ancient Egyptians as symbolic of immortality. Always facing away from his burden he maneuvered this way and that, a creature of jewel-like beauty. Black turned to emerald, and emerald to amythest, and then to gold.

We listened. Silence lay everywhere.

"Spring cannot end in a sweltering stupor!" My thoughts raced back over ninety days, back to the first day of spring and we stood on the chilly bank of the Sabine River where crystal dewdrops trembled on every leaf and stem. Then we were wrapped in the crisp scent of pines and listened to mockingbirds, titmice, blue jays and Carolina wrens boisterously salute the dawn of spring. One wood thrust sang its cool pure melody that rose and fell unhurriedly with slow-paced intervals between phrases.

Since that dawn we had worked with stiffened fingers on the Aransas Refuge and the Edwards Plateau and buttoned our coats snugly against the cold night wind in the Basin of the Big Bend. Suddenly heat had swept over Texas, and we sweltered on the lomas and the bird islands, in the Panhandle and the Trans-Pecos, but neither cold nor heat had kept us from filling every hour of each day with rewarding field work.

Now many of the young herons we watched break out of eggs were adventuring far from their island birthplaces. Golden-cheeked warblers in the juniper-oak thickets west of Austin had been weaned and were on their own. Terns, mottled gray and white, were testing their wings. Big ungainly turkey poults bristled as sheaths broke away from their pinfeathers. Fat white-winged dove squabs with funny short tails had left their flimsy nursery platforms in Bentsen State Park. Hopefully somewhere in the Big Thicket the nearly extinct ivory-billed woodpeckers had raised a young or two. In the Panhandle youthful white-necked ravens followed their heedless parents until they became so hungry they searched for their own food. Along the Canadian River juvenile Mississippi kites had mastered the art of resting on thermals.

Many young birds had already paid the final price for inexperience and become meals for other birds, snakes and mammals. In every one of the varied habitats across the great expanse of Texas there were birds and burgeoning life, but here, in the intense heat of that record-breaking spring afternoon, vitality was brought to a standstill, and all life was silent, torpid, hidden from the ardent sun.

"Let's cross the highway and walk toward the mountains."

"All right, but we may pass out first," Allan muttered.

Staggering under the weight of the remorseless heat, we turned toward the Franklin Mountains. They wavered strangely behind the flickering ghostly shimmer of heat waves. Brown, yellow and russet, they looked to us a treeless desolation and their serrated crests jutted against the sky like giant shark's teeth.

Between us and the mountains the land sloped upward in a series of folds dotted by tumbled rocks and boulders and streaked by twisting gouges dug by long dry streams. A few small yuccas and dwarfed catclaw and mesquite grew here, most of them close to the edges of the empty stream beds. Creosote bushes, the plant botanists consider an indicator of a true desert, grew at widely spaced intervals as if planted by a precise gardener who carefully marked off the distance between each with a tape measure. This spacing of creosote bushes was a means of survival for each thirsty bush had an enormous root system that enabled it to soak up sufficient water during the brief rains to survive the long periods of drought.

There had been one good rain in early spring and the creosote bushes had clothed themselves richly with yellowish-green, resin-coated leaves. Shortly five-petaled, clear-yellow flowers had opened. Now the bushes were hung with seeds. Though considered evergreen since they seldom shed all their leaves at once, the creosote bushes most thickly hung with fuzzy gray seeds had dropped most of their foliage.

We had often watched ground squirrels climb nimbly into the flexible branches of these bushes to eat the seeds. That torrid afternoon all resident ground squirrels had sought the comfort of their burrows. Under one creosote bush were the tracks of a quail, possibly scaled but more likely a Gambel's; but the shade it found there was too slight, and it had sought a denser covert.

We saw the lacelike chain of a lizard's tracks. At right angles came the purposeful prints of a roadrunner. The lizard tracks vanished in a whirling blur and we suspected their maker had become a roadrunner's dinner. Not a lizard did we see. No doubt they were there hidden under stones or plastered tightly against the shady side of a creosote branch where they would remain immobile until the heat moderated.

Not a song or even a cheep reached our ears. The sky was empty. Heat, thorns and sand surrounded us. Our feet dragged, and as they scuffed through the sand it smoked up behind our heels in little puffs. We descended into the trough of one of the desert folds. Allan, wiping perspiration from his face, said we had better turn back.

We swung about and froze in our tracks, dazed and speechless before the glittering iceballs that sparkled like Christmas-tree ornaments. Every small fuzzy seed on the creosote bushes was back-lighted by the long low shafts of the sun and, as if by magic, flared with icy radiance. From ordinary shrubs with a pleasantly pungent scent, the creosote bushes had been transformed by the quality of light into beauty more subtle and impressive than the famed desert flower fields. They displayed a cold crystalline beauty incongruous on the fevered desert that has haunted our thoughts since. Whenever we are in desert country and the sun is low either morning or evening, we seek out creosote bushes laden with seeds to enjoy again the frosty glitter, the antithesis of the burning desert.

Only long, low rays of the sun transform the seeds into sudden beauty as Cinderella was changed by the wand of her fairy godmother for a limited time. Flat-lighted or at midday the seeds are dull whitish balls and nothing more. As we gazed at the unpretentious shrub transformed with arresting spangles by the declining sun, we wondered how many other modest plants and animals were overlooked by us and have been unnoted and unsung by poets.

The time of singing birds had been too short. Each day hurried past on wings that reduced them to minutes. Day followed day as telephone poles seen from an express train appear to draw close together as the pickets of a garden fence. Now as the sun slipped to the horizon and the frosty gleam of the creosote seeds dimmed, those days that had flashed by as meteors flame across the sky; rich full days, now stretched back forever into limitless time.

The summer solstice was riding high and in the desert sucked dry by the thirsty sun, birds were silent. The heat would grow, then fade, and winter would chill the land. Another spring with its eternal mysteries was waiting quietly in the wings to make its appearance nine months in the future. What marvelous sights and strange adventures awaited us then? We found their promise in the fine theatrical icy glitter of a desert shrub as the Texas spring ended.

Index